History

for the IB Diploma

Independence Movements

(1800–2000)

Allan Todd and Jean Bottaro
Series editor: Allan Todd

Cambridge University Press's mission is to advance learning, knowledge and research worldwide.

Our IB Diploma resources aim to:

- encourage learners to explore concepts, ideas and topics that have local and global significance

- help students develop a positive attitude to learning in preparation for higher education

- assist students in approaching complex questions, applying critical-thinking skills and forming reasoned answers.

CAMBRIDGE
UNIVERSITY PRESS

CAMBRIDGE
UNIVERSITY PRESS

University Printing House, Cambridge CB2 8BS, United Kingdom

One Liberty Plaza, 20th Floor, New York, NY 10006, USA

477 Williamstown Road, Port Melbourne, VIC 3207, Australia

4843/24, 2nd Floor, Ansari Road, Daryaganj, Delhi – 110002, India

79 Anson Road, #06–04/06, Singapore 079906

Cambridge University Press is part of the University of Cambridge.

It furthers the University's mission by disseminating knowledge in the pursuit of education, learning and research at the highest international levels of excellence.

Information on this title: education.cambridge.org

© Cambridge University Press 2015

First published 2011
Second edition 2015
20 19 18 17 16 15 14 13 12 11 10 9 8 7 6 5 4

Printed in the United Kingdom by Latimer Trend

A catalogue record for this publication is available from the British Library

ISBN 978-1-107-55623-2 Paperback

....

Contents

Contents

Overview

This book is designed to prepare students taking the Paper 2 topic *World History Topic 8: Independence movements (1800–2000)* in the IB History examination. It will examine themes relating to independence movements in Africa and the Middle East, Asia, the Americas and Europe. The themes are organised within chapters focusing on case studies across these regions. Chapters 2–4 deal with African and Asian states that moved from colonial rule to independence in the period after the Second World War. Chapter 5 covers the struggle for Cuban independence from Spain during the 19th century, while Chapter 6 covers the struggle for Irish independence from 1800 to 1932.

The African, Asian, Americas and European examples – Zimbabwe, India and Pakistan, Vietnam, Cuba and Ireland – have much in common with each other. Each was a colonial possession under the control of a European power. They all gained independence from colonial rule in the late 19th or 20th centuries. These chapters will help you analyse and evaluate the reasons for historical change in these countries and acquire historical perspective by comparing and contrasting each of the case studies.

Figure 1.1 Indians celebrate the independence of their country from British rule in 1947

1

Introduction

Africa, Asia and the Americas – decolonisation

Four case studies have been selected from Africa, Asia and the Americas – Rhodesia/Zimbabwe, India and Pakistan, Vietnam, and Cuba. They were all subject to **colonialism**, but emerged as independent states either before the First World War or after the Second World War in a process that is often called **decolonisation**.

Each case study has been selected because of the manner of its transition from colonial rule to independence. In the Americas, Cuba began its struggle for independence from Spain in the second half of the 19th century. While in the late 19th century, Britain, France and other European states engaged in a 'scramble' to colonise the areas of Africa and Asia that remained independent. This 'new' **imperialism** expanded European control over these regions. More formal empires were established or consolidated, and various forms of administration were imposed on the **indigenous** populations.

By 1945, however, these colonial empires were coming under increasing pressure. Indigenous groups in the colonies had begun to form independence movements. These opposition groups were often led by Western-educated élites. The ideologies of the independence movements sometimes drew upon the intellectual bases of the European left, including the works of Karl Marx. However, **Marxism** was not a major factor in most independence movements, and only grew more significant in some states after 1945 as a result of the developing Cold War.

The two world wars of the 20th century had an impact on colonial empires across the world. The rhetoric that followed the end of the First World War (1914–18) emphasised self-determination and national identity – concepts at odds with the European colonial domination then prevalent. Failure to address the demands of indigenous nationalist leaders in the decade after the war only intensified activity on the part of these independence movements to bring an end to European colonial rule.

The Second World War (1939–45) had an even more fundamental impact. The two chief colonial powers of the mid-20th century, Britain and France, suffered greatly during the war. Britain only just survived the onslaught of the Axis powers (Germany and its allies) and emerged from the conflict almost bankrupt. British possession of India had also been threatened by Japan. France suffered even more. Metropolitan France had been occupied by German forces, and its Southeast Asian colonies had been conquered by Japan. When the rhetoric of self-determination emerged again in the post-1945 period, nationalist movements realised that their colonial masters were now ill-equipped in terms of economic and military power to resist moves towards independence.

The transition to independence in these regions must also be studied against the backdrop of the **Cold War** between the USA, the **USSR** and their allies.

This book examines the origins and rise of the independence movements in these regions, the methods they used to achieve their goals, and the reasons for their success. It also explores the challenges these newly independent states faced in the first ten years of their existence and how they responded to those challenges.

Europe – the struggle for Irish independence

The case study in Chapter 6 covers events in Ireland from 1800 to 1932. Ireland finally came under English control during the 16th century and was, in many ways, Britain's first colony. Problems of economic underdevelopment, landownership, poverty and religion increasingly combined to create a clear Irish nationalism and a growing desire for independence. Britain's response was a mixture of repression and reform but, as the 19th century progressed, those desiring a fully independent Irish republic increased in number. The methods used in this emerging struggle were a mixture of peaceful agitation for reform and violent conflict. Although at first the constitutional approach predominated, those favouring violent methods increasingly came to the fore during the early 20th century.

Beginning in 1916 with the Easter Rebellion, revolutionary republicans waged a guerrilla war against British forces. This military conflict continued until 1922, when a limited form of independence was achieved. However, this was accompanied by the splitting of Ireland into what soon became two separate states: the Irish Free State in the south, and Northern Ireland. Many republicans were deeply disappointed by this outcome, leading to a short civil war in the Irish Free State. Although the south of Ireland finally achieved complete independence in 1949, the issue of a divided Ireland continued to cause problems – including further violence.

Themes

To help you prepare for your IB History exams, this book will cover the themes relating to independence movements in Africa, Asia, the Americas and Europe, as set out in the IB History Guide. For ease of study, this book will examine each state in terms of a series of major themes subdivided by region. The three major themes that will be examined are:

- the origins and rise of independence movements
- methods of achieving independence, including the role and importance of leaders; and the reasons for success
- the challenges faced in the first ten years after independence, and the responses to those challenges.

Separate units within Chapters 2–6 explore these themes within the context of each case study to help you focus on the key issues. This approach will enable you to compare and contrast developments in the various states, and to spot similarities and differences.

All the main events, turning points and key individuals will be covered in sufficient detail for you to be able to access the higher markbands – provided, of course, that your answers are both relevant and analytical!

Where appropriate, each chapter will contain visual and written sources, both to illustrate the events or issues under examination, and to provide material for exam-type questions. These will help you gain practice in dealing with the questions you will face in History Papers 1 and 2.

Cold War: the term used to describe the tension and rivalry between the USA and the USSR between 1945 and 1991. 'Cold war' refers to relations that, although hostile, do not develop into a 'hot war' (involving actual military conflict). The term was popularised in the years 1946–7 by US journalist Walter Lippmann and US politician and businessman Bernard Baruch. With regard to our study, the USSR became a champion of independence movements, providing political, financial and military support for geopolitical and ideological reasons.

USSR: the Union of Soviet Socialist Republics. The USSR was the first communist state to develop, in 1917. It emerged from the First World War with considerable influence in Europe, although it had less influence than the USA across the world in general. Unlike the USA, which was a global superpower, the USSR was essentially a regional superpower.

Key Concepts

To perform well in your IB History examinations, you will often need to consider aspects of one or more of six important Key Concepts as you write your answers. These six Key Concepts are:

- Change
- Continuity
- Causation
- Consequence
- Significance
- Perspectives.

Sometimes, a question might require you to address two – or more – Key Concepts. For instance: 'Why did Irish republicans launch the Easter Rising in 1916? What were the most significant consequences of this action for the struggle for Irish independence between 1916 and 1922?'

It is immediately clear with this question that the Key Concepts of Consequence and Significance must be addressed in your answer. However, it is important to note that although the word 'causes' doesn't explicitly appear in the question, words such as 'why' or 'reasons' nonetheless are asking you to address Causation as well.

To help you focus on the six Key Concepts, and gain experience of writing answers that address them, you will find a range of different questions and activities throughout these chapters.

Theory of Knowledge

Alongside these broad key themes, all chapters contain Theory of Knowledge links to get you thinking about aspects that relate to history, which is a Group 3 subject in the IB Diploma. The Independence Movements topic has clear links to ideas about knowledge and history. The events discussed in this book are recent phenomena and form good case studies for understanding the nature of the historical process. Thus, the questions relating to the availability and selection of sources, and to interpretations of these sources, have clear links to the IB Theory of Knowledge course.

For example, when investigating aspects of the nature of decolonisation, or the motives and influence of individuals (such as Mahatma Gandhi or Ho Chi Minh), institutions (such as ZANU-PF) or states (such as colonial powers or Cold War rivals), historians must decide which primary and secondary evidence to select and use – and which to leave out – to make their case. But in selecting what they consider to be the most important or relevant sources, and in making judgements about the value and limitations of specific sources or sets of sources, how important are these historians' personal political views? Is there such a thing as objective 'historical truth'? Or is there just a range of subjective opinions and interpretations about the past, which vary according to the political interests and leanings of individual historians?

You are therefore encouraged to read a range of books offering different interpretations of independence movements in Africa and the Middle East, Asia and Oceania, the Americas and Europe. This will help you gain a clear understanding of the **historiography** of the events studied, as well as equipping you with the higher-level historical skills needed to gain perspective on the events of the second half of the 20th century as a whole.

Historiography: differing historical debates; in particular, those historians who focus on the problems of the imperial powers and those who emphasise the importance of developments in the various colonies in the move to independence.

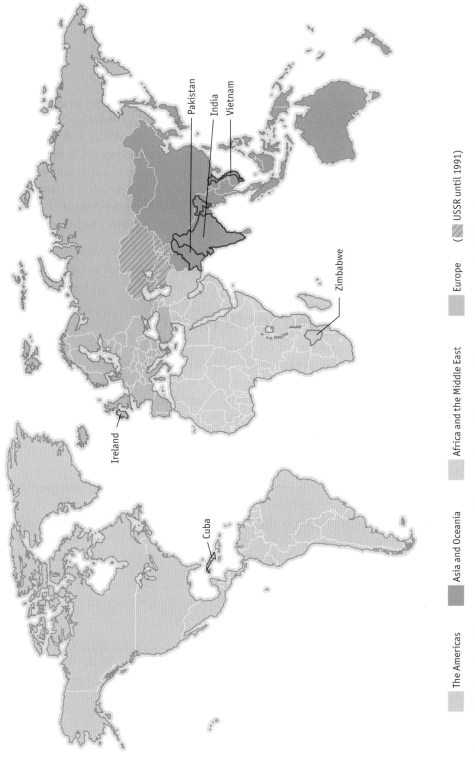

Figure 1.2 The four IB regions are shown on this map, along with some of the states covered in this book

The Americas

Asia and Oceania

Africa and the Middle East

Europe

(USSR until 1991)

Pakistan

India

Vietnam

Zimbabwe

Ireland

Cuba

IB History and regions of the world

For the purposes of study, IB History specifies four regions of the world:

- Europe
- Asia and Oceania
- the Americas
- Africa and the Middle East.

Where relevant, you will need to be able to identify these regions and to discuss developments that took place within them. Besides the states covered in this book, you may also study other examples of independence movements in Africa and the Middle East, Asia and Oceania, the Americas and Europe specifically identified in the IB History Guide. These may include the Algerian struggle against French colonial rule, led by Ahmed Ben Bella; the leading role played by Kwame Nkrumah in the nationalist movement in Ghana; the role of Jean-Jacques Dessalines in the struggle for independence in Haiti; or the struggle for Greek independence and the role played by Theodoros Kolokotronis.

Remember, when answering a question that asks you to choose examples from *two* different regions, you *must* be careful – failure to comply will result in limited opportunities to score high marks.

Exam skills needed for IB History

Throughout the main chapters of this book, there are various activities and questions to help you develop the understanding and the exam skills necessary for success. Before attempting the specific exam practice questions at the end of most chapters, you might find it useful to refer to Chapter 7 *first*. This suggestion is based on the idea that if you know where you are supposed to be going (in this instance, gaining a good grade) and how to get there, you stand a better chance of reaching your destination!

Questions and markschemes

To ensure that you develop the necessary understanding and skills, each chapter contains a number of comprehension questions in the margins. In addition, three of the main Paper 1-type questions (comprehension, cross-referencing and reliability/utility) are dealt with at the end of Chapters 2–6. Help for the longer Paper 1 judgement/synthesis questions, and the Paper 2 essay questions, can be found in Chapter 7 – the final exam practice chapter.

For additional help, simplified markschemes have been put together in ways that should make it easier to understand what examiners are looking for in your answers. The actual IB History markschemes can be found on the IB website.

Finally, you will find examiners' tips and comments, along with activities, to allow you to focus on the important aspects of the questions and answers. These should help you avoid simple mistakes and oversights that, every year, result in some otherwise good students failing to gain the highest marks.

Terminology and definitions

In order to understand the case studies that follow, it is important to grasp a few general definitions. These terms are often more complex than they first appear, and will be developed in relation to the specific case studies chosen for this book. It is useful, however, to understand some of these terms before you embark on your detailed survey.

Many of the ideological concepts that underpin this study derive from 19th-century European political philosophy. In a European context, such concepts influenced thinking and subsequent actions with very little modification. In the African, Asian and Americas case studies, however, these ideologies were substantially modified. The reasons for this were both social and economic. The situations in the African, Asian and American countries under consideration in this book were very different from the European political, economic and social conditions in which these ideologies originated.

Nationalism

Nationalism underpins all the movements under consideration in this book. It has its origins in the early 19th century and is, in part, a product of the French Revolution (1789–99). Nationalism is a political ideology founded on the belief that people should have political self-determination based on their nation. However, nationalism also involves issues such as a common history and shared culture and values.

SOURCE A

Thus was the German nation placed – sufficiently united within itself by a common language and a common way of thinking, and sharply enough severed from the other peoples, in the middle of Europe, as a wall to divide races.

An extract from Johann Gottlieb Fichte's 'Thirteenth Address' in 1806. Fichte was a German nationalist writing at the time of the Napoleonic Wars. Quoted in G.A. Kelly (ed.) (1968), *Addresses to the German Nation*, New York: Harper Torch, pp. 190–1.

The problem with this ideology is that it is difficult to define 'nation'. This has been done – for example by Johann Gottlieb Fichte (see **Source A**) – by variously applying ethnic or cultural definitions to nationhood. In the final analysis, this definition of nation is crude in the extreme, a position outlined by historian Patrick J. Geary in his book *The Myth of Nations*. However, nationalism became a powerful social, cultural and political force in the 19th and 20th centuries. In the African, Asian and Americas case studies, nationhood was very difficult to define. All the countries in this book had problems developing a homogenous concept of nationhood because they were composed of many ethnic groups with distinct cultures and histories.

Some independence movements in Africa and Asia were heavily influenced by Marxism. The problem was that communism was ill-suited to practical application in the agrarian societies that formed the colonial possessions under study.

Colonialism

'Colonialism' is a key term that dominates our analysis of the African and Asian case studies. In the 19th century it developed into a form of imperialism that attempted to create more formal empires. Colonialism involved the administration of distant parts of the globe from a home country, often called the metropolitan area. Colonies took many forms, but in general terms their peoples and economies were exploited to provide resources for the colonial power. These resources were frequently turned into manufactured goods and sold back to the colonies. An example of this is British India, which supplied cotton to Britain's industries and then bought the finished products back from the colonial power.

Introduction

Decolonialism

'Decolonisation' is the process of transition from colonial rule to independence. This concept is at the core of many IB History questions associated with the African and Asian part of this book. Scholars debate why decolonisation occurred and the relative impact of indigenous independence movements as opposed to the economic necessities of the colonial power (See **Source B**).

SOURCE B

The end of the colonial era is celebrated in the history books as a triumph of national aspiration in the former colonies and of benign good sense on the part of the colonial powers. Lurking beneath, as so often happens, was a strong current of economic interest – or in this case, disinterest.

John Kenneth Galbraith, an influential economic thinker during the 1960s, comments on colonialism. J.K. Galbraith (1994), *A Journey Through Economic Time: A Firsthand View*, Boston: Houghton Mifflin, p. 159.

Neo-colonialism

'Neo-colonialism' is a term applied to post-colonial states like those covered in the case studies that follow. It refers to the continuing economic control exerted by industrialised countries over their former colonies (See **Source C**).

SOURCE C

The result of neo-colonialism is that foreign capital is used for the exploitation rather than for the development of the less developed parts of the world.

Kwame Nkrumah, who became leader of the first newly independent African country, Ghana, in 1957, comments on neo-colonialism. K. Nkrumah (1965), *Neo-colonialism: The Last Stage of Imperialism*, London: Thomas Nelson & Sons, p. 1.

In your study of the post-colonial African and Asian states, you might consider whether the old colonial rulers simply changed the way they influenced events. For example, did the use of capital from the West in the form of investments and loans once more tie the new post-colonial states to their former masters?

History and changing perspectives

Historians often change their views of past events. This may occur as new primary sources come to light or simply because new perspectives emerge. An analysis of these changes (historiography) is a higher-level historical skill.

In the African, Asian and Americas case studies, a broad theme is our perception of colonial empires in general. There are several different interpretations of the impact of colonialism, the move towards independence and post-colonial developments. Imperialist historians stress the positive role played by the colonial powers in bringing change, in the form of infrastructures such as railways and communications systems, political ideologies, health care, education and the concept of the nation-state. They also focus on the policies of the colonial powers during the decolonisation process. Nationalist historians – whether Asian or African – often focus on the role played by leaders and nationalist groups in the move towards independence, and question the perceived benefits of colonial rule. Revisionist historians also question these benefits, viewing the colonial infrastructure as rudimentary, the services minimal and the education inappropriate. They see such moves as promoting the interests of the colonial powers, leaving many colonies unprepared for self-government and ill-equipped for independence.

Historians of the more recent 'subaltern studies group' focus on the role played by ordinary people in the independence struggle in India, and how they too were agents of political and social change. In this context they use the term 'subaltern' to refer to those who hold inferior positions in society in terms of race, class, gender, sexuality, ethnicity and religion. More recently this approach has been extended to historical studies of other parts of the world.

Another view, based partly on Marxist perspectives, regards the colonial empires as essentially exploitative. This perspective questions whether the process of decolonisation and subsequent independence was beneficial to the indigenous peoples of the post-colonial states. It is from this perspective that the theory of neo-colonialism has developed. This view is linked to the general **globalisation** of the world economy. It believes that Western states and corporations use their capital, in the form of investment, loans and even economic aid, to control and further exploit post-colonial states. From this perspective, prime minister Robert Mugabe's actions in Zimbabwe – despite the damage they have done to his country – could be seen as an attempt to fight back against this development.

Globalisation: the term used to describe economic and cultural developments in the later 20th century, in which the world's economies and cultures became homogenised. This has created great interdependence between all areas of the globe. Due to the Western states' superior economic capacity, globalisation may have created a new form of power for them. China, however, is fast catching up, and both China and the US, for example, might be seen as using their economic superiority to advance their geopolitical goals through the process of globalisation.

Summary

By the time you have worked through this book, you should be able to:

- show a broad understanding of the nature of decolonisation in the African and Asian states
- understand the reasons for the emergence and rise of independence movements
- understand and explain the various reasons why the countries in the African, Asian, Americas and European case studies emerged as independent states
- evaluate the significance of the roles played by specific individuals
- show an understanding of the challenges faced by the newly independent states in these four regions
- analyse the effectiveness of those independent states that emerged during the first ten years of their existence
- understand and explain all the case studies in the context of the impact of the various relevant wars.

2 Zimbabwe

Introduction

Until the Second World War, most of Africa was ruled by European colonial powers. After the war, however, the growth of African nationalism led to decolonisation and independence. In 1957, Ghana became the first independent state in sub-Saharan Africa. For most African countries the path to independence was a peaceful one, following constitutional negotiations. However, for colonies with large numbers of European settlers who were reluctant to accept majority rule, the process involved lengthy wars of liberation. The Algerians fought an eight-year war against France before becoming independent in 1962. In Kenya, a determined resistance from landless peasant farmers, called the Mau Mau Uprising, forced Britain to accept the principle of black majority rule in 1963. Independence for the Belgian Congo (later called Zaire and then the Democratic Republic of Congo) was accompanied by violence and civil war, aggravated by superpower intervention. Portugal was initially determined to maintain control of its colonies, and it was only after lengthy wars of resistance to Portuguese rule that the colonies became independent in 1975. In Angola this was followed by a decades-long civil war, prolonged by Cold War politics and foreign intervention.

The last British colony to become independent was Rhodesia/Zimbabwe in 1980. Nationalist movements in Zimbabwe waged a long struggle against white rule to achieve this in the area of central southern Africa that British settlers called Rhodesia. This independence movement involved peaceful political organisations, strikes and eventually a bitter armed struggle against a white minority government that was unwilling to surrender political power and economic privilege.

Zimbabwe was the name of an African kingdom that dominated trade in the area between the 13th and 15th centuries. The capital at Great Zimbabwe was built by ancestors of the Shona people. The kingdom controlled the export of ivory and gold from the interior to the Swahili city states on the eastern coast. In the 1960s, nationalist organisations chose the name Zimbabwe as it symbolised African achievement and heritage, and had links to the pre-colonial past.

African nationalists rejected the name Rhodesia because of its obvious links to imperialism and white domination. Some historians use the name Zimbabwe exclusively when discussing the history of the area. For the sake of clarity, however, this chapter uses the names by which the region was officially known at different times: Southern Rhodesia (until 1965); Rhodesia (between 1965 and 1979); Zimbabwe-Rhodesia (1979–80); and Zimbabwe (1980 onwards).

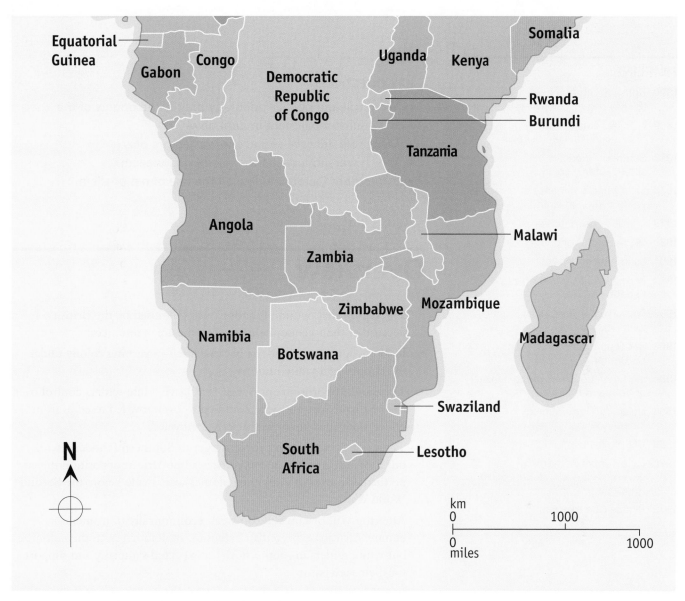

Figure 2.1 A map showing the states of southern Africa in 2015

1 Unit

The origins and rise of independence movements in Zimbabwe

TIMELINE

1890 British South Africa Company (BSAC) begins colonising Rhodesia.

1896–7 BSAC crushes uprisings by Shona and Ndebele peoples.

1923 Southern Rhodesia becomes self-governing colony.

1930 Land Apportionment Act reinforces white control of land.

1939 Bledisloe Commission.

1939–45 Second World War.

1951 Land Husbandry Act.

1953 Formation of Central African Federation.

1962 Formation of Rhodesian Front by white extremists.

1963 Break-up of Central African Federation.

1964 Ian Smith becomes prime minister of Southern Rhodesia.

1965 Unilateral Declaration of Independence.

1966 UN applies economic sanctions.

1970 Land Tenure Act; Smith government declares Republic of Rhodesia.

1972 Pearce Commission.

KEY QUESTIONS

- What role did political ideology play in the origins of the nationalist movement in Zimbabwe?
- What role did race and economic factors play?
- Which wars influenced the rise of nationalism?
- What other factors influenced the rise of nationalism?

Overview

- The region that became Rhodesia was colonised by the British because of their economic interest in the area's resources.
- In 1923, Southern Rhodesia became a self-governing colony under the control of a white minority.
- The Land Apportionment Act of 1930 gave white settlers control over the best land. Africans were confined to overcrowded reserves from which their movement was strictly controlled.
- There was white support for a merger of Southern Rhodesia with other British colonies in central Africa but African opposition meant no further moves to unify the colonies were made before the Second World War.
- After the war, Britain was too weak economically to maintain its empire; Africans expected an extension of democracy to the colonies; but white settlers in southern Africa expected sympathy and support for their viewpoint.
- In 1953, Britain created the Central African Federation (CAF), joining Southern Rhodesia, Northern Rhodesia and Nyasaland.
- Widespread protests and resistance by African nationalists in Northern Rhodesia and Nyasaland forced Britain to break up the CAF in 1963, creating the independent states of Zambia and Malawi respectively in 1964.
- Whites in Southern Rhodesia were not prepared to accept plans for majority rule, but Britain was not willing to grant independence to a white minority government. Talks between the two governments reached a stalemate.
- In 1965, the right-wing Rhodesian Front government, led by Ian Smith, made a Unilateral Declaration of Independence (UDI), cutting off ties with Britain.
- The new Rhodesian state was not officially recognised, and UDI was condemned by Britain and the United Nations (UN).

- The 1970 Land Tenure Act consolidated white control of the land; the government declared the Republic of Rhodesia.
- In 1972, a settlement that would ensure the continuation of white minority control was rejected by the African majority in a report by the Pearce Commission.

2.1 What role did political ideology play in the origins of the nationalist movement in Zimbabwe?

Zimbabwe is named after the stone ruins of Great Zimbabwe, the centre of a thriving empire that dominated the region more than 500 years ago. The Shona descendants of the builders and rulers of Great Zimbabwe continued to live in the area after its decline. In the 19th century, Ndebele people from the south moved into the western part of Zimbabwe.

Rhodes and the British South Africa Company

British interest in the area was sparked by hopes of finding gold deposits to match the substantial gold discoveries that had been made in the South African Republic. However, the British government itself did not colonise the region. In 1889, the government granted a charter to **Cecil John Rhodes** and his private company, the British South Africa Company (BSAC), to exploit the resources in the area that became known as Rhodesia.

White settlers started moving into the area in 1890, and in 1896–7 the BSAC crushed uprisings by the Ndebele and Shona people to secure white control. Using a mixture of force and diplomacy, Rhodes rapidly carved out his own empire. The white settlers and BSAC administrators used a ruthless combination of land seizure, taxation and forced labour to impose a system of harsh control over the people of Zimbabwe. By 1914, a minority of 25,000 white settlers dominated the land, which had been organised into large ranches. In the process, the local people lost their independence and freedom, as well as their land.

White settlers opposed continuing BSAC rule. They saw the BSAC as dominating the economy of the region for the benefit of its shareholders to the detriment of their own interests. In 1922, in a **referendum** conducted by the British government, the settlers rejected a proposal to make Rhodesia a province of South Africa. Instead, when the BSAC charter expired the following year, Southern Rhodesia became a self-governing British colony.

Although it was to be many years before a nationalist movement emerged, the establishment of a colony in Southern Rhodesia and the ideology associated with colonialism laid the foundations for African resistance in future years.

Theory of Knowledge

History and language: The white settlers in Rhodesia called the 1896–7 uprisings the 'Ndebele Rebellion' and the 'Shona Rebellion', but the local people themselves referred to them as the *Chimurenga*, or 'struggle'. Use this example, and others you can think of, to explain how terminology can be linked to bias in history.

Figure 2.2 Cecil John Rhodes (1853–1902)

A British businessman and politician, Rhodes established a huge commercial empire for himself in southern Africa based on mining. He was so powerful in the area that the whole region under BSAC control was named after him. Southern Rhodesia was the area between the Limpopo and Zambezi Rivers; Northern Rhodesia lay to the north.

Referendum: the approval of a law or political action by direct public vote.

Figure 2.3   A poster released by the Empire Marketing Board in the early 1930s, showing a tobacco plantation in Southern Rhodesia

2.2 What role did race and economic factors play?

The British colony of Southern Rhodesia

The establishment of Southern Rhodesia as a self-governing British colony in 1923 placed great power in the hands of the white settlers. Britain had a supervisory role, but the white population effectively controlled the colony. The constitution gave power to an elected legislative (law-making) assembly, led by a prime minister. The constitution did not specifically prohibit Africans from voting, but the franchise qualifications were so high that very few black people qualified. Thirty years later only 560 Africans, out of a population of four million, had the right to vote. The constitution gave Britain little control over the white government, which could effectively implement its own policies. Elsewhere in the empire – for example in Kenya – the British government had sought to protect the rights of the indigenous population. In Southern Rhodesia, however, the structure actually encouraged the domination of whites over blacks.

A key development in reinforcing white domination was the Land Apportionment Act of 1930. This formally divided the land between the African population and white settlers. Although a minority, white settlers gained more than half the land, while Africans were marginalised into the poorer and more arid regions, or 'reserves'. Africans could not own land outside these reserves and had to have an official document, or 'pass', to allow them to leave in search of work in the towns. The unfair distribution of land was a deep-seated issue that would resurface again and again.

The division of the land caused a massive economic crisis for black farmers. The reserves were overcrowded, overstocked and over-grazed. In order to survive during the difficult years of the **Great Depression** in the 1930s, black farmers had to farm intensively what land they had, resulting in severe ecological damage. This led to famine and great hardship. At the same time, the white minority grew richer, increasing political tensions in the colony.

White settlers had earlier rejected a proposed union with Northern Rhodesia, but after the discovery of vast copper deposits in the north, the issue resurfaced. Large numbers of white miners and farmers from Southern Rhodesia migrated to the 'Copperbelt', as it became known. Links between the two colonies had also been strengthened by the merging of their two railways into 'Rhodesia Railways'. When the imperial authorities in London proposed the formation of a 'Greater Rhodesia', to include the two Rhodesias and Nyasaland, white settlers in the three colonies supported the idea. They felt that such a union would protect their interests from African political activity. The British government appointed the Bledisloe Commission to investigate the issue. The Bledisloe Report, published in 1939, stressed the economic interdependence of the three territories, but noted the concerns of Africans that such a union would not be in their interests. Africans feared that such a move would lead to the extension of racial segregation from Southern Rhodesia to the other two territories.

SOURCE A

The African possesses a knowledge and shrewdness, in matters affecting his welfare, with which he is not always credited. It would be wrong to assume that his opposition to the amalgamation of Northern and Southern Rhodesia is based to a very large extent on ignorance or prejudice or an instinctive dread of change.

Extract from the Bledisloe Report (1939). Adapted from R. Blake (1977) *History of Rhodesia*, London: Methuen Publishing, p. 226.

The Bledisloe Report, which noted the viewpoint of the black majority, meant that African opinions were heard in London for the first time. The report caused concern among the more liberal civil servants in Britain, but its conclusions were totally at odds with the views of the settlers. Although the outbreak of the Second World War in 1939 postponed any further discussion about a possible merger, the idea of federation did not die.

Economic changes after the Second World War

The war created an economic boom in Southern Rhodesia. The growth of white commercial farming and the establishment of manufacturing industries resulted in increased demand for cheap African labour. In response to this, the government introduced the Land Husbandry Act in 1951. This Act enforced a radical change in the traditional system of land tenure in the African reserves, dividing the communally owned land into individual smallholdings. Only adult males and widows living in the reserves at the time were included in the scheme.

The Act was intended to force those unable to acquire land to work in the towns and on white commercial farms. The result was a huge increase in the number of landless people, many of whom moved to the towns to seek work. In the towns, social problems such as poverty and poor living conditions fuelled growing discontent. This formed the basis for the growth of African nationalism as a mass movement.

Great Depression: following the 1929 Wall Street Crash (see Chapter 3, section 3.2, Social and economic developments), the entire world entered a prolonged economic downturn that resulted in a contraction of economic activity and mass unemployment. This became known as the Great Depression.

QUESTION

What disadvantages did the black majority in Rhodesia face in the period before the Second World War?

Theory of Knowledge

History and language: Although historians today would consider the language used in the extract from the Bledisloe Report shown in **Source A** to be patronising, it is important to take into account the time and context in which a statement was made or written. Why do you think this is? In what ways, and by whom, would this statement have seemed dangerously liberal at the time?

KEY CONCEPTS QUESTION

Consequences: What were the political and economic consequences of the land policies of the colonial government in Southern Rhodesia?

Establishment of the Central African Federation, 1953

The Second World War (1939–45) had a massive impact on the British Empire and the expectations of its population. Britain emerged from the conflict economically weakened, and it was clear that the empire would not be able to survive in the same form as it had before the war began. White settlers in Southern Rhodesia hoped that the contribution of Rhodesian and South African troops to the Allied war effort would win them support and sympathy. As a result they assumed that they would not be subject to the post-war move towards decolonisation that was sweeping the British Empire. They hoped that, if independence came to the British colonies in Southern Africa, it would be in the form of white-dominated states with close ties to Britain.

After the war, white settlers revived the idea of a closer union of the three British colonies, wanting to create an economically powerful, white-controlled state. They put strong pressure on the British government to make the necessary constitutional changes. Africans, however, were strongly opposed to the idea and the Labour government was hesitant about proceeding. However, the election of a Conservative government in 1952 changed this. Despite continuing African protests, in 1953 Southern and Northern Rhodesia and Nyasaland were joined as the Central African Federation (CAF).

The federal parliament was made up of thirty-five members, of whom only six were African – two from each territory. African representative councils in Northern Rhodesia and Nyasaland selected their delegates, but the African delegates from Southern Rhodesia were elected by white voters. Federation led to a further economic boom in Southern Rhodesia, and this assisted the government's policy of encouraging white immigration.

Majority rule: when a government has been elected by the majority in an election in which all adults have the right to vote, regardless of race. In the context of post-colonial Africa, this meant a black government. Minority rule means rule by a white minority, who dominate political power and deny others the right to vote, except perhaps in insignificant numbers. Rhodesia had a white minority government until 1979, as did apartheid South Africa until 1994.

Federation also allowed whites to strengthen their hold on power. Originally Britain had intended that the federation would begin the transition to **majority rule**. However, this development was halted by whites in Southern Rhodesia, who had already established a self-governing state under white domination and hoped to extend this to the other two territories. In 1953, the white population in Southern Rhodesia numbered 150,000, out of a total population of just over four million, but white immigration during the 1950s pushed this number up to about 250,000. There were far fewer white settlers in Northern Rhodesia and, especially, Nyasaland.

The origins of black nationalist organisations

Before the Second World War, there were no large-scale African political organisations. African dissatisfaction with colonial rule and economic exploitation was voiced mainly through societies known as Welfare Associations, which focused on issues such as voting rights for Africans, or educational and social reforms. Independent African churches also provided an outlet for discontent and defiance.

There was also support from urban workers for industrial organisations, and branches of the Industrial and Commercial Workers' Union (ICU) held mass meetings and called for improved working conditions. However, all of these were on a regional rather than a national scale. The first attempt to create a nationwide nationalist movement was the formation in 1934 of the Southern Rhodesian African National Congress (SRANC). This was cautious and conservative in its approach, and failed to gain a mass following, appealing instead to an educated élite.

Several factors hindered the development of black political organisations. Most Africans lived in the reserves or on land owned by white settlers, and it was illegal for Africans to have permanent residence in any of the urban centres. Political activity is most easily facilitated in dense population centres, not among farm labourers or rural dwellers dispersed across the countryside. Africans were also denied education on a large scale. African schools run by missionaries had focused initially on teaching basic literacy, as well as practical subjects such as carpentry, agriculture and domestic science.

The poor standard of education prevented the development of a large independence movement and also deprived the economy of black skilled workers and professionals. After the war, however, the number of potential leaders increased rapidly as larger numbers of Africans began to receive secondary education.

The development of nationalist movements was also negatively affected by the segregationist and repressive policies of the government, which wanted to prevent the spread of political opposition. Godfrey Huggins, prime minister of Southern Rhodesia from 1933 to 1953, and of the Central African Federation from 1953 to 1956, was a strong supporter of maintaining white domination.

Figure 2.4 A school in Rhodesia in 1959; before the Second World War few black Rhodesians received any formal education, but standards of education improved after the war

ACTIVITY

'The open expression of these racial views was the prelude to inevitable repression, conflict and bloodshed. In the retrospect of a later "forgive and forget" culture about imperialism it is important to recall the sheer demeaning contempt such attitudes conveyed.'

G. Arnold (2006), *Africa: A Modern History*, London: Atlantic Books, p. 286.

How do the attitudes shown in **Sources B** and **C** help to explain African opposition to the creation of the Central African Federation? Read and comment on the views of historian Guy Arnold, and explain how they relate to the sources. Suggest what he means by 'a later "forgive and forget" culture about imperialism'.

Self-determination: people's right to rule themselves. This became a key demand in Asian and African colonies after the Second World War.

SOURCE B

Partnership between black and white is the partnership between a horse and its rider.

Godfrey Huggins. Quoted in G. Arnold (2006), *Africa: A Modern History*, London: Atlantic Books, p. 286.

2.3 Which wars influenced the rise of nationalism?

The impact of the Second World War and the Cold War

The Second World War exposed the horrors of Nazi race policies, and so after the war there was a worldwide condemnation of racism and a greater awareness of human rights. Furthermore, during the war, the wartime Allied leaders, Winston Churchill and Franklin D. Roosevelt, had confirmed their support for **self-determination** in the Atlantic Charter, a joint declaration of Allied war aims. By 1945, therefore, Africans in colonial empires hoped that the end of the war would mean an end to colonialism and white domination.

The Second World War made a significant contribution to the growth of African nationalism in Southern Rhodesia. Black soldiers from Southern Rhodesia had fought with some equality alongside whites in East Africa and Burma. On their return home they found it impossible to revert to their previous subservient position. They had been part of the Allied fight for freedom, and they now wanted to know why liberation and democracy did not extend to African colonies. This new mood was reflected in the revival of the SRANC after 1945, and an increasing number of strikes by workers. Despite this, the Huggins administration ignored any claims the African population made for greater rights, and continued a policy of strict social and economic segregation.

SOURCE C

We believe that the African should be given more say in the running of the country, as and when he shows ability to contribute more to the general good, but we must make it clear that even when that day comes, in a hundred or two hundred years' time, he can never hope to dominate the partnership. He can achieve equal standing, but not go beyond it.

Roy Welensky, prime minister of the Central African Federation, 1956–63. Quoted in G. Arnold (2006), *Africa: A Modern History*, London: Atlantic Books, p. 286.

After 1945, some members of the new Labour government in Britain grew concerned about developments in the British colonies in southern Africa, and wanted to work towards a multiracial settlement there. However, with the start of the Cold War, colonial affairs became secondary to the development of a Western alliance and containment of the perceived threat of the USSR. Indeed, the white-dominated colonies of southern Africa were seen as partners in this struggle. Thus, from 1945, the British government put little pressure on the Southern Rhodesian government to curtail its race polices. At the same time, however, Britain was concerned that continued segregationist policies would alienate the black majority and deny them any democratic route to self-determination. The British government feared that desperation might push Africans into a guerrilla war, which would lead to instability and even communist involvement in the region.

2.4 What other factors influenced the rise of nationalism?

The break-up of the Central African Federation

Even before the establishment of the Central African Federation, there had been strong opposition from African nationalist organisations in Northern Rhodesia and Nyasaland by those who feared the extension of white minority rule from Southern Rhodesia to the two northern territories. When Britain ignored their concerns and went ahead with the formation of the CAF in 1953, opposition intensified. Protests by the Nyasaland African Congress gained momentum after 1958, when Dr Hastings Kamuzu Banda became an outspoken critic of federation. In Northern Rhodesia, Kenneth Kaunda formed the Zambia African National Congress (ZANC) to step up protests and force Britain to grant independence to the territories.

The British government feared that the protests would turn into armed resistance, which would be more difficult to control and would divert Britain's military and economic resources from the Cold War. Britain also believed that governments led by Banda and Kaunda would be viable solutions to the problems in the region. Not only did these men have mass support, but they were considered to be politically moderate leaders who would block communist influence in the region.

In 1960, the British government set up a commission to review the workings of the CAF. The commission recommended that, as African opposition to it was so strong, each colony should be given the right to secede (withdraw from the federation). The British government readily accepted this recommendation and on 31 December 1963 the CAF was formally dissolved. In 1964, Northern Rhodesia and Nyasaland became the independent states of Zambia and Malawi respectively, under majority rule governments.

Southern Rhodesia remained a self-governing British colony, however. The British government would not grant independence to a white minority government, and this government in turn was determined not to allow majority rule. From the perspective of white Rhodesians, Britain had ignored their concerns by creating two new black African states along their northern frontier. They believed that their future now lay in cooperation and closer links with the apartheid government in South Africa. This reinforced the siege mentality that was deeply ingrained in the minds of white settlers, and led directly to UDI and a break with what they saw as a meddling colonial power.

Fact: The segregationist policies applied in Southern Rhodesia were very similar to the discriminatory race policies in South Africa. After 1948, when the Afrikaner Nationalist Party was voted into power in South Africa, this policy became known as apartheid, an Afrikaans word meaning 'separateness'. In theory it segregated the white and black populations; in reality it created extreme political, social and economic inequality, with the white population benefiting disproportionately from the arrangement.

Theory of Knowledge

Historical interpretation: The Nigerian historians A.E. Afigbo and E.A. Ayandele believe that Britain's decision to break up the Federation and recognise majority rule in Northern Rhodesia and Nyasaland was influenced by British experiences during the Mau Mau Uprising in Kenya and French experiences in Indochina and Algeria. They think these showed that *'attempts to suppress political ambitions of the majority in colonial countries could lead to expensive and futile wars'*. How valuable to historians is hindsight when they analyse the reasons for decisions in the past?

Figure 2.5 These maps show Rhodesia/Zimbabwe at the time of the Central African Federation (left) and after the Unilateral Declaration of Independence (right)

The Unilateral Declaration of Independence, 1965

Since 1961, the government of Southern Rhodesia had been negotiating with the British government regarding full independence, but the British government insisted that certain guarantees must be made before independence could be granted. One of these was eventual progress to majority rule. As the white government's main reason for wanting independence was to maintain white supremacy, it would not agree to this. As protests and acts of resistance by black nationalist groups intensified, white Rhodesians turned to a new political party, more right-wing and racist than its predecessors – the Rhodesian Front.

In 1962, a Rhodesian Front government was elected to power, and in 1964 **Ian Smith** became its leader and prime minister of Southern Rhodesia. He adopted a hard-line policy towards the nationalist movements, banning them and imprisoning hundreds of their leaders. The government also introduced harsh security laws, including a compulsory death sentence for many political offences. Under Smith, negotiations between the British government and the white administration in Southern Rhodesia rapidly broke down, especially after the election of a Labour government in Britain in 1965. Rhodesians began to talk openly about declaring independence unilaterally.

On 11 November 1965, Smith made a Unilateral Declaration of Independence (UDI), formally severing his country's ties with Britain. In 1970, the Rhodesians took this a step further, breaking all legal ties with Britain and becoming the Republic of Rhodesia. The result of these acts was to place Rhodesia on a collision course with neighbouring African states and to intensify armed resistance to the white minority regime.

International reactions to UDI

UDI was condemned immediately by the United Nations Security Council, which called on all countries not to recognise the 'illegal racist minority regime' and to refuse to give it any assistance. UDI was also condemned by the Organisation of African Unity (OAU) and the Commonwealth. No country in the world, not even apartheid South Africa, officially recognised the Smith regime.

Britain regarded the declaration as illegal and moved to impose economic and diplomatic sanctions. In previous situations where the peaceful transition from colonial rule to independence had broken down, the British had been ready to use force. However, the special circumstances in Rhodesia prevented this. Firstly, Southern Rhodesia had been autonomous for almost forty years rather than ruled directly from London. Secondly, there was a racial dimension to the decision. The presence of a large white minority in Rhodesia created fears in the British government that public opinion in Britain would not tolerate a military solution to the problem. There is even some evidence to suggest that ministers feared the British army would not carry out orders directing it to fight the white settlers. As a result, the British government decided that military force would only be used if civil order collapsed in Rhodesia.

Britain decided that a combination of political and economic pressures might achieve its aims, and rallied support for **economic sanctions** at the United Nations (UN). More than forty countries agreed to isolate Rhodesia politically and, critically, economically. The UN passed a resolution implementing restrictions on the supply of arms, financial services and oil to Rhodesia. Later that year the embargo was extended to include a range of essential goods, and by mid-1967 the embargo was made total. At first sight

Fact: Unilateral means 'made by one side only'. In other words, this was a one-sided decision, made by white settlers in Southern Rhodesia without the agreement of the British government, which did not recognise the legality of the declaration. The previous occasion on which British colonists had made such a move was when settlers in North America made their famous Declaration of Independence in 1776, resulting in the establishment of the United States of America.

Ian Smith (1919–2007)

He was the leader of the Rhodesian Front political party. He became prime minister of Southern Rhodesia in 1964, and after UDI in 1965 he was prime minister of Rhodesia until the end of white minority rule in 1979. After independence, he remained a member of the Zimbabwean parliament until 1987.

Economic sanctions: also known as trade embargoes, these ban trade with a particular country, and are used as a means of putting pressure on a country to change its policies.

Zimbabwe

Fact: The Organisation of African Unity (OAU) was established in 1963 by the thirty-two African states that were independent at that time. One of its aims was to eradicate colonialism in Africa by giving support to the liberation movements fighting white minority rule in southern Africa, including the nationalist organisations in Rhodesia, and putting pressure on the UN to support independence movements. Zimbabwe joined the OAU after independence in 1980. In 2002, the OAU was replaced by the African Union.

Figure 2.6 White voters arrive at a polling station in Salisbury, Rhodesia, in November 1964, to cast their votes in a referendum about independence

these economic sanctions should have created economic collapse in Rhodesia, but they had limited impact. Instead, they helped to reinforce a siege mentality among whites.

There were specific problems involved in the implementation of economic sanctions against Rhodesia that made them far less effective than they might have been. Although Britain was empowered by the UN to enforce oil sanctions, it turned a blind eye to exports into Rhodesia by British oil companies via the Mozambican port of Beira, which was connected to Rhodesia by a pipeline. Thus, Rhodesia was never really cut off from the key resource of oil. The British did not want to destroy the Rhodesian regime; rather they wanted to make life so difficult that Smith would be forced back to the negotiating table.

Another major obstacle to the successful implementation of sanctions was South Africa, which until the 1970s continued to supply goods and financial credit to this other white minority regime. In addition, Portugal, a country sympathetic to the Smith regime, was in control of Mozambique until 1975. Some American and other Western companies also needed Rhodesia's valuable mineral exports, such as chromium, and continued to buy them secretly despite the sanctions.

Finally, the Rhodesians had the means to retaliate. Many neighbouring African states were linked to Rhodesia's economy and infrastructure, making them vulnerable. A good example is Zambia, which was almost totally dependent on Rhodesia for coal to power its vital copper industry, and on the Rhodesian rail routes for the export of its copper. In an effort to help Zambia break its dependence on Rhodesia and South Africa, China financed the building of a railway linking the Zambian Copperbelt with the Tanzanian port of Dar es Salaam, called the TanZam Railway. The rail link covered 1,800km (1,100 miles) over extremely rugged terrain. It was China's most ambitious foreign aid project and built at a time when China was competing with the USA and Soviet Union for influence in Africa. Historians such as Neil Parsons believe that the real victim of sanctions was Zambia. Although the Rhodesian economy was severely damaged by sanctions, the government was in no danger of a sudden collapse.

Attempts at a negotiated settlement

In spite of UDI, the British government continued to hold talks with Smith in an attempt to negotiate a settlement. The Rhodesian government, however, stubbornly refused to make meaningful concessions and showed that it had no intention of relinquishing white control. In 1970, the Land Tenure Act replaced the Land Apportionment Act of 1930, consolidating white control over more of the land. This Act formed the basis of a new constitution, designed to maintain white supremacy, which declared Rhodesia to be a republic.

Finally, in 1971, the two sides agreed on a proposed settlement. Although this made provision for eventual majority rule, it effectively maintained white domination for the foreseeable future. Despite this, the British government insisted that the agreement should have the support of the majority of people in Rhodesia, and in 1972 it sent the Pearce Commission to investigate. Even though the nationalist organisations had been formally banned and their leaders in prison, there were widespread demonstrations, strikes and mass meetings showing overwhelming opposition from Africans to the proposed settlement. This was a major setback for the white minority government, which had hoped to gain international recognition of its regime.

KEY CONCEPTS ACTIVITY

Causes and consequences: Design a spider diagram to analyse the causes and consequences of UDI.

ACTIVITY

Explain the similarities and differences between the significance of the Bledisloe Commission of 1939 and the Pearce Commission of 1972.

SOURCE D

The whole Pearce Commission exercise proved a disaster for the Smith government… It showed Britain, South Africa and the world at large the depth and extent of African rejection of white minority rule in Rhodesia. It showed that the regime would be unlikely to survive for very long even if it gained legal independence. Finally it showed Africans who disliked the regime that this hatred was shared by almost every other African throughout the land. It thus played a very important part in preparing the ground for the spread of the liberation struggle.

A.E. Afigbo et al. (1986), *The Making of Modern Africa, Volume 2: The Twentieth Century,* London: Longman, p. 276.

Historical interpretation: Although the Smith regime was ultimately overthrown in 1979, it seems that economic sanctions were not a major reason for this. In a study for the Harvard Center for International Affairs, Robin Renwick, head of the Rhodesian department of the British Foreign Office, reports that between 1965 and 1974 Rhodesia's real output increased by 6 per cent per year 'despite the depressing effect of sanctions'; the value of exports more than doubled between 1968 and 1974 and continued to rise afterwards, although much more slowly. How valuable are statistics such as these to historians investigating the impact of economic sanctions?

End of unit activities

1   Create a spider diagram to examine the political, economic and social advantages that white settlers had in the colony of Rhodesia.

2   The historian Guy Arnold has argued: 'The history of Rhodesia is the history of Anglo-Saxon racialism in Africa. Two factors operated throughout the colonial period: white control of African education in order to limit advance and white control and demarcation of the land.' Write an argument to support this view.

3   The historian Kevin Shillington believes that the creation of the Central African Federation was designed to benefit the white settlers of Southern Rhodesia, at the expense of the black inhabitants of all three territories. Find out what you can about the Central African Federation (1953–63), and work out an argument to support or oppose this view.

4   'Britain should have played a more decisive role in the early 1960s to force the government of Southern Rhodesia to accept majority rule.' Divide into two groups. One group should develop an argument to support this statement, and the other group an argument to oppose it.

5   Write a short report to explain whether the policies applied towards the African majority by successive white administrations between 1890 and 1970 represented change or continuity.

KEY QUESTIONS

- What role did non-violent protest play in the struggle for independence?
- What was the role of armed struggle in achieving independence?
- What other factors played a role in the success of the nationalist movement?
- What part did Robert Mugabe play in the struggle for independence?
- Why did the nationalist movement succeed?

Overview

- A strong nationalist movement emerged despite government efforts to suppress it. Several nationalist groups were formed and later banned by the government throughout the 1950s and 1960s.
- Africans formed political organisations such as the Zimbabwean African People's Union (ZAPU) and the Zimbabwean African National Union (ZANU). When they were banned by the government in 1964, these groups resorted to an armed struggle.
- In 1966, the guerrilla movements Zimbabwe People's Revolutionary Army (ZIPRA) and Zimbabwe African National Liberation Army (ZANLA) began a fourteen-year war of resistance to gain majority rule in Zimbabwe.
- The Smith government tried to counter support for the nationalist movement by attacking guerrilla bases in neighbouring states and moving the rural population into 'protected villages'.
- There were divisions within the nationalist movement, with leadership struggles and competition for power and influence between ZAPU and ZANU.
- The independence of neighbouring Mozambique under a FRELIMO government in 1975 gave a boost to the Zimbabwean nationalist movement, providing economic and military support.
- As a result of pressure from Zambia and other frontline states, ZAPU and ZANU joined together in 1976 to form the Patriotic Front (PF), to strengthen the liberation movement.

TIMELINE

1957 Southern Rhodesian African National Congress (SRANC) re-launched – but banned in 1959.

1960 Formation of National Democratic Party (NDP) – but banned in 1961.

1962 Formation of Zimbabwean African People's Union (ZAPU).

1963 Formation of Zimbabwean African National Union (ZANU).

1964 ZAPU and ZANU banned by the government.

1966 Start of guerrilla war.

1974 South Africa begins to put pressure on the Smith government.

1975 Mozambique achieves independence under FRELIMO government.

1976 Talks between Smith and Nkomo break down; South Africa steps up pressure on Smith government; formation of Patriotic Front between ZANU and ZAPU.

1977 Guerrilla war intensifies.

1978 Internal Settlement between Smith and 'moderate' leaders.

1979 Elections won by Muzorewa; establishment of Zimbabwe-Rhodesia; Internal Settlement rejected by Patriotic Front and international community; Lancaster House talks.

1980 Elections won by Mugabe and ZANU-PF; independence of Zimbabwe.

- In the climate of the Cold War, the West wanted to prevent the spread of communist influence in a strategically vital region, and this influenced policies towards the Smith government.

- South Africa played a key role in events, initially supporting the Smith regime but later increasing the pressure for reform, mainly to prevent a Marxist victory in Rhodesia, which would weaken South Africa.

- In the face of mounting military incursions and a declining economy, the Smith government concluded an 'Internal Settlement' with moderate black leaders in an effort to prevent a PF victory.

- Smith met nationalist leaders at Lancaster House in London, and the parties agreed on a settlement that was acceptable to both blacks and whites.

- Robert Mugabe played a decisive role in the nationalist struggle, and he and ZANU-PF won independent Zimbabwe's first election; he played a dominating role in subsequent developments there.

- Many factors – both internal and external – played a role in the success of the nationalist movement.

Figure 2.7 Demonstrators gather at Rhodesia House in London in protest against the British government's policies towards Rhodesia

2.5 What role did non-violent protest play in the struggle for independence?

Before the 1950s there were no effective nationwide African political organisations. The Southern Rhodesian African National Congress (SRANC), which had been formed in 1934, was cautious and conservative in its approach and failed to gain a mass following, appealing instead to an educated urban élite. The development of a mass-based movement was hampered by the rural base of most of the population and the repressive policies of the government.

The growth of a nationalist movement in the 1950s

During the 1950s, however, this situation began to change when developments in other parts of Africa inspired the birth of a nationalist movement in Southern Rhodesia. Since the Second World War there had been increasing resistance to colonial rule all over Africa, and in the 1950s African nationalism became a powerful force. In South Africa, too, there was a mounting spirit of defiance towards the imposition of stricter segregation laws, while in Northern Rhodesia and Nyasaland, nationalist leaders were demanding an immediate end to federation and majority rule. Nationalists in Southern Rhodesia were also motivated by a growing economic disparity. In 1961, for example, the average wage for black workers was less than £90 per annum, while whites earned more than £1,250. There was no indication that the white minority intended to surrender their economic privileges or political control, and this intensified resistance to the white Rhodesian regime.

In 1955, a militant organisation, the City Youth League, was launched in Salisbury (Harare), and in 1957 it merged with Bulawayo-based organisations to form a re-launched SRANC, led by Joshua Nkomo. The policy of the SRANC was moderate, and it stressed non-racialism and the right of all – black and white – to be citizens of the country. With growing landlessness and unemployment, it rapidly grew into a mass-based organisation with support in both urban and rural areas.

However, the Southern Rhodesian government was not prepared to tolerate protests and opposition, and so in 1959 it banned the SRANC and introduced restrictions on political organisations. This move only served to intensify opposition. In 1960, the National Democratic Party (NDP) was formed, also under the leadership of Nkomo, and proposed a policy of more active resistance to white minority rule. Growing unrest and protest actions around the country led to the banning of the NDP in December 1961.

It was re-launched a week later, in January 1962, as the Zimbabwe African People's Union (ZAPU). ZAPU's first president was Joshua Nkomo with the Reverend Ndabaningi Sithole as chairman and Robert Mugabe (see Section 2.6, Rivalry between ZAPU and ZANU) as secretary. Its programme was much more confrontational and it organised Land Freedom Farmers who occupied unused government or white-owned land.

Historical interpretation: Historian David Leaver has argued that both whites and blacks either created myths or used history to legitimise their struggles. The myth of white supremacy was based on their control of the land and the concepts behind segregation and minority rule. Black nationalists emphasised the greatness of Great Zimbabwe as a legitimate black state long before the colonists arrived. As Leaver states: 'To African nationalist movements of the 1960s and 1970s, Great Zimbabwe proved what most whites sought to deny – that blacks had, could, and would create a great nation. From the early 20th century, there never was any doubt about the site's African origins: colonial mythmaking was believed by those who needed or wanted to believe it.'

QUESTION

Is Leaver's view convincing? As you read other case studies in this book, try to find parallels with this view of Rhodesia/Zimbabwe.

QUESTION

What factors played a role in hindering the emergence of a strong national independence movement in Rhodesia/Zimbabwe?

Among ZAPU members there were differences of opinion about the tactics to use to achieve majority rule. Some, including Nkomo, were prepared to compromise with Britain and the Southern Rhodesian government to negotiate a constitutional solution. Others urged more active forms of confrontation and began a campaign of sabotage, targeting railway lines, electrical installations and government forests. ZAPU was banned in September 1962, but survived under the name of the People's Caretaker Council (PCC).

2.6 What was the role of armed struggle in achieving independence?

Rivalry between ZAPU and ZANU

Even though ZAPU had embarked on a campaign of sabotage and the occupation of unused land, **Joshua Nkomo** had also been prepared to negotiate a settlement with Britain. Others distrusted Nkomo's leadership and supported more radical solutions and this led to a split in the organization. In 1963 Sithole and other leaders, including **Robert Mugabe**, broke away to form a separate nationalist organisation, the Zimbabwe African National Union (ZANU). It supported a policy of more militant confrontation with the white-minority government.

A struggle began between ZAPU and ZANU to gain the support of people in the townships. In time, regional differences between them intensified. ZANU was seen to represent the interests of Shona-speakers based mainly in the eastern part of the country, and ZAPU the interests of Ndebele-speakers in the western areas. Disagreements over policies and regional rivalries between the two organisations reduced their effectiveness at a crucial time in the early 1960s, when the Central African Federation was breaking up and constitutional negotiations were taking place. When Ian Smith and the right-wing Rhodesian Front Party were elected in 1964, they banned both ZANU and ZAPU/PCC, and imprisoned hundreds of their leaders, including Nkomo, Sithole and Mugabe.

Figure 2.8   Robert Mugabe (b. 1924)

He emerged as one of the primary figures in the independence movement as leader of ZANU, a splinter group of Joshua Nkomo's ZAPU. He was prime minister of Zimbabwe from 1980 to 1987, and president with special powers from 1987.

The move to guerrilla warfare

When the Rhodesian Front government banned ZAPU and ZANU in 1964, both organisations realised that a constitutional solution was unlikely and began an armed struggle. ZAPU formed the Zimbabwe People's Revolutionary Army (**ZIPRA**), and ZANU formed the Zimbabwe African National Liberation Army (ZANLA). ZAPU aligned itself with the USSR and encouraged an uprising by urban workers. Its armed wing, ZIPRA, later received Soviet support and funding. ZANU, on the other hand, aligned itself with China and attempted to mobilise the rural peasantry. It believed that the low urban density of Rhodesia, and the ease with which the authorities could monitor and control town-dwellers, meant that ZAPU's strategy was doomed to failure. ZANU and its military wing ZANLA received support and training from China.

The first real clash between guerrilla fighters and the Rhodesian army came in April 1966, when ZANU guerrillas crossed into Rhodesia from Zambia to blow up power lines and attack white farms. They were wiped out by the Rhodesian army in what was later referred to as the Battle of Sinoia. Although this event demonstrated how effective the Rhodesian armed forces were at countering insurgent activity, it also showed how vulnerable the white farming community was.

In addition, the Rhodesian government realised it would face problems in the future if the guerrilla attacks became better organised and supported. In 1967 and 1968, the tempo increased, with attacks on urban targets such as hotels and cafés. In August 1967, a combined force of **ZAPU** and African National Congress guerrillas from South Africa attacked targets in Rhodesia. This force was defeated, but it drew South African forces into the conflict. For the next few years, South African paramilitary units were stationed in Rhodesia.

These early attacks showed the nationalist organisations that large-scale incursions into Rhodesia would not be successful on their own. They were inviting a devastating military response from the government, which the guerrillas could not hope to resist. However, if large areas of the countryside could be brought over to support the resistance movement, and if attacks in the cities were coordinated, then perhaps the government would lose control of the situation. This was the path increasingly followed by **ZANU**, which infiltrated Rhodesia with small numbers of guerrillas – sometimes single individuals.

ZANU and its military wing **ZANLA** were applying **Maoist** techniques borrowed from the Chinese. These involved creating a strong powerbase among the peasants, making control of the countryside impossible for the government. ZANLA even enlisted the aid of traditional leaders and local spirit mediums. The powerbase they created was initially political, but eventually it involved arming large numbers of men and women who supplemented the more formally trained ZANLA guerrillas. By 1972, the peasants of north-eastern Rhodesia had been heavily politicised and were prepared to support guerrilla operations. The guerrilla war intensified when ZANLA launched a series of attacks on white farmsteads that the Rhodesian security forces found difficult to contain.

Government attempts to crush the uprising

Even though the period of national service required by the white population was extended, the Rhodesian government simply did not have enough troops to protect the scattered white farming communities. The government therefore launched Operation Hurricane, a plan to strike the guerrilla bases in neighbouring Zambia and Mozambique. It also closed the border with Zambia to all goods except copper. These actions left no room for negotiation and served to alienate Zambia and extend the war's geographic area. The South African government was also concerned by these actions, fearing destabilisation of the whole region. The Rhodesian attempt to eliminate guerrilla bases in neighbouring countries was thus not successful.

The government next focused on the peasants, who were providing vital support for ZANLA. The government imposed collective fines on entire regions, confiscated cattle as a punishment and closed key facilities such as shops, clinics, schools and churches. The most extreme measure was the creation of 'protected villages' – entire communities were uprooted and moved out of the war zone. This created vast unpopulated regions along the Mozambique frontier, allowing the Rhodesian military to sweep the countryside for guerrillas. Although this measure had an impact on ZANLA operations, it also alienated the rural population to such an extent that many more joined the resistance. It has been

ZAPU: Zimbabwe African People's Union

ZANU: Zimbabwe African National Union

ZIPRA: Zimbabwe People's Revolutionary Army (the armed wing of ZAPU)

ZANLA: Zimbabwe African National Liberation Army (the armed wing of ZANU)

Maoist: relating to the policies and tactics used by Chinese communist leader Mao Zedong. Working in a pre-industrial agrarian society, he modified classic Marxism to fit China's circumstances. He argued that communist activity could prepare the peasant population for a full-scale uprising against the ruling class.

Fact: Events would prove ZANU right – it was in the countryside that the guerrillas stood the best chance of success. It was harder for the Rhodesian armed forces to maintain control over large rural areas. The presence of friendly states, especially Mozambique after 1975, along all except the southern border of Rhodesia also created safe havens for the guerrillas.

Zimbabwe

Fact: The uprisings against
colonial rule that had taken
place in 1896–7 had been
called the *Chimurenga*,
which means 'struggle' in
Shona. Although they had
been crushed, the resistance
provided inspiration to
future freedom fighters.
The uprising against white
minority rule between 1966
and 1980 was referred to as
the Second *Chimurenga*.

QUESTION

What strategies
did the Rhodesian
government use in an
attempt to crush the
resistance movement?
How successful were
they?

Theory of Knowledge

History and language:
An example of bias in
historical terminology
is the use of the word
'terrorist'. White Rhodesians
referred to ZANU and
ZAPU as terrorists, while
the nationalist movements
saw themselves as freedom
fighters. What term could
be used that would be more
neutral than either of these?

Figure 2.9   ZANLA guerrillas in the Zambezi Valley region of Rhodesia

estimated that 240,000 Africans were uprooted by this scheme. Although some of the
settlements to which they were relocated were an improvement on their original homes,
in general the new protected villages were of very low quality and living conditions
were poor. In an attempt to win support, the government offered rewards to villagers for
informing on ZANLA operations. This had limited success and its effects were largely
offset by the negative policy of the protected villages.

The increased tempo of the war began to have a significant effect on the white
population. Rhodesia's critical shortage of troops resulted in extreme measures to fill
the ranks of the army. The draft age for white settlers was extended to thirty-eight, and
mixed-race Rhodesians were also conscripted. As time went on, this placed an increasing
drain on the economy as more of the skilled workforce was called up for military
service. The regular army was also expanded, but it was clear that a military force capable

of waging a long-drawn-out war would be prohibitively expensive. ZANLA's operations, therefore, were slowly undermining the white regime.

Divisions among the nationalists

In 1975, the nationalist organisations and the Smith government, under pressure from Zambia and South Africa respectively, agreed to a ceasefire. From the nationalist point of view, the ceasefire looked like – and was depicted as – a victory. The nationalists, however, faced problems of their own. The movement had already divided into ZANU and ZAPU; now there was infighting within ZANU's military wing, ZANLA. This was the so-called Nhari Rebellion of 1975.

The Nhari Rebellion was essentially a confrontation between the ZANU high command and a group of ZANLA guerrillas. The guerrillas were led by Thomas Nhari, who complained about the lack of sophisticated weapons, ammunition and supplies reaching the guerrillas while the leaders enjoyed comfortable lives in the Zambian capital, Lusaka. Eventually Nhari was arrested and executed together with sixty ZANLA fighters who had supported him.

This did not solve the divisions within ZANLA, however, and in 1975 its charismatic leader, Herbert Chitepo, was assassinated. Much later it was discovered that Chitepo's death was a result of Rhodesian undercover operations, but at the time it was blamed on ZANLA infighting. The Zambians stepped in to restore order and forced the ZANLA leadership to leave for Mozambique. Zambian actions also began to starve ZANU of money. Funds for the guerrilla war went through a nationalist umbrella organisation called the African National Council, headed by Bishop Abel Muzorewa. Under Zambian pressure he withdrew funding for ZANU.

At this stage there was also a change of leadership within ZANU. Many in the organisation had come to believe that Sithole was out of touch with the fighters in the ZANLA camps in Mozambique, and he was replaced as leader of ZANU by Robert Mugabe. Sithole continued to lead a significant minority claiming to be the real ZANU. In 1975, Mugabe and a fellow ZANU leader, Edgar Tekere, were under house arrest in Mozambique. This was ostensibly for their own safety, but may also have been because Mugabe was regarded with some suspicion by Mozambican leaders. These problems within ZANU shifted the power in the nationalist movement to Nkomo's ZAPU. ZAPU's military wing, ZIPRA, was almost wholly based in Zambia and received full support from Kenneth Kaunda.

This division of effort between ZAPU and ZANU weakened the effectiveness of the resistance movement. Eventually pressure from the **frontline states** led to the establishment of the Patriotic Front between ZAPU and ZANU in October 1976. This was not a union of the two organisations, but an agreement to work together. Although differences between the two continued – with ZANU openly critical of détente – by this time there was widespread support for both organisations throughout Zimbabwe.

Developments after 1976

From 1976, members of the guerrilla organisations and the black population in general increasingly looked to Mugabe as the nationalist leader who would succeed in gaining majority rule. His position was further strengthened when the frontline states of Zambia and Mozambique finally allied themselves to ZANU. This development proved critical in bringing down white minority rule in Rhodesia. Despite the formation of the Patriotic

Frontline states: these were the independent states that were geographically close to Rhodesia – Mozambique, Zambia, Botswana, Angola and Tanzania – and which were affected by the ongoing guerrilla war. Three of them shared borders with Rhodesia, and Tanzania provided the nationalist forces with support and bases. The frontline states played an influential role in urging unity among the nationalist groups and an acceptance of a negotiated settlement.

Front, friction within the nationalist ranks continued, but ZANU managed to strengthen its position and create a military threat that the Rhodesian government could not overcome.

Between 1977 and 1979, the guerrilla war intensified. ZIPRA forces from Zambia and Botswana and ZANLA forces from Mozambique launched full-scale incursions into Rhodesia. This created considerable tensions within the ruling Rhodesian Front party when extremists demanded mass conscription and a huge expansion of the army. There was even talk of a military coup against Smith. Neither came about.

The Rhodesian security forces also stepped up their attacks on guerrilla bases outside the country. In November 1977 they launched a massive raid on Chimoio, a ZANLA camp 90km (56 miles) inside Mozambique. Using ground troops and the entire Rhodesian air force, they killed more than 1,200 people. They also attacked ZIPRA camps in Zambia.

The nationalists reacted by increasing the conflict, declaring 1978 as the 'year of the people' and sending thousands of guerrillas into Rhodesia. With increasingly sophisticated weapons, including Soviet-made surface-to-air missiles, ZIPRA forces shot down two Air Rhodesia passenger planes, killing dozens of passengers. ZANLA forces blew up the oil storage tanks in an industrial area of the Rhodesian capital, Salisbury. By 1979, the nationalist guerrillas were on the brink of victory.

2.7 What other factors played a role in the success of the nationalist movement?

FRELIMO: the Frente de Libertaçâo de Moçambique, or Mozambican Liberation Front. This group was formed in 1964 to fight Portuguese control in Mozambique. During the 1960s and early 1970s, Portugal waged fierce wars against resistance groups in all three of its African colonies – Mozambique, Angola and Guinea-Bissau. These resistance movements forced the Portuguese to grant independence in 1975.

Détente: an attempt by all sides in the Cold War, including China, to ease the tension and create an atmosphere of mutual tolerance and acceptance. Vorster saw parallels in its application to the affairs of southern Africa.

The independence of Mozambique

Unlike other parts of Africa that had become independent in the 1950s and 1960s, the colonies of southern Africa did not make the transition to independence smoothly. Portugal was fighting to retain control of Mozambique and Angola, and Namibia was under the control of South Africa. In Mozambique, which shared a long border with Rhodesia, the Portuguese were fighting a losing war against **FRELIMO**. In 1975, Portugal withdrew and Mozambique became independent under a FRELIMO government. This gave a significant advantage to Zimbabwean nationalists. FRELIMO trained guerrilla fighters and provided safe havens for operations across the border into Rhodesia. The new Mozambican government also placed an economic embargo on trade with Rhodesia at considerable cost to its own economy. Eventually, ZANLA guerrillas began to infiltrate Rhodesia from Mozambique's Tete province in such numbers that they posed a serious military threat to the Smith regime.

The role of South Africa and Zambia

Portugal's withdrawal from southern Africa and the independence of Mozambique under a socialist FRELIMO government in 1975 forced the South African government to reassess the situation. The South African leader, John Vorster, realised the significance of developments in Rhodesia. He decided on a policy of **détente** – called the 'Outward Policy' – to establish better relations with the independent African states in the region.

The Outward Policy involved negotiation with neighbouring governments in an effort to secure regimes that were at least neutral to South Africa. Vorster hoped to achieve this through a combination of diplomacy and the wielding of South Africa's economic power. South Africa was the dominant economy in the region and its cooperation was essential for the economic well-being of all the southern African states.

Smith's government threatened Vorster's plans for two reasons. Firstly, the actions of the Rhodesian army along its borders were causing major diplomatic problems. Secondly, it seemed to Vorster that Rhodesia's defeat was inevitable in the long term, and that the longer the guerrilla struggle went on, the more likely it was that an extreme Marxist regime would come to power in Rhodesia. This would be a direct threat to South Africa's security. It would be in South Africa's best interests if a moderate black government came to power in Rhodesia by negotiation.

Zambia's leader, Kenneth Kaunda, also wanted the war to end as soon as possible so that Zambia could focus on its own pressing economic problems. The presence of ZANU and ZAPU leaders and their guerrilla armies was creating tensions, and they were a target for cross-border raids into Zambia by the Rhodesian security forces. By the end of 1974, Kaunda and Vorster had reached an agreement to attempt to stop the fighting in Rhodesia. As part of the process of détente, they put pressure on their respective allies. Kaunda and the leaders of the other frontline states urged the leaders of the nationalist organisations to negotiate. Under pressure from South Africa, Smith agreed to release ZAPU and ZANU leaders from prison. By 1975 a ceasefire of sorts was in place.

However, the ceasefire did not last and the independence struggle continued. Any chance of fruitful discussions between the two sides was prevented by Smith's refusal to make meaningful concessions. As guerrilla attacks continued, the shortage of Rhodesian troops, the economic cost of the war and the strain it placed on the white minority became more obvious. Smith's confidence was severely damaged by the pressure put on him by the South African government.

Fact: By 1979, conscription of white Rhodesians had been extended from age thirty-eight to fifty, placing a huge strain on the economy. It also contributed to increasing numbers of whites emigrating from Rhodesia. Soon Rhodesia was conscripting black soldiers, who were obviously not committed to the fight. The protected villages scheme was extended, and by 1979 more than half a million people had been relocated.

The Cold War and events in Angola

The guerrilla war in Rhodesia was also linked to the Cold War. Southern Africa supplied key minerals to the world economy, and the value of its strategic position was recognised by the USSR and China, as well as by the West. Soviet and Chinese support for ZAPU and ZANU respectively created the potential for future communist influence in the region, a situation that the West feared would be exploited by its enemies in the Cold War.

SOURCE A

Finally, the Rhodesian conflict constituted a chapter in the global Cold War, with the Soviet bloc and China supporting the two guerrilla armies and the United States and its allies backing white Rhodesia and South Africa as strategic, resource-laden bastions of anti-communism.

J. Mtisi, M. Nyakudya and T. Barnes (2009), 'War in Rhodesia' in B. Raftopoulos and A. Mlambo (eds.) *Becoming Zimbabwe: A History from the Pre-colonial Period to 2008*, Harare, Zimbabwe: Weaver Press, p. 144.

Zimbabwe

QUESTION

Why was the role of South Africa critical in forcing Smith's government into talks with the nationalists?

KEY CONCEPTS QUESTION

Significance: What was the significance of the Cold War in influencing the independence struggle in Zimbabwe?

Events in Angola brought the politics of the Cold War closer to Southern Africa. When Angola, another former Portuguese colony, gained independence in 1975, a civil war broke out between the socialist People's Movement for the Liberation of Angola (MPLA), which had Soviet backing, and the National Union for the Total Independence of Angola (UNITA). Anxious to prevent an MPLA victory, South Africa invaded Angola to support UNITA, while the MPLA received substantial support from communist Cuba, including 20,000 Cuban troops. Under international pressure, South Africa withdrew its army from Angola, although its support for UNITA continued. The USA also worked to oppose an MPLA victory in Angola, although it did not send troops to intervene there.

South Africa feared that the new MPLA government in Angola would extend its operations south into South African-controlled Namibia, where a nationalist movement called the South West African People's Organisation was struggling for independence. It foresaw a hostile alliance of states in southern Africa, allied to the USSR. This would obviously not be in South Africa's interests. It feared that continuing raids by the Rhodesian army into neighbouring states would serve to create such an alliance, and so was anxious to see a resolution to the ongoing war in Rhodesia. Vorster used Rhodesia's dependence on its rail link through South Africa to put pressure on Smith to agree to a negotiated settlement. Matters came to a head in August 1976, when Rhodesian forces attacked a camp at Nyadzonya in Mozambique, killing hundreds of people. The Rhodesian government claimed that it was a ZANLA training camp; ZANU insisted that it was a refugee camp. Whatever the truth, Vorster decided that the time had come to declare South African support for majority rule in Rhodesia, totally isolating Smith's government.

Vorster also came under pressure from the US. American foreign policy had failed to prevent a communist government coming to power in Angola and the new US secretary of state, Henry Kissinger, believed that open support for majority rule in Rhodesia would serve American interests if it prevented the nationalist movements from drawing closer to the communist bloc. He put pressure on Vorster to help deliver majority rule in Rhodesia, by promising to tone down America's anti-South Africa rhetoric. In September 1976, Vorster threatened to cut off supplies to Rhodesia if Smith failed to move to majority rule.

In addition, by this time ZANLA raids from Mozambique were increasing. The combination of South African pressure and an intensification of the guerrilla war forced Smith's hand. He offered majority rule in return for the West lifting sanctions and making funds available for development. In reality, however, Smith was not prepared to accept full majority rule. Rather, he believed that some small concessions could be made to the black majority without relinquishing white control. He also believed that the nationalist movement remained so divided that it would be unable to push for full majority rule.

The failure of negotiations

Under pressure from Zambia and South Africa, Smith and Nkomo had several rounds of talks in an effort to reach a settlement, including one in a railway carriage on the Victoria Falls Bridge, high above the Zambezi River, between Rhodesia and Zambia. However, these talks had all broken down when the Smith government predictably failed to make significant concessions that would lead to black majority rule. Another meeting between Vorster, Smith and Kissinger in Pretoria also failed to convince Smith of the urgent need for reform.

When Britain convened a conference in Geneva between October and December 1976, there still seemed little prospect of a lasting settlement. The USA convinced Smith that a compromise could be reached with the nationalists. Smith, however, saw the talks as a chance to buy a two-year cessation of economic sanctions, during which time the Rhodesian security forces could destroy the guerrilla movement. The Americans had not discussed their proposals with the nationalist leadership or with the presidents of the frontline African states. The Geneva conference ended in deadlock.

International pressures

On the international scene, pressure on Smith's government increased. The new Democratic administration in the USA, under President Jimmy Carter, worked with the British government to create a new plan for Rhodesia. In July 1978, the US Senate voted against the lifting of sanctions. In Angola, the Soviet Union was creating

Figure 2.10   A ZANU poster deriding the Internal Settlement of 1979

Zimbabwe

a communist ally with the aid of the Cubans. South Africa was becoming ever more concerned about a total Marxist victory in the region, and from 1978 the new South African premier, P.W. Botha, put more pressure on Smith.

This international pressure together with the escalation of the guerrilla war forced the Smith government into a deal with moderate black leaders – those who had no military backing, and who, like Smith, were opposed to the Patriotic Front. In 1978, an 'Internal Settlement' was reached between Smith, Muzorewa, Sithole and Chief Jeremiah Chirau. They agreed to a transition to majority rule but with the white political position protected by constitutional guarantees. In 1979, elections were held in which Muzorewa's United African National Council won 67 per cent of the vote. Muzorewa briefly became prime minister of 'Zimbabwe-Rhodesia', although whites retained control of the army, police, civil service and economy. The Patriotic Front had called on its supporters to boycott the election. It rejected the Internal Settlement and stepped up the guerrilla war.

Britain, the United States and the rest of the world also refused to recognise the Internal Settlement, and the frontline states, supported by the OAU, confirmed their support for the Patriotic Front. At a Commonwealth conference held in Lusaka in August 1979, African leaders put pressure on the British prime minister Margaret Thatcher, saying that it was Britain's responsibility to resolve the crisis. Nigeria, Britain's biggest trading partner in Africa, even threatened to block British investments in Nigeria. Thatcher agreed to convene a constitutional conference in London.

QUESTION

How did a combination of internal and external pressures force the Smith government into negotiations?

At the same time, there were increasing pressures on the Rhodesian government and on the Patriotic Front. By late 1979, with more than 20,000 guerrillas active within the country, Smith saw the futility of his position and agreed to negotiate a settlement. Mozambique and Zambia, both of which had suffered heavy damage as a result of raids by Rhodesian security forces, and needed peace to rebuild their own economies, put pressure on the nationalist leaders to negotiate. The result was the Lancaster House conference in 1979.

The Lancaster House talks and the election of 1980

Robert Mugabe was extremely reluctant to attend the Lancaster House talks, and it was only under extreme pressure from Kenneth Kaunda of Zambia and Samora Machel, the president of Mozambique, that he reluctantly agreed to negotiate. They could no longer afford to sustain their support for the nationalist movements operating from their countries. At the Lancaster House talks in London, the parties signed a ceasefire in a war in which about 27,000 people had lost their lives. Even at the last minute, Mugabe was reluctant to sign the ceasefire agreement: it was only a threat from Samora Machel to cut off all support for ZANU that forced him to agree.

KEY CONCEPTS QUESTION

Causes and consequences: What were the causes and consequences of the Lancaster House talks?

The parties attending the Lancaster House talks drew up a new constitution and prepared for all-party elections in 1980. In the meantime, the Smith government formally surrendered its independence and handed over power to a transitional government under British control. The constitution established a parliamentary democracy with twenty of the one hundred seats reserved for whites for at least seven years, giving the white minority disproportionate power in the new state. The issue of land created the greatest disagreement. The Patriotic Front wanted the new government to take over and redistribute unused farmland to resettle war veterans. However, the constitution stipulated that, for the first ten years, land could not be confiscated but could only change hands on the principle of 'willing seller, willing buyer'. The British and American governments offered to make funds available to implement this, but no details were clarified or agreed. The unresolved land issue was to create problems in the future.

As the election approached, the Patriotic Front disintegrated, and ZANU and ZAPU fought the election as separate parties – **ZANU-PF** and PF-ZAPU respectively.

SOURCE B

The wrongs of the past must now stand forgiven and forgotten. If ever we look to the past, let us do so for the lesson the past has taught us, namely that oppression and racism are inequalities that must never find scope in our political and social system. It could never be a correct justification that because the whites oppressed us yesterday when they had power, the blacks must oppress them today because they have power. An evil remains an evil whether practised by white against black or black against white.

Speech by Robert Mugabe pledging reconciliation, 18 April 1980. Quoted in M. Meredith (2005), *The State of Africa*, Cape Town, South Africa: Jonathan Ball Publishers, p. 328.

White Rhodesian (and South African) hopes of a victory by the moderates were shattered by the outcome of the election. Mugabe's ZANU-PF won fifty-seven seats, Nkomo's PF-ZAPU won twenty seats, and the moderate Muzorewa's UNAC won only three. The twenty seats reserved for whites all went to Smith's Rhodesian Front party. All except one of PF-ZAPU's seats were won in Matabeleland in the west, and ZANU-PF won all the seats in the northern region of Mashonaland, a development 'boding ill for the post-independence period', according to historians Mtsi, Nyakudya and Barnes. On 18 April 1980, Robert Mugabe was installed as the first prime minister of independent Zimbabwe.

2.8 What part did Robert Mugabe play in the struggle for independence?

Mugabe's role in the nationalist movement

Robert Mugabe is of Shona origin and his ethnic background has influenced his politics. Like many other independence leaders, he received a Western education in mission schools, in his case Catholic, and qualified as a teacher after graduating from university at Fort Hare in South Africa in 1951. He also studied at Oxford University in Britain in 1952. He has two law degrees and is a Master of Science. His education brought him into contact with many future African leaders, including Julius Nyerere and

ZANU-PF: Zimbabwe African National Union – Patriotic Front

ACTIVITIES

Was the Lancaster House agreement of greater benefit to the white minority or to the black majority nationalist movement?

Explain the possible reactions to the speech quoted in **Source B** by different groups of people hearing it at the time: guerrilla soldiers who have spent many years in camps in exile; members of the Rhodesian Front; black farmers who have lost their land and been moved to protected villages; and members of the British government.

Fact: A song by the Jamaican reggae singer Bob Marley called 'Zimbabwe' had been an inspiration to guerrilla fighters during the nationalist struggle. Marley and his group The Wailers were invited to Zimbabwe to participate in the Independence Day celebrations in Salisbury on 18 April 1980, where they performed this song.

Zimbabwe

Figure 2.11 Robert Mugabe (left) with George Silundika (centre) and Joshua Nkomo (right) in a photograph taken around 1960

Kenneth Kaunda. In the late 1950s, Mugabe taught in Ghana, where he was influenced and inspired by Kwame Nkrumah. These early years influenced his political thinking, pushing him towards the left and Marxism.

After his return to Zimbabwe in 1960, Mugabe joined the National Democratic Party, which soon developed into Nkomo's ZAPU organisation. In 1963, Mugabe left ZAPU to join Sithole's ZANU party, and in 1964 he was arrested and imprisoned for his political views. During this period he experienced at first hand the restrictions of the Rhodesian government – he was not even allowed to attend the funeral of his four-year-old son.

Mugabe's early life was thus dominated by two forces – first, an extensive period of education and second, a long period of imprisonment. It was during this latter period that he came to two conclusions about the route to majority rule. He recognised that a more conventional, Soviet-style revolutionary movement would fail in the face of the poverty and lack of political consciousness of Zimbabwe's peasant class. He also saw that the white regime was so extreme in its position that considerable force would have to be applied to bring about any kind of change within the country. He concluded, therefore, that a Maoist (see Section 2.6, The move to guerrilla warfare) approach to insurgency was necessary to politicise the mass of the black rural poor and to conceal political activity so that it could not be easily countered by the Rhodesian regime.

Mugabe's time in prison greatly increased his prestige within ZANU. He was released in 1974, after South African pressure on the Smith government to reach an agreement with the Zimbabwean independence movements. When Sithole was overthrown as leader of ZANU in 1974, Mugabe emerged to take his place. The problem Mugabe faced, however, was that he and his organisation were largely ignored by other African leaders. Thus, when he travelled to Zambia in the same year, Kaunda refused to recognise his position. At that time ZAPU was seen as the best hope for achieving independence in Zimbabwe. Mugabe had no military experience and was eyed with suspicion by other African leaders. He was a dedicated Marxist and he had an inflexible approach to the problem of gaining independence.

Mugabe consolidated his control of ZANU in 1975. This takeover was accompanied by political assassination and intimidation, which showed him that leaders had to be ruthless to achieve their goals, a view that has since dominated his political life. He then focused on defeating ZAPU to push forward his model of the fight for independence. His bid for dominance was successful, and ZANU played a vital role in the final phases of the guerrilla war. By the time of the Lancaster House negotiations, Mugabe had become a key player in events.

The Lancaster House talks demonstrated Mugabe's diplomatic skill. The events of 1979 were complex; ZAPU and ZANU were waging a guerrilla war that was wearing down the Rhodesian regime but not defeating it. Left to its own devices, there is a good argument that Ian Smith's regime would have continued the fight against the nationalist organisations. However, outside pressures in the form of the UN and South Africa had created the conditions in which Smith might be prepared to deal with Mugabe. It was at this point that the ZANU leader made two key concessions. He agreed both to the creation of a parliament in which the white population was disproportionately represented, and to place a ten-year moratorium on changes to landownership. These concessions reassured whites and allowed them to reach an agreement that led to the formation of an independent Zimbabwe a year later. Subsequent events, however, showed that Mugabe never stopped opposing white supremacy and that in the long-term he was determined to end white domination not only of political power but also of the economy.

Mugabe's role after independence

After 1980, Mugabe became more dictatorial and more isolated even from ZANU-PF. His position within a ring of close confidantes made it difficult for him to fully appreciate the extent of the economic crisis that later affected Zimbabwe. Furthermore, the power, wealth and position of the political élite depended on the patronage of Mugabe, so few of them were willing to challenge him. In addition to this, a cult of personality was established that made it difficult for him to reverse his earlier policies and be seen to be wrong. This restricted the ability of his regime to implement 'sensible' policies to solve the economic problems.

It is possible to argue that Mugabe was determined to hold on to power at all costs. Proof of this may lie in the political and economic crises that Zimbabwe faced after ten years of independence. Some argue that Mugabe was determined to socially engineer Zimbabwe to become a peasant republic. On the other hand, others believe that he was

ACTIVITY

Go to the website www.newsday.co.zw and enter 'Tekere' into the search box to read the article 'Why Mugabe "hated" Tekere'. Edgar Tekere was a former comrade of Mugabe's in the ZANU leadership, and later the leader of a group opposed to Mugabe. He had written a book, *A Lifetime of Struggle*, which critically examined how Mugabe rose to his leadership position in ZANU and then Zimbabwe.

Explain why he was so critical of Robert Mugabe. What does his criticism suggest about the state of democracy in Zimbabwe?

Figure 2.12 Robert Mugabe reviews troops on parade during the 28th anniversary celebrations of Zimbabwe's independence in 2008

simply rewarding his followers with land, or buying political support. An extreme view is that he had little choice in the matter and that he was a figurehead for a ZANU-PF élite so embroiled in corruption that they could not let go of power. Some historians, such as Guy Arnold, believe that the reasons why Mugabe maintained support have their roots in Zimbabwe's colonial past (see **Source C**).

SOURCE C

The Zimbabwe crisis at the end of the century raised many questions that were not addressed in the West. It was, of course, about a dictatorial ruler using every weapon at his disposal to hold onto power: these included violence and intimidation of his opponents, altering the constitution or ignoring it; destroying the independent judiciary; and seeking popular support by deploying as weapons the two highly emotive issues of land redistribution and the control of land by the white farmers. But Mugabe was also using as a weapon the deep underlying resentments of past colonialism and the ingrained bitterness resulting from a century of the racial arrogance and contempt that had been second nature to the majority of the white settlers.

G. Arnold (2006), *Africa: A Modern History*, London: Atlantic Books, p. 904.

Of all the nationalist leaders in this book, Mugabe is the most difficult to analyse. It is clear that he was intelligent and well-educated, and it is easy to understand how he formed his political views – not only about the best road to independence but also about the form of a post-colonial Zimbabwe. He was clearly both a ruthless and a sophisticated political operator. The manner in which he eliminated potential rivals and opposition proves the former; his subtle handling of the white minority at the Lancaster House talks and in the first decade of his premiership suggests the latter. He clearly was an accomplished leader in the 1980s, a decade that saw Zimbabwe prosper. His role in his country's subsequent problems was far more difficult to establish.

2.9 Why did the nationalist movement succeed?

It was a combination of factors – both internal and external – that contributed to the success of the nationalist movement in Zimbabwe:

- The support of the rural population was crucial to the success of the guerrilla campaign. Mugabe had realised early on the importance of winning over the peasant farmers. Furthermore, many of them were alienated by the government's policies, especially the 'protected villages' scheme, and so were ready to assist the nationalist movement. Historians Mtisi, Nyakudya and Barnes comment that 'whether or not coercion was used, the "cooperation" between guerrillas and peasants was important in ensuring the success of the armed struggle'. They also note that many ordinary people 'made significant sacrifices for the liberation of the country'. [Source: J. Mtisi, M. Nyakudya and T. Barnes (2009), 'War in Rhodesia' in B. Raftopoulos and A. Mlambo (eds.), *Becoming Zimbabwe: A History from the Pre-colonial Period to 2008*, Harare: Weaver Press, p. 155.]

- The unwillingness of the Smith government to make meaningful concessions strengthened the hand of the nationalist movement. This undermined the position of moderate blacks who supported the idea of negotiations rather than armed conflict and strengthened support for the nationalist movement.

- Although there were divisions among the nationalists, their guerrilla fighters posed a mounting military threat that the government could not eliminate. Isolated white farms in rural areas came increasingly under attack, leading to mounting emigration rates.

- Sanctions also had an effect on weakening the position of the Rhodesian government, although they did not succeed in their original target of forcing the Smith government to negotiate soon after UDI. As exports decreased and the war escalated, the cost to the economy mounted. The white population had to pay higher taxes to meet the 45 per cent increase in the defence budget and this in turn contributed to the rise in emigration.

- The contribution of the frontline states, notably Zambia and Mozambique, played a critical role in the success of the nationalist movement. From the beginning of the guerrilla campaign, the nationalist movements were based in Zambia, where their presence caused considerable tension as well as expense, but afforded both organisations a protected base from which to operate. The independence of Mozambique in 1975, and the re-location of the ZANU headquarters there, meant that guerrilla incursions along the long eastern border became much easier.

ACTIVITY

The role of Mugabe is at the core of this unit. Did he have an elaborate plan to portray himself as a moderate before embarking on more radical policies? Or were his actions logical and just all along, intending to redistribute the wealth of the country to the black majority? Was Mugabe simply a pawn, used as a front to cover the activities of a clique of ZANU-PF members who used their position to their own benefit? In this view, Mugabe could not stand down or act against their wishes for fear of the political consequences. Which of these views do you think is the most accurate assessment of Mugabe's role?

- International pressures also played a key role. Critical to this was the change in South Africa's policies from one of active support for the Smith government to support for a negotiated settlement, and the application of economic pressures. The US and Britain also played important roles in applying pressure on Smith and facilitating negotiations that in the end favoured the nationalist movement.

End of unit activities

1 Draw up a table to highlight the differences between ZANU and ZAPU. Include information on leadership, support base, ideology, tactics, allies, effectiveness and any other categories you think are important.

2 Write a report about the involvement of Mozambique and Zambia in the Zimbabwean independence struggle. Include an analysis of the negative impact that their support had on their own countries.

3 Draw a spider diagram to analyse the factors that finally forced the Smith government to agree to black majority rule. Include the following factors plus any others you can think of:

- sanctions
- the guerrilla war
- collapsing economy
- pressure from South Africa
- impact of the Cold War
- world opinion.

4 'The key factor responsible for the attainment of majority rule in Zimbabwe was the heroism of the nationalist organisations.' Divide the class into two groups. One group should prepare an argument to support this statement, and the other an argument to oppose it.

5 Find out what daily life was like for ordinary civilians, black and white, who lived in Rhodesia/Zimbabwe between 1965 and 1980.

6 Enter '4 March' on the BBC's 'on this day' page (http://news.bbc.co.uk/onthisday) to read a 1980 news report written on the day of Zimbabwe's first democratic election. Use the information here, together with information from this unit, to write a newspaper editorial commenting on the historical significance of the ZANU-PF victory in the election.

Challenges and responses in post-colonial Zimbabwe

KEY QUESTIONS

- What economic and cultural challenges did Zimbabwe face after independence?
- What political and racial challenges did Zimbabwe face after independence?
- What were the successes and failures of the new government?
- What challenges remained unresolved after 1987?

TIMELINE

1980 Zimbabwe becomes an independent state.

1982 Violence breaks out between ZANU and ZAPU supporters in Matabeleland.

1987 Mugabe and Nkomo sign Unity Accord; Mugabe's powers as president are significantly strengthened.

1992 Land Acquisition Act.

1997 Land Redistribution Act.

1999 Formation of Movement for Democratic Change.

Overview

- Newly independent Zimbabwe faced many challenges in 1980, including economic reconstruction, political transformation, inequity in the ownership and control of land, and racism.

- The new government needed the cooperation of the white minority, which still controlled key areas of the economy.

- The government applied moderate economic policies and sought to retain the cooperation of white business and agriculture.

- There were significant improvements in education and health care, but these improvements were unevenly distributed, and key areas of the economy remained under foreign ownership.

- Efforts by the government to implement a programme of land reform and redistribution met with limited success.

- Rivalry and tensions between Robert Mugabe's ZANU–PF and Joshua Nkomo's PF–ZAPU surfaced once again, based on political rivalry between the two leaders and parties, as well as ethnic and regional differences between their supporters.

- In 1982, Nkomo was dismissed from the government and PF–ZAPU accused of planning a coup. The Fifth Brigade, a ruthless North Korean-trained militia, waged a war of violence and intimidation against ZAPU supporters in Matabeleland.

- The crisis ended in 1987, when Mugabe and Nkomo signed a Unity Accord, merging the two parties and increasing Mugabe's powers.

- Relations between the government and the white community deteriorated, with accusations of racism adding to tensions rooted in white economic privileges.

- After 1990, ZANU–PF consolidated its hold on power, winning all elections using violence, intimidation and vote-rigging.

- Despite the difficulties, there was opposition to Mugabe's rule, notably from the Movement for Democratic Change (MDC), which was formed in 1999 under the leadership of Morgan Tsvangirai.
- Land reform became the key issue in Zimbabwe in the late 1990s, culminating in the occupation by force of many white-owned farms by groups of landless peasants and war veterans.
- Throughout the 1990s the economy declined, causing real hardship to the people of Zimbabwe.

2.10 What economic and cultural challenges did Zimbabwe face after independence?

Economic challenges

The new state of Zimbabwe faced many challenges in 1980. The country had emerged from more than fifteen years of civil war, which had caused severe damage to the economy and infrastructure. The country also needed to be reintegrated into the world economy after many years of trade sanctions. The new government's main concern was economic reconstruction, but the white minority still controlled key areas of the

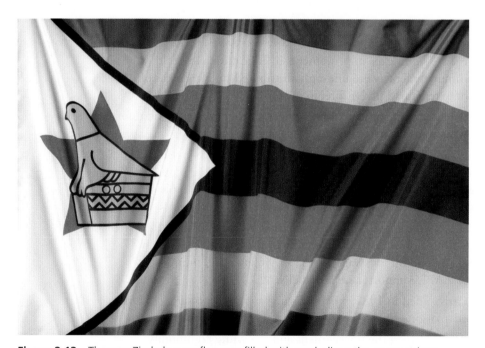

Figure 2.13 The new Zimbabwean flag was filled with symbolism: the green stripes represent the land; the yellow stripes the mineral wealth; the red stripes the blood that was shed; black represents the black majority; the white triangle represents peace; the red star symbolises internationalism; and the Zimbabwe bird represents the pre-colonial history of the empire of Great Zimbabwe

economy so their cooperation was vital. Furthermore, the new Zimbabwe was as reliant on South Africa for economic activity as its Rhodesian predecessor had been. These factors hindered the ability of the new government to fulfil many of the wishes of its followers, especially the redistribution of land.

Cultural challenges

The government also faced the problem of nation-building in a society 'deeply divided along the lines of race, class, ethnicity, gender and geography', according to historian James Muzondidya. The government adopted as its national symbols emblems associated with the empire of Great Zimbabwe, as reminders of the pre-colonial past. The Zimbabwe bird is depicted on the flag, coat of arms and coins, and features of the ruins of Great Zimbabwe on the banknotes and coat of arms. The languages of the two main ethnic groups, Shona and Ndebele, were adopted as official languages, along with English.

2.11 What political and racial challenges did Zimbabwe face after independence?

Political challenges

Another challenge was to transform the colonial state from an authoritarian white minority regime to a more democratic form of government. There was also serious inequity in ownership and control of land and resources. Whites still controlled much of the economy because, as a result of colonial land policies, they owned the bulk of the fertile agricultural land. Robert Mugabe was initially committed to gaining the confidence of the 6,000 white commercial farmers who were a critical factor in the economic well-being of the country. He also attempted to reassure white-controlled businesses that the government would apply market rather than socialist solutions to the country's problems. For the white minority, the new regime initially brought many advantages. Their businesses no longer had to fight against the impact of economic sanctions and they were no longer drafted into the military. There was an economic boom between 1980 and 1982, with growth at a record 24 per cent. Whites were the major beneficiaries of this.

Issues of race

The inequality enshrined in the Lancaster House constitution, which protected the political and economic power of the white minority, was another challenge. Firstly, whites controlled 20 per cent of the seats in parliament and were thus grossly overrepresented. This concession could be reviewed after seven years. Secondly, the Lancaster constitution banned the government from forcibly seizing land for at least ten years. The government could buy land, but only at market prices, and based on a system of 'willing seller, willing buyer'. The sheer scale of such an investment meant

Fact: As part of the process of transformation, many of the place names associated with colonial rule were replaced by African names. The capital city, which had been named Salisbury in honour of the British prime minister at the time of the takeover of the area by the British South Africa Company in 1890, was renamed Harare in 1992, after the Shona chieftain Neharawa, who had lived there with his people in pre-colonial times.

QUESTION

What were the economic, political and social problems facing the new government?

Fact: There were some remarkable improvements in education. Between 1980 and 1990, the number of schools increased by 80 per cent. Between 1979 and 1985, enrolment in primary schools rose from 82,000 to more than 2.2 million, and in secondary schools from 66,000 to 482,000.

Historical debate:
Historian James Muzondidya believes that the main obstacle to successful land reform was the *'willing-seller, willing-buyer'* principle in the Lancaster House constitution, which protected the interests of white commercial farmers: *'Conscious of the racial protection guaranteed by the constitution, white farmers were generally reluctant to relinquish their colonially inherited privilege.'* Another view, voiced by Martin Meredith, is that ZANU-PF politicians made more effort to acquire farms for themselves than to distribute them to landless peasants, and that by 1990, 8 per cent of commercial farmland was owned by politicians, senior civil servants and security-force officials.

QUESTION

How successful was Zimbabwe in its first decade of independence?

that the nationalisation of this key resource and its redistribution to the black majority was impossible. Initially, therefore, the white minority had considerable political and economic influence.

Continuing racism was another issue that needed to be faced. Historians Terence Ranger and Ibbo Mandaza have described the post-independence attitude of the remaining white population as a legacy of 'settler culture', based on a desire to maintain their privileged lifestyles and positions. Another historian, James Muzondidya, suggests that whites made little effort to contribute to nation-building or to rectify the racial imbalances inherited from the past. Most whites retained their privileged economic positions, while the bulk of the population lived in poverty. These unresolved issues became major problems in the 1990s.

2.12 What were the successes and failures of the new government?

For the first decade after independence, Zimbabwe followed a fairly moderate course. This was partly due to the Lancaster House constitution, which had given key concessions to the white minority. This placed a brake on radicalism in the new state, and acted as a counterbalance to the more Marxist or African nationalist policies of ZANU-PF. Initially Mugabe attempted to include whites in his government, and there were two white cabinet ministers. He also retained the white heads of the armed forces and the intelligence services, and even struck up a working relationship with Ian Smith.

There was remarkable progress in the provision of education and health services, especially in areas neglected by the colonial administration or damaged by years of guerrilla warfare. This was helped by almost £900 million of aid that poured into Zimbabwe, especially from Scandinavian countries. Work was also done on building or repairing infrastructure, such as roads, clinics, fencing and boreholes, and in providing safe drinking water to 84 per cent of the population. Altogether there were some notable economic and social achievements in the first few years, although many challenges remained. The economic gains were unevenly distributed and society remained very unequal, with millions of rural dwellers still desperately poor. Control over key areas of the economy remained in foreign hands, mainly British or South African-based multinational companies. In 1985, 48 per cent of Zimbabwe's manufacturing industry was owned by foreign companies or individuals.

The new government also started on a process of land reform. This was a pressing issue: four million Zimbabweans lived on overcrowded communal land and black peasants had a disproportionate amount of poor land frequently threatened by drought. With financial aid from Britain, the government began to resettle black families on formerly white-owned land that had been abandoned during the war. None of this broke the ten-year moratorium on the seizure of white land. However, progress was slow, and by 1990 only 6.5 million hectares of land had been acquired and 52,000 families resettled. In addition, much of the land that had been redistributed was in areas unsuited to agriculture.

Political developments: the move to authoritarian rule

The political situation in Zimbabwe was deeply affected by its history. For many decades the white minority had used repressive laws to crush protests, detain political opponents and silence opposition. In the liberation movement, too, there was a tradition of intolerance, where opponents were viewed as enemies and treated with a mixture of violence and intimidation, and the use of force was often seen as the only way to achieve results. These traditions continued in post-independence Zimbabwe.

Mugabe had often stated that he wanted to establish a one-party state under ZANU-PF. The chief obstacle to this was Joshua Nkomo's PF-ZAPU. Rivalry between the two nationalist movements went back a long way, but they had united to form the Patriotic Front under pressure from the frontline states in 1976. They had contested the 1980 election as separate parties but, despite ZANU-PF's convincing majority, Mugabe had included Nkomo in a coalition government. However, not long after independence, tensions and rivalries between the two parties began to surface once more. Friction surrounding the integration of the two guerrilla forces, Nkomo's ZIPRA and Mugabe's ZANLA, to form a new national army soon turned into violence.

Figure 2.14   ZANU-PF supporters welcome Mugabe back to Zimbabwe at the time of independence in 1980

Zimbabwe

The government called the crushing of opposition in Matabeleland the *Gukurahundi* operation, a Shona word meaning 'the rain that sweeps away the chaff'. What do you think is the symbolism implied in this term?

Theory of Knowledge

History and ethics: Mugabe justified the violence by accusing the opposition of plotting to overthrow the state. He claimed that it was necessary to defend the gains that the liberation movement had achieved. Can you think of other examples in history where dictators have used the notion of a threat to the security of the state to justify violence? Can violence ever be justified? Is it acceptable to use violence to save lives, or to intervene to prevent a greater evil from happening?

The political conflict and personal rivalry between the two parties and their leaders also had ethnic and regional aspects. Most of PF-ZAPU's supporters were Ndebele speakers, living predominantly in Matabeleland in the western part of the country. They believed that ZANU-PF was putting the interests of the majority Shona-speakers ahead of others. In October 1980, Mugabe signed a secret agreement with the communist dictatorship in North Korea whereby the Koreans would train a Zimbabwean brigade in internal security tactics. This unit, drawn exclusively from Shona-speakers, came to be known as the Fifth Brigade.

By 1982, Mugabe felt strong enough to move against Nkomo, and he accused ZAPU of planning a military coup. Nkomo was expelled from the government and his party's property was seized, ruining the livelihoods of many ex-ZIPRA guerrillas. In the army, former ZIPRA soldiers were targeted, many were beaten up and some were killed. As a result, many former ZIPRA guerrillas fled into the bush, taking their arms with them. By late 1982, concentrations of these refugees had become a serious threat to public order in Matabeleland. The Fifth Brigade was sent in to destroy the 'dissidents', as they were labelled by Mugabe.

The Fifth Brigade attacked not only armed ex-ZIPRA soldiers, but also the civilian population. About 2,000 people died within six weeks, and 20,000 between 1982 and 1987. The situation was made worse by drought and, by 1984, 400,000 people in southern Matabeleland were almost entirely dependent on relief supplies. When the Fifth Brigade stopped the movement of these supplies, the entire region was threatened with famine. In addition to the actions of the Fifth Brigade, Mugabe's secret police rounded up thousands of civilians and interned them in camps where beating and torture were routine and many died. This violence and intimidation intensified in the run-up to the 1985 election. The government used the 'Matabeleland Crisis' or the 'Dissidents' War' – as the whole operation was called – as a means of ridding itself of opposition.

The violence in Matabeleland only ended when Mugabe and Nkomo signed the Unity Accord in December 1987. This formally merged ZANU and ZAPU into a single party, which retained the title of ZANU-PF. Zimbabwe was now effectively a one-party state, a situation that had been achieved by wearing down ZAPU, its officials and ex-guerrillas. At least 20,000 civilians had died as a result of this infighting.

Nkomo became one of two vice-presidents in the new party and was given a senior post in the government, together with two other former ZAPU leaders. As Mugabe's power became more secure, he and ZANU-PF grew in confidence. On 30 December 1987, Mugabe was declared executive president by parliament, a position that merged the roles of head of state, the government and the armed forces. He was also given the powers to dissolve parliament, declare martial law and hold office for an unlimited number of terms. In effect, Mugabe had become a dictator, and the key offices of state were controlled by a new élite whose members owed their positions of power to him.

The infighting between ZANU-PF and ZAPU had a negative effect on the white minority. In order to secure its victory, ZANU-PF had taken control of the state's media so it could advance its cause with propaganda. This propaganda openly referred to whites as racists and, as a result, a greater rift developed between the black and white communities. Other factors also contributed to this rift. White voters continued to support Smith and his uncompromising Rhodesian Front, and in parliament the overrepresented white community regularly criticised the ZANU-PF government. Their continued privileged position added to the tensions, although half of the white population had emigrated within three years of independence and by 1985 only 100,000 remained. Adding to the suspicions were undercover military operations by the apartheid government in South Africa in an attempt to hinder Zimbabwe's development. During 1987, the reservation of twenty seats for white voters was abolished (as had been decided in the Lancaster House constitution) and so they lost their overrepresentation in parliament.

After 1987, ZANU-PF strengthened its hold on power, and in the 1990 election it won 117 of the 120 seats. However, there were signs of discontent with the state of affairs. Edgar Tekere, a former ZANU leader and member of Mugabe's government, broke away and formed the Zimbabwe Unity Movement (ZUM). Tekere ran unsuccessfully against Mugabe in the 1990 presidential election, but ZUM won 20 per cent of the votes in the parliamentary elections. Anti-government protests by students at the University of Zimbabwe led to its closure by the government for six months in 1990–1. When the Zimbabwe Congress of Trade Unions (ZCTU) sympathised with the students, its leader Morgan Tsvangirai was arrested and detained for six weeks.

> **QUESTION**
> How did the ZANU-PF government use violence as a means of consolidating its power?

2.13 What challenges remained unresolved after 1987?

Threats to democracy

Despite growing dissatisfaction with the government, ZANU-PF continued to win elections that were marred by violence. Mugabe too was re-elected in 1996, but with only 32 per cent of the electorate casting their votes. As the state of the economy deteriorated in the late 1990s, there was increasing criticism of government policies. As concerns mounted, a new political movement was formed in 1999. This was the Movement for Democratic Change (MDC), a coalition of civic groups, churches, lawyers and trade unionists opposed to ZANU-PF. One of its leaders was Morgan Tsvangirai. Despite government attempts to intimidate voters, the MDC attracted large crowds to its meetings and managed to win 47.06 per cent of the votes in the next election, with ZANU-PF winning 48.45 per cent. Fearing the strength of the opposition, the government constantly harassed Tsvangirai. It also acted against independent newspapers that were critical of its policies, threatening to silence them. The printing presses of one such newspaper, the *Daily News*, were blown up. During 2001, the government moved against the judiciary, which had until then managed to retain a degree of independence. The chief justice was forced out of office and two other judges retired early, leaving the Supreme Court with a ZANU-PF majority in favour of government actions.

> **ACTIVITY**
> Use the information in this section to explain why Zimbabwe can be considered an example of an authoritarian state, but not a one-party state.

Zimbabwe

Mugabe referred to the 2002 election as the 'Third *Chimurenga*', or struggle. The first one had been the uprising against the imposition of colonial rule in 1896–7; the second the guerrilla war against the Rhodesian Front government between 1966 and 1980. What is the significance of the use of the term in the context of the 2002 election? What propaganda function would it serve?

How might the influences referred to in **Source A** affect our ability to find historical truth?

SOURCE A

I don't think that anyone could fail to notice how central to ZANU-PF's [election] campaign was a particular version of history. I spent four days watching Zimbabwe television which presented nothing but one 'historical' programme after another. Television and newspapers insisted on an increasingly simple and monolithic history. Television constantly repeated documentaries about the guerrilla war and colonial brutalities. The newspapers regularly carried articles on slavery, colonial exploitation and the liberation struggle. I recognised the outlines of many of my own books but boiled down in the service of ZANU-PF.

Extract from 'The Zimbabwe elections: a personal experience', an article written by Terence Ranger, a leading historian of Zimbabwe, at the time of the 2002 presidential election. Quoted at http://africalegalbrief.com.

Subsequent elections were marked by violence, intimidation and serious irregularities. A new and sinister development in the 2002 election was a threat by the army to step in if ZANU-PF lost. When the MDC retained the support of all the main towns in the 2005 election, the government struck. In a brutal display of state-sanctioned violence, Mugabe's police and youth militia attacked the poor inhabitants of informal settlements on the fringes of the towns. Houses were bulldozed, markets destroyed, the goods sold by street vendors confiscated or burnt, and people left to fend for themselves. A UN investigation estimated that 700,000 lost their homes and livelihoods, and that another 2.4 million people were affected indirectly. According to historian Martin Meredith, the purpose of the operation was to make clear the fate of anyone who voted against Mugabe. In spite of this, the MDC won a majority in the 2008 elections, and Tsvangirai won the first round of the presidential election. However, a re-run of this election was 'won' by Mugabe, after some of the worst political violence since the Matabeleland campaign in the 1980s. After this, Mugabe reluctantly agreed to a form of power-sharing with the MDC in an 'inclusive government'.

International observers watched political developments in Zimbabwe with grave concern. Western countries suspended aid and the European Union applied 'smart sanctions' against Mugabe and other top ZANU-PF leaders, prohibiting travel and freezing overseas bank accounts.

The issue of land

Although some progress had been made on the land issue in the first decade of independence, it was not nearly enough to tackle the inherited problem, which was aggravated by population growth in rural areas. The fact that 4,500 white farmers owned eleven million hectares of the best farmland, while more than a million black farmers shared sixteen million hectares, was an issue that obviously had to be addressed. This fact, together with years of reluctance on the part of white farmers to compromise on the issue of land, became the main political prop of Mugabe's regime. Britain provided £44 million for land resettlement – a figure that fell far short of the funds needed to effect any meaningful redistribution of land. Mugabe was able to use the land issue as a political weapon to keep himself in power – with disastrous economic consequences.

The Lancaster House provisions protecting the white ownership of land and guaranteeing full compensation for it expired after ten years. In 1992, they were replaced

Fact: When landless peasants invaded and occupied white-owned farms, many of them claimed to be 'war veterans' of the independence struggle in the 1970s. Many guerrilla fighters had left school early to join up, had little education and few skills, and had struggled to survive after independence. Initially loyal supporters of Mugabe, they began to protest in the late 1990s at the government's apparent indifference to their situation. Critics of Mugabe believed that condoning the land invasions was his government's way of attempting to solve this issue.

Figure 2.15 Children watch a stall burning during the violent government attacks in 2005, which the government claimed was designed to clear Zimbabwe's slums

by the Land Acquisition Act, which gave the government the right to purchase half of the land still owned by white farmers for the resettlement of small-scale black farmers. However there was widespread criticism when it emerged that, rather than peasant farmers, the political élite loyal to Mugabe was acquiring the leases to some of the farms. In 1997, the Land Redistribution Act listed 1,503 white farms for compulsory purchase and reallocation, including some of the largest and most productive commercial farms in the country. War veterans began to invade white-owned farms and threaten farmers and their workers with violence. Over the next few years, the war veterans became increasingly hostile. Historian Guy Arnold poses the question of whether Mugabe controlled the war veterans or whether he was in fact their prisoner: 'He had unleashed a demand and with it a sense of grievance that could not be bottled up or contained.' The government condoned the often violent invasion of farms by landless peasants, many of whom claimed to be war veterans. By the middle of 2001, 95 per cent of all white farms had been occupied or listed for resettlement.

KEY CONCEPTS
QUESTION

**Causes and
consequences:** What
were the causes and
effects of the land
reform crisis that
affected Zimbabwe in
the 1990s?

These events affected not only the white farmers themselves but also their farm workers. Many were assaulted and about 20,000 were evicted from the farms where they had lived all their lives. The land seizures were not accompanied by back-up services to help small farmers. Large tobacco and dairy farms were often dismantled in a piecemeal manner and handed over to small peasant farmers, many of whom lacked experience of commercial farming. Once again, claims were made that many of the most productive farms went to high-ranking politicians and ZANU-PF supporters. In this way, the redistribution of land – although welcomed with great joy by the bulk of Zimbabwe's people and in many ways a fair outcome after years of injustice – had a catastrophic effect on agricultural production and contributed to the collapse of the economy.

Economic decline and collapse

The unresolved challenges and political extremism in Zimbabwe resulted in the country's economic collapse. The health and education systems – real achievements of the new government in the 1980s – started to collapse as funds dried up. Rising unemployment and dissatisfaction with working conditions led to widespread industrial unrest and strikes in the early 1990s. As the economic situation deteriorated, there were accusations of corruption against senior officials. There was also criticism of the government for its misuse of funds to benefit senior politicians at a time when the population as a whole was suffering. Towards the end of 1997, the Zimbabwean currency collapsed after a government decision to compensate ex-guerrilla soldiers for their role in the independence struggle. The economic situation deteriorated even further when the Zimbabwean government decided to provide military aid to Congolese president Laurent Kabila in a civil war in the Democratic Republic of Congo. As the defence spending escalated to support this, Zimbabwe saw increasing unemployment, inflation at 70 per cent and shortages of fuel, electricity and other commodities. The effects of AIDS

Figure 2.16   A banknote to the value of $100 million Zimbabwean dollars, issued in 2008; even higher values were issued later as Zimbabwe battled to control inflation

added to the problems facing Zimbabwe – by 1999, 1,700 people a week were dying as a result of the disease.

From 2000, the economy declined even further, with rising food prices and a collapsing currency. Income from tourism dropped drastically as visitors stayed away, scared by the political violence and instability. Foreign investment dried up as banks and companies feared risking money in a politically and economically unstable environment.

The disruption to agriculture caused by the land invasions resulted in food shortages and starvation, with millions of people living in desperate poverty. With skyrocketing unemployment, town-dwellers in particular found themselves badly hit by the economic problems. By the end of 2002, an estimated three million Zimbabweans had fled as refugees or illegal immigrants to neighbouring countries, especially South Africa, and more were to follow in the next few years as the economy declined further and Mugabe clung to power despite mounting opposition.

QUESTIONS

Why was land such an emotive issue in Zimbabwe?

What factors contributed to the ongoing political and economic crises in Zimbabwe?

ACTIVITY

Look back at the historian Guy Arnold's assessment of Mugabe's rule (Section 2.8, **Source C**). How accurate do you think it is? Refer to the post-colonial history of Zimbabwe in your answer.

End of unit activities

1   Draw up a table to summarise the challenges facing Zimbabwe after independence, how the government tried to deal with them, and what the results were.

2   Read the article at www.independent.co.uk/news/world/africa/zimbabwes-last-white-ruler-the-man-who-defied-the-world-758891.html, written at the time of Ian Smith's death in 2007. Explain why the writer argues that Smith was a good role model for Robert Mugabe. Comment on the view expressed in the concluding paragraph that 'in struggling so long to ensure that whites in Zimbabwe clung on to everything, Smith finally ensured that they lost everything'.

3   Find out what you can about the Movement for Democratic Change (MDC) and its leader Morgan Tsvangirai.

4   Joshua Nkomo, the former leader of ZAPU and vice-president under Mugabe, died in 1999. Work out a list of questions you would like to have asked him before his death, and compose the answers you think he may have given. Enter 'Obituary: Joshua Nkomo' into the search box at www.bbc.co.uk to read more about him.

5   'The problems of post-independence Zimbabwe can undoubtedly be attributed to the legacy of colonial and white supremacist rule.' Divide the class into two groups. One group should work out an argument to support this statement and the other an argument to oppose it.

6   Write two speeches, one criticising and one defending the developments in Zimbabwe since 1980. One should be written from the perspective of a white farmer who has recently lost his land, the other from a ZANU-PF veteran who has recently acquired land.

2

End of chapter activities

Paper 1 exam practice

Question

What, according to **Source A** below, was the Soviet government's attitude to UDI?

[3 marks]

SOURCE A

The racialist regime in Southern Rhodesia ... constitutes a hotbed of danger for all other African peoples, including those which have already freed themselves from colonial oppression. It is a bayonet pointed at the heart of liberated Africa, a constant threat to peace on the African continent and a threat to world peace. The Soviet government, guided by its principled stand in questions of abolishing colonialism, strongly condemns the new crime against the peoples of Africa and declares that it does not recognise the racialist regime which has usurped power in Southern Rhodesia. The Soviet Union fully supports the decisions adopted by the United Nations Security Council and General Assembly on the situation in Southern Rhodesia and will carry them out unswervingly.

Extract from a Soviet government statement referring to UDI. From *Soviet News*, No. 5206, 16 November 1965, p. 70.

Skill

Comprehension of a source.

Examiner's tips

Comprehension questions are the most straightforward questions you will face in Paper 1. They simply require you to understand a source and extract two or three relevant points that relate to the particular question.

As only three marks are available for this question, make sure you don't waste valuable exam time that should be spent on the higher-scoring questions by writing a long answer here. Just write a couple of short sentences, giving the necessary information to show you have understood the source. Try to give one piece of information for each of the marks available for the question.

Common mistakes

When asked to show your comprehension/understanding of a particular source, make sure you don't comment on the wrong source! Mistakes like this are made every year. Remember, every mark is important for your final grade.

Simplified markscheme

For each item of **relevant/correct information** identified, award one mark – up to a maximum of three marks.

Student answer

According to Source A, the Soviet government was against UDI, and so it 'strongly condemns' what it saw as a 'new crime against the peoples of Africa'. It accused the Rhodesian government of being a threat to peace in Africa and to world peace.

Examiner's comments

The candidate has selected two relevant and explicit pieces of information from the source – this is enough to gain two marks. However, as no other reason/information has been identified, this candidate fails to gain the other mark available for the question.

Activity

Look again at the source and the student answer above. Now try to identify one other piece of information from the source, and so obtain the other mark available for this question.

Summary activity

Copy this diagram and, using the information in this chapter, make point form notes under each heading.

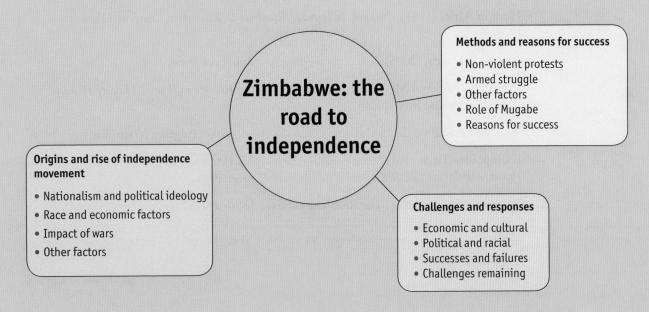

Methods and reasons for success
- Non-violent protests
- Armed struggle
- Other factors
- Role of Mugabe
- Reasons for success

Zimbabwe: the road to independence

Origins and rise of independence movement
- Nationalism and political ideology
- Race and economic factors
- Impact of wars
- Other factors

Challenges and responses
- Economic and cultural
- Political and racial
- Successes and failures
- Challenges remaining

Paper 2 practice questions

1 'Armed struggle was the main reason for the eventual independence of Zimbabwe in 1980.' To what extent do you agree with this statement?

2 Examine the political problems faced by Rhodesia/Zimbabwe in the second half of the 20th century.

3 Evaluate the successes and failures of Robert Mugabe as ruler of a newly independent Zimbabwe.

4 Examine the reasons for the decline of colonial control in Rhodesia/Zimbabwe.

5 Compare and contrast the roles played by Joshua Nkomo and Robert Mugabe in the independence struggle in Zimbabwe.

6 Evaluate the success of the Zimbabwean government in dealing with the problems presented by independence.

Further reading

Try reading the relevant chapters/sections of the following books:

Arnold, Guy (2006), *Africa: A Modern History*, London: Atlantic Books.

Curtin, P., Feierman, L.T. and Vansina, J. (1995), *African History from the Earliest Times to Independence*, 2nd edn, London and New York: Longman.

Dowden, Richard (2008), *Africa: Altered States, Ordinary Miracles*, London: Portobello Books.

Hudson, Miles (1981), *Triumph or Tragedy? Rhodesia to Zimbabwe*, London: Hamish Hamilton.

Meredith, Martin (2005), *The State of Africa*, London: Free Press.

Moorcraft, Paul and McLaughlin, Peter (2008), *The Rhodesian War: A Military History*, Barnsley: Pen and Sword Books.

Nugent, Paul (2004), *Africa since Independence*, Basingstoke: Palgrave Macmillan.

Raftopoulos, Brian and Mlambo, Alois (eds) (2009) *Becoming Zimbabwe: A History from the Pre-colonial Period to 2008*, Harare, Zimbabwe: Weaver Press.

Verrier, Anthony (1986), *The Road to Zimbabwe 1890–1980*, London: Jonathan Cape.

India and Pakistan

Introduction

During the 19th century, when most of Africa and much of Asia were colonised by European powers, a large area of South Asia became the British colony of India. In all the colonial empires, resistance to the imposition of foreign rule took many forms, ranging from uprisings and armed rebellion to acts of defiance or the creation of anti-colonial literature, art and music. In India after the First World War, a strong nationalist movement developed, determined to end British rule. This was finally achieved after the Second World War, when India and Pakistan became independent countries. The success of the Indian nationalist movement inspired similar movements in other Asian and African colonies.

India emerged as a stable democracy, but Pakistan was not as successful in its transition to independence, lacking many of the advantages held by India. India has since developed into the world's largest democracy, and, with China, is well-placed to emerge as one of the most powerful and influential states in the 21st century. Pakistan, on the other hand, still faces considerable political, social and economic problems.

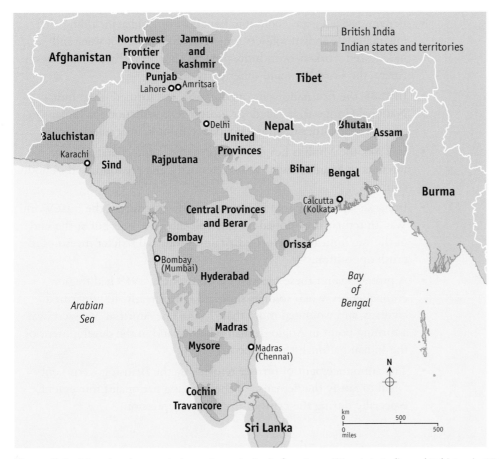

Figure 3.1 Map showing pre-independence India, before its partition into India and Pakistan in 1947

TIMELINE

KEY QUESTIONS

- What role did nationalism and political ideology play in the origins of the nationalist movement in India?
- What role did race, religion and social and economic factors play?
- Which wars influenced the rise of nationalism?
- What other factors influenced the rise of nationalism?

Overview

- India's complex cultural history is critical to understanding the development of the Indian nationalist movement and the progress towards independence from colonial rule.

- Until 1947, India was a British colony. Colonial rule was efficient but authoritarian, and Indians themselves had no meaningful representation.

- Britain derived great economic benefits from India, including raw materials. Indian soldiers fought Britain's colonial wars, and indentured workers from India provided labour in British colonies in Africa, the Caribbean and other parts of Asia.

- In 1885, the first nationalist organisation was formed – the Indian National Congress. It called for greater representation for Indians in government, rather than independence from British rule.

- In 1906, the Muslim League was formed to protect and advance the interests of Muslims, who were a minority in a predominantly Hindu country.

- Indians played a key role in supporting Britain during the First World War. In return, they hoped for self-rule after the war; but at the end of the war, instead of reform, Britain introduced stricter measures to crush opposition.

- A protest against these measures at Amritsar in 1919 had tragic consequences, when soldiers shot and killed nearly 400 unarmed civilians, and wounded more than 1,000. The Amritsar Massacre was a turning point in Anglo–Indian relations and in the development of the Indian nationalist movement.

- The announcement of further reforms by the British government failed to satisfy the demands of the growing nationalist movement, especially during the crisis of the Great Depression.

- Between the two world wars, Britain introduced some constitutional reforms but the pace of change was too slow to satisfy Indian nationalists.
- Needing support against Japan in the Second World War, Britain committed itself to independence for India once the war was over.
- India played a significant role in the Allied war effort, and by the end of the war was economically stronger. By contrast, Britain emerged from the war in a weak position and was ready to negotiate the end of its Indian empire.

3.1 What role did nationalism and political ideology play in the origins of the nationalist movement in India?

India before the British

The area of Asia in which India, Pakistan and Bangladesh are situated today is often referred to as the 'subcontinent' or South Asia. Over the centuries, many different people moved into this region, bringing with them their languages, traditions and religions. As a result, the area contains a rich mixture of people and cultures. At first the main religion was Hinduism, and Hindu princes ruled most of the region. Later, Muslim invaders brought Islam to the subcontinent and established the powerful Mughal Empire, which lasted for more than three centuries (1526–1858). Although the rulers of the empire were Muslim, most of the local leaders and the general population remained Hindu. The Sikhs were a much smaller, but significant, religious group.

British rule in India

British interest in India began when the English East India Company (EIC) set up trading posts along the coast from the beginning of the 17th century. EIC rule gradually expanded into the interior, and by the middle of the 19th century the company controlled large parts of India. Although there was still a Mughal emperor, he had no real power. However, an uprising against EIC control in 1857–8 resulted in the intervention of the British government, which sent troops to crush the uprising and take over control from the EIC.

The Mughal emperor had supported the uprising, and after its failure he was removed from power and sent into exile. India became part of the British Empire. Large parts of the country were placed under direct British administration, but some areas remained under the control of hereditary Indian rulers, with whom the British signed treaties that recognised their autonomy over local affairs. There were more than 500 of these 'princely states', as they were called. India was ruled by a **viceroy** and an administration of 5,000 officials sent from London, who provided efficient, but authoritarian, government. Indians themselves had no meaningful representation in this government,

Theory of Knowledge

History and language: Indian nationalists regarded the uprising as the First War of Independence. The British, however, referred to it as the Indian Mutiny, because it started among sepoys – Indian soldiers serving in the army of the English East India Company. The uprising had broad-based support, however, from a wide range of Indians, including peasants, workers, landlords and princes. As a result, historians now describe it as the Indian Uprising. Use this example, and others you can think of, to explain how terminology can reflect bias in history.

Viceroy: the highest official in the colonial administration, who ruled India on behalf of the British monarch. Although there was a great deal of status, material comfort and wealth attached to the position, the viceroy had limited power to influence policy, which was decided by the British government in London and implemented by the secretary of state for India.

although they later formed the bulk of the junior staff in the Indian Civil Service. British control over 300 million Indians was enforced by a large army, staffed by British officers and Indian troops. The administration and the army were financed out of taxes paid by Indians.

Britain derived great economic benefits from its Indian empire. Money, collected from peasants in the form of taxes, was transferred to London to fund the British government's purchase of EIC shares, finance capital investments (especially railways) and provide funds for the administration of India. Critics felt that the money could have been better used for internal investments in India itself. Britain also benefited from the balance of trade with India, which supplied raw materials – mainly cotton, jute, indigo, rice and tea – to British factories. In return India bought manufactured goods such as textiles, iron and steel goods and machinery, and by 1914 was the biggest export market for British goods. As a result, India under colonial rule was no longer an exporter of cloth to European markets. Instead it produced raw cotton that was manufactured into cloth in British factories and re-exported to Asia. In this way, colonial rule 'de-industrialised' India. Another disadvantage for India was that land formerly used to grow grains for staple foods was now used for commercial cash-crop production, making peasants dependent on foods grown elsewhere.

India also served Britain's political and economic interests in other parts of the empire. Indian soldiers, paid for by Indian taxpayers, were used to protect trade routes and serve British interests in China, East Africa and the Middle East. India also served as a source of indentured labourers for British colonies in the West Indies, Africa and other parts of Asia. By 1920, however, the system of indenture was stopped, partly as a result of criticism from Indian nationalists, who saw it as one of 'imperial exploitation that brought shame to India', according to Barbara and Thomas Metcalf. These historians also note that the plight of **diaspora** Indians was a 'critical stimulus to Indian nationalism'.

Diaspora: a scattering of people around the world, away from their country or continent of origin. Partly as a result of the system of indentured labour, there are substantial Indian minorities living in other parts of the world today. One such Indian community is in South Africa, where Mohandas Gandhi, later to become the dominant figure in the Indian nationalist movement, spent 20 years and developed his political ideas.

Fact: The caste system in India developed about 2,500 years ago. It divided society into a hierarchy of levels called castes. Status, occupation, rights, privileges and opportunities in life were all determined by the caste into which one was born. The caste system is usually associated with Hindu tradition but, according to historian Mridula Mukherjee, it was prevalent among Sikhs, Christians and Muslims too.

3.2 What role did race, religion and social and economic factors play?

After the harsh suppression of the 1857–8 uprising, British power in India seemed to be secure. The British brought certain benefits to India. These included an efficient administration and judicial system, a good railway network and Western education for some. However, British rule was always based on an assumption of superiority, as the statement in **Source A** by a British official, quoted by historian Lawrence James, shows.

QUESTION

How can the ideas expressed in **Source A** be considered a form of 'cultural imperialism'?

SOURCE A

We must rule our Asiatic subjects with strict and generous justice, wisely and beneficently, as their natural superiors, by virtue of our purer religion, our sterner energies, our subtler intellect, our more creative faculties, our more commanding and indomitable will.

Quoted in L. James (1997), *Raj: The Making and Unmaking of British India*, London: Abacus, p. 297.

Indians resented the harsh realities of colonial control and the superior attitudes of the colonising power towards them. This view was later explained by Jawaharlal Nehru, who became a leading figure in the nationalist movement against British rule (see **Source B**).

SOURCE B

We in India have known racialism in all its forms since the beginning of British rule. The whole ideology of this rule was that of the master race, and the structure of government was based upon it; indeed the idea of the master race is inherent in imperialism. There was no subterfuge [nothing hidden] about it; it was proclaimed in unambiguous language by those in authority. More powerful than words was the practice that accompanied them and, generation after generation and year after year, India as a nation and Indians as individuals were subjected to insult, humiliation, and contemptuous treatment. The English were an imperial race, we were told, with the god-given right to govern us and keep us in subjection. As an Indian I am ashamed to write all this, for the memory of it hurts, and what hurts still more is that we submitted for so long to this degradation. I would have preferred any kind of resistance to this, whatever the consequences, rather than that our people should endure this treatment.

J. Nehru (1946), *The Discovery of India*, London: Meridian Books.

KEY CONCEPTS ACTIVITY

Consequences: Compare and contrast the views expressed in **Sources A** and **B**. Explain the consequences of colonial attitudes about race on the growth of nationalism and resistance in India.

The influence of religion on the early nationalist movement

The British believed that government should be firm and vigilant against the rise of any resistance to their rule. Above all, they wanted to prevent the formation of a united opposition movement. To this end, they stressed differences between people – significantly differences of religion and also of caste. They regarded caste as a form of fixed identity, instead of something that had developed and changed over time. According to the historian Thomas Metcalf, the British saw caste as a 'concrete, measurable "thing" that could be fitted into a hierarchy able to be ascertained and quantified in reports and surveys'. The result of this colonial policy was to create and intensify existing differences in Indian society (see **Source C**).

SOURCE C

Having unified India, the British set into motion contrary forces. Fearing the unity of the Indian people to which their own rule had contributed, they followed the classic imperial policy of divide and rule. The diverse and divisive features of Indian society and polity were heightened to promote cleavages among the people and to turn province against province, caste against caste, class against class, Hindus against Muslims, and the princes and landlords against the nationalist movement.

B. Chandra, M. Mukherjee and A. Mukherjee (2000), *India after Independence: 1947–2000*, London: Penguin, p. 18.

QUESTIONS

What is meant by a policy of 'divide and rule'? How and why did the British use this policy in India?

How could a nationalist movement overcome such tactics?

Towards the end of the 19th century, there was a growing feeling among educated Indians that there should be more Indian representation in government. In 1885, they formed a nationalist organisation called the Indian National Congress (INC). In its early stages, the Congress represented the interests of the wealthy middle class and it did not have mass support. Most of the founding members were graduates and all spoke English. They saw themselves as a bridge between the Indian masses and the colonial power. As a result, the existence of the Congress tended to limit the development of more radical nationalist groups.

The élitist nature of the early Congress made it very conservative in its goals, and it used petitions to try to achieve them. It did not question the continuation of British rule, but called rather for greater Indian representation in the legislative councils, easier access to the Indian Civil Service and less expenditure on the army. Most of its membership was Hindu, although it also had Muslim members. Right from the start, Congress leaders made explicit efforts to draw Muslims into their meetings, and members of the organisation believed that the interests of caste or religious affiliation should be secondary to the needs of the Indian nation as a whole.

However, in 1906, Muslims established their own political organisation, the Muslim League, believing that this was the only way to protect the interests of the Muslim minority. At first the League was dominated by a similar middle- and upper-class leadership to the Congress.

> **QUESTION**
>
> How did class and religion affect the make-up of the early nationalist movement in India?

Conflict in Bengal and its impact on religious differences

Serious nationalist opposition to colonial rule in India started when the British decided to partition the province of Bengal in north-eastern India. Bengal had been the first region to come under British control, and its main city, Calcutta, was the capital of British India. The province had a population of more than eighty million people, the majority of whom were Bengali-speaking Hindus. In 1905, the British viceroy announced that the province would be divided into two, in order to provide more efficient administration. This partition created an eastern province with a Muslim majority, and a western part in which Bihari- and Oriya-speaking Hindus were in the majority. Bengali-speaking Hindus saw the partition as a threat to their position in the region and a deliberate attempt by Britain to weaken Bengali nationalism.

The partition prompted Congress into action. An anti-partition movement expressed its opposition using petitions, protests in the press and rallies. When these failed, protestors organised a boycott of British goods. They made public bonfires of manufactured goods from Britain and urged Indians to use local products instead. This boycott proved to be very effective. British imports into India dropped by 25 per cent, and the economy of some areas – such as the city of Bombay on the west coast – expanded as Indian industries developed to take advantage of the gap. The British authorities reacted to the anti-partition protests with mass arrests, which had limited impact. The events had significant results: Congress realised the political power of an economic boycott, and nationalists in other parts of India were united in support for the Bengali cause.

Fact: In recent years, many place names in India have been changed. In this chapter, we have used the names that were in use at the time of the historical events discussed. Among other changes, Calcutta is now Kolkata and Bombay is now Mumbai.

The confrontation over Bengal radicalised parts of the Congress and a revolutionary wing, called the New Party, emerged. This faction was especially strong in Calcutta, Poona (Pune) and Lahore. This development was significant because it seemed that the more moderate leaders were being marginalised in favour of radicals such as **Bal Gangadhar Tilak**, who urged more active opposition to British rule. Another more radical group favoured assassination and sabotage as forms of protest against colonial policies and actions.

SOURCE D

We have a stronger weapon, a political weapon, in boycott. We have perceived one fact; that the whole of this administration, which is carried on by a handful of Englishmen, is carried on with our assistance. We are all in subordinate service. This whole government is carried on with our assistance and they try to keep us in ignorance of our power of cooperation between ourselves by which that which is in our own hands at present can be claimed by us and administered by us. The point is to have the entire control in our hands.

Extract from Tilak's address to the Indian National Congress, 1907. Quoted in W.T. De Bary (1958), *Sources of Indian Tradition*, New York: Columbia University Press, pp. 719–20.

Muslims in Bengal became increasingly unnerved by the developments, and by the appeals to Hindu nationalism made by some anti-partition protestors. Support for the Muslim League increased as the Islamic minority sought to safeguard its own interests. Representatives met with the viceroy and stressed the view that Muslims were a distinct community that needed separate representation for its own protection.

The strength of opposition to the partition of Bengal forced Britain to reassess its policies in India. At first it tried to crush the protests, and by 1909 large numbers of Bengalis were in prison and the situation seemed to be running out of control. Then, in a change of policy, the secretary of state for India, John Morley, decided that concessions should be made to the nationalists so that Britain could maintain its control of the subcontinent. These reforms gave Indians some representation in government, and in 1910 elections were held for the central and provincial legislative councils. Muslims were given separate representation – separate electorates and reserved seats – in a move that shaped future political developments. Indians now had the power to question the decisions of colonial officials and debate the budget for the country.

In addition to this, Bengal was reunited and the capital of India was moved from Calcutta, the site of anti-British activism, to the city of Delhi, which had been the capital of the Mughal Empire. This move pleased Muslims. The Morley reforms cooled the situation in the subcontinent and restored the more moderate elements of Congress to power.

Bal Gangadhar Tilak (1856–1920)

He was the first leader of the Indian National Congress to gain popular support. He demanded self-rule – or *swaraj* – from the British, who saw him as a dangerous troublemaker, and in 1908 sentenced him to prison for sedition (treason). He was released in 1914.

QUESTION

In what ways is Tilak's address critical of Indians themselves, rather than of the British?

KEY CONCEPTS ACTIVITY

Significance: Explain the significance of each of these:

- the anti-British boycotts
- separate representation for Muslims and Hindus
- the movement of the capital from Calcutta to Delhi.

Figure 3.2 In an elaborate ceremony incorporating many features of the Mughal past, the British king George V was crowned emperor of India in 1911

Social and economic developments

During the First World War (1914–18), key industries in India, such as cotton textiles, iron and steel, experienced a boom as manufacturers took advantage of the increased demands caused by the war. Agriculture, however, remained the dominant sector of the economy, and it faced increasing problems after the war. Food production could not keep up with the high population growth rate. In addition, India was badly affected by the Depression, which followed the **Wall Street Crash** in 1929. Overseas markets for India's exports declined, and the value of export crops dropped substantially. This forced Indian peasants to borrow to survive and, when debt became unmanageable, they were thrown off the land, creating masses of rural unemployed. As a result, millions of peasants migrated to the cities in search of work, adding to the numbers of urban unemployed. The impact of the Depression on India was one of the causes of civil unrest in the 1930s, as dissatisfied and unemployed people joined the nationalist movement.

Wall Street Crash: the collapse of the New York stock exchange in 1929 caused a banking and economic crisis in the United States and spread to the rest of the world. It resulted in the Great Depression, which lasted for much of the 1930s.

3.3 Which wars influenced the rise of nationalism?

The impact of the First World War

The First World War was essentially a conflict between European powers, but it involved their overseas empires as well. When war broke out in 1914, Britain expected support from its colonies, and India supplied large numbers of soldiers and huge amounts of resources to the cause. Some nationalists viewed the war as an opportunity to press for greater independence, but most Indians, including radicals such as Tilak, urged support for Britain's war effort.

However, as the war dragged on, dissatisfaction grew, partly due to heavy wartime taxation and increased efforts at recruitment. The war also caused a conflict of loyalties for Muslims in India, because the Ottoman Empire – the world's leading Islamic power – had an alliance with Germany. By the end of the war it had become obvious to many Indians just how dependent Britain had been on their help to secure victory over Germany. Indian soldiers returning from Western Europe passed on their experience of the high living standards and wealth of even the poorest classes in Britain and France when compared to the people of India. Indians hoped that their sacrifices in the war would result in reforms that would give them greater representation in government.

In this way, the experiences of the war heightened nationalist sentiments and many hoped that the British would soon allow India a greater degree of independence. Indeed, in 1917 the British government announced its intention to encourage 'the gradual development of self-governing institutions' in India. The proposals, however, were rejected by both Congress and the Muslim League as not going far enough. Then, in 1918, instead of reform a series of harsh repressive measures was introduced to crush opposition. The anger at this situation was compounded by the effects of the worldwide 1918 influenza epidemic, which killed twelve million Indians.

The Amritsar Massacre (1919)

There were protests all over India against the new measures. A new form of protest was a nationwide *hartal*, or work stoppage, as well as large marches in major cities. Ignoring a ban on public meetings, a crowd of 5,000 gathered at Amritsar, where the British officer in charge, General Reginald Dyer, ordered his troops to open fire on the unarmed protestors. The soldiers killed 379 people and wounded more than 1,000 more in ten minutes. Many of those killed were women and children who had been trapped because soldiers had blocked the exits. Indians were shocked at the news of the massacre, and more especially by British reactions to it.

The British government ordered an inquiry into the incident and Dyer was forced to resign from the army, but some British officials expressed approval of his actions, some settlers in India regarded him as a saviour, and he was welcomed back in England as a hero.

After the massacre, many more people began to support Congress and its call for an end to British rule. Among the new supporters were moderate members of the

Fact: One and a half million Indians volunteered to serve in the British army during the First World War – the largest volunteer army in history. They fought on the Western Front, in Gallipoli, Palestine and North and East Africa. Indian troops won 13,000 medals for bravery, including 12 Victoria Crosses. About 65,000 Indian soldiers were killed in the war, and an equal number wounded.

Fact: Indian national pride was strengthened when Rabindranath Tagore (1861–1941), a Bengali poet, novelist, musician and playwright, was awarded the Nobel Prize for Literature in 1912, becoming the first Asian Nobel laureate. He was later knighted by the British king, but returned his knighthood in protest after the massacre of hundreds of unarmed civilians in 1919 by British troops at Amritsar.

Figure 3.3 An illustration from a German satirical magazine, 21 January 1920, showing British general Reginald Dyer surveying the aftermath of the massacre at Amritsar

QUESTIONS

Why is the Amritsar Massacre considered to be a turning point in the development of the Indian nationalist movement?

How did differences between British and Indian perspectives of the massacre create further support for the nationalist movement?

Indian élite who until that point had considered themselves to be loyal British subjects. One of the Congress leaders who was outspoken in his condemnation of the Amritsar Massacre was Mohandas Gandhi. From this point, Gandhi emerged as the dominant figure in the nationalist movement (you will learn more about him in the next unit).

Constitutional developments between the two world wars

In 1919, the British parliament passed the Government of India Act, which was regarded as a first step in the progress towards self-government for India. Although the central government in Delhi remained under British control, certain responsibilities in the provinces – such as agriculture, education and health – were given to Indian ministers. Crucially, however, the British retained control of the police and the justice system. About 10 per cent of the adult male population was given the right to vote for provincial legislatures. However, these tentative steps towards reform did not satisfy Indian nationalists.

In 1927, the British government appointed the Simon Commission to make recommendations for further constitutional reform. However, no Indians were included in the commission so the nationalists rejected it and called instead for dominion status and full self-government. When the British ignored the call and instead made vague statements about future constitutional developments, impatience at the slow pace of reform increased. The stagnation of British policy in the 1920s helped to foster the demands of the nationalist movement for complete independence for India.

In 1935, the British parliament passed the Government of India Act, a new set of constitutional reforms that gave more control in the provinces to elected Indian ministers. However, the Act ensured that Britain retained control through emergency powers, which could be imposed whenever it was deemed necessary. Although both Congress and the League condemned these measures as inadequate, they decided to participate in the provincial elections held in 1937. The right to vote was based on a property qualification, and so was limited to thirty-five million of the wealthier part of the Indian population, including women. In the elections, Congress emerged as the strongest political force, gaining a landslide victory with 70 per cent of the popular vote. In stark contrast, the Muslim League did not do well in the elections, winning barely 5 per cent of the total Muslim vote.

On the eve of the Second World War, the situation in India was a complex one for Britain. On the one hand, the lack of unity among the nationalists seemed to serve Britain's interests. On the other hand, growing tensions and divisions had the potential to cause unrest that would be difficult to contain. The outbreak of war in 1939 meant a postponement of the further constitutional reforms laid out in the 1935 Government of India Act.

The impact of the Second World War

When the Second World War started in 1939, the British viceroy committed India to fight on the Allied side against Germany without consulting the Indian legislative council. This act was legal and constitutional, but it emphasised India's subservience to the colonial power. This strengthened the resolve of the nationalist movement to continue the independence struggle. In December 1941, Japan entered the war on Germany's side with a series of successful military strikes across East Asia. The Japanese rapidly overran European colonies in Indochina, the Malayan peninsula and Burma, bringing their armies to the border of India, and severely denting Britain's military and imperial prestige.

The war created political opportunities for the Indian nationalists. The British simply did not have the resources to suppress a potential nationalist rising in India while they were fighting the war. Consequently, Britain decided to make political concessions to Congress and the Muslim League. Although this seemed a wise decision – after all, neither Indian independence party was radical, nor were they champions of armed resistance – the British government was not prepared to make significant concessions. In 1941, the British prime minister, Winston Churchill, signed the Atlantic Charter, a document that supported the right of all peoples to political self-determination. However, shortly afterwards, Churchill told the British parliament that this provision did not apply to India. It was clear that the British

Figure 3.4 Sikh soldiers serving alongside the British 8th Army in Italy during the Second World War

attitude towards India had changed little by 1941. Indian nationalists were outraged by this turn of events.

By 1942, however, Japan's sweeping victories in Asia forced Churchill to change his position. He recognised the urgent need to gain the support of Indian leaders in fighting Japan. In March 1942, he sent Stafford Cripps, a member of the British government, to India to negotiate with the nationalist leaders. Cripps made the commitment to grant India independence but only after the war was over. In return, Congress was to commit itself fully to the British war effort. (You will learn about the responses of the nationalist leaders to these conditions in the next unit.)

3.4 What other factors influenced the rise of nationalism?

The post-war situation in India

India made a major contribution to the Allied victory in the war. Not only did Indian soldiers fight in North Africa, Italy and Burma, but also the Indian economy was a significant factor in the final defeat of the Axis powers. An example is the Jamshedpur steel complex, which became the largest producer of steel in the British Empire for the duration of the war. The war transformed India's economic relationship with Britain. Before the war, India had been in debt to Britain. However, during the war, Britain's need to fund the war forced it to borrow heavily from India – so much so that by 1945 the economic relationship between the two states had been reversed, with Britain owing India huge sums of money.

The war also placed strains on India. Two million people died in the great Bengal Famine of 1943, which was caused partly by the loss of rice imports from Japanese-occupied Burma and partly by a British administrative decision to divert food from the Bengal countryside to feed the military instead. However, the war also brought opportunities. The economic demands of the conflict encouraged industrialisation on a scale unknown before 1939, and Bombay became a major centre of light engineering and manufacturing of pharmaceuticals and chemicals.

The Second World War had a negative impact on the British economy. Although Britain emerged victorious, the burden of sustaining the war effort proved costly. By 1945, Britain's economy was on the brink of collapse, and it became apparent that it would be impossible to maintain a global empire. Furthermore, in order to maintain Indian support in the war against Germany and Japan, the British had made serious commitments to the nationalist movement. With the defeat of the Axis powers in 1945, it was time for Britain to make good its promises of independence and negotiate with the nationalist leaders.

End of unit activities

1   'The British derived more benefits from India than Indians did from Britain.' Divide into two groups. One group should prepare an argument to support this statement, and the other group should prepare an argument to oppose it.

2   Find out what you can about the experiences of Indian soldiers during the First World War by looking at www.bbc.co.uk/history/worldwars/wwone/india_wwone_01.shtml. Explain how their exposure to new ideas, customs and perspectives might have affected them on their return to India after the war.

3   Draw up a table to contrast the Indian National Congress and the Muslim League, using the following categories: support base; political outlook; attitude towards the British; political aims.

4 Write a short report to explain whether British policy towards India between 1909 and 1947 represented change or continuity.

5 In class, divide into small groups. Each group should prepare ten cards, each with a question based on this unit, that requires a single relevant fact as an answer. Each group exchanges cards with another group. The answers can be scored as a fun quiz activity. This is an example:

> *What global event in 1929 had an impact on the Indian economy?*
>
> *Answer: Wall Street Crash*

As an extension activity, after discussion, each group should write a short paragraph for each card. The paragraph should explain how each fact fits into the general historical process studied in this unit, showing how it relates to the Indian independence movement. This is an example:

> *The Wall Street Crash created unemployment in India, both rural and urban, as markets shrank. The crisis in the global economy hindered India's ability to trade its way out of the crisis. Poverty and unemployment created political unrest and strengthened calls for independence.*

KEY QUESTIONS

- What methods did the Indian nationalist movement use to achieve independence?
- What role did Mohammad Ali Jinnah play in the struggle for independence?
- What role did Mohandas Gandhi play in the struggle for independence?
- Why did the Indian nationalist movement succeed?

TIMELINE

1920–2 Gandhi's first non-cooperation campaign begins.

1929 Congress demands complete independence for India.

1930 Salt March.

1937 Congress wins elections for provincial legislatures.

1939 Second World War begins.

1942 'Quit India' resolution by Congress.

1943 Bose forms Indian National Army under Japanese command.

1945 Second World War ends.

1946 Direct Action Day triggers widespread communal violence.

1947 Mountbatten arrives as last viceroy of India; Pakistan and India become independent.

Overview

- Mohandas Gandhi, his philosophy of *satyagraha* and his campaigns of non-cooperation were at the core of the independence movement in India.

- Indian nationalists were frustrated by the slow pace of constitutional reform, and in 1929 Congress demanded complete independence.

- The 1930 Salt March gained worldwide attention and forced Britain to start negotiations with the nationalists at a series of Round Table conferences in London.

- There were increasing political tensions in the 1930s, and the Muslim League made calls for the recognition of their identity as a separate nation.

- In 1942, Congress adopted the 'Quit India' campaign to force Britain to leave India immediately.

- The Muslim League cooperated with Britain during the war and so was in a stronger position at the end of the war, when negotiations about independence began.

- Between 1945 and 1947, British control of India collapsed, as anti-British protests mounted and demands for independence grew.

- However, there were differences of opinion between Congress and the Muslim League about the form that an independent Indian state should take.

- The Muslim League's call for 'direct action' led to an outbreak of communal violence in which thousands died.

- As tensions rose, Congress accepted the concept of partition, and India and Pakistan became separate independent states in August 1947.

- Both Jinnah and Gandhi played critical roles in the independence movement, but they differed fundamentally about the form that an independent Indian state should take.

- The success of the nationalist movement was due not only to the strength of the movement itself, but must also be seen in the wider context of the time.

3.5 What methods did the Indian nationalist movement use to achieve independence?

The person who transformed the Indian National Congress into a mass nationalist movement after the First World War was Mohandas Gandhi. Until then, support for Congress had come from the Indian élite, so, for the movement to succeed in challenging British rule in India, it needed to expand its appeal. This was Gandhi's great achievement.

Gandhi and *satyagraha*

Gandhi championed a form of non-violent resistance, or civil disobedience, to colonial rule that stemmed from an Indian concept called *satyagraha*, or 'soul force'. It was based on the belief that ordinary people can bring about political change by using peaceful means to fight for justice.

SOURCE A

Soul force, or the power of truth, is reached by the infliction of suffering, not on your opponent, but on yourself. Rivers of blood may have to flow before we gain our freedom, but it must be our blood… The government of the day has passed a law which I do not like. If, by using violence, I force the government to change the law, I am using what may be called body-force. If I do not obey the law, and accept the penalty for breaking it, I use soul force. It involves sacrificing yourself.

Gandhi describes the concept of satyagraha. Quoted in J. Bottaro and R. Calland (2001), *Successful Human and Social Sciences Grade 9*, Cape Town, South Africa: Oxford University Press, p. 45.

Theory of Knowledge

History and ethics:
Gandhi believed that the authorities could be forced to give in, by the firm yet peaceful demonstration of the justice of a cause. How could *satyagraha* be an effective moral force to bring about political change? Can you think of other contexts in 20th-century history where non-violent resistance has been used effectively?

Satyagraha involved a campaign of non-cooperation with the British administration, boycotts of British schools, universities and law courts, and, critically, boycotts – called *hartal* – of British goods. Gandhi consciously rejected Western values and adopted the dress and lifestyle of a simple peasant. He established an ashram, or community, committed to non-violence and self-sufficiency using traditional methods. This appeal to traditional cultural values allowed him to connect to the mass of the Indian peasantry. He also identified with the problems of specific groups, earning their respect and support: tenant farmers exploited by landlords, industrial workers involved in disputes with factory owners, and poor farmers unable to pay taxes after bad harvests.

This non-violent opposition stemmed in part from the fact that armed resistance was not practical given the military power of the British. *Satyagraha* would exploit Britain's greatest weakness in India – the British economy's reliance on the subcontinent. Simply boycotting British goods would have a massive effect on the colonial power's ability to trade successfully, and non-cooperation in the form of strikes would severely damage

British-owned companies. Non-violent resistance also suited the Indian élite, who feared that an armed struggle would destabilise India so much that potentially radical groups and individuals might gain a foothold and threaten their position in Indian society.

Gandhi changed Congress from a narrow, élite organisation into a mass nationalist movement that incorporated all sectors of Indian society. This inclusiveness was not only based on class, but also crossed ethnic and religious lines. After the First World War, one of Gandhi's strongest sources of support was the **Khalifat** movement, led by the brothers Mohammed and Shaukat Ali. Historians Sugata Bose and Ayesha Jalal describe the 'courageous display of unity among Hindus, Muslims and Sikhs' that existed at this period. Although the British tried to crush resistance by implementing harsh laws and jailing Gandhi and other leaders, the movement gained increasing support.

The non-cooperation campaign, 1920–2

In 1920, Congress formally agreed to support Gandhi's plan for a campaign of non-cooperation, which now included a call for *swaraj* (self-government) as well, through legitimate and peaceful means. The boycott of British goods and institutions had some success. The British reacted to the campaign by arresting 20,000 protesters, but this only

Khalifat: 'caliph' is a Muslim term for a supreme political and spiritual leader in the Muslim world. The Khalifat movement among Muslims in India wanted to protect the Ottoman Empire by putting pressure on the British. When the Ottoman Empire was broken up after the First World War, and Turkey became a secular state, the movement lost its primary goal and became part of the wider nationalist movement in India.

Figure 3.5 Gandhi at his spinning wheel; his promotion of spinning had symbolic significance rather than practical use – hand-woven cloth symbolised a rejection of foreign manufactured goods and the promotion of self-reliance; the spinning wheel became the symbol of the Indian nationalist movement

3

'**Untouchables**': the lowest category in the caste system, they traditionally suffered many forms of discrimination. They could not own land, enter temples or use common resources such as village wells or roads. They performed all the menial work, such as carrying water, tanning leather and working the land, usually as sharecroppers. The British colonial administration referred to them as the 'depressed classes'. Gandhi fought for their rights and called them *Harijans*, or children of God.

Fact: *Hindutwa*, or the promotion of Hindu values and the creation of a state modelled on Hindu beliefs and culture, was the aim of a militant Hindu nationalist group, the Rashtriya Swayamsevak Sangh (RSS), which was formed in 1925. It was a member of the RSS who later assassinated Gandhi because of his tolerant attitude towards Muslims. The ideas of *Hindutwa* re-emerged as a powerful political force in Indian politics in the 1980s, in the Bharatiya Janata Party (BJP), the political group associated with Hindu nationalism.

QUESTION

Explain the dilemma facing Muslims in India during the 1920s.

prompted further resistance. However, when protests got out of control and protesters turned to violence, Gandhi called off the campaign. A month later, Gandhi was arrested and sentenced to six years in prison. Although he was released after two years for health reasons, he abstained from direct political activity until 1929. During this period he abandoned any political action and withdrew to fast and to meditate. He called for a 'constructive programme' of local hand-weaving industries and social programmes to promote self-reliance.

During this period, Gandhi fought for greater rights for the '**Untouchables**' and managed to negotiate some reforms to the caste system in the province of Travancore, allowing freedom of movement. By championing their cause, Gandhi encouraged social integration and, critically, sent out a significant signal that post-colonial India would be a modern state based on the values of social equality for all.

Communal tensions

A feature of the early non-cooperation campaign had been the unity between Hindus and Muslims. For example, the Khalifat leader Mohammed Ali had served as president of Congress as well. However, a disturbing development in the mid-1920s was the growth of tension and violence between religious communities. This was partly due to the emergence of a politicised form of Hinduism, called *Hindutwa*, which promoted an anti-Muslim message.

The 1920s also saw a strengthening of the Muslim League, as the Khalifat movement declined with the collapse of the Ottoman Empire. Mohammed Ali Jinnah, the leader of the League, offered to cooperate with Congress to draw up proposals for constitutional reform, in return for safeguards for the Muslim minority. But, under pressure from Hindu nationalists, Congress rejected this offer. Tensions between the two communities were heightened in some regions by economic factors. In many – but certainly not all – provinces, many of the landlords and traders were Hindu, while the Muslims were peasant farmers or poor workers.

SOURCE B

I have a culture, a polity, an outlook on life – a complete synthesis which is Muslim. Where God commands I am a Muslim first, a Muslim second, and a Muslim last, and nothing but a Muslim... But where India is concerned, where India's freedom is concerned, where the welfare of India is concerned, I am an Indian first, an Indian second, an Indian last, and nothing but an Indian.

Mohammed Ali, commenting on the conflicting sense of identity facing Muslims in India in the 1920s. Quoted in S. Bose and A. Jalal (1996), *Modern South Asia*, London: Routledge, p. 143.

In 1927, when the British government was investigating constitutional reform in India, **Motilal Nehru** drafted a proposed constitution that called for **dominion status** and full self-government. Younger and more radical members of Congress, such as Subhas Chandra Bose and Jawaharlal Nehru, went even further and called for complete self-government outside the British Empire. At the same time, Jinnah and the Muslim League were insisting that Muslims should be given separate representation to protect their position as a minority.

During 1928, there were radical protests by students and urban youth and a series of strikes by workers in Bombay, backed by the Communist Party of India. The British authorities responded by charging thirty-one trade union leaders with planning to overthrow the government, although they were eventually freed after their trials collapsed. At the 1929 session of Congress, Gandhi backed the demand for *purna swaraj*, or complete independence. The failure of Britain to negotiate meaningfully with the nationalists had pushed Congress into radical action. Even Gandhi had, to a degree, become more radical as a result of the slow pace of reform in the 1920s.

The development of a mass-based nationalist movement

The move to a mass-based nationalist movement in the 1930s started with the Salt March. Gandhi chose to make salt the issue upon which he would base his second great *satyagraha* campaign. Salt was a vital commodity in India, a basic life-sustaining resource. Not only did the British tax it heavily but its production was a state monopoly – it was illegal for ordinary Indians to manufacture or sell salt. In March 1930, Gandhi began a march of nearly 400km (250 miles) to the coast. Crowds gathered to support him and the event received media coverage all over the world. When Gandhi arrived at the sea, he picked up a lump of natural salt, symbolically breaking the law. The authorities made no attempt to stop this act, so powerful was the message that the protest action sent out to millions of Indians and to people around the world. Soon the protests spread, and thousands of people began to break the salt laws. Eventually, the authorities reacted by imprisoning thousands of protesters, including Gandhi. His arrest prompted nationwide strikes and rioting in the larger urban centres. By the end of 1930, 100,000 people had been arrested and one hundred had been killed by the police.

Eventually the British decided on negotiation, and a Round Table conference was held in London. However, without any representatives from Congress – which boycotted the meeting – little progress was made. In 1931, Irwin, the viceroy of India, released Gandhi and began talks with him in Delhi. Given Irwin's previous opposition to reform in India, this shows just how seriously the British viewed the situation. Irwin and Gandhi reached an agreement: Gandhi called off the civil disobedience campaign and, in return, the British recognised the development of a local Indian manufacturing economy and invited Gandhi to London for a second round of talks. The second Round Table conference in London did little to advance India's cause, and on his return to India, Gandhi called for renewed civil disobedience.

Increasing political tension

In 1932, Gandhi was arrested and imprisoned once again, leading to widespread resistance to the colonial power. Peasants refused to pay taxes and support for the boycott of British goods increased. During this period another 80,000 Indians were imprisoned. As well as repression, Britain also resorted to 'political engineering to divide and deflect the nationalist challenge', according to Bose and Jalal. This took the form of the Communal Award, a voting formula that confirmed separate electorates for religious minorities, such as Muslims and Sikhs, and also for the 'depressed castes' (the Untouchables). Gandhi viewed this development as a serious challenge to the unity of the nationalist movement, and threatened to fast to death in his prison cell. The fast had a wide impact on public opinion and eventually led to an agreement between Gandhi and Dr B.R. Ambedkar, the leader of the Untouchables, that a separate electorate would

Motilal Nehru (1861–1931)

He was an early leader of the Indian nationalist movement, a leader of the Indian National Congress and founder of the influential Nehru-Gandhi family. His son, Jawaharlal Nehru, was independent India's first prime minister (1947–64); his granddaughter, Indira Gandhi, was prime minister from 1966 to 1977 and from 1980 to 1984; and his great-grandson, Rajiv Gandhi, was prime minister from 1984 to 1989.

Dominion status: gave colonies autonomy to run their own affairs. They were linked to Britain as members of the empire but not ruled by Britain. Australia, New Zealand, South Africa and Canada had dominion status; British colonies in Asia and other parts of Africa did not.

Historical debate:
There are different interpretations of modern Indian history. Imperialist historians focus on the role of the British in the progress towards independence. Indian nationalist historians focus on the role played by Indian leaders such as Gandhi and Nehru in the independence movement. Historians of the more recent 'subaltern studies' group focus on the role played by ordinary people in this struggle, and how they too were agents of political and social change. The word 'subaltern' is a military term meaning someone of inferior rank, but in this context it is used to refer to anyone who holds an inferior position in society in terms of race, class, gender, sexuality, ethnicity or religion.

ACTIVITY

In pairs create a chart. On one side list Gandhi's actions and policies, on the other rate their effectiveness in bringing about an end to British domination in India from 1 (very ineffective) to 5 (very effective).

Figure 3.6 A significant feature of the salt campaign was the involvement of large numbers of women as marchers and speakers

be abandoned in favour of a larger number of reserved seats. Some more traditionalist Congress members were troubled by Gandhi's pact with Ambedkar and his championing of the depressed castes.

Around this time, the Muslim League began calling for a separate Muslim state as part of the process of decolonisation. During the First World War, the League and Congress had made an agreement, the Lucknow Pact, to cooperate in striving for independence. However, this agreement had later collapsed and the two organisations became alienated from one another. After the failure of the Round Table talks in 1930, the League drafted its first demands for an independent Muslim state, which it called Pakistan. The name means 'land of the pure' in the Urdu language, and was made up from the initial letters of the Muslim-majority provinces of Punjab, the Afghan frontier, Kashmir and Sind. The aspirations of the League were further reinforced in 1932 with the British government's announcement of the Communal Award.

Nationalist leaders from both movements condemned the British government's proposals in the 1935 Government of India Act as too little too late. Nehru called the act a 'charter of slavery'; Bose dismissed it as a scheme 'not for self-government, but for maintaining British rule'; and Jinnah described it as 'most reactionary, retrograde, injurious and fatal to the interest of British India vis-a-vis the Indian states'. Nevertheless, Congress and the League decided to participate in the provincial elections held in 1937. But the success of Congress in winning 70 per cent of the popular vote in these elections, and the failure of the League to win much support at all, added to the tensions between the two movements.

Growing divisions

Although the League had fared badly in the elections, Jinnah hoped that the League could form part of coalition governments in the provinces that had large Muslim minorities. Having won the elections so convincingly, however, Congress was not prepared to compromise with the League in this way. It turned down Jinnah's offer of cooperation, although it did appoint some of its own Muslim members to provincial governments. Historians such as Barbara and Thomas Metcalf refer to the attitude and actions of Congress towards the League at this time as arrogant and 'high-handed', and say that they caused the League to strengthen its efforts to gain a mass following. In some provinces, Muslim leaders complained of favouritism towards Hindus, and the promotion of Hindu symbols and the Hindi language, although this was never Congress policy. Using the slogan 'Islam in danger' as a rallying call, Jinnah tried to build up his powerbase by uniting all Muslims within the League. Support for the idea that India's Muslims were a distinct nation entitled to a separate state gained ground, especially as the election results had revealed the electoral dangers that Muslims faced as part of a

SOURCE C

I am proud of being an Indian. I am proud of the indivisible unity that is Indian nationality… Islam has now as great a claim on the soil of India as Hinduism. If Hinduism has been the religion of the people here for several thousands of years, Islam has also been their religion for a thousand years. Just as a Hindu can say with pride that he is an Indian and follows Hinduism, so also we can say with equal pride that we are Indians and follow Islam.

Statement by Maulana Azad, president of the Indian National Congress, 1940. Quoted in B. Metcalf and T. Metcalf (2006), *A Concise History of Modern India*, Cambridge: Cambridge University Press, p. 198.

QUESTION

Compare and contrast the views expressed in **Sources B** and **C**. How might Jinnah have responded to this statement by Maulana Azad? What response would a supporter of *Hindutwa* make to it?

single state. However, some Muslims continued to support the goal of a united India, as the statement by Maulana Azad, president of Congress in 1940, shows (**Source C**).

By the late 1930s there was growing conflict between the left- and right-wings within Congress itself. The most prominent leaders in the left-wing were **Jawaharlal Nehru** and the more radical **Subhas Chandra Bose**. They were impatient with the cautious and conservative approach advocated by Gandhi and others. Gandhi tried to maintain unity by ensuring that first Nehru (in 1936–7) and then Bose (in 1938) served as president of Congress.

In 1939, Bose was re-elected as president of Congress in the first contested election in the history of the movement. He was supported by the youth, trade union and peasant wings of the party. It seemed that elements within Congress had run out of patience and were moving towards support for a more radical revolutionary – and potentially violent – solution to British domination of India.

However, Bose's re-election was opposed by Gandhi and many of the most powerful figures in Congress, and the election threatened to split the party in two, weakening the nationalist movement. When Bose realised he would not have the cooperation of the moderates in Congress, he left to form the revolutionary Forward Bloc Party. These developments showed that, despite the emergence of radical forces, the moderates managed to maintain control of the nationalist movement. But the tensions and divisions threatened the unity of the nationalist movement at a critical time when the Second World War was starting in Europe.

The nationalist movement during the Second World War

The war created political opportunities for the Indian nationalists when it became obvious that Britain needed the full support of India in the war against Japan. The Cripps mission offered the nationalists independence after the war, in return for support for the British war effort.

Congress rejected the offer. It accepted that, in the long term, a Japanese victory in Asia would simply replace one form of colonial domination with another; however, the postponement of independence seemed unreasonable. As a result, Congress began to campaign actively for immediate independence from Britain. In August 1942, it adopted the 'Quit India' resolution and re-launched the campaign of non-cooperation with the colonial power. Britain reacted by imprisoning Congress leaders and banning the organisation. As Britain's repressive policy took hold, almost 60,000 Indians, including Gandhi and Nehru, were detained without trial. British attempts to control the increasingly dangerous situation in India led to more than 1,000 people being killed.

SOURCE D

India will attain her freedom through her non-violent strength, and will retain it likewise. Therefore, the committee hopes that Japan will not have any designs on India. But if Japan attacks India, and Britain makes no response to its appeal, the committee will expect all those who look to the Congress for guidance to offer complete non-violent non-cooperation to the Japanese forces, and not to render any assistance to them. It is no part of the duty of those who are attacked to render any assistance to the attacker. It is their duty to offer complete non-cooperation.

Extract from *Gandhi's 'Quit India' resolution*, 1942.

The war also created opportunities for the Muslim League. The League's leader, Jinnah, at first approached Congress with an offer of cooperation in the face of British repression. When Congress rejected this offer, the Muslim League continued to cooperate with Britain. Jinnah accepted Cripps's offer of delayed independence, but he demanded a two-state solution after independence. As the situation in India grew increasingly tense, and Congress became the target of British repression, the League moved to give full support to the British war effort. In return, Britain gave serious consideration to a two-state solution to the problem. The League was therefore in a strong negotiating position at the end of the war. Its support for Britain's actions in India would be a key factor in the emergence of the separate Muslim state of Pakistan after independence.

The move to independence, 1945–7

After the end of the Second World War, anti-British feelings in India intensified. In 1945, Indians who had fought in Bose's Indian National Army alongside the Japanese were put on trial for treason. The trial turned them into national heroes – they were seen as fighters for Indian freedom who were now being unfairly tried by the colonial power. Massive protests followed, and the British were forced to reduce the punishment to suspended sentences. This failed to stop the protests, which included a mutiny in the Royal Indian Navy involving twenty naval bases and seventy-four ships. Faced with a rapidly deteriorating situation, the British government realised the importance of reaching a settlement in India urgently. Britain had been seriously weakened by the war, and did not have the economic resources to maintain control in these uneasy circumstances.

The situation in India was further complicated by differences of opinion over the specific form of a post-colonial state. Congress wanted the creation of a single, secular state, in which religious affiliation would not be significant. The Muslim League, however, wanted India to be divided. Muslims formed only about 20 per cent of the population at that stage, and they feared that their interests would be neglected in a Hindu-dominated state. They wanted a separate country, Pakistan, to be created in the northern parts of the subcontinent, where most Muslims lived. Congress vigorously opposed the concept of a divided India. Congress leaders, such as Gandhi and Nehru, tried to persuade Muslim leaders that they would be safe in a united India.

The leader of the Muslim League, Mohammed Ali Jinnah, put pressure on Britain to support the creation of two separate states. The League also appealed to popular fears and prejudices – Muslims of all classes flocked to join the organisation, believing that Islam was in danger. In **Source E**, historian Ramachandra Guha analyses the contrast between the election messages of Congress and the League in the 1946 elections for provincial assemblies.

Fact: Subhas Chandra Bose viewed the war as an opportunity to force Britain to grant independence immediately. He allied himself with the Axis powers, and tried unsuccessfully to raise an Indian Legion in Europe to fight for the Germans. When the Germans transferred him to Southeast Asia by submarine in 1943, he formed a 60,000-strong Indian National Army (INA) among Indian prisoners of war and civilians there. He also established a Free India government in the Burmese capital of Rangoon. The INA fought Allied forces in Burma, and invaded and briefly captured parts of north-eastern India, before being defeated.

QUESTION

Comment on whether the course of action outlined in Gandhi's 'Quit India' resolution is consistent with his philosophy of *satyagraha*.

QUESTION

Does **Source E** show a biased view? Explain how it can be argued that the language used in the source can contribute to bias. How could one establish whether it is an accurate and reliable interpretation of the situation?

SOURCE E

The world over, the rhetoric of modern democratic politics has been marked by two rather opposed rhetorical styles. The first appeals to hope, to popular aspirations for economic prosperity and social peace. The second appeals to fear, to sectional worries about being worsted or swamped by one's historic enemies. In the elections of 1946 the Congress relied on the rhetoric of hope. It had a strongly positive content to its programme, promising land reform, workers' rights, and the like. The Muslim League, on the other hand, relied on the rhetoric of fear. If they did not get a separate homeland, they told the voters, then they would be crushed by the more numerous Hindus in a united India.

R. Guha (2007), *India after Gandhi: The History of the World's Largest Democracy*, London: Macmillan, p. 28.

Communalism: the belief in promoting the interests of one ethnic, religious or cultural group rather than those of society as a whole. Communal groups were responsible for promoting violence between Hindus, Muslims and Sikhs.

Communal violence

As negotiations between the British government and Indian representatives dragged on, tensions mounted. Fearing that Britain and Congress would push forward with plans for a single state, Jinnah called for 'direct action' in support of the Muslim League's demand for partition. He wanted to show the other parties that Muslim aspirations could not be ignored.

On 16 August 1946, or 'Direct Action Day', there was rioting in Calcutta, which soon turned into widespread **communal** violence between Muslim and Hindu communities, with both sides committing atrocities. In this Great Calcutta Killing, as it became known, more than 4,000 people were killed and thousands more wounded or made homeless. There were violent clashes between Hindus and Muslims in other parts of India as well, and thousands more were killed. The British interpreted the violence as a sign that there were irreconcilable differences between Hindus and Muslims, an interpretation that is questioned by many historians today.

Independence and partition, 1947

In an atmosphere of escalating violence, Congress reluctantly came to accept that partition was the only viable solution and that British India would be divided into two separate states. The violence also exposed the weakness of Britain's position in the subcontinent, and the British decided to quit India as soon as possible.

In February 1947, Lord Louis Mountbatten was sent as the last viceroy of India, to facilitate and oversee the handover of power by June 1948. He later brought the date forward to 15 August 1947. In only six months, therefore, Mountbatten had to decide whether power would be handed over to one, two or more states, where the borders between them would be, and what was to happen to the 'princely states' – those parts of India that had remained under the control of hereditary rulers.

Mountbatten opted for the Muslim League's two-state solution and created two enclaves in north-western India and eastern Bengal, containing large numbers of Muslims, to form Pakistan. The rulers of the princely states were allowed to choose which state to join. The problems were not, however, solved by the partition plan. The ethnic and religious mix of the subcontinent was far more complex than implied by the simple geographic division devised by the British. For the partition plan to work, millions of people would have to relocate to one country or the other, depending on their ethnicity and religion.

In August 1947, British rule came to an end when the subcontinent became independent as two separate states: India and Pakistan. But the challenges facing the new states, especially in the immediate aftermath of independence and partition, were immense. (You will read about them in the next unit.)

3.6 What role did Mohammad Ali Jinnah play in the struggle for independence?

Mohammad Ali Jinnah (1876–1948) was an important figure in the Indian independence movement. Like many other nationalist leaders, he had a Western education. After studying at Bombay University, he trained as a lawyer in London in the 1890s where he was influenced by British liberal ideas. As a result he came to believe that the Indian independence struggle should use constitutional methods. He was a member of the Indian National Congress from 1896, but only became active in Indian politics after defending the leading nationalist Tilak who was arrested and charged with sedition at the time of the conflict in Bengal in 1905.

In 1913, Jinnah joined the Muslim League and in 1916 became its president for the first time. He believed that India had a right to independence, and argued that Indians were entitled to agitate for this goal. However, he also recognised the benefits that British rule had brought to India in the form of law, culture and industry. In many ways these were the views of most Indian nationalist leaders at the time. At the same time, Jinnah was also a member of the Home Rule League, which wanted India to be given dominion status. This would give India autonomy rather than complete independence within the British Empire. Initially Jinnah had been a moderate liberal Anglophile, but Britain's failure to give independence to India after the First World War caused him to adopt more radical views.

In 1920, when the Indian National Congress launched a non-cooperation campaign, Jinnah resigned from Congress. He thought that Gandhi's tactics of non-cooperation could destabilise the political structure. He was also uneasy about Gandhi's public image as a traditional Hindu holy man. But the key difference between Jinnah and other Congress leaders was his promotion of a two-state solution for India after independence. He claimed that, in a single post-colonial state, Muslims would be swamped by the Hindu majority. Congress continued to believe firmly in a united India.

Under Jinnah, the Muslim League became an alternative pressure group that the British sometimes played off against Congress. Throughout the 1920s and 1930s Jinnah campaigned for independence, but he became disillusioned at the slow pace of reform. He fought successfully for separate Muslim representation in elections, but was bitterly disappointed about the poor performance of the League in the 1937 elections. From then on, he set out to build up support for the League as the sole representative of Indian Muslims.

During the Second World War, Jinnah astutely supported the British, and this strengthened the position of the League in later negotiations. In 1941, he started a newspaper, *Dawn*, to spread the League's views, and he put considerable pressure on Cripps during the British representative's visit to accept the concept of a separate Muslim state. During this period, Gandhi tried unsuccessfully to come to an agreement with Jinnah, but there were fundamental differences in their ideas about partition.

In the tense period after the war, Jinnah took advantage of the confusion to continue to demand a separate Muslim state. On 16 August 1946, he instructed his followers to engage in 'direct action'. This led to strikes and protests and, eventually, communal violence on a large scale.

Eventually the British and Congress leaders accepted the partition of India, with Pakistan as a separate Muslim state. Jinnah became its first leader, but died of tuberculosis within a year. The new state of Pakistan, for which he had fought so hard, was a fragile political entity, with its Western and Eastern zones separated by 1,500km (930 miles) of Indian territory.

Historical debate:
Some historians believe that it was Jinnah's call for direct action that caused much of the violence and bloodshed that followed. Metcalf believes that, perhaps unintentionally, Jinnah's call precipitated the *'horrors of riot and massacre that were to disfigure the coming of independence'*. Ramachandra Guha states that Jinnah was deliberately trying to *'polarise the two communities further, and thus force the British to divide India when they finally quit'*. However, other historians, including Bose and Jalal, believe that Jinnah's intentions have been misinterpreted and that he was merely trying to ensure *'an equitable share of power for Muslims'* in a united India, and not the creation of a separate Islamic state.

Historical debate:
There is some debate about whether Mohammad Ali Jinnah wanted a secular or an Islamic state in Pakistan. He died before he could put policy into action. Many scholars believe that he wanted a state similar to modern Turkey. It is interesting to note Jinnah's comments on the nature of the state he envisaged for Pakistan in **Source F**, in an address he made to the first meeting of the Pakistan Constituent Assembly, on 11 August 1947.

SOURCE F

You are free to go to your temples, you are free to go to your mosques or to any other place of worship in this state of Pakistan… You may belong to any religion or caste or creed – that has nothing to do with the business of the state… We are starting with this fundamental principle that we are all citizens and equal citizens of one state.

Mohammad Ali Jinnah, quoted in S. Bose and A. Jalal (1996), *Modern South Asia*, London: Routledge, p 194.

Many historians are critical of Jinnah for his insistence on a two-state solution. Some also argue that he encouraged communal violence in the final months before independence. Others, however, believe that that it would have happened anyway, given the tensions at the time. Other historians believe that Congress should share the blame for the partition of India. Scholars such as Seervai and Jalal argue that Jinnah never really wanted partition but used the concept of it as a means to try to force Congress to share power with the Muslim League and in this way get political rights for Muslims, but that Congress leaders would not accept this.

3.7 What role did Mohandas Gandhi play in the struggle for independence?

Mohandas Gandhi (1869–1948) is one of the outstanding figures of the 20th century, so much so that it is difficult to evaluate objectively his impact on the Indian nationalist movement and India's final transition to independence in 1947. In many ways he was similar to Jinnah. He certainly had the same liberal Western-influenced background. Where he differed from the Muslim leader, however, was in his public image as a Hindu holy man. In addition, his policies of *satyagraha* were directly opposed to Jinnah's more constitutional political approach.

Gandhi was born into a middle-class Indian family; his father had been a high-ranking official in Porbander, one of the princely states. Gandhi was brought up in the Jain religious tradition, which influenced his later political belief in *satyagraha*. He trained as a lawyer at University College London. One of his first legal positions was in South Africa, where he experienced racial discrimination at first hand. He also saw the British colonial authorities in South Africa use extreme violence to quell opposition to its rule, in the ruthless suppression of a Zulu rebellion in 1906. These formative years led Gandhi to reject racism and injustice, not only for Indians but for all people. These experiences, together with his religious background, convinced him that the most effective way of fighting colonial oppression was by non-violent methods. He believed that any other strategy in India might lead to the same violent response by the British that he had seen in South Africa.

He returned to India in 1915, and spent more than a year travelling around the country assessing local conditions. He also focused on issues of self-reliance and social mobility, encouraging the building of schools, hospitals and clean water facilities. From this early period there was a combination of Western liberal thought and an Indian approach to non-violent protest in his actions. By 1918, Gandhi had led the first non-violent acts of non-cooperation in the Champaran agitation. The success of this event established his reputation as an effective leader of mass civil disobedience. The strategy was very effective when used against a liberal democracy like Britain, where suppressing such protests was a difficult public-relations problem for the British to solve.

Gandhi became a national figure following the Amritsar Massacre in 1919, after which he launched his first all-India non-cooperation campaign. Through this and later campaigns he was able to transform the nationalist struggle into a mass movement. Gandhi also proved to be adept at propaganda. The Salt March of 1930 is an excellent example of this (see Section 3.5, The development of a mass-based nationalist movement). By marching hundreds of kilometres in full view of the media to collect salt illegally, Gandhi made a most effective political statement. The salt tax was patently unfair and Gandhi responded with non-violent protest. The British reaction, imprisoning more than 60,000 people, only served to damage their credibility as rulers of the subcontinent. Gandhi was imprisoned several times during the independence struggle and he used hunger strikes – both inside and outside prison – as a form of political and social protest.

Gandhi can be seen as a social liberal. He certainly wanted reform of the Indian caste system to create greater equality, and his liberal attitude also extended to the emancipation of Indian women. He was partly successful on both counts, which is significant given the deeply rooted cultural attitudes that he was challenging.

Fact: The Champaran agitation was one of Gandhi's first major successes. He supported the cause of peasant farmers in the Champaran district of Bihar, who were being forced to grow indigo for British planters, instead of food crops for their own use.

Figure 3.7 Mohammad Ali Jinnah and Mohandas Gandhi in 1944

Historians often debate the impact of individuals on the historical process. One school of thought is that certain individuals can change the course of history; Gandhi is one of these individuals. Another argues that developments in social, cultural and economic structures are the key part of the historical process. In this perspective, individuals such as Gandhi are nothing more than actors in a play whose lines have already been written. Re-read this unit and decide which school of thought you most favour.

ACTIVITY

Read the news report published on the 50th anniversary of Gandhi's death on www.bbc.co.uk (enter 'The lost legacy of Mahatma Gandhi' into the search box to find the report).

How valid are the criticisms of Gandhi from left- and right-wing perspectives? Does he deserve the title of 'father of the nation'? How appropriate is the title of this article?

Gandhi took advantage of Britain's involvement in the Second World War to increase the pressure for independence in the 'Quit India' campaign. He has been criticised for this because of his failure to make a stand against Nazism. He was, however, quite correct in pointing out the inconsistencies of the British position in fighting Nazism without giving self-determination to the Indian population. The events of the First World War period had also taught him that British promises could not necessarily be relied upon.

Gandhi has been criticised too for his attitude to the form of the post-colonial state in India. India was a diverse society, but 80 per cent of the population was Hindu. Many of the ethnic and religious minorities – especially Muslims – genuinely feared Hindu domination in an independent India. Gandhi has been accused of not fully understanding the depth of Muslim fears. When Congress considered the idea of a federated India in 1934, in which Muslims would have some autonomy in Muslim majority provinces, Gandhi made his opinions public by resigning from the party in protest. The result of this failure to compromise arguably contributed to the final division of the subcontinent into India and Pakistan, an event that was accompanied by considerable bloodshed.

Gandhi was assassinated in 1948 by a Hindu extremist, Nathuram Godse, who felt that Gandhi had weakened India by upholding secular rather than Hindu nationalist values. (You will read more about this in Unit 3) In India, Gandhi is seen as the father of the nation. Although he was not the originator of non-violence as a means of political action, he was the first to apply it successfully on a large scale. He became the pre-eminent independence politician of the day, and a great spiritual and moral leader. He became known as the 'Mahatma' – a semi-religious term meaning 'great soul'.

3.8 Why did the Indian nationalist movement succeed?

Some historians emphasise the role played by Gandhi in the success of the Indian nationalist movement. There can be no doubt that his leadership and actions played a big part in it, especially by turning what had been a small organisation dominated by élite middle-class leaders into a mass movement. By appealing to traditional cultural values and identifying with specific groups and their problems, he generated wide support for the Congress movement. However, there were other very astute and able leaders in Congress who also played important roles in the success of the nationalist movement, one of them being to recognise and use Gandhi's broad-based appeal.

However, the success of the Indian nationalist movement cannot simply be accounted for by the actions and appeal of the 'Great Men'. Some historians believe that it was the pressure from below – the 'subalterns' – that made the British position untenable in the end. These came in the form of peasant resistance, strikes by workers and actions by individuals, both non-violent and violent. The sheer numbers involved gave the nationalist movement increasing momentum.

Source G suggests that we also need to examine the wider context to understand why the nationalist movement succeeded:

SOURCE G

The reasons for independence were multifaceted and the result of both long and short-term factors.

The pressure from the rising tide of nationalism made running the empire politically and economically very challenging and increasingly not cost effective. This pressure was embodied as much in the activities of large pan-national organisations like the Congress as in pressure from below – from the 'subalterns' through the acts of peasant and tribal resistance and revolt, trade union strikes and individual acts of subversion and violence.

There were further symptoms of the disengagement from empire. European capital investment declined in the inter-war years and India went from a debtor country in World War One to a creditor in World War Two…

Britain's strategy of a gradual devolution of power, its representation to Indians through successive constitutional acts and a deliberate 'Indianisation' of the administration, gathered a momentum of its own. As a result, India moved inexorably towards self-government.

The actual timing of independence owed a great deal to World War Two and the demands it put on the British government and people. The Labour party had a tradition of supporting Indian claims for self-rule, and was elected to power in 1945 after a debilitating war which had reduced Britain to her knees. Furthermore, with US foreign policy pressurising the end of western subjugation and imperialism, it seemed only a matter of time before India gained its freedom.

C. Kaul (2011), 'From empire to independence: the British Raj in India 1858–1947', www.bbc.co.uk/history/british/modern/independence1947_01.shtml.

ACTIVITY

Use the information in the text and in **Source G** to make a spider diagram to analyse the reasons why the Indian nationalist movement succeeded.

End of unit activities

1   Working in small groups, debate the effectiveness of *satyagraha* as a political tactic. Refer to events in Gandhi's fight against British rule in India to support both sides of the argument. Report your conclusions to the rest of the class.

2   Write two letters to the press that might have appeared in *The Times of India* in 1942. The first should urge support for the 'Quit India' campaign launched by Congress. The second should argue that the special circumstances of the war require patience, restraint and loyalty to king and empire.

3   Draw up a table to compare the views of Gandhi and Jinnah. Use the example below as a model:

Views about:	Gandhi	Jinnah
Political tactics		
Britain and British rule		
The place of religion in society and state		
Visions for the future of India		

India and Pakistan

4 'Britain had hoped to continue to rule India after the war, but Indian nationalists hoped for change.' Write a response to this statement, explaining whether continuity or change was a more realistic hope in the aftermath of the Second World War.

5 'The Muslim League emerged from the Second World War in a far stronger position than it had held in 1939.' Do you agree with this view? Write a paragraph to support your answer.

6 Work in small groups of four or five. Each student should assume a role and prepare to defend the policies and actions of that role. Examples could be Gandhi, Bose, Nehru, Jinnah or Mountbatten. In turn, each character should make a short presentation, explaining his beliefs, policies and actions, and then defend them when cross-questioned by the rest of the group.

TIMELINE

1947 India and Pakistan become independent; refugee crisis in Punjab; war between India and Pakistan over Kashmir.

1948 Assassination of Gandhi; death of Jinnah.

1949 UN arranges ceasefire in Kashmir.

1950 India's first constitution ratified.

1964 Death of Nehru.

1965 War between India and Pakistan over Kashmir.

1971 East Pakistan becomes Bangladesh.

1984 Assassination of Indira Gandhi sparks anti-Sikh attacks.

1992 Hindu extremists destroy Ayodhya mosque.

1998 Hindu nationalist BJP comes to power in India; India and Pakistan become nuclear powers.

1999 War between India and Pakistan over Kashmir.

2001 US-led invasion of Afghanistan – start of 'War on Terror'.

KEY QUESTIONS

- What were the problems resulting from partition?
- What challenges did independent India face and how did it respond?
- What challenges did independent Pakistan face and how did it respond?

Overview

- After independence, violence between Hindus and Muslims led to the flight of fifteen million refugees across the borders between the new states.

- India and Pakistan went to war over the state of Kashmir, which was eventually partitioned between them by the United Nations.

- Independent India faced several challenges that threatened its survival as a secular democracy, including political extremism, language divisions, communalism and Sikh separatism.

- The new government implemented policies to promote industrialisation, institute land reform, deal with rural poverty and increase food production.

- Social challenges facing the government were the position of women, inequalities resulting from the caste system, high rates of illiteracy, inadequate health services and high population growth rates.

- Pakistan faced severe problems as a result of partition, with serious economic problems, political inexperience and disputes over assets with India.

- Internal tensions in Pakistan resulted in the secession of East Pakistan as the independent state of Bangladesh.

- Pakistan struggled to establish a strong tradition of democratic government, with the army frequently intervening to establish military rule.

- The dispute between India and Pakistan over Kashmir resulted in three wars and ongoing tensions in the region.

- As an ally of the United States, Pakistan was significantly affected by the politics of the Cold War, which had a destabilising effect militarily, politically and economically.

Theory of Knowledge

Historical interpretation: Some historians think that the reality of the partition of India cannot be understood by simply examining the political events that led up to it or that followed it. They believe that this approach omits the 'human dimension', or the 'history from below' focus. Urvashi Butalia has constructed a history of partition based entirely on interviews with people who actually experienced it, called *The Other Side of Silence: Voices from the Partition of India*. What are the advantages and disadvantages of using oral evidence in history?

3.9 What were the problems resulting from partition?

Partition created immense problems for the two newly independent states. The two areas where partition was most complex were in the provinces of Punjab in the west and Bengal in the east. Both had mixed populations, so it had been decided to divide each of them between India and Pakistan.

Figure 3.8 A convoy of refugees trying to reach East Punjab in 1947; partition led to a desperate migration of people anxious not to be caught on the wrong side of the border

Matters were further complicated by the fact that the new borders dividing these provinces were announced only a few days after independence. Millions of Hindus and Muslims found themselves on the wrong side of the border and tried desperately to get to safety. About fifteen million people abandoned their homes and belongings in a panic-stricken scramble to get to the other side.

The situation in Punjab was also complicated by the presence of the Sikhs, who were scattered throughout the province. Their demands for their own state had been ignored, and they feared that the partition of the province would leave their community powerless and split between two states. When the border was finally announced, they streamed eastwards out of West Punjab, along with millions of Hindus. This added to the violence. At the same time, millions of Muslims were moving westwards towards the border of Pakistan. Law and order broke down entirely, and up to a million people were killed in communal attacks. As a result of this mass migration, East Punjab ended up with a population that was 60 per cent Hindu and 35 per cent Sikh, while the population of West Punjab was almost totally Muslim. This process was similar to the **ethnic cleansing** that has occurred in more recent times.

Ethnic cleansing: the expulsion of a population from a certain area, or the forced displacement of an ethnic or religious minority. The term was widely used to refer to events in the civil wars in Yugoslavia in the 1990s.

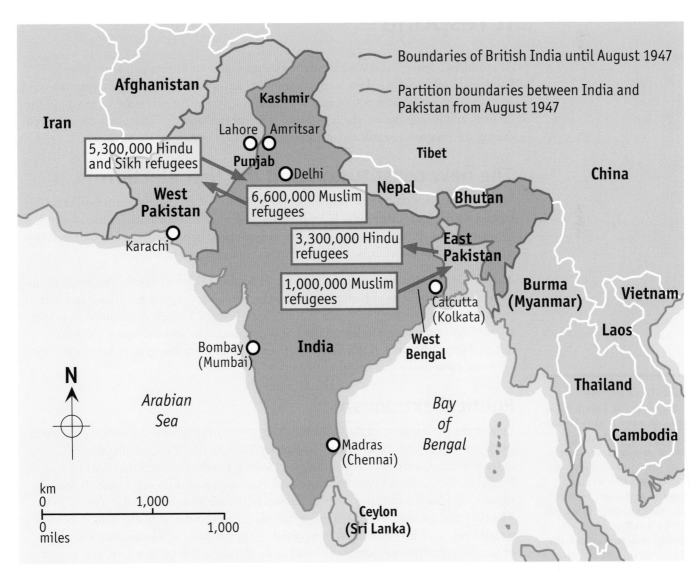

Figure 3.9 Map of the subcontinent after independence, showing the flow of refugees

The province of Bengal was also partitioned and Hindu refugees fled from East Pakistan into West Bengal, with Muslim refugees moving in the opposite direction. However, the migration in Bengal was a more gradual process and not accompanied by as much violence and death as in Punjab.

By the end of 1947, the new governments were able to contain the violence and restore order and control. Despite the mass migration, about forty million Muslims remained in India, and several million Hindus in Pakistan. The resettlement of refugees was a huge financial burden for the new states, which also had to manage the economic consequences of the abrupt partition on existing patterns of communication, infrastructure, agriculture, irrigation and trade.

3.10 What challenges did independent India face and how did it respond?

After independence, India was dominated by the figure of its first prime minister, Jawaharlal Nehru, who led the country until his death in 1964. During this period India emerged as a stable democracy – a notable achievement given the large size of the country and its population, the legacies of colonial rule and the difficulties encountered during the progress towards independence.

The new constitution and the first election

India's first constitution came into effect on 26 January 1950. The constitution was secular, which meant there was to be no state religion, a complete separation of religion and state, and a secular school system. The constitution recognised equality and freedom of religion for all individuals, and any citizen could hold public office.

The Congress Party won an overwhelming majority in the first election in 1952, gaining 75 per cent of the seats in parliament. It had enormous prestige as the leader and heir of the nationalist movement as well as its links with Gandhi. Congress remained in power because the opposition was fragmented, and it managed to win successive elections during Nehru's lifetime. But it faced continuing problems relating to political extremism, separatist movements and communalism.

Political extremism

One of the most urgent challenges facing the new government was political extremism and right-wing Hindu nationalism. In January 1948, less than six months after independence, Gandhi was assassinated by a young Hindu extremist. His assassin was Nathuram Godse, an active supporter of the Rashtriya Swayamsevak Sangh (RSS), a right-wing Hindu nationalist group, opposed to the creation of a secular state in India. The RSS had promoted a campaign of hatred against Gandhi, accusing him of being a traitor because of his willingness to negotiate with the Muslim community. The shock of Gandhi's death strengthened the hand of secularists in the government, and helped to calm communal tensions within the new Indian state.

Fact: The Rashtriya Swayamsevak Sangh (RSS) was an openly anti-Muslim group with a vision of India as a land of – and for – Hindus. Its members portrayed Muslims as a hostile and alien element in Indian society. Claiming to be a cultural not a political organisation, the RSS formed uniformed paramilitary cells.

Figure 3.10 Mourners surround the body of Mohandas Gandhi as it lies in state at his funeral in 1948

Sikh separatism

The Sikhs made up a distinctive religious group, numbering about ten million, with their own history, culture and identity, as well as their own language, Punjabi. Many of them resented the fact that, while Hindus and Muslims had been accommodated in the partition plan, Sikh demands for their own state were ignored. When partition came, millions of them left their farms and villages in West Punjab and went to India as refugees. By 1951, they formed a third of the population of Indian Punjab, and held prominent positions in politics, business and the army. The main Sikh political party was the Akali Dal, which wanted more control for the Sikhs in Punjab. Some even wanted an independent Sikh state, to be called Khalistan.

When the Akali Dal held mass demonstrations in 1955, the Indian government ordered the army to invade the Golden Temple in Amritsar, the Sikhs' most sacred holy place, which the government believed was the centre of the protests. In 1965, the Indian government finally agreed to create a smaller Punjab state with a Sikh majority, after the Sikh leader Fateh Singh threatened to fast to death unless the government recognised Sikh demands. Punjab was split into a new state called Haryana, which was mainly Hindu, and a smaller Punjab, where Sikhs formed the majority. The position of the Sikhs, however, remained unresolved, and led to problems for future Indian governments. In the 1980s, a violent campaign for the creation of a separate Sikh state led to the assassination of the Indian prime minister Indira Gandhi.

Fact: Some historians and politicians incorrectly refer to India as a 'Hindu state'. In fact, India is a secular state. After partition, forty million Muslims remained in India, compared to sixty million in Pakistan. According to the 2001 census, although the population is more than 80 per cent Hindu, there are sizeable religious minorities in India, including 138 million Muslims, 24 million Christians and 19 million Sikhs.

Fact: Nehru's daughter, Indira Gandhi (prime minister 1966–77 and 1980–4), was assassinated by her Sikh bodyguards after she had ordered troops to storm the Golden Temple at Amritsar to arrest the leader of a militant Sikh separatist group. Thousands were killed in the process. After her death, at least 2,000 Sikhs were murdered and many more made homeless in anti-Sikh riots in Delhi and elsewhere.

Communalism and Hindu nationalism

The Bharatiya Jan Sangh (BJS) was a Hindu nationalist party that challenged the secular nature of the Indian state. Most of its leaders were also members of the militaristic Hindu nationalist group RSS. The BJS promoted Hindu culture, religion and traditions and, using the slogan 'one country, one culture, one nation', attempted to unite all Hindus. The group treated India's Muslims with suspicion, questioning their loyalty to India. In the 1952 general election, the BJS won only 3 per cent of the vote, indicating that there was little support for a communalist Hindu party at that stage. According to historian V.P. Kanitkar, Mohandas Gandhi's assassination had discredited right-wing Hindu organisations, diminishing their political influence.

The BJS was later succeeded by the Bharatiya Janata Party (BJP) as the main Hindu nationalist party. *Hindutwa*, or the promotion of Hindu values and the creation of a state modelled on Hindu beliefs and culture, emerged in the 1980s as a powerful force in Indian politics, as support for the BJP grew. The movement was stridently anti-Muslim, and triggered communal violence. In 1992, Hindu extremists demolished a mosque in Ayodhya, claiming that it was built on one of the holiest Hindu sites. This action started a wave of violence between Hindus and Muslims in which more than 3,000 people were killed. In the 1998 general election, the Congress Party suffered its worst-ever defeat when the BJP emerged as the largest single party and ruled India as part of a coalition. Although the BJP was defeated by Congress in the 2004 election, it emerged again as the strongest party in the 2014 elections.

Problems of consolidation

At the time of independence, there were 550 'princely states' that occupied about 40 per cent of British India, and their rulers had to decide which state to join. All except three of them voluntarily decided to join either India or Pakistan, in return for the right to retain some of their wealth and privileges. Two of the exceptions were Hyderabad and Junagadh, where Muslim princes ruled over large Hindu populations. Both were annexed to India by force, against the wishes of their Muslim rulers, in moves generally welcomed by their people. The third exception was Kashmir, a large state, strategically placed in the north-west and bordering both India and Pakistan. It had a Hindu prince ruling over a predominantly Muslim population. India and Pakistan fought a war for control of Kashmir between December 1947 and January 1949, before the United Nations arranged a ceasefire and divided Kashmir between the two. This result satisfied neither side, nor the people of Kashmir.

The consolidation of India was completed when small areas that had remained under colonial control were incorporated. France handed over Pondicherry and other small French enclaves in 1954, and when Portugal was reluctant to withdraw from Goa, the Indian army invaded and united it with the rest of India in 1961. The dispute with Pakistan over Kashmir remained unresolved.

Economic challenges

The main economic challenges facing India were poverty, unemployment, landlessness and an unequal distribution of resources. The government aimed to address these problems by introducing a series of Five-Year Plans to promote economic growth. However, this was offset by high population growth rates. Efforts at land reform and rural development schemes had limited success in reducing inequality or poverty among

Historical debate:
Historians debate the reasons for the rise of Hindu nationalism. Thomas Blom Hansen sees it as a response to the economic pressures created by globalisation. Others, such as Bose, see it as a reaction against the political mobilisation of lower-caste parties.

Fact: When the BJP emerged as the strongest party in the 2014 elections, its leader, Narendra Modi, became prime minister. One of the issues which he had to face was a campaign led by Mohan Bhagwat, the leader of the RSS, for the forcible conversion of Muslims and Christians to Hinduism. Crises such as these threatened the tradition of secular democracy in India.

the millions of landless villagers. The Five-Year Plans were more successful in industry, however, and helped to promote growth. Much of the industrialisation was financed from abroad, but Nehru was careful to limit foreign influence and avoid the dangers of **neo-colonialism**, through high tariff barriers and government control of key industries.

The focus of economic policy from the late 1960s shifted from industry to agriculture in an attempt to make India self-sufficient in food production. This was the 'Green Revolution', which used high-yielding seed varieties, irrigation schemes and chemical fertilisers to increase agricultural output by impressive amounts. However, it intensified regional inequalities as well as social divisions. Certain regions were not suited to the new methods of agriculture, and wealthier farmers, with access to capital, larger farms and entrepreneurial skills, were the ones who benefited. Government controls over the economy were relaxed in the 1980s, as India sought to become part of the world capitalist system. Despite initial problems, the Indian economy has grown at an exponential rate since the 1990s, and India is fast becoming one of the key players in the world economy.

Neo-colonialism: literally, a new form of colonialism. It refers to the economic control that industrialised countries and international companies have over developing countries. The term was first used by the Ghanaian leader Kwame Nkrumah to refer to Africa's continuing economic dependence on Europe.

Figure 3.11   Villagers in India study by the light of lanterns at a night school in 1953

Fact: India is referred to as one of the BRICS countries, an acronym that covers the rapidly emerging economies of Brazil, Russia, India, China and South Africa. Some economists believe that these nations have the potential to form a powerful economic bloc that could be wealthier than the current dominant economic powers by the middle of the 21st century.

Social challenges

With India's low literacy rate of 16 per cent, one of the biggest challenges was improving the state of education. Efforts to increase the number of children attending school had some success, but the aim of compulsory education for all was not achieved. However, many new universities, institutes of technology and higher research establishments were established, with an emphasis on science and technology, to support the economic goals of industrialisation and modernisation.

After independence, there were dramatic changes in the status of women. Despite strong opposition from Hindu traditionalists, new laws gave women equal rights with men in the inheritance and ownership of property, as well as greater rights in marriage. But although the legal position of women improved, it was very difficult to change traditional attitudes, especially in rural areas. There was an improvement in the number of girls attending school, although educational opportunities for girls in rural areas lagged far behind those for boys. Even decades later, the literacy rate for women in India was significantly lower than that for men.

Another social challenge was the caste system, especially the position of the Untouchables. The 1950 constitution specifically abolished this class and the practice of 'untouchability' was forbidden. Members of this caste were now free to use the same shops, schools and places of worship as any other citizen. Special government funding was set aside to give them access to land, housing, health care, education and legal aid.

However, the new laws and the special aid did not abolish social disadvantages and discrimination, and caste oppression was still common in rural areas, where acts of brutal violence sometimes occurred. In some cases these were caused by the resentment over the preferential treatment decreed by government policies.

In 1950, India had a population of 350 million, with an average life expectancy of thirty-two years. Millions of people died each year in epidemics of smallpox, plague, cholera and malaria. The government allocated funding to improve health services, train more doctors and nurses, and build hospitals and clinics. But this resulted in rising population growth rates, putting more pressure on land and resources. The government tried to control this by offering incentives for smaller families and promoting sterilisation programmes, to which there was considerable resistance. Between 1947 and 2010, the average life expectancy in India more than doubled to sixty-six years, and literacy rates improved dramatically, to 61 per cent. However, in the same time, the population tripled to nearly 1.2 billion people.

Cultural challenges

One of the biggest cultural challenges facing India was the issue of language. There were many hundreds of languages in India, and part of the colonial legacy was English as the language of government, the law courts and of higher education, as well as that of the educated middle and upper classes. The most widely used language was Hindi, spoken in the north, but it was used by only half of the people in India. The constitution recognised fourteen major languages, and made Hindi and English the official languages. However, it also allowed the Indian parliament to alter state boundaries, and this opened the way for different language speakers to press for changes. The Teluga-speaking Andhras of southern India were the first to campaign for a state of their own. Violent riots took place after an Andhra leader fasted to death, following which the state of

Theory of Knowledge

History and ethics:
The policy of the Indian government towards the lower castes is a form of 'affirmative action'. What does this mean? How can a policy of affirmative action be justified? Does it conflict with the principle of equal opportunity?

ACTIVITY

How successfully did India respond to the challenges that it faced?

Andhra Pradesh was created in 1953, in an area formerly part of the state of Tamil Nadu. At the same time, Tamil Nadu was recognised as a Tamil-speaking state. Protests over language also led to the division of the state of Bombay to satisfy the demands of Gujarati and Marathi speakers.

The constitution had made provision for the phasing out of English as an official language and for Hindi to take its place completely by 1965. Tamil-speakers in southern India protested violently against the use of Hindi, and several demonstrators burned themselves to death. As a result, English was retained as the language of communication between the different regions. The continued use of English perpetuated a further division in Indian society, between the educated 5 per cent who spoke it and the rest of the population.

3.11 What challenges did independent Pakistan face and how did it respond?

Pakistan did not make the transition to independence as smoothly as India. The problems facing the new Muslim state included the impact of partition, military dominance in politics, the dispute over Kashmir and the impact of the Cold War.

The legacies of partition

Economic and social challenges

At the time of partition, more than 90 per cent of industries in the region were in India, as well as most of the railways and hydroelectric plants. The large cities of South Asia – Delhi, Bombay and Calcutta – were all in India. Lahore was the only city of economic and cultural significance in Pakistan. Pakistan's economy was mainly agricultural, there were few exports and most people were poor farmers.

Both countries faced the challenge of settling millions of refugees, but for Pakistan it was particularly difficult, because the refugees formed a larger percentage of the population than they did in India. In addition, many of those coming into Pakistan were unskilled rural labourers, while many who fled from Pakistan to India were professionals, skilled workers and traders. This contributed to a shortage of skills to staff the new administration.

Although the majority of the population shared a common religion, Islam, there were vast linguistic and cultural differences, not only between the people of East and West Pakistan, but also within West Pakistan, where the people of the northern frontier areas bordering on Afghanistan were accustomed to a greater degree of autonomy.

Disputes over assets

There were bitter disputes over assets and territory between India and Pakistan. As a result of its size and geographical position, India inherited most of the administrative

3

India and Pakistan

QUESTION

Why were some of the challenges facing Pakistan more complex than those facing India?

ACTIVITY

Historians Talbot and Singh believe that the break-up of Pakistan, and the creation of Bangladesh as an independent country in 1971, proved that ethnicity was a more enduring bond than religion. What evidence could be used to support this argument? Work out a counter-argument to this view.

infrastructure of British India, whereas Pakistan had to build up its government structures from scratch. There was suspicion and resentment over the division of assets, including financial reserves and government property. Pakistan believed that the Indian government intended to undermine it right from the start, by denying it a rightful share of these assets. In the end Pakistan reluctantly accepted what it regarded as an unfair division. Although Pakistan covered 23 per cent of the land area of the subcontinent, it only received 17.5 per cent of the financial assets. India was reluctant to hand even these over, and only did so after a fast by Gandhi put pressure on it.

The Indian Army had been the basis of British control over India, and there were disagreements too over its division. Although an agreement was reached that Pakistan would receive one-third of the troops and military equipment, most of the military stores were in Indian territory, and the transfer was plagued with difficulties. The outbreak of fighting with India over Kashmir in 1947 underlined the vulnerability of Pakistan's position, and so, according to historians Talbot and Singh, its government started to use scarce resources to build up its military forces 'at the cost of dependence on foreign aid and economic and social development'.

There was also a sense of injustice over the territorial division of India. In Pakistani eyes, some strategically important regions with Muslim majorities had been given to India. Pakistan's determination to unite Kashmir under Pakistani control must be understood in the light of these circumstances.

A divided state

Pakistan itself was divided into two parts, East and West Pakistan, separated by 1,500km (930 miles) of Indian territory. More than half of the Pakistani population lived in East Pakistan, an economically underdeveloped region with very high population densities, which was subject to natural disasters such as regular flooding.

The people of the two regions had little in common except their religion. The Bengali-speaking people of East Pakistan had their own culture and history, and a strong sense of national identity. They resented the political and economic dominance of the Urdu-speaking people of the western regions. Bengalis were underrepresented in the armed forces and in the administration. To them it seemed as though East Pakistan was little more than a colony, providing tax revenues and foreign exchange from the export of jute for the benefit of West Pakistan. A Bengali party, the Awami League, wanted greater autonomy, but West Pakistan maintained control by arresting its leaders and crushing protests. In 1971, West Pakistani troops crushed an uprising demanding the secession of East Pakistan. As a result, about ten million refugees fled into India to escape the fighting. This prompted the Indian government to intervene. Indian troops crossed the border into East Pakistan, 93,000 Pakistani soldiers surrendered unconditionally, and the people of East Pakistan declared their independence as the state of Bangladesh.

Political challenges

Pakistan did not have the same continuity of leadership experienced by India after independence. Jinnah, the founder of Pakistan and its first leader in 1947, died of tuberculosis a year later. His successor, Liaqat Ali Khan, was assassinated in 1951. His death was partly motivated by a religious backlash to his secular policies, and a reaction by extremists to a perceived weakness in his negotiations with Nehru over Kashmir.

Another advantage that India had was the long experience of Congress in building up structures of leadership in the nationalist movement. Many of these leaders took positions in government after independence. The Muslim League, however, did not have this experience. The heartland of support for the League had been in the province of Uttar Pradesh, which was now part of India. Muslims from this region had moved westwards as refugees to Pakistan, and once there they had to compete with local people for access to land and employment, which put them at a disadvantage.

There were also problems surrounding the adoption of a constitution. The first drafts were rejected by Bengalis as giving too much power to the central government, and by prominent Muslim leaders who felt that the drafts did not sufficiently incorporate the principles of Islam. A constitution was finally approved in 1956, but it did not provide a stable foundation for democracy. Two years later the constitution was suspended when the head of the armed forces, General Ayub Khan, took over the government in the first of several spells of military rule. The circumstances of Pakistan's beginnings as an independent state – its weak economy, the dispute over Kashmir and the belief that its borders were insecure in the face of a strong and hostile neighbour – put the military in a strong position. The army frequently justified its intervention in politics on the pretext of stamping out corruption. From the 1950s onwards there were several long periods of military rule, interspersed with interludes of weak civilian government.

The position of the military was strengthened by outside circumstances, such as the Cold War. Realising its important strategic position in relation to the Soviet Union, the US formed alliances with Pakistan and supplied it with substantial military and financial aid. This aid significantly strengthened the position of the military in Pakistan and contributed to the weakness of democracy. The government used the aid to create an army that it hoped would be strong enough to recover Kashmir, and also provide it with protection against perceived Indian aggression. Pakistan was also negatively affected by the 'War on Terror', when the US led an invasion of Afghanistan in 2001 after the 9/11 Al-Qaeda attacks on the World Trade Center in New York. This was to have a destabilising effect on Pakistan, militarily, politically and economically.

The problem of Kashmir

When the United Nations divided Kashmir in 1949, a UN peacekeeping mission remained in Kashmir to monitor the border between the two. The issue proved to be more politically divisive in Pakistan than in India. Many Pakistanis firmly believed that all of Kashmir, with its predominantly Muslim population, rightfully belonged in Pakistan. However, Pakistan did not have the military might to seize the parts of this region occupied by India by force, and this failure proved to be a source of embarrassment to a succession of Pakistani governments, undermining their authority and credibility.

Since 1949, India and Pakistan have fought two more wars over Kashmir – in 1965 and 1999. As both states became nuclear powers in the 1990s, the ongoing conflict over Kashmir became one of grave concern to the international community. Since 1987, a Muslim separatist group has been fighting a campaign in the Indian part of Kashmir to try to force the Indian government to withdraw from Kashmir altogether. Pakistan has provided support and funding to the Kashmiri militants, a source of ongoing tensions with India.

Fact: Pakistan's alliance with the West and the continuing presence of Western forces in Afghanistan intensified instability in the northern areas of Pakistan. Militant Islamist groups conducted campaigns of political violence and terror directed at government forces. Many civilians became victims of these attacks, including 132 students who were massacred by suicide killers at a school in Peshawar in December 2014.

QUESTION

Why is the dispute over Kashmir so difficult to resolve?

End of unit activities

1 'Although the consequences of partition were worse for Pakistan than they were for India, Pakistan would not exist as a state if it were not for partition.' Write an argument to support or to criticise this view.

2 Research the circumstances of Gandhi's assassination and write a newspaper report explaining the events leading up to it, and the impact of his death.

3 Read 'The hidden story of partition and its legacies', by historian Crispin Bates, on www.bbc.co.uk (enter the title into the search box to find the article). In what ways does this historian blame the British for the upheavals that accompanied independence in India? According to this article, what are some of the unresolved issues from the time of partition?

4 'The violence and bloodshed that accompanied independence and partition can be attributed largely to British policies and mismanagement.' Divide the class into two groups. One group should prepare an argument to support this statement, and the other an argument to oppose it.

5 Draw a spider diagram to evaluate the policies implemented by the Indian government after independence. Include categories on territorial consolidation, constitutional developments, and economic, social and foreign policies.

6 Draw up a table to show the challenges facing Pakistan after independence, including a column to show how it responded to each of these challenges.

7 Write an obituary for Mohammad Ali Jinnah, evaluating his role in the history of South Asia.

End of chapter activities

Paper 1 exam practice

Question

Compare and contrast what **Sources A** and **B** reveal about attitudes towards the continuation of British rule in India.

[6 marks]

SOURCE A

The committee is of the opinion that Britain is incapable of defending India. It is natural that whatever she does is for her own defence. There is the eternal conflict between Indian and British interests. Japan's quarrel is not with India. She is warring against the British Empire. India's participation in the war has not been with the consent of the representatives of the Indian people. It was purely a British act. If India were freed, her first step would probably be to negotiate with Japan. The Congress is of the opinion that if the British withdrew from India, India would be able to defend herself in the event of the Japanese, or any aggressor, attacking India.

Extract from *Gandhi's 'Quit India' speech*, 5 August 1942.

SOURCE B

It is, therefore, plain beyond doubt that Indian self-government is assured as soon as hostilities are over. A promise has been made and that promise will be carried out. Is it reasonable then for people of India, while hostilities are continuing, to demand some complete and fundamental constitutional change? Is it practical in the middle of a hard-fought war in which the United States, China and Britain are exerting all their strength to protect the Eastern world from domination by Japan? Gandhi has asked that the British government should walk out of India and leave the Indian people to settle differences among themselves, even if it means chaos and confusion. There would be no authority to collect revenue and no money to pay for any government service. The police would cease to have any authority, courts of justice would no longer function, and there would be no laws and no order.

Extract from the response to Gandhi's speech by Stafford Cripps, the British government's special envoy to India, 6 August 1942.

Skill

Cross-referencing/comparing and contrasting.

3

Examiner's tips

Cross-referencing questions require you to compare and contrast the information/content/nature of two sources relating to a particular issue. Before you write your answer, draw a rough chart or diagram to show the similarities and the differences between the two sources. That way, you should ensure you address both aspects/elements of the question.

Common mistakes

When asked to compare and contrast two sources, make sure you don't just comment on one of them. A few candidates make this mistake every year – and lose four of the six marks available.

Simplified mark scheme

Band		Marks
1	Both sources linked, with **detailed references** to BOTH sources, identifying **both** similarities and differences.	6
2	Both sources linked, with **detailed references** to BOTH sources, identifying **either** similarities or differences.	4–5
3	Comments on **BOTH** sources, but treats each one **separately**.	3
4	Discusses/comments on **just one source**.	0–2

Student answer

Source A states that Britain is motivated by self-interest and cannot defend India. It had involved India in the war against Japan without consultation with the Indian people. Britain should withdraw from India immediately, and leave Indian leaders either to negotiate with the Japanese or to defend India.

Source B responds by stating that Britain has committed itself to self-rule for India but only after the war is over. There cannot be fundamental constitutional changes while the war is still on. If Britain withdraws immediately, the administration will collapse and there will be chaos.

Examiner's comments

The answer simply paraphrases both sources without making any attempt to compare or contrast them. There is no attempt to link the sources, or to comment on them. The candidate has thus only done enough to get into Band 3, and so be awarded only three marks.

Activity

Look again at the two sources, the simplified markscheme, and the student answer above. Now try to rewrite the answer, linking the two sources by pointing out similarities and differences between them, and referring to the sources without simply paraphrasing them.

100

Summary activity

Copy this diagram and, using the information in this chapter, make point form notes under each heading.

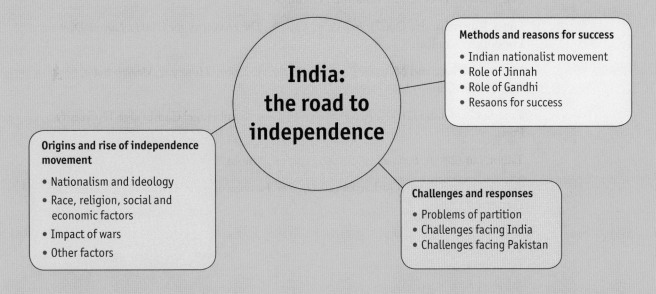

India: the road to independence

Methods and reasons for success
- Indian nationalist movement
- Role of Jinnah
- Role of Gandhi
- Resaons for success

Origins and rise of independence movement
- Nationalism and ideology
- Race, religion, social and economic factors
- Impact of wars
- Other factors

Challenges and responses
- Problems of partition
- Challenges facing India
- Challenges facing Pakistan

Paper 2 practice questions

1 Examine the impact of the two world wars on the rise of the independence movement in India.

2 Examine the reasons why India and Pakistan were granted independence as separate states in 1947.

3 Evaluate the effectiveness of India's response to the political, economic and social challenges it faced after independence.

4 Examine the role and importance of Jinnah in the creation of the state of Pakistan.

5 Examine the impact of British policy and actions in India on the rise of the nationalist movement.

6 'The success of the independence movement in India cannot be attributed solely to the part played by Gandhi.' To what extent do you agree with this statement?

Further reading

Try reading the relevant chapters/sections of the following books:

Bates, Crispin (2007), *Subalterns and Raj: India since 1600*, London: Routledge.

Bose, Sugata and Jalal, Ayesha (1998), *Modern South Asia*, London: Routledge.

Butalia, Urvashi (2000), *The Other Side of Silence: Voices from the Partition of India*, Durham: Duke University Press.

Chandra, Bipan, Mukherjee, Mridula and Mukherjee, Aditya (2000), *India after Independence: 1947–2000*, London: Penguin.

Guha, Ramachandra (2007), *India after Gandhi: The History of the World's Largest Democracy*, London: Macmillan.

Metcalf, Barbara and Metcalf, Thomas (2006), *A Concise History of Modern India*, Cambridge: Cambridge University Press.

Pandey, Gyanendra (2001), *Remembering Partition*, Cambridge: Cambridge University Press.

Talbot, Ian (2000), *India and Pakistan*, London: Arnold.

Talbot, Ian and Singh, Gurharpal (2009), *The Partition of India*, Cambridge: Cambridge University Press.

Vietnam

4

Introduction

Vietnam, Cambodia and Laos together make up the region known as Indochina. Vietnam lies to the south of China and to the east of India, and it has been influenced by both these countries. The geography of Vietnam is diverse, and at times throughout its history the varying political and cultural beliefs of inhabitants in the different regions of Vietnam have developed into ideological divisions that have split the country.

The geography and climate of Indochina as a whole have also had a significant impact on the economy of the region. Indochina has a tropical monsoon climate, with high levels of heat and humidity, and a rainy season that stretches from May to October. This climate is ideal for the production of rice if managed properly.

During the 20th century, important national independence movements developed in both Cambodia and Laos. However, the focus in this chapter will be on Vietnam – the most important of France's colonies in Indochina.

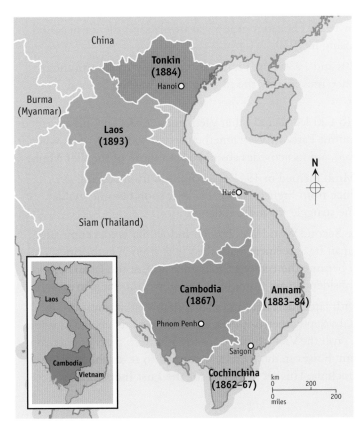

Figure 4.1 Map showing the regions of French Indochina, with the dates they were colonised by the French; Tonkin, Annam and Cochinchina eventually became Vietnam which, after 1954, was split into North and South Vietnam; the inset map shows the countries as they are today

1 Unit The origins and rise of independence movements in Vietnam

KEY QUESTIONS

- What political, economic and social factors led to the development of an independence movement in Vietnam before 1946?
- What external factors influenced the rise of the independence movement?

Overview

- In 1893, France – which had already established control of Vietnam, Cambodia and Laos – joined these countries together to form the French Indochinese Union.

- The nationalist revolution in China in 1911 inspired a rebellion in Vietnam in 1916; this was quickly suppressed by the French.

- In the 1920s, the first Indochinese nationalist movements were formed, despite the cultural and social divisions within the region. These included the Cao Dao in 1926 and the Nationalist Party of Vietnam in 1927. The latter group was involved in the unsuccessful Yen Bai Rising in 1930.

- In the 1920s and 1930s, the French found it easy to control these independence movements; the turning point was the Second World War.

- In 1930, Ho Chi Minh and other Vietnamese exiles in China formed the Communist Party of Vietnam; the party lasted until 1945, when it was dissolved and its activities absorbed into those of the Viet Minh.

- The Viet Minh formed in 1941 as a common front seeking independence from French colonial rule. It soon became the key group in the struggle for independence.

- During the Second World War, French Indochina was occupied by Imperial Japan by agreement with the Vichy French authorities. The Viet Minh became the centre of resistance against the Japanese, and received considerable aid from the Allied powers in their struggle.

- In 1945, with Japan defeated, an independent Vietnam was briefly established. In September, however, Britain used French and Japanese soldiers to push the Viet Minh out of the southern parts of Vietnam. At this point, however, the French attempted to re-establish colonial rule in Indochina. This set the scene for the First Indochina War.

4.1 What political, economic and social factors led to the development of an independence movement in Vietnam before 1946?

In 1884–5, France defeated China in the Sino–French War, gaining control of northern Vietnam. Between 1887 and 1893, France established a federal protectorate over the three main areas of Indochina. Local rulers were usually left in place, but they were mere figureheads and real power lay with the French government. Vietnam was close to the markets of China, while Indochina in general was important for rubber production. Indochina, and especially Vietnam, was therefore one of France's most prized colonial possessions. France controlled its Indochinese territories by the policy of 'divide and rule', setting one part of the region against another, emphasising the cultural differences between them. This policy hindered the development of a coherent nationalist movement.

Although this policy mostly worked well for France, there were several limited uprisings against French rule before 1939. There was a nationalist rebellion in Vietnam from 1885 to 1895, led by Phan Dinh Phung. During and after the First World War, nationalist sentiments grew and there were further uprisings, but the French refused to make concessions. Not surprisingly, the political opposition to French rule in Vietnam continued to grow.

The political origins of Vietnamese nationalism

The opposition felt by many Vietnamese to French rule stemmed from several sources. The Vietnamese had a history of resistance to the imposition of foreign rule, and the French colonial system exploited the indigenous population. The Vietnamese people were forced to pay for the development of their country in the interests of the colonial power. In particular, taxes had to be paid in hard currency, which placed serious strain on the subsistence-farming economy that dominated the region. Peasants were forced to work on French-owned plantations and in French mines in order to meet these tax demands. The French also imposed a monopoly on the sale of salt, opium and alcohol, for which they then demanded exorbitant prices. The effect of these policies was to impoverish the region and place a significant economic burden on the indigenous population. Eventually this led to political opposition.

Fact: The French had first become interested in Vietnam – and the rest of Indochina – as a result of their ambitions in mainland China. In the past, Chinese emperors had controlled northern Vietnam as well as Korea. In 938 AD, after nearly 1,000 years of struggle, the Vietnamese had won their independence from China, but they remained subject to several invasions by the Chinese between that time and the arrival of the French in the 1850s. However, in the latter part of the 19th century China was in chaos, and the **Great Powers** sought to take advantage of this by wresting territory and trade concessions from the Chinese.

Great Powers: the major states of the world. In the 19th century, these were Britain, France, the USA and Russia. After the Second World War, the world's major states were the USA and the USSR; Britain and France only fitted this description to a limited extent. Later, communist China became increasingly powerful and important. After 1945, the Great Powers became involved in Indochina to further or protect their own economic, military or ideological interests.

SOURCE A

In your eyes we are savages, dumb brutes, incapable of distinguishing between good and evil. Some of us, employed by you, still preserve a certain dignity … and it is sadness and shame that fills our hearts when we contemplate our humiliation.

Part of a letter written in the early 1900s by Phan Chu Trinh, a minister at the imperial court, to the French governor. Quoted in S. Karnow (1984), *Vietnam: A History,* Harmondsworth: Penguin, p. 118.

Figure 4.2   Ho Chi Minh (1890–1969)

He was a Vietnamese patriot and independence leader. He led the Viet Minh from 1941 onwards, defeating both the Japanese and then the returning French colonialists in the post-war period, and establishing the Democratic Republic of Vietnam (North Vietnam). In 1911, he left Indochina, and visited many countries. Ho lived and worked in France from 1919 to 1923, and was amazed to see Europeans doing manual labour. He became interested in radical politics and Vietnamese nationalism while in France. At first, he joined the French Socialist Party but in 1920 he became one of the founder members of the French Communist Party. He left France in 1923 to study in the USSR and then visited China before returning to Vietnam. During the Second World War, his military campaigns were assisted by intelligence from the US, but Ho became increasingly disillusioned with America after 1945. He had stepped into the background politically by 1960, but remained very much a figurehead for his country.

In the 1920s and 1930s, the French had found it easy to break up and suppress opposition groups, but anti-French feeling grew increasingly strong in the region. In 1930, Vietnamese soldiers in the French colonial army in Yen Bai mutinied, under the leadership of the Viet Nam Quoc Dan Dang (VNQDD), the Vietnamese Nationalist Party. This uprising was easily crushed by the French, and a wave of brutal suppression of opposition followed.

Eventually, in 1930, a new force appeared in Vietnamese politics that was more successful in fighting the French colonial power. This was the Communist Party of Vietnam, formed by the merger of three different communist parties. It was renamed the Dang Cong San Dong Duong (Indochinese Communist Party) later that year. The party was established by **Ho Chi Minh** and others while they were in exile in China. By 1945, the party had been dissolved and its activities absorbed into those of the nationalist–communist Viet Minh (formally the Viet Nam Doc Lap Dong Minh Hoi – the Revolutionary League for the Independence of Vietnam), which had been formed four years earlier.

Social divisions within Indochina

Indochina is not a homogeneous region, and the diversity of peoples and cultures has had a fundamental impact on its history. During the period under study, these divisions led to the emergence of the three states of Indochina: Vietnam, Laos and Cambodia. In Vietnam, in the Red River Delta in the north, the people of the Tonkin region were ethnically and culturally very homogeneous. The southern part of the country, however, had a more diverse cultural and religious make-up.

Regional rivalries, long simmering below the surface, often boiled up into conflicts. Later, in the post-war period after 1945, France found it impossible to control these rivalries, and this structural weakness became one of the main factors in the nationalists' victory over and ejection of the French from the region in 1954. However, this did not result in independence for Vietnam – it would take another twenty years of political and military struggle before full independence was finally achieved.

4.2 What external factors influenced the rise of the independence movement?

Nationalism began to increase during the Second World War, after Indochina was conquered by the Japanese in 1940. In many respects, during the first phase of the struggle for independence, external factors seemed the most significant influence on the emergence and rise of an independence movement in Vietnam in the period before 1946.

The impact of the Second World War

The internal politics of Vietnam, and Indochina generally, were radically changed by the outbreak of the Second World War in 1939. In the spring of 1940, France was attacked by Germany and rapidly defeated. This created a new political situation.

To Indochinese nationalists, France's prestige had been fatally compromised. Vietnamese nationalists were drawn together into the Viet Minh by Ho Chi Minh. The group began to step up resistance activities against the Vichy administration in Vietnam. Japan's rapid victories over European colonial powers in the region also destroyed the myth of Western and white superiority.

In September 1940, the situation changed again when Japanese troops entered Indochina – initially with Vichy cooperation – and established control over the region. Just over a year later, on 7 December 1941, Japan attacked the US Pacific naval base at Pearl Harbor, triggering the USA's entry into the Second World War. Ho quickly realised that the Second World War presented Vietnam with the chance of gaining independence. At this point, the communists became the only viable indigenous resistance group, and when Ho formed the Viet Minh in 1941, he immediately received the backing of the Allied powers. Thus, factors outside Vietnam helped create the formidable independence movement that France was unable to defeat in the post-war period.

The Viet Minh's position was now transformed. It was the only organisation able to effectively resist the Japanese in Indochina, and, despite its communist leanings, it continued to receive aid and encouragement from the Allied powers. Viet Minh fighters were trained in China by one of Jiang Jieshi's warlords, and the USA supplied Ho's guerrillas with equipment. The Viet Minh's anti-Japanese guerrilla warfare during the war was mainly limited to the Tonkin region, in the far north of the country, but these operations legitimised the Viet Minh's claim to be the leaders of the Vietnamese people and a potential post-colonial government.

The Viet Minh's immediate task was to fight the occupying Japanese forces. France, which had been defeated by Germany in 1940, offered no resistance. The Viet Minh was not the only nationalist group active around this time, however. Several others existed, often with a religious base and focused mainly in the south, but almost all of them collaborated with the Japanese and, later, with the Viet Minh. The Cao Dai, officially established in 1926, became the third largest religion in Vietnam, after Buddhism and Catholicism. It split in 1946, and most of its members supported the French, although a small section continued to work with the Viet Minh. The Hoa Hao, founded in 1939, developed its own private army, but split in 1947, with most supporting the French. The Binh Xuyen was essentially a bandit army that, like the other two groups, decided to collaborate with the French in 1948.

The Viet Minh's real chance of gaining independence for Vietnam came in the last year of the Second World War, when Japan's position became increasingly precarious. Allied strategy to defeat Japan involved two thrusts across the Pacific towards the Japanese home islands. As Japan attempted to resist the main Allied attacks, areas such as Indochina became secondary to Japan's main military effort. In Vietnam, the Japanese sought to reduce their military presence by replacing the Vichy French regime with a nominally independent Vietnam under a French-controlled 'puppet' leader, the Vietnamese emperor Bao Dai. Thus, as the war came to an end, the Japanese had created a difficult problem for the post-war French re-imposition of colonial rule.

In August 1945, the USA dropped atomic bombs on the Japanese cities of Hiroshima and Nagasaki. Japan collapsed quickly in the wake of the disaster, leaving most of its former empire without central direction. The Allies were not numerous enough to quickly occupy this empire by force, and for a period of time Ho Chi Minh and his Viet Minh guerrillas had a free hand. By August 1945, they controlled most of

---

KEY CONCEPTS ACTIVITY

Carry out research on the economic and social features of Vietnam before 1940. Then write a couple of paragraphs to show how significant these factors were in hindering the emergence of a nationalist movement in the 1920s and 1930s.

Fact: In Europe, Germany occupied the north of France, while the south was governed by the pro-German Vichy regime. Vichy also controlled France's overseas empire.

Fact: Although the British, French and Dutch tried to re-establish their former colonies after 1945, by 1961 the entire region had been decolonised.

Theory of Knowledge

History and language: The colonial powers often used language as a means of control, by insisting on the use of European languages in their colonies. Ho Chi Minh's father lost his job as a teacher because, as a means of protest, he refused to learn French. Ho Chi Minh, however, mastered French and lived in Paris for several years, where he was a founder member of the French Communist Party. How does this information about Ho's family history illustrate the saying that 'language is power'?

Vietnam

QUESTION

Why did many Vietnamese tend to support the Viet Minh rather than other nationalist leaders before 1945?

Fact: The Viet Minh also provided a model for other countries in Indochina – especially as many other nationalist leaders tended to collaborate with the French and Japanese, seriously damaging their credibility in the eyes of the general population.

Theory of Knowledge

Emotion and beliefs: According to G.W.F. Hegel (1770–1831), 'Nothing great is accomplished in the world without passion.' Yet Bertrand Russell (1872–1970) believed that 'opinions held with passion are always those for which no good ground exists'. Nationalism is clearly a cause about which many people feel extremely emotional – leading some to be willing to die, and to kill, for their nationalist beliefs. Apart from the nationalism that emerged in Vietnam, make a list of the nationalist movements in other counties you have studied. Which of the two views above do you think is more valid in relation to nationalist beliefs?

Vietnam and, in the middle of that month, they marched unopposed into Hanoi, the capital of French Indochina. This became known as the August Revolution. On 2 September Ho declared the whole country as the new Democratic Republic of Vietnam. However, the French did not recognise the Viet Minh as legitimate rulers. US president Franklin D. Roosevelt had supported the idea of an independent Vietnam, and Ho had hoped for continued US support after the war. However, the USA's attitude changed in the wake of Harry Truman's succession to the presidency and the onset of the Cold War.

SOURCE B

For more than eighty years, the French imperialists … have violated our fatherland and oppressed our fellow citizens… They have enforced inhuman laws: to ruin our unity and national consciousness. They have carried out three different policies in the north, the centre and the south of Viet-nam… In the autumn of the year 1940 … the French imperialists … surrendered, handing over our country to the Japanese… From that day on, the Vietnamese people suffered hardships… The result of this double oppression was terrific … two million people were starved to death in the early months of 1945… We declare to the world that Vietnam … has in fact become a free and independent country.

An extract from Ho Chi Minh's speech declaring Vietnamese independence, 2 September 1945. Quoted in C.A. Buss (1958), *Southeast Asia and the World Today*, Princeton: D. Van Nostrand, pp. 154–5.

The emperor Bao Dai had predicted this turn of events and quickly abdicated. This, together with the Viet Minh's military record in the war years, left Ho without significant Vietnamese opponents to his seizure of power. He began to implement communist reforms, redistributing land and promising elections. He also embedded his control in the countryside, establishing military cells in peasant villages. The Viet Minh suppressed other nationalist opposition groups, such as the Constitution Party and the Party of Independence.

While Ho Chi Minh was busy establishing the Democratic Republic of Vietnam, the major powers had very different ideas about what should happen to Vietnam in the aftermath of the Second World War. The Western Allies had agreed that northern Vietnam should be given to the Chinese, while Britain had been allocated responsibility for implementing post-war arrangements in southern Vietnam. However, Vietnam was not high on Britain's list of strategic objectives. On 12 September 1945, a small British military force arrived in southern Vietnam, but was not nearly strong enough to secure control over the whole of the country. Despite this, and with the help of French and Japanese soldiers, the British managed to push the Viet Minh out of the south and secure Saigon. They then sat back and awaited the arrival of French reinforcements.

Although northern Vietnam had been allocated to the Chinese, **Jiang Jieshi** was facing civil war against the communists in his own country, and was unable to maintain significant forces in Vietnam for long. Once again Ho and his guerrillas were given time to consolidate their control over the north. The French began to arrive in force in early 1946, and it was clear they meant to re-establish control of Vietnam. However, it was equally clear that very few Vietnamese wanted the French back.

The French continued the British policy of clearing the Viet Minh from the south, and re-established a substantial military presence in both Laos and Cambodia. In March 1946, Ho reached an agreement with the French. He was to be allowed an army, and the territorial integrity and independence of the Democratic Republic of Vietnam was to be maintained, although it would remain a French protectorate as part of the French Union. At first it seemed that Ho had achieved an independence of sorts, but later France refused to honour these promises to grant local autonomy. Instead, the French created the Indochinese Federation, over which they retained substantial control. The Viet Minh, however, demanded full independence, and Ho Chi Minh went to France to negotiate a more permanent settlement.

The French government, under premier Charles de Gaulle, was determined to recover as much of its pre-war colonial empire as possible, partly for economic reasons but also to restore some of France's international prestige – which had taken a severe battering by the country's defeat and occupation by Germany. Furthermore, French settlers in Cochinchina in southern Vietnam were pushing for the re-establishment of French colonial power in the region. As a result, French troops were ordered north to reoccupy Tonkin in the first steps towards re-establishing colonial rule. In November 1946, the French took Hanoi and bombarded the port city of Haiphong. In December they overthrew Ho's government, the Viet Minh withdrew to their village strongholds and a full-scale war broke out.

In conclusion, the Second World War gave the Viet Minh a huge boost. It allowed the group to gain legitimacy and for a period of time it had established an independent state in the Tonkin region. The power of the French had been eroded by the war – and not only in Indochina. The French domestic economy and the prestige of their armed forces had been severely damaged. Ho and his guerrillas had taken full advantage of this opportunity, and they would prove more than a match for the French army in Vietnam after 1946.

Independence postponed

Although in March 1946 it seemed that Vietnam had at last gained independence, that hope was soon shattered. Instead, first France and then the US stepped in to deny independence to Vietnam. It would take another thirty years of bitter military conflict and destruction before, in 1975, a united Vietnam finally achieved total independence.

Fact: The French Union was set up by the government of France in October 1946. It was intended as a replacement for the old colonial system and included France itself, along with its overseas territories. Former colonies such as Vietnam became protectorates and were ostensibly granted a degree of self-government. The Indochinese states left the French Union in 1954.

Jiang Jieshi (1887–1975)

Also known as Chiang Kai-Shek, he was the leader of the Guomindang, the Chinese nationalist party, which engaged in a lengthy civil war with the Chinese communists. The nationalists were defeated by the communists in 1949, and Jieshi was forced to retreat to the island of Formosa (Taiwan).

QUESTION

What were the main consequences of the Second World War for the nationalist Viet Minh and their struggle for independence?

End of unit activities

- Read the extract at www.rationalrevolution.net/war/collection_of_letters_by_ho_chi_.htm entitled 'In France, December 26, 1920'. Using the information, draw a spider diagram to examine the impact of French colonisation on the people of Indochina.

- Working in pairs, work out a dialogue between two American State Department officials, discussing the wisdom of supplying weapons to the Viet Minh during the Second World War.

4

Vietnam

QUESTION

To what extent was there continuity between the Vietnamese nationalist movements before and after 1930? Remember: to answer such a question means you need to show both change and continuity.

ACTIVITY

'Historical development is evolutionary rather than revolutionary.'

Carry out some further research on the history of Vietnamese nationalism from 1900 to 1946. Then explain and discuss your response to the quotation above with other members of your class.

- Find out what you can about the Japanese occupation of Southeast Asia during the Second World War. 'The attitude and actions of the French after the Second World War were the main cause of the outbreak of war in Vietnam in 1946.' Divide into two groups. One group should prepare an argument in support of this statement, and the other group an argument to oppose it.

- Read up on the early life of Ho Chi Minh, noting information about his education, his travels and any other factors that you think contributed to the development of his ideas. You can start by looking at the website: www.historylearningsite.co.uk (enter 'Ho Chi Minh' into the search box).

- 'To what extent was the Second World War the most significant turning point in the fortunes of the Vietnamese nationalists?' This type of question demands that you place a historical development in context. It also challenges the nature of the historical process. Is historical change caused by long-term developments or by rapid spurts of development usually caused by a single cataclysmic event – in this case a war? Divide into groups and brainstorm two responses to the question, one affirmative and one negative, creating a spider diagram for each. Then create a balanced response with a third spider diagram by rating each of the ideas in the original exercise on a scale of one to five, from unconvincing (one) to very convincing (five). From this, create an essay plan and then write the essay.

KEY QUESTIONS

- What methods were used in the struggle for Vietnam's independence?
- How significant were the roles played by Ho Chi Minh and Vo Nguyen Giap in the struggle for independence?
- Why did the independence movement succeed?

Overview

- During the period 1946–75, two wars were fought in Indochina – the First and Second Indochina Wars.
- The first war took place between the Viet Minh and the French. By the end of 1954, after the Battle of Dien Bien Phu, the French had been defeated and their colony in Indochina had been destroyed.
- Developments in Vietnam started to cause concern in the West, where the 'domino theory' of states falling one after the other to communism began to take hold.
- At the end of the First Indochina War, the Geneva Conference outlined the structure of Vietnam. A two-state solution was agreed, with a communist North and a pro-Western South Vietnam.
- The agreements at Geneva disappointed both sides, and soon war broke out again, with the North attempting to reunite the country.
- In the first phase of fighting, Ho Chi Minh's leadership was critical to northern victories.
- In the early 1960s, pressure from the North increased and the flimsy political structure of the South appeared to be on the brink of collapse.
- This caused the USA to intervene in the conflict to prop up the southern regime and to prevent the communist domination not only of Vietnam but of the whole of Southeast Asia.
- In 1965, the first major battle involving American troops took place. As the decade went on, US commitment to the conflict increased.

TIMELINE

1946 French troops reoccupy Indochina; First Indochina War breaks out.

1954 Battle of Dien Bien Phu; defeat of France; Geneva Conference.

1955 US recognises the Republic of South Vietnam.

1957 Formation of the Viet Cong (VC).

1959 Start of Second Indochina War; VC begins guerrilla war in South Vietnam.

1960 National Liberation Front in South Vietnam formed; Cambodian Communist Party formed.

1963 Demonstrations begin in Vietnam against Ngo Dinh Diem regime; Diem ousted by a military coup; John F. Kennedy assassinated; Lyndon B. Johnson becomes president of the USA.

1964 Gulf of Tonkin Incident; USA begins bombing North Vietnam; Gulf of Tonkin Resolution.

1965 US ground troops fight first large battle of the Second Indochina War; Battle of Ia Drang.

1967 Operations Cedar Falls and Junction City clear the Iron Triangle.

1968 Battle of Khe Sanh; Tet Offensive; massive domestic opposition to the war in the USA; Richard Nixon elected president.

1972 The Army of the Republic of South Vietnam (ARVN), backed by massive US air power, stops major North Vietnamese Army (NVA) invasion of the South.

1975 NVA forces enter Saigon, ending the Second Indochina War with communist victory.

- In 1968, the Tet Offensive ended in military defeat for the communists, but US television coverage of the event caused a major backlash at home and forced the US to begin the process of disengagement.

- In the early 1970s, this disengagement was facilitated by the 'Vietnamisation' of the conflict. However, this failed and, in a major offensive in 1975, the North overran the South and created a united Communist Republic of Vietnam.

- The USA, a superpower, had been defeated by a country in the developing world.

4.3 What methods were used in the struggle for Vietnam's independence?

Two phases: these two conflicts are known as the Indochina Wars because nationalist movements appeared in all three Indochinese states. However, most of the early fighting took place in Vietnam.

In 1946, the struggle for Vietnamese independence entered the first of **two phases**. The First Indochina War (1946–54) was the conflict that eventually eliminated French colonial control. This was followed by the Second Indochina War (1959–75), which aimed to eliminate Western – and especially US – influence in the area and establish an independent and unified Vietnam. Although the Vietnamese succeeded in driving out the Japanese and then the French, it took almost another thirty years of painful and costly armed struggle to banish US influence and involvement.

The First Indochina War, 1946–54

In November 1946, the French attacked the port of Haiphong, killing many civilians and sparking the First Indochina War. By December 1946, the situation across the region had deteriorated. The Viet Minh were massing for a full-scale uprising and the French were pouring troops into the region. For the next eight years, the French increasingly struggled to maintain their strongholds in urban areas, while the Viet Minh quickly established widespread popular support in the rural agricultural areas. By the time the conflict ended, the French had suffered 92,000 killed, 114,000 wounded and more than 20,000 missing.

Initially the French were confident that the size of their army and their superior weapons technology would enable them to defeat the Viet Minh easily. Strategically, too, the French had the upper hand because they controlled the major towns and the communications infrastructure of Vietnam. This was even true in the northern Tonkin region, a Viet Minh stronghold. The French controlled all the economically valuable parts of the country, while the Viet Minh were forced to shelter in the highland regions, which were little more than wilderness.

From guerrilla tactics to conventional warfare

Fact: These raids failed due to the dense terrain, which favoured Vo Nguyen Giap's guerrilla army. The French simply policed the region as best they could with garrisons and outposts. Thus, after some initial French success, the situation soon reached a stalemate.

At first, France's optimism seemed well-founded. In late 1946 and early 1947, the Viet Minh suffered a series of serious military defeats. The French, however, did not have the military might to hold the entire country, and the highlands became safe havens for the Viet Minh. The French tried to change the strategic situation in October and November

1947 by launching a series of major raids into the area to the north of Hanoi, with the objective of capturing Viet Minh leaders.

In the following months, the Viet Minh began building up their strength. In 1949, Mao Zedong and his communists emerged as victors in the Chinese Civil War, and declared the People's Republic of China – creating a sympathetic communist state on Vietnam's northern border. This gave Vo Nguyen Giap's soldiers bases from which to operate, as well as access to Chinese-supplied weapons of increasing sophistication, including heavy artillery. In 1950, Giap switched his strategy to a more conventional form of warfare.

This was successful at first, with victories along the China–Vietnam border at Lang Son and Cao Bang. Having secured his supply lines, Giap then sought to liberate the entire Red River Basin (see Figure 4.5). However, the Viet Minh suffered a series of serious defeats in conventional battle against the French line of defence around Hanoi. A reversion to guerrilla tactics allowed the Viet Minh to rebuild their strength and slowly extend their influence over the next three years. The events of 1950 showed that, although the Viet Minh could be defeated on the battlefield – especially if they engaged in conventional stand-up fights – they always had the option to go to ground and recover. The French, and later the Americans, would learn that military strategy had to be accompanied by political initiatives if they were to capitalise on their victories.

From the start of the First Indochina War, the French had been at a political disadvantage in Vietnam. The Second World War, and the power vacuum created by the withdrawal of Japanese forces in 1945, had allowed the Viet Minh to become firmly established in the northern Tonkin region. Furthermore, the Viet Minh had acquired substantial military strength as part of a more general Allied war effort against the Japanese. France's political strategy was ineffective and the regime under the emperor, Bao Dai (see Section 4.2, The impact of the Second World War), was so obviously under French influence that it did not draw many non-communist Vietnamese nationalists away from the Viet Minh. As the cost of the conflict escalated – in both men and resources, the French attempted to negotiate with the Viet Minh. This came to nothing, as Ho Chi Minh sought to wear down his enemy's resolve through **guerrilla warfare**.

Dien Bien Phu, 1954

In 1952, **Vo Nguyen Giap** pushed into Laos. Late the following year, French colonial troops were parachuted into the hill country around Dien Bien Phu, on the Vietnam–Laos border, to establish a fortified position in an attempt to disrupt Viet Minh supply routes from Laos. The French reasoned that if the base posed a serious threat, it might draw the Viet Minh into a set-piece battle where superior French firepower – especially from air attacks – could inflict a serious defeat and return the strategic and political initiative to France.

Aware of the French presence in the area, Giap surrounded the base and, in January 1954, launched his first attack at Dien Bien Phu. On 7 May, he captured the base. The fall of Dien Bien Phu was attributed to several factors (see **Source A**). However, one of the main reasons for the Viet Minh's victory was that Giap went to immense efforts to drag Chinese-made field and anti-aircraft artillery to the area. In particular, he organised 80,000 peasants to deliver food, weapons and ammunition through the jungle on bicycles.

Fact: The Red River Basin was strategically important to the French. Its high agricultural output would provide a vital food supply to the Viet Minh, and the French also feared the region's ten million inhabitants falling under the control of the Viet Minh should it be captured. Some historians have suggested that the need to maintain French troops in the Red River Basin rather than sending them as reinforcements to Dien Bien Phu may have contributed to the French defeat there.

Guerrilla warfare: a method of waging warfare that places emphasis on small raids, assassination and sabotage. Guerrilla soldiers do not wear uniforms and blend into the local population.

Vo Nguyen Giap (1911–2013)

He was highly educated and a graduate of Hanoi University. He had originally been a teacher, but rose to be the Viet Minh's military leader after joining the Indochinese Communist Party in 1931. He was a student of military history, with a special interest in Napoleon and Sun Tzu. He had practical military experience fighting the Japanese in the Second World War. He was a gifted military commander and leader of the communist armies throughout the two Indochina wars. His most notable victory was that at Dien Bien Phu.

Vietnam

Significance: Why did the Viet Minh win the First Indochina War?

Remember, questions like this require you to consider the relative significance of a range of different factors.

Theory of Knowledge

History, language and perspective:
The choice of words to describe a historical event can affect your perspective on it. To the Viet Minh, the Battle of Dien Bien Phu was seen as a 'victory'. To the French and the Americans, it was a 'disaster'. Language and historical bias are thus closely linked. How might you describe the result of the battle in neutral language?

SOURCE A

Dien Bien Phu highlighted the shortcomings of French strategy. Located near the Laotian border in a rugged valley of remote north western Vietnam, Dien Bien Phu was not a good place to fight. The base depended almost entirely on air support for supply. The French occupied the place to force a battle, but they had little to gain from such an engagement. Victory at Dien Bien Phu would not have ended the war; the Viet Minh would have retired to their mountain strongholds. On the other hand, the French had much to lose, in manpower, equipment, and prestige.

V.H. Demma (1989), *American Military History*, Washington, DC: Center of Military History, US Army, p. 340.

Figure 4.3 French troops being led to a prison camp after their capture during the Battle of Dien Bien Phu

France's colonial army in Indochina was shattered by the defeat at Dien Bien Phu, and its reputation lay in tatters. Once again, it looked as if Ho Chi Minh's dream of an independent Vietnam was about to be realised.

The impact of the Cold War on the Vietnamese struggle for independence

The history of Vietnam – and of Indochina – cannot be fully understood without a general survey of the Cold War. In the immediate post-Second World War era, the world had quickly polarised into a Western bloc led by the USA, and a communist-dominated Eastern bloc. In 1939, the only communist state in the world had been the USSR; by 1945 this state had emerged as a regional superpower that dominated half of Europe.

By 1954, the situation in Indochina seemed to the West to have further developed in favour of communism. By 1949, Mao Zedong's Chinese Communist Party had emerged victorious from its struggle with Jiang Jieshi's nationalist regime to establish the People's Republic of China. In 1950, the **Korean War** began, as communist-dominated North Korea attacked the pro-Western South. The United States and its allies had been able to contain this attack only with considerable military effort.

From an American perspective, communism appeared to be a growing threat across the globe but particularly in Asia. Indochina was seen by the government in Washington as part of this anti-Western development, and the victories of the Viet Minh were viewed with some alarm by the US administration. As a result, following its policy of containment, the US increasingly placed the events unfolding in Indochina within a broader global perspective, seeing the region as the front line in a larger conflict between the opposing ideologies of capitalism and communism. This perspective began to condition American reactions to developments within Indochina in general and specifically in Vietnam.

In the US, the fear of the spread of communism took the form of the '**domino theory**', which underpinned policies throughout the administrations of both John F. Kennedy and his successor **Lyndon B. Johnson**. Thus, Vietnamese communism, which was essentially a nationalist movement with very limited objectives – the independence of Vietnam from its former colonial masters – was perceived by the US as a direct threat to its own interests in the region.

The Geneva Conference, 1954

France began to negotiate a settlement at an international conference convened in Geneva in 1954 to discuss the general situation in the Far East. The USSR had managed to add Indochina to the agenda and in fact, prior to the talks, Britain and France supported this, hoping that an agreement could be reached to bring about a ceasefire. Initially the Americans believed it would be bad for US interests for France to pull out of Indochina; the US hoped that a military solution was still possible.

However, the Viet Minh victory at Dien Bien Phu occurred just as the Geneva delegates were preparing to meet, leaving American policy in tatters. The US had propped up French colonial rule in Indochina, but now it seemed that the Viet Minh had been completely successful. The first domino was about to fall. It is important to understand

Korean War: a war fought in 1950–3 between communist North Korea backed by the People's Republic of China, and the pro-Western South Korea backed by the USA. The North came close to victory before the conflict ended in a stalemate.

Domino theory: this envisaged one state after another falling in sequence to communism, like a line of dominoes. It appeared especially relevant in Southeast Asia when US President Dwight D. Eisenhower advanced a scenario in which first Vietnam 'fell', and then in turn Laos, Cambodia and Thailand, with the process culminating in a communist takeover in Australia.

Lyndon B. Johnson (1908–73)

As a Democrat member of the House of Representatives (1937–48) and then the Senate (1948–60), Johnson became known as a liberal. However, this reputation and his 'Great Society' programme were overshadowed by his escalation of the USA's involvement in the Second Indochina War, which he began after assuming the presidency in 1963. Under him, the war became increasingly costly and unpopular and, in March 1968, he announced that he would not stand for re-election.

Figure 4.4 Delegates arrive for the Geneva Conference in 1954, including (left to right on the steps in the foreground) Viet Minh leader Pham Van Dong, French prime minister Pierre Mendès France and British minister of foreign affairs Anthony Eden

just how concerned the US was about a possible French defeat at Dien Bien Phu. The joint chiefs of staff – the main military planning body in the USA – seriously considered giving US air support to the French, and the deployment of American ground troops was also discussed.

17th parallel: a line of latitude dividing North and South Vietnam. The demilitarised zone to the south was intended to act as a buffer and prevent communist incursion to the south. In fact, the communists simply went round it, through Cambodia.

On 21 July 1954, the Geneva Accords ruled that Indochina should be divided into its constituent parts: Vietnam, Laos and Cambodia. Furthermore, Vietnam should be temporarily divided in two along the **17th parallel**. The Viet Minh would hold the north of Vietnam, and withdraw from the south, as well as from Cambodia and Laos. French troops would withdraw to the south. There would be a demilitarised zone (DMZ) in between the two parts. This would create the conditions for a ceasefire and, once accomplished, elections would be held in Vietnam by July 1956, as the first step to creating a united country again.

Both the US and the Viet Minh accepted the Geneva Accords. Although by this time the Viet Minh controlled nearly 75 per cent of Vietnam, they had come under pressure from their Soviet and Chinese backers to make peace. Both these powers feared full-scale US intervention in the region, and China in particular felt vulnerable to such a development. The Viet Minh also needed time to reconstruct their army and economy. The main reason for Ho's acceptance of the accords, however, was that he was genuinely convinced he could win the planned elections in view of the strong nationalist feeling in the country. Fear of this outcome was why, in the event, the US and South Vietnam refused to hold the elections. Eisenhower later conceded that Ho would have won 80 per cent of the vote had the elections been allowed to take place.

ACTIVITY

In pairs, discuss and write down at least three different reasons why Vietnam – and Indochina in general – was such a significant region in the Cold War.

SOURCE B

We did not sign the Geneva Agreements … we will struggle for the reunification of our homeland. We do not reject the principle of free elections as peaceful and democratic means to achieve that unity. Although elections constitute one of the bases of true democracy, they will be meaningful only on the condition that they are absolutely free. Faced now with a regime of oppression as practised by the Viet Minh, we remain sceptical concerning the possibility of fulfilling the conditions of free elections in the North.

Comments made on 16 July 1954 by Ngo Dinh Diem, prime minister of South Vietnam. Quoted in A.B. Cole (ed.) (1956), *Conflict in Indo-China and International Repercussions*, New York: Cornell University Press, pp. 226–7.

Instead of the promised elections, a permanent partition of Vietnam was created and the situation was formalised in June 1955, when the USA gave its support and recognition to **Ngo Dinh Diem** as leader of the new Republic of South Vietnam. This was one of the main causes of further conflict in the region, as the North Vietnamese attempted to unite the entire country through force. It would lead to the Second Indochina War, in which America would play such a key and costly role.

With Ho Chi Minh and the Viet Minh in control of North Vietnam, the USA rushed to give South Vietnam support – military, political and financial – and set up a pro-Western regime. Once committed to supporting this state, which should have been reunited with the North according to the Geneva agreement, the US found it difficult to disengage. It would be drawn deeper and deeper into the politics of the region until, by the 1960s, it was forced to deploy US ground forces in support of South Vietnam.

North Vietnam after the Geneva conference

North Vietnam – the Democratic Republic of Vietnam – was recognised by all the communist states, but faced considerable problems in the immediate post-Geneva period. The division of the country along the 17th parallel cut the northern population off from the main rice-growing areas in the Mekong Delta, and the threat of famine was very real. In addition, much of the fighting in the recent war had taken place in the North, and all the damage inflicted would have to be repaired before the country could function properly. Finally, although the North was backed by the USSR and communist China, neither saw the region as a priority. The North Vietnamese also viewed China with considerable suspicion given its historical interest in the region.

Ngo Dinh Diem (1901–63)

He came from a Catholic background and had worked at the emperor's court. He established himself as a champion of Vietnamese independence and resigned his cabinet post in the 1930s in protest at French failures to increase the region's autonomy. In the Second World War he had, unlike Ho, stood aside from guerrilla activity and in 1950 he emigrated to America. While there he was introduced to the Kennedy family – who were also Catholics – and cultivated an image of the 'acceptable' face of Vietnamese nationalism.

Vietnam

Fact: In some ways, Vietnam became entangled in the Cold War by accident. Many Vietnamese nationalists were communists, and a communist state – China – abutted the region. However, without the actions of the French and, later, the Americans, it is highly unlikely that Indochina would have become one of the major battlegrounds of the Cold War.

Fact: Compared to the significant economic aid offered to the South by the USA, North Vietnam's communist allies were of limited use.

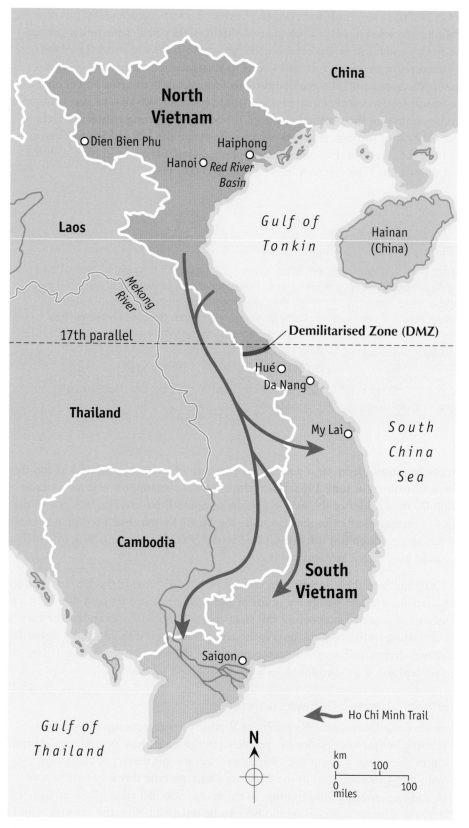

Figure 4.5 North and South Vietnam during the Second Indochina (Vietnam) War

At first, Ho concentrated on establishing control in the North, rather than spreading revolution southwards. He moved to eliminate the influence of French sympathisers – sometimes via executions. The Catholic Church was also brought under control. Ho initiated a programme of land reform, and the redistribution of land from rich landlords was popular, as was the abolition of rents. However, this policy was accompanied by the execution of thousands of the wealthier landlords, in an action decided on by groups known as People's Agricultural Tribunals. In some places, local leaders widened the net to include those who had not been significant landowners, and these actions disrupted agricultural production. In August 1956, Ho and Giap publicly admitted these 'errors', and production was increased. Later, however, when Ho began to implement the **collectivisation** of agriculture along Chinese lines, the move was less popular, and met with considerable resistance from those peasants who simply wanted land redistribution, not to be herded into huge collective farms under state control. In all, about one million refugees fled from North to South Vietnam.

Ho also sought to take advantage of the North's limited mineral wealth and encourage the development of industry. To do this he needed the support of the Soviets. Following the collapse of Sino–Soviet relations in the 1950s, this was a difficult objective to achieve without alienating the Chinese, who were a much more important and immediate military ally than the USSR. Given the mainly agricultural economy of the Tonkin region, this attempt at industrialisation had a negligible effect and in no way prepared North Vietnam for the conflict ahead. At the same time, Ho attempted to rebuild the army, placing an almost unbearable burden on the economy of the North.

So the new state of North Vietnam was not well placed to wage a war against a new enemy, the Republic of South Vietnam, now backed by the powerful USA. The task facing Ho was far more difficult than forcing the French out of the region. However, Ho helped the Viet Cong in the South form the National Liberation Front – a coalition of nationalists and communists. He also helped the construction of what became known as the Ho Chi Minh Trail through Laos and Cambodia, along which supplies could reach the Viet Cong.

Collectivisation: a method of organising agriculture by grouping farms into large, state-owned collectives. The method was first used in the USSR in the late 1920s.

ACTIVITY

In pairs, establish a case that in the mid-1950s North Vietnam was essentially too weak to wage a war of liberation in the South.

Figure 4.6 A Viet Cong supply convoy, using reinforced bicycles

4

South Vietnam after the Geneva Conference

The regimes in the South – before and after 1954 – had one thing in common: they were corrupt, undemocratic and brutal. In 1949, the French had installed Bao Dai, the Vietnamese emperor, to be the puppet leader. However, he had been weak (and was blamed for his collaboration with the Japanese), and the French had been forced to withdraw, despite receiving $3 billion from the US in their fight against the Viet Minh. It was difficult to select a leader for South Vietnam, as there was simply no one with Ho Chi Minh's stature in the pro-Western camp. In 1954, the US convinced Bao Dai to recall Ngo Dinh Diem as his prime minister, but the following year Diem ousted Bao Dai and, after a clearly rigged referendum, declared the independent republic of South Vietnam with himself as president.

On the face of it, Diem was a good choice. He was pro-Western, conservative and had connections in America. In reality his Catholic background – a northern trait – made him unacceptable to the bulk of the Buddhist South Vietnamese. He was also highly élitist; he has been described as a mandarin (a bureaucrat of Chinese or Vietnamese origin), and lacked the common touch so important in the world of modern politics.

Fact: Diem was inclined to talk over others and was a poor listener. He was, however, a survivor, and with American aid he thwarted a series of attempted coups between 1960 and 1963.

Another problem faced by the new republic was the displacement of large numbers of Catholic Vietnamese from the north. During the French occupation the colonial power had sought to convert the indigenous population to Catholicism, with some localised success in the Tonkin area. The virtual mass migration of these people – 850,000 moved south – added a new dimension to the already volatile ethnic mix in the South. Measures taken by Diem's government to grant the Catholic refugees land in the Mekong Delta only increased the tension.

Vietnam was also divided internally. The French had encouraged the growth of a series of religious 'sects' that possessed huge private armies and considerable political influence. The most powerful of these were the Cao Dai and Hoa Hao (see Section 4.2, The impact of the Second World War). The former had two million followers and could command an army of 20,000 men; it controlled much of the Mekong Delta. On top of this, a mafia-style organisation called the Binh Xuyen had an army of 25,000 men and considerable assets in the form of gambling and prostitution rackets in Saigon. Each of these organisations demanded recognition by the government and virtual independence within their local areas of influence. Diem crushed these groups with his army, but at considerable cost in lives and money.

Army of the Republic of South Vietnam (ARVN): South Vietnam's standing army was equipped to high standards by the USA. Some ARVN units were very effective, but most suffered from poor motivation and leadership. The army was heavily infiltrated by the Viet Cong.

Diem also had problems with the **Army of the Republic of South Vietnam (ARVN)**. It was large – numbering over 250,000 men – but morale was low and corruption was common at all levels. What is more, the French had taken all the ARVN's equipment with them when they left. However, by 1960, the US mission in Vietnam, with the help of $85 million per year, had created a fairly effective and modern army. The ARVN still had weaknesses – its officer corps was ineffective and the training given was more suited to a conventional battlefield than to the counterinsurgency warfare needed to stop the Viet Minh.

The southern economy had also been badly damaged in the fighting. Once again, the USA stepped in with aid, rebuilding the infrastructure and subsidising the economy.

It was in the area of politics that the most serious problems lay. Diem and his brother, Ngo Dinh Nhu, rejected any notion of democracy and established a dictatorship. Diem's family dominated the government and, although Diem himself was an honest man, this gave the impression of corruption. Furthermore, his government ignored the needs of the people.

In particular, Diem had a very different approach to the land question than that followed by the Viet Minh in North Vietnam, and this lost him popularity among the peasant classes. Up until 1954, the Viet Minh had redistributed 600,000 hectares of land in the south to the landless peasants and had abolished high rents. Diem, however, sided with the large landowners and thwarted attempts by the peasants to acquire their own land. In 1955, Diem reversed the Viet Minh's earlier redistribution policy and ordered the peasants to resume paying rents. In 1958, he forced them to buy the land they farmed in six annual instalments. This was very costly, and alienated most of the peasant population. Against this backdrop, the Viet Minh agenda, which emphasised the redistribution of land and wealth, had real influence on the affiliation of the southern peasantry.

The final reason for Diem's unpopularity was that he gave the best positions in the government to Catholics rather than to Buddhists – even though Buddhists made up about 90 per cent of the population. Diem held on to power by ruthless suppression of all political opposition, but this created even more widespread

Figure 4.7 Troops of the Army of the Republic of South Vietnam (ARVN) man a machine gun in Danang

Viet Cong (VC): the name given by Diem and the US to the guerrilla movement based in the South. The term Viet Cong (short for 'Vietnamese communists') was an attempt to label all resistance as communist. In fact, the locally born VC drew recruits from a broad section of the South Vietnamese population. It consisted of three groups: main-force units of regular soldiers, provincial forces and part-time guerrillas. The part-time guerrillas – men and women – farmed by day and fought by night. The VC generally avoided large-scale military operations, favouring guerrilla tactics.

National Liberation Front (NLF): a political coalition of communists and other nationalists, intended to unite the southern resistance. It also had growing links with the North Vietnamese Army (NVA) and North Vietnamese government.

QUESTION

Given that one of the USA's stated aims has long been to promote and defend democracy, why did it support Diem's regime in South Vietnam? Can you think of other undemocratic regimes supported by the US in the period 1945–2000?

resistance to his regime. His refusal to hold the elections agreed to in the Geneva Accords also played into the hands of the growing opposition. Although the Viet Minh had withdrawn from the South, the group's southern Vietnamese members – as many as 15,000 of them – had remained. In 1957, these nationalists and communists formed the **Viet Cong (VC)**. The VC was the core of the new resistance to Diem's government in South Vietnam.

The VC began to assassinate government officials and, in the villages, the group often formed alternative political bodies to undermine the central government and to get local peasants involved. They used terror against government officials, but their operations usually left ordinary villagers untouched, unlike those carried out by the ARVN and US troops.

At first the VC comprised largely autonomous cells working independently of each other – and of North Vietnam. This structure meant that if any VC members were caught by the ARVN or US troops, they could not yield much information, even under torture. Members of the VC were therefore very difficult to identify. Although they soon received military supplies from the North, most of their operations were decided and designed by local commanders, who had good knowledge of their areas. In 1960, the **National Liberation Front (NLF)** was formed as the political arm of the VC.

SOURCE C

I saw that the Diem government made many fundamental errors: First, it was a government of one family. Second, Diem suppressed many patriots who participated in the war against the French. Third, he put the Christian religion above the interest of the nation. I am personally not a Buddhist, but eighty percent of the Vietnamese population are Confucian or Buddhist.

From 1958 some resistance was formed, which led to the formation of the National Liberation Front in December 1960... I had been the comptroller of a large bank, and later became Director General of the Sugar Company of Vietnam and secretary-general of the Self-Determination Movement.

The mobilisation committee for the [NLF] was formed by intellectuals: the architect Huynh Tan Phat; the doctor Phung Van Cung; the lawyer Trinh Dinh Thao; myself; and others... Our idea of independence came from what we saw in free countries in the West... I was not a Communist.

Comments made by Truong Nhu Tang, a founding member of the NLF. Quoted in A. Santoli (1985) *To Bear Any Burden*, New York: E.P. Dutton, pp. 76–7.

The US decided to support the Diem government, much as it had done the French. From 1955 to 1961 the US poured $1 billion into South Vietnam, and more than 1,500 Americans were present in the country, offering support in various ways. From 1956, the US took over responsibility from the French for training the ARVN. Without this US support, the Diem regime would have collapsed.

Thus, by the early 1960s the Republic of South Vietnam had made progress in many areas, but there were inherent weaknesses in the state. These would encourage the growth of opposition and severely hinder the Republic's ability to resist it. This situation did not change over time, and is one of the reasons why the US was drawn ever deeper into the war in Indochina.

The origins of the Second Indochina War 1959–75

Within just a few years after the end of the First Indochina War in 1954, the Second Indochina War broke out – for people in the rest of the world, this is better known as the Vietnam War. This time, Vietnamese nationalists fought against the US in order to achieve independence.

The Americanisation of the conflict

After Geneva, the USA became more directly involved in Indochina, as the main supporter of South Vietnam. The VC began operations in the South as early as 1957, with the assassination of local officials and attacks on government buildings. North Vietnam pledged support and began to construct the routes needed to supply and support the VC in South Vietnam. These routes became known as the **Ho Chi Minh Trail.**

In 1960, the political wing of the VC – the NLF – was formed with the objective of achieving an independent and reunited Vietnam. Despite this, the North grew afraid that the situation would lead to conflict before it had recovered enough to fully support the armed struggle in the South. The impact of the VC was obvious – in 1958, 700 government officials were assassinated, rising to 4,000 in 1961.

QUESTION

Why couldn't South Vietnam maintain a democratic form of government?

Ho Chi Minh Trail: a series of communication and supply routes through Laos and Cambodia, which connected the VC in the South to their allies in the North.

Figure 4.8   Viet Cong guerrillas advance through the jungle

4

The success of the VC was due mainly to the alienation of the peasant class. They did not benefit at all under Diem's regime, and these peasants were described at the time as 'a mound of straw ready to be ignited'. The VC was careful to target recognisable supporters of the government, whereas Diem's army was indiscriminate in its reaction – shelling and strafing villages with little regard for the civilian population. Soon the VC had thousands of supporters in the countryside. To deprive the VC of its bases, the US and the South Vietnamese government attempted to isolate the peasant population from the VC by relocating whole villages to areas that could be more easily policed by the ARVN. In theory these new settlements – known as 'strategic hamlets' – were supposed to have new schools, medical facilities and electricity, but this was rarely achieved. Furthermore, the peasants resented being removed from their homes, which had strong religious connections with their ancestors. The strategic hamlets were also regularly patrolled by the ARVN, whose behaviour alienated the peasants even more, increasing support for the VC.

Alongside this, Diem faced rising opposition from other quarters. In 1960, he clamped down on journalists, students and other groups opposed to his regime, imprisoning many. The Washington administration was warned by the **CIA** of the impending collapse of Diem's regime. In November 1960, there was an abortive army **coup**.

Religious tensions

The existing Civil Guard – a sort of badly armed local militia – had been expanded and re-equipped. New ARVN Ranger Battalions were created and trained by US specialists. By 1961, the number of US military advisors in Vietnam had risen to 800, in total disregard of the agreements made at Geneva. The situation began to spiral out of control in 1963, when it became obvious that the inherent religious tensions had reached crisis point, with outright opposition to the Diem regime by thousands of Buddhists.

Buddhists had been historically suppressed by Vietnam's rulers, who preferred the Chinese philosophy of Confucianism. Diem was a Catholic, and hundreds of thousands of other Catholics had migrated south after Geneva. The tension was partly caused by ideological differences, but the biggest factor in Buddhist opposition was the monopoly of power held by Catholics in government.

The first major demonstrations came in May 1963 in the Hué region. The government reacted with vicious counter-measures, sending armoured vehicles against the demonstrators, killing many and arresting hundreds. This simply encouraged greater opposition and the demonstrations spread to Saigon. Again the South Vietnamese security forces, under the control of Diem's brother Nhu, attempted to crush the anti-government campaign by force. As well as marching in the streets, the Buddhists also lobbied the administration and allies within the army. The most striking example of their opposition to Diem was the self-immolation (suicide by burning to death) of a Buddhist monk, Thich Quang Duc, on 11 June 1963. This act was broadcast around the world, along with the Buddhists' message of protest against Diem's authoritarian rule. It seemed that Diem was losing control, jeopardising US influence in Vietnam.

On 21 August 1963, Diem ordered the ARVN to attack Buddhist temples in Hué. Many Buddhists were killed or arrested, and more monks set themselves on fire. It was a public-relations disaster, and the US ambassador to Vietnam, Henry Cabot

CIA: the Central Intelligence Agency, the USA's spy and covert operations organisation.

Coup: a seizure of political power by an army, usually by force.

Theory of Knowledge

History and religion: Religion and religious persecution have sometimes been a powerful force in history. What role did they play in the downfall and death of Ngo Dinh Diem?

Lodge, decided that Diem must be removed from power. The nature of Diem's fall is of great importance. At first the US simply pressured Diem to resign, but when this failed, President Kennedy gave tacit support to an army coup. On 1 November 1963, the generals made their move – backed by the CIA – and Diem was deposed. He and his brother, Nhu, were shot. General Duong Van Minh became the new leader of the junta (military-led government), but he failed to unite the regime or gain popular support. In 1964, five more coups took place. Eventually, in 1965, General Nguyen Van Thieu became president of South Vietnam, but he still led a corrupt and brutal regime.

The North Vietnamese leadership in Hanoi was not blind to these developments, and ordered regular **North Vietnamese Army (NVA)** units to the South to reinforce the VC. This order began to affect events in the South within a year and, by 1964, the government in South Vietnam (and the US) was faced with a situation that was spiralling out of control.

North Vietnamese Army (NVA): the NVA was the regular army of North Vietnam. It was well equipped, with high morale and good leadership. From 1964 onwards, the NVA was found in ever-increasing numbers fighting alongside the Viet Cong in South Vietnam.

Peasant support

After Diem was killed, there were some attempts at land reform in the South. In 1954, 60 per cent of peasants had been landless and 20 per cent had less than a hectare. Tenant farmers had been forced to pay almost 75 per cent of their annual crop to landlords. This was why the Viet Minh's redistribution of land in the 1940s and 1950s had been so popular among the peasant class. After 1954, the VC continued to support these redistribution policies, and so maintained popularity with many peasants. To reduce this support, in 1968, Thieu gave land to 50,000 families; in 1970, the Land-to-the-Tiller Act ended rent payments and gave ownership to those who worked the land, with a maximum holding of fifteen hectares. In all, by 1972, 0.6 million hectares had been

Figure 4.9 The Buddhist monk Thich Quang Duc burned himself to death in protest at the persecution of Buddhists by Diem's government

distributed to 400,000 landless peasants. By 1973, all but 7 per cent of peasants in the South owned land.

Main stages of the Second Indochina War

As early as 1957, the VC had begun assassinating public officials. In the spring of 1959, the VC began to engage the ARVN in direct combat using guerrilla tactics. The ARVN was not trained to cope with this method of warfare. In addition, many of the South's army officers had gained their posts through family influence or corruption, rather than as a result of competence. The ARVN was also often infiltrated by the VC.

The government in North Vietnam decided to renew the conflict in 1959. While this decision was clearly tied to Cold War politics, it was also very much a continuation of the struggle for an independent Vietnam. In July 1959, the Central Committee of the Workers' Party in the North met to formalise the reopening of hostilities in this second phase of Vietnam's fight for independence. The group believed that reunification was necessary in order to achieve socialism.

Despite attempts at land reform, the corruption and brutality of the government and the ARVN continued, alienating many in the South. In addition, the VC and the NVA were determined to continue the struggle for an independent and united Vietnam. The events of the Cold War, combined with the incompetence of the ARVN, caused the US to step up its aid and eventually to commit troops to the conflict in Indochina. This growing US involvement turned a war of independence into an anti-imperialist war, in which it would be necessary to expel the US if the nationalist aim of an independent Vietnam were ever to be achieved. Consequently, the North began to send men and supplies to the VC in the South via the Ho Chi Minh Trail.

From 1964 onwards, the USA became increasingly involved in the struggle in Vietnam. With South Vietnam unable to cope, and in fear of Vietnam becoming the first communist 'domino' (see Section 4.3, The impact of the Cold War on the Vietnamese struggle for independence), the US appealed to the Southeast Asia Treaty Organisation (SEATO), established in 1954 to stop the spread of communism in the region, to send troops. Soon, Australia and New Zealand – which feared a communist Vietnam backed by the USSR and China – had also sent troops to fight alongside American forces.

Escalation and Operation Rolling Thunder, 1964–5

In March 1964, NVA regulars began to infiltrate South Vietnam via the Ho Chi Minh Trail. By this time, an estimated 170,000 VC guerrillas were operating in the South. The trail was located for the most part in Laos, and US president Lyndon Johnson made it clear that he was prepared to support ARVN raids into Laos to disrupt this activity. On 2 August 1964, the Gulf of Tonkin Incident took place when the American destroyer USS *Maddox* was fired upon by North Vietnamese patrol boats in the Gulf of Tonkin. *Maddox* had been in – or very near – North Vietnamese territorial waters and had been supporting South Vietnamese naval operations in the area. On 4 August, Johnson ordered US war planes to attack targets in the North, dramatically escalating the war. On 7 August 1964, the US Senate passed the Gulf of

Tonkin Resolution, giving the president a free hand to prosecute the war in Vietnam as he saw fit.

As 1964 went on, tension continued in the South. An attempt to introduce a new constitution in August prompted more student and Buddhist demonstrations and sparked off another coup, out of which Air Marshal Nguyen Cao Ky emerged as leader. VC activity increased, and US troops were actively targeted. In December, the Brink Hotel in Saigon, which was used as US officers' quarters, was bombed. In February 1965, a major VC attack on a US base at Pleiku killed eight American servicemen. On 2 March, the US launched Operation Rolling Thunder, a major air offensive against the North. Next, the USSR began to supply increasingly sophisticated military equipment to the North Vietnamese. By July 1965, the NVA was deploying Soviet-made surface-to-air missiles to defend their airspace.

SOURCE D

The US can go on increasing aid to South Vietnam. It can increase its own army. But it will do no good. I hate to see the war go on and intensify. Yet our people are determined to struggle. It is impossible for westerners to understand the force of the people's will to resist and to continue.

Comments made by North Vietnamese politician Pham Van Dong, 1964. Quoted in M. Chandler and J. Wright (1999), *Modern World History*, Oxford: Heinemann, p. 110.

On 8 March 1965, the first large-scale deployment of US troops took place. This development soon led to the commitment of US army and marine forces to full-scale battle. At first, skirmishes between marine patrols and VC guerrillas took place around Da Nang in the south-central region of Vietnam, but on 18 August 1965, a full-scale marine attack took place on a VC regiment located 20km (12 miles) south of the American base at Chu Lai. Within three and a half years, half a million US ground troops would be committed to fighting the VC and the NVA.

Search and destroy

The early part of 1966 was fairly static. The NVA had been severely damaged by the events of 1965, and was rebuilding its forces. However, guerrilla activity did not cease. From mid-1966, the first large-scale US **search and destroy** operations were put into effect. These operations aimed to seal off areas of South Vietnam and to saturate them with US troops. The first of these operations, El Paso, took place in May and June in the area around Loc Ninh.

Search and destroy had a limited effect. The strategy did result in the capture or death of many VC guerrillas and severely disrupted the VC's military infrastructure. However, its political effects were less convincing, sometimes even counterproductive. The US could clear large areas of South Vietnam of VC and NVA soldiers, but it could only hold on to these areas by permanently garrisoning them. Once the US forces had left an area, the VC slowly crept back in and recommenced guerrilla operations. Furthermore, both phases of these operations could be very damaging to the civilian

Search and destroy: an anti-guerrilla strategy used by the USA, search and destroy involved sealing off large areas of territory and then searching for and defeating the enemy in battle. In practice, it often resulted in the destruction of Vietnamese villages and the deaths of civilians.

population, often driving them to support the VC. It was not uncommon for entire villages to be destroyed, while the fighting killed many civilians and damaged their property.

In other areas of the country, Australian troops used the different strategy of **counterinsurgency**. This also involved military operations – for example, the Australians won a major battle against the VC on 18 August 1966 at Long Tan. However, their tactics were coordinated with extensive civic-aid programmes designed to improve the living conditions of the peasants through provision of better medical care, education and living standards. The local populations thus equated progress with cooperation with the Australians, making it far more difficult for the VC to re-establish control. The problem was that this strategy only worked effectively in very small, self-contained areas.

Counterinsurgency: a method of combating guerrilla warfare that uses a mixture of military action and socio-economic improvement for peasant communities.

Fact: The best that US air power could achieve was to disrupt communications and supply routes from China, and wage a fairly ineffective campaign to bring down the morale of the northern population.

Historical debate: Historians have debated the relative successes and failures of each side during the military engagements of the war, and most agreed that it was a serious defeat for the US. Recently, historians such as William Duiker and Robert Buzzanco have argued that Tet was a massive setback for the Viet Cong. The most serious challenger to the received wisdom is C. Dale Walton, who argues that it was possible for the US to have won the war on the battlefield as it was actually successful in most of its military operations. If you believe these authors then you must look beyond the battlefield to find reasons for nationalist victory.

Figure 4.10　An Australian soldier helps a young Vietnamese girl; Australian medical teams worked in South Vietnam as part of counterinsurgency operations to improve the lives of local people

The US carried out a series of major air attacks on North Vietnam throughout 1967. Similar operations had been ongoing since 1965, but the strategic impact on the North had been minimal. North Vietnam simply did not have the industrial base to provide easy targets, and it was almost impossible to disrupt agriculture by air attacks. In 1967, the North began to develop improved air defences based on surface-to-air missiles. It also established its own air force. NVA airmen were now using sophisticated Soviet-supplied MiG-21 interceptor aircraft, and by the end of 1967, 455 US planes had been lost. Once again, the limits of a purely military solution to the situation in Vietnam had been demonstrated. On the ground in South Vietnam more search and destroy operations were launched in 1967. VC/NVA units were badly damaged but not destroyed, and, despite strenuous US efforts, survivors were able to retreat to the safety of Cambodia.

SOURCE E

Vietnam is thousands of miles from the USA... Contrary to the 1954 Geneva conference, the USA has ceaselessly intervened in Vietnam. The US government has committed war crimes... Half a million US troops have resorted to inhuman weapons... Napalm, toxic chemicals and gases have been used to massacre our people, destroy our crops and raze our villages to the ground... US aircraft have dropped thousands of bombs, destroying towns, villages, hospitals, schools. We will never submit to force; never accept talks under threat of bombs.

Comments made by Ho Chi Minh in 1967. Quoted in B. Walsh (2001), *Modern World History*, London: John Murray, p. 360.

Khe Sanh and the Tet Offensive

From January to April 1968, the Battle of Khe Sanh took place. Khe Sanh was a US base in the central highlands near the demilitarised zone, and was intended to block the infiltration of the NVA from the Ho Chi Minh Trail into the central coastal plain. The NVA high command reasoned that the strategic situation of Khe Sanh was so similar to Dien Bien Phu – isolated in the dense terrain of the central highlands – that they could impose a second conventional defeat on their enemies. In April, the NVA sent two full divisions to Khe Sanh. The battle raged for months, but the US managed to destroy the NVA's heavy artillery. In April, after very hard fighting, the NVA retreated – leaving an estimated 20,000 dead. The battle was a major defeat for the North.

At the same time as the Battle of Khe Sanh was being fought, the Viet Cong launched the Tet Offensive, which proved to be the turning point of the war. It was a massive and widespread offensive, intended to attack military and political targets across South Vietnam. The offensive was timed to coincide with Tet, the Vietnamese New Year, which was normally a time of truce. The Viet Cong thus hoped to catch ARVN forces offguard and to encourage a general rising of the South Vietnamese population through a display of massive military power. The VC attacked on 31 January, deploying 84,000 troops. However, the ARVN managed to hold out until US reinforcements arrived, and the offensive failed.

SOURCE F

Tet was a great loss for the NLF forces. Our forces had to be restructured afterward. There were three phases of fighting during the offensive: During the first phase in my area the NLF forces did the fighting. We lost too many men and in the second phase had to be reinforced by North Vietnamese units. And in the third phase, the fighting was done exclusively by North Vietnamese units... The southern forces were decimated ... and from that time on mostly served as intelligence, logistics, and saboteurs for the northerners.

Comments by Nguyen Tuong Lai, a Viet Cong guerrilla leader. Quoted in A. Pollock (1995), *Vietnam: Conflict and Change in Indochina*, Melbourne: Oxford University Press, p. 77.

Historical debate:
The impact of the media on the eventual outcome of the war has been the focus of historical debate. Peter Braestrup argues that media coverage of the Tet Offensive and My Lai moulded opinion and helped tip the US public against the war. William Hammond, however, argues that the media supported the war until the politicians in Washington changed their position, claiming that the media reacted to public opinion rather than moulding it. The same debate has surrounded the widespread anti-war protests. Melvin Small argues that the protests greatly influenced the US administration, whereas Adam Garfinkle claims that the protesters were so radical that they outraged public opinion and actually prolonged the war.

Tet was a serious strategic defeat for the Viet Cong, which suffered high casualties (more than 40,000 dead), and was never able to regain its previous strength. By abandoning its guerrilla tactics and coming out into the open, the VC was badly mauled by superior US firepower and mobility. In particular, the VC's overall structure was shattered by the defeat. A good example of this is the subsequent recapture of the northern capital, Hué, by US marines after a month-long battle that left more than 5,000 Viet Cong dead. The US suffered 147 dead and 857 wounded. However, while the Tet Offensive was a disaster for the VC, it was an important development for the independence movement. NVA troops moved in to take the place of the defeated Viet Cong, and they were much better matched to the conventional methods of warfare used by the ARVN and US troops.

However, the main effect of Tet was not military but political, as it helped turn US public opinion – appalled by the images of the offensive that were broadcast into American homes – against the war.

Figure 4.11   Viet Cong guerrillas lie dead after the failure of the Tet Offensive

Fragging: US slang for killing an unpopular officer with a grenade.

Increasing opposition in the US was just one factor that adversely affected the morale of US troops. Among others were the impact of VC booby traps, and the growing numbers of casualties, both of US troops and of civilians. The '**fragging**' of officers became more common, as did drug-taking. There was a rise in racial tension within the army. Desertion and outright insubordination increased.

The My Lai Massacre

In March 1968, the impact of the Tet Offensive was deepened by the notorious massacre at My Lai, in which US troops killed 400–500 civilians. This further encouraged the rural Vietnamese in the South to side with the VC, as well as reinforcing opposition to the war in the US. Furthermore, the American commander in Vietnam, William Westmoreland, demanded more troops – 206,000 – and permission to attack into Cambodia and Laos to capitalise on the success of Tet. The American public was outraged at the massacre and strongly objected to the drafting of yet more American troops to this foreign battlefield.

Figure 4.12   Victims of the My Lai Massacre

Politically, the US now began to look for a way out of Vietnam. On 31 March 1968, President Johnson announced that all bombing of the North would be suspended. In May, the first peace talks opened in Paris; they lasted until 1973. After Richard Nixon became president, the US representative at the talks was the secretary of state, Henry Kissinger. The North was represented by Le Duc Tho.

Vietnamisation and the end of the war

The Nixon administration took office in January 1969, and soon announced plans for a phased withdrawal of US troops in Vietnam – 25,000 to leave in 1969, with 150,000 more in 1970. At the same time, the US was entering a period of the Cold War known as détente (see Chapter 2, Section 2.2.3, The role of South Africa and Zambia). During this time, the USA attempted to improve relations with the two great communist powers, the USSR and China, to create greater global stability and open up markets for American trade. However, 'Vietnamisation' – the attempt to make the ARVN capable of fighting the NVA without US troops – proved ineffective due to the inherent problems within the ARVN, and the political and social structure of Vietnam. It soon became

Historical debate:
There is discussion about Richard Nixon's contribution to the outcome of the war. Jeffrey Kimball argues that Nixon made up policy as he went along, and withdrew from Vietnam in a messy and badly planned way. Larry Berman and Melvin Small argue that Nixon was motivated by the need to achieve *'peace with honour'* as a solution to the crisis. Ted Morgan argues that Nixon had no other choice but to expand the war into Cambodia in order to cover the US retreat from the main theatre of war in Vietnam.

Historical interpretations and language: Historians are still divided as to whether or not the US was actually defeated in Vietnam. While some see it as a clear defeat for the US, others see it as – at worst – a forced withdrawal. How important do you think the choice of terms is when writing – and reading – history?

Fact: The USSR and China both forced the government of North Vietnam to make an agreement. They wanted better relations with the USA, and the events of 1972 had shown that total military victory would be difficult to achieve.

ACTIVITY

In groups, prepare a chart. On one side list the military events of the Second Indochina War. On the other side, decide who came out best from each event – the NVA/VC or the US/ARVN.

apparent that the US would be forced to withdraw from South Vietnam, leaving the region without the strength and unity to resist a concerted VC/NVA attack.

North Vietnam wanted the withdrawal of all US troops and the replacement of the government in the South with a coalition. As the ARVN and US suffered more defeats, the pressure on the US to withdraw increased. By 1971, this was being openly discussed and the North withdrew its demand for a coalition government, improving the atmosphere of the talks. However, when the US permitted South Vietnam to make some changes to preliminary agreements, the North withdrew from the talks. The US followed up with an intensive bombing campaign, which succeeded in driving the North back to the negotiating table.

By 1972, the VC/NVA had rebuilt their forces after the defeat in the Tet Offensive. NVA regulars moved into South Vietnam, fighting a guerrilla campaign to begin with but soon waging more conventional warfare. The renewed US bombing of the North eventually drove all sides into a negotiated settlement at the talks in Paris.

On 27 January 1973, formal agreements were made that would allow the US to disengage from the conflict. The Agreement on Ending the War and Restoring Peace in Vietnam was signed by South and North Vietnam, the NLF and the USA. The US agreed to withdraw all troops within sixty days, and a ceasefire was set to begin on 28 January. By March 1973, all US and SEATO troops had left Vietnam.

By 1975, Vo Nguyen Giap had accumulated enough NVA reserves to begin a protracted conventional campaign, and the war for reunification resumed. The North already had troops south of the border, and the Paris agreements had resulted in the withdrawal of vital US air support.

The government in the South was corrupt and unpopular. Food shortages and inflation further eroded support. At the same time, increasing numbers of ARVN troops deserted. In March 1975, the NVA launched its final campaign. Despite some isolated victories, the ARVN proved unable to stop the advance of the NVA; many ARVN units simply disintegrated, and the South collapsed after only two months. Thieu resigned on 21 April and fled to Taiwan. NVA and VC troops entered Saigon on 30 April 1975 completely unopposed. The war was finally over, and the early nationalist aims of an independent and reunified Vietnam were finally achieved.

4.4 How significant were the roles played by Ho Chi Minh and Vo Nguyen Giap in the struggle for independence?

While objective factors – such as economic crises or military strategies and tactics – are important in historical developments, another important factor in any struggle is often the roles played by individuals. In Vietnam, the two outstanding individuals in the independence movement were Ho Chi Minh and Vo Nguyen Giap.

Ho Chi Minh

An important factor in the success of the communist resistance, first to the French and then to the Republic of South Vietnam and its US backers, was the leadership of Ho Chi Minh. He was charismatic, intelligent and ruthless. He had been educated in France and had joined the French Communist Party in 1920. He had spent the early 1920s in Moscow, where he had made strong contacts with the Russian Bolshevik Party. During his time in Russia, Ho had formulated a model of communist revolution based not on a rising of industrial workers but on an organisation based around agricultural peasants. Thus, like Mao in China, he modified classic Marxism to fit into a developing-world context. In 1924, he travelled to Canton – a Chinese communist stronghold – and there began to form his Vietnamese communist organisation.

In 1941, Ho returned to Vietnam and led the guerrilla war against the Vichy French and the Japanese. His movement was supported in these operations by the USA. With the defeat of Japan in 1945, he emerged as leader of an independent Vietnam after ruthless purges of his opponents. Ho was initially friendly towards the US, which he saw as an opponent of European colonial empires, but his communist credentials ruled out any possibility of US support for the newly created Vietnam. Thus, in 1950, he successfully negotiated with the USSR and the People's Republic of China for support against French attempts to reinstate colonial rule in Indochina. He attempted to strike a deal with the French, but talks broke down due to the unwillingness of the former colonial power to negotiate. Ho devised the general direction of the war against the French but wisely left the details of military planning to his minister of war, Vo Nguyen Giap.

With the defeat of the French in 1954 and their replacement by the Republic of South Vietnam, the war for independence took a new direction. Ho remained staunchly opposed to any negotiated settlement while foreign troops remained in South Vietnam. This was even the case when wider strategic considerations caused his Soviet and Chinese backers to pressure him to compromise with the South. Even in the dark days of 1967, Ho realised that US public opinion would not support the war forever and that South Vietnam and its army were fundamentally weak. He put in place the long-term strategy of attrition that would eventually lead to victory. He authorised the Tet Offensive and began the Paris talks that were the outcome of this public-relations disaster for the US government.

Ho Chi Minh did not live to see the fruits of his efforts, dying in September 1969. His death was greeted with shock by his people and his successes as leader created a cult around him.

Vo Nguyen Giap

The military leader of the Viet Minh was Vo Nguyen Giap, and he proved to be a gifted general. When the Viet Minh made their bid to take over Vietnam in 1945, Giap was made minister of war. For the first four years, he concentrated on building up the Viet Minh army and gathering peasant support. Initially, he followed a guerrilla strategy in the First Indochina War, but in the later phase of the conflict he switched to more **conventional warfare**. By 1954, Giap commanded 117,000 troops, against 100,000 French plus 300,000 Vietnamese in France's colonial army.

ACTIVITY

Carry out some further research on the activities of Ho Chi Minh. Then, in pairs, draw up a list of developments associated with him, and try to place these points in order of significance. Finally, write a short paragraph to support and justify the aspect which you have placed in first position.

Conventional warfare: warfare between well-defined, uniformed forces fighting set-piece battles. On several occasions, wars in Indochina began as guerrilla wars before entering a conventional phase.

4.5 Why did the independence movement succeed?

Apart from the individual contributions made by Ho Chi Minh and Vo Nguyen Giap, there are several other reasons why Ho and his mainly communist movement were more successful than other nationalist groups. Parts of Ho's nationalist movement were socialist in nature, but at first it limited its objectives to creating an independent Vietnam. The organisation established itself in northern Vietnam, and its leaders were educated Vietnamese – teachers, indigenous colonial administrators and low-ranking officers in the colonial army. However, it soon became clear that the real strength of the movement was its communist roots. This created a strongly disciplined organisation characterised by a unity that previous nationalist movements had lacked. Furthermore, the Vietnamese communists were supported by both the USSR and the Chinese communists. The former supplied aid and the latter gave Ho and his people a safe haven from which to operate against the Japanese.

SOURCE G

The Communist Party of Indochina is the party of the working class. It will follow these slogans:

- To overthrow French imperialism and the reactionary Vietnamese capitalist class.
- To make Indochina completely independent.
- To establish a worker-peasant and soldier government.
- To confiscate the banks and other enterprises belonging to the imperialists and put them
- under the control of the worker-peasant and soldier government.
- To confiscate all of the plantations and property belonging to the imperialists and the Vietnamese reactionary capitalist class and distribute them to poor peasants.
- To bring back all freedom to the masses.
- To carry out universal education.
- To implement equality between man and woman.

A draft programme for Indochinese communists, written by Ho Chi Minh in 1930. Quoted at www.fordham.edu/halsall/mod/1930hochiminh.html.

Fact: Cells were the smallest organisational units in communist parties, and were the basis for all communist work and actions – such as propaganda, recruitment of new members and organising strikes. In situations such as those existing in French-controlled Vietnam, they had to be secret, and members of one cell would often not know members of other cells. Thus, if anyone was captured – and probably tortured – they would be unable to reveal many names. Eventually, these cells built up into a national network.

Ho was aided by French suppression of anti-colonial elements, which destroyed moderate nationalist groups whilst strengthening the hand of the more radical communists. In 1930, an abortive anti-colonial rising in Vietnam was crushed by the French, removing many of Ho's nationalist rivals. As the 1930s progressed, the communists attempted to infiltrate Vietnamese society. They followed the typical pattern of establishing cells within villages and began to organise the peasants into potential resistance groups. This had a limited impact, and once the French became aware of these activities they easily destroyed the local cells. Ho was forced to flee the country. When he returned to Vietnam in 1940 and attempted to organise another uprising, he and his organisation were once more defeated with relative ease.

At first the reasons for the North's victory may seem obvious. Despite overwhelming military and financial might from the USA, the South was unable to sustain a war against the forces of the VC and NVA. In addition, many in the US – and the rest of the world – had come to see American interference in Vietnamese affairs as damaging and unnecessary. In particular, the war in Vietnam was viewed as essentially a war of national liberation begun by Ho Chi Minh rather than the attempted communist conquest of another country from outside, as portrayed by the US government.

After Tet and the My Lai Massacre, the war became politically untenable for the US and it began to withdraw from the conflict. The South – wracked by internal divisions – was unable to resist on its own, even with a massive injection of US military aid in the final stages of the war. But this analysis, although convincing, needs to be developed and placed in a more rounded historical context.

Military factors

It is clear that in the First Indochina War the communists won the upper hand militarily. They were fighting against a weakened European power emerging from the Second World War – France had been under German occupation for almost four years, and simply did not have the military will or economic reserves to sustain a war in Indochina. Thus, the guerrilla tactics wore down the French willingness to fight, and the catastrophic defeat at Dien Bien Phu made the war politically unsustainable for France.

SOURCE H

We cannot help draw the conclusion that our armed forces are not suited to this kind of war... This was partly because of the nature of the conflict. It was both a revolutionary war fought at knife-point during the night within the villages. It was also a main force war in which technology could make a genuine difference. Both sides had trouble devising tactics that would be suitable for each type of warfare. But we and the South Vietnamese had more difficulty with this than the other side.

Draft of a memo from US secretary of state Henry Kissinger to President Gerald Ford, titled 'Lessons of Vietnam', 12 May 1975. Presidential Country Files for East Asia and the Pacific, Gerald R. Ford Library.

However, during the Second Indochina War this analysis does not apply. The problem was not wholly a military one, and the US armed forces could not defeat the VC/NVA outright. The VC/NVA could always retreat to a network of safe havens in the wake of defeat, where they could re-evaluate and regroup. It was only later in the war that Nixon ordered ground forces into Cambodia to deny the VC/NVA such refuges. Even so, North Vietnam remained out of bounds for US ground forces and the US was never able to totally cut off the Ho Chi Minh Trail, which connected the NVA's bases in the North to their VC allies fighting in the South. Furthermore, the methods used to fight the large battles of the war tended to alienate the rural peasantry of the South, who made up the bulk of the population. Thus, although severely damaged, the VC could always recruit new fighters and rely on the local population to support their guerrilla operations.

The structures and ideologies of the North and South Vietnamese states

North Vietnam was better suited to fighting a war of attrition. This state had a quite definite strategic goal – the reunification of Vietnam under communist rule. Ho Chi Minh provided strong leadership in pursuit of this goal. The nature of the state also helped towards victory – the Tonkin region was very culturally homogeneous compared with the southern part of the country. North Vietnam's communist ideology and the fact that its government had emerged from a revolutionary struggle also created unity. Both these factors created great social discipline, and the sharp focus of the struggle for unification kept internal disunity to a minimum. North Vietnam did, however, face problems. The country, a developing-world state with almost no industry, was fighting the most powerful economy in the world. The support of China and the USSR was also, therefore, a significant factor in the North's success.

On the other hand, the North's largely agricultural economy was very difficult for the US to damage, and its massed air raids on the North – which dropped three times the tonnage of bombs that had been used on Germany in the Second World War – were not a decisive factor in the outcome of the war. On balance, therefore, the unity of purpose of the North Vietnamese equipped them better for the long-drawn-out war of attrition that their fighters had created by their tenacious struggle in the South.

Because decisive victory could not be achieved on the battlefield alone, the political weaknesses of the Republic of South Vietnam became key to the outcome of the conflict. In theory, the war of attrition this created should have been won by the USA, with its vastly superior resources. However, this proved impossible. The ethnic, political and cultural differences within the South created so many divisions that South Vietnam could not survive without direct US military support. This can be seen by comparing the events of 1972 to those of 1975. In 1972, a large communist attack was halted by the use of massed US air power. In 1975, despite massive US aid to the ARVN, the NVA swept all resistance aside. Thus, one of the major reasons for the North's victory in the war was the failure of the emergence of a coherent state in the South – the reasons for which were deeply rooted in Vietnamese history.

The influence of the Cold War

The conflict in Indochina cannot be analysed in isolation from the Cold War. The Cold War conditioned US reaction to events in Vietnam and Indochina. In particular, the USA's policy of containment and belief in the domino theory resulted in support for pro-Western factions whatever the cost.

When an independent Vietnam emerged from the Second World War, Ho Chi Minh genuinely believed that the US would maintain its support, as it claimed to be an anti-colonial force. The Cold War also brought the large communist powers of China and the USSR into the conflict as supporters of the North. The ideological nature

Historical debate: The historian George Herring argues the case that some US politicians believed foolishly that military success could offset the inherent weakness of the South Vietnamese regime. Robert Thompson modifies this, arguing that military action, especially aerial bombing, only served to force the rural population into the arms of the Viet Cong. Larry Cable believes that the Americans should have concentrated more on counterinsurgency and abandoned their damaging search and destroy strategy.

Fact: China and the USSR had their own interests, which sometimes conflicted with those of North Vietnam. There are points in the history of the conflict when the USSR limited its backing due to international considerations. The limit on support applies even more to China, which had historical interests in Vietnam that Ho and his regime actually perceived as imperialistic.

Figure 4.13   North Vietnamese tanks move through the streets of Saigon in May 1975

of the war thus gave the North access to large amounts of money and modern weaponry. This is especially interesting given China's rather ambiguous role in the region and general Vietnamese fears that, by relying on China, they were encouraging a re-imposition of its historical dominance over their country. Thus, despite the battering that VC/NVA forces received at the hands of America's armed forces, they were always able to survive.

SOURCE I

During the 1950s and 1960s, the Vietnamese Communists confronted formidable enemies, the French and the Americans, in their quest for national unification. Ho Chi Minh avidly sought advice and weapons from China. But sentiments of distrust were never far below the surface. The Chinese, for instance, were suspicious of Hanoi's intentions to incorporate Laos and Cambodia in an 'Indochinese Federation', while the North Vietnamese guarded closely their 'special relationship' with Laos when China increased its aid to the Pathet Lao.

Q. Zhai (2000), *China and the Vietnam Wars, 1950–1975*, Chapel Hill: University of North Carolina Press, p. 119.

QUESTION

Why was North Vietnam finally able to win its war of independence?

Conclusion

The outcome of the war was the result of a combination of factors, but at its heart lay the North's extreme resilience. US and ARVN forces could inflict debilitating defeats on the VC/NVA, but due to the existence of safe havens and the willingness of the North Vietnamese to continue the struggle, they always re-entered the conflict once they had rebuilt their strength. The North Vietnamese could tolerate the war of attrition, whereas the US could not. The failure of the US to create a South Vietnamese state with a similar resilience meant that, once domestic opinion about the conflict turned against Washington, the war was effectively lost.

End of unit activities

- Draw a spider diagram to compare the two sides in the First Indochina War, showing the disadvantages facing the French and the advantages of the Viet Minh. Include information on military strength, tactics, allies and foreign aid, support from the Vietnamese people, political factors and any other considerations that you think are relevant.

- Draw up a table to contrast the two Vietnamese states in the period after the Geneva Conference of 1954. Use the table below as an example, and add any other categories that you think are necessary.

	South Vietnam	North Vietnam
Problems facing the country		
Economic situation		
Political structure		
Quality of leadership		
Foreign aid		

- In 1960, opponents of Diem formed the National Liberation Front (NLF), the armed wing of which was the Viet Cong. Read about the NLF on at least two of the websites listed below, and make notes to answer these questions: How did the NLF try to win over the peasants? How did the Viet Cong operate? Why were they able to resist US forces?

  www.spartacus.schoolnet.co.uk

  www.historylearningsite.co.uk
  (Enter 'National Liberation Front' into the search box for the above websites.)

  www.pbs.org/battlefieldvietnam/guerrilla/index.html

- 'North Vietnam won the war because the government in the South was seen as an unpopular regime propped up by the US.' Divide into two groups. One group should work out an argument in support of this statement; the other group should work out an argument to oppose it.

- Use the information in this chapter, from books and from the internet to find out about the impact of the war on the people and environment of Vietnam.

- It is 1969. The Paris peace talks have started and there are signs that the new Nixon administration will soon begin to scale down American involvement in Vietnam. Imagine that you are a journalist working in North Vietnam. Prepare a list of questions that you would have liked to ask Ho Chi Minh about his political career and achievements, and compose the answers that you think he may have given.

ACTIVITY

Read this unit again. Why do you think historians have come up with such radically different interpretations of the impact of the media on the war in Vietnam?

KEY QUESTIONS

- What political challenges did Vietnam face after independence?
- What economic and social challenges did independent Vietnam face after 1975?
- How did Vietnam's government respond to these challenges?

Overview

- After 1975, Vietnam attempted to reconstruct its economy, which had been badly damaged by the war, using the USSR as a model. This was at best only partly successful.

- The social impact of the North's victory took its toll on the South and further restricted economic activity. As a reaction, thousands of Vietnamese fled the country in small boats, many of them dying in the attempt.

- Vietnam emerged as a genuinely independent state; it was not a satellite of the USSR and was prepared in 1979 to defend its frontiers successfully against a much more powerful China.

- The situation in post-war Indochina was desperate, partly because of the social and economic dislocation caused by the war and partly due to ill-conceived policies by the communist successor regimes in the region.

- By 1990, Vietnam had begun to introduce economic reforms and to intervene in the politics of its neighbours.

- By the later 20th century, the region was beginning to recover.

4.6 What political challenges did Vietnam face after independence?

After 1975, Vietnam proved able to remain independent of its backers, especially China. In fact, in 1978, Vietnam invaded Kampuchea (Cambodia) and overthrew the tyrannical government of the Khmer

Rouge leader Pol Pot, who had aligned himself with the Chinese communist regime. In addition to concerns about China's political influence, the new Vietnamese government also faced internal political challenges.

Vietnam and China

For centuries, Vietnam had been under the influence of Imperial China. Although the Viet Minh had received help from China after the communist victory in 1949, Vietnamese nationalists were keen to limit Chinese influence. Conflicts with China over Cambodia, and Vietnam's alliance with the USSR, led to a three-week border war with its powerful northern neighbour in 1979. China attempted to enforce its influence in the region but its invading army was badly beaten in the jungles of northern Vietnam against a determined and experienced Vietnamese army. Although there had been no more fighting, relations remained strained.

The border war highlights several important factors relating to Vietnam's position after it achieved independence. First, Vietnam was a Soviet, not a Chinese, ally. Second, Vietnam was so distant from the USSR that it was essentially a sovereign state, with none of the problems of satellite status experienced by the countries of Eastern Europe. Third, Vietnam's historical antipathy towards China surfaced almost as soon as the war was over. The border war of 1979 shows how foolish US strategy in Vietnam had been from the start. The US had propped up the South in order to prevent the expansion of Chinese power into the region. Ironically, as soon as the US had withdrawn and Vietnam was united, China attempted to reassert its influence in the region.

This increased the traditional historical tensions between Vietnam and China, and in 1979 there was a series of major clashes along the Sino–Vietnamese border, as the newly created united Vietnam successfully repelled Chinese incursions into its territory. Thus, Vietnam did not become a puppet of the larger communist states as American strategists had feared throughout the 1950s.

Internal political problems

Many South Vietnamese who were closely associated with the previous regime had fled with the Americans. There were, however, about 300,000 individuals who were considered by the communists to be members of the bourgeoisie, and thus class enemies. These people – including civil servants, army officers and the professional classes of the South – were quickly identified and arrested. Large numbers were forcibly re-educated in camps where conditions were atrocious and beatings commonplace. By 1990, international pressure forced the regime to allow these people to emigrate. Most of them did, depriving Vietnam of the skilled people required to run a modern economy.

The secret police – known as the Cong An – helped maintain order, and kept a close watch on any potential anti-government activity. To remove colonial, imperialist and Western capitalist influences, pre-1975 art and literature were banned. All new works had to be sanctioned by the government, which insisted on pro-nationalist and pro-communist messages. The new government also controlled or supervised the new agencies, and owned the newspapers as well as the radio and television services.

Fact: Soviet aid to Vietnam after 1979 was significant. As well as military aid and technical training, the Soviet Union provided Vietnam with more economic aid than any other country and became its biggest trading partner, a role it maintained until the late 1980s.

QUESTION

Were earlier US fears about Vietnam becoming a puppet of the USSR or China borne out after 1975?

Theory of Knowledge

History and empathy: The historian R.G. Collingwood (1889–1943) is associated with a theory of history that stresses the importance of attempting to use empathy in order to understand the motives and actions of people in the past. To what extent can you empathise with political actions taken by the rulers of Vietnam after 1975? Is it even appropriate that such an attempt should be made?

4

4.7 What economic and social challenges did independent Vietnam face after 1975?

Although Vietnam was at last united and independent after 1975, it faced many economic and social challenges. In addition, a US trade embargo on the new communist state made recovery from the war even slower and more difficult than it would otherwise have been. It is only now that Vietnam is beginning to prosper.

Figure 4.14 Civilians survey the wreckage of their bomb-damaged homes in Hué, South Vietnam, in 1968

Economic impact of the war

The cost of the war for all sides was enormous. Fifty-eight thousand US soldiers were killed or missing and 300,000 sustained wounds. In South Vietnam, 220,000 soldiers were killed, and more than 5,000 of America's allies – from Thailand, South Korea, Australia and New Zealand – were also dead. The North Vietnamese suffered appallingly, with up to a million military dead (NVA and VC). The combined total of Vietnamese civilian deaths has been estimated at 400,000, and it is believed that more than a million South Vietnamese civilians were injured between 1964 and 1975. In Cambodia, between 500,000 and a million died. Economically, the US spent $150 billion and this commitment of resources was one of the main contributing factors in the worldwide recession of the 1970s.

Vietnam's post-war economy

The country's economic problems were rooted in the damage done by the long-drawn-out war of independence, the essentially agrarian nature of the united Vietnam and the political alienation of the southern middle classes. Even the most advanced states would have found it difficult to rebuild an economy that had been so badly damaged. Post-war Vietnam was in ruins. The war had taken its toll on the population and had shattered the economy of the entire country. Furthermore, there were extreme political and social divisions, as the population of the South had to be incorporated into a united communist state. This was not too difficult in the countryside, but in the urban areas of the South, where the population had led a more Western lifestyle, it caused extreme social instability.

The Northern government also had problems switching to functioning as a peacetime administration. The communists had effectively been at war since 1941 and they found rebuilding the country a huge challenge. This situation was exacerbated by the USA's blockade of Vietnam and its diplomatic efforts to ensure that most of the West placed an embargo on trade with the new country.

Social challenges

As 90 per cent of Vietnamese were from the same ethnic group, there were no significant problems with ethnic or racial minorities. However, religious groups were brought under government control, with only state-controlled churches allowed to function. The Protestant Montagnard of the central highlands (many of whom had worked with US forces) and the Hoa Hao Buddhists in the South protested about persecution and the seizure of their lands.

The most visible expression of the social backlash against the North's victory was the 'boat people'. Social and economic conditions in Vietnam became so bad that between 1975 and 1990 more than a million people attempted to leave the country in small boats. The number of boats used for this mass exodus was so large that it had an impact on the country's fishing economy. Many of the 'boat people' died in their attempt to leave their homeland. Others ended up in Australia, New Zealand or the USA. In 1990, Vietnam agreed to allow voluntary migration, and the phenomenon of the boat people stopped.

> **QUESTION**
>
> What do you understand by the term 'boat people'?

4.8 How did Vietnam's government respond to these challenges?

Politically and socially, the impact of the North's victory was immediate and far-reaching. After 1975, the North imposed a single-party state and communist policies in the South, such as forced collectivisation and the expansion of heavy industry. In 1976, the whole country was renamed the Socialist Republic of Vietnam. About 80 per cent of the population of this new state were poor peasants living in rural areas. The government was based on elected legislative and executive bodies, but the Communist Party decided who could be candidates. However, unlike many other recently unified and independent states, the North Vietnamese leadership was experienced in administration.

To overcome the various political, economic and social challenges Vietnam faced after 1975 – and to implement communist policies – the new government moved to a centralised economy. From 1975 to 1985, heavy industry was developed, and state-owned agricultural collectives were established in the countryside. The latter policy brought about the biggest changes for the peasants. Private businesses were nationalised, and the government attempted to oversee the entire war-shattered economy. As a way of recovering as quickly as possible, Vietnam joined **Comecon** and, until Mikhail Gorbachev took over as leader of the USSR in 1985, Vietnam received $3 billion a year in aid from the Soviet Union, and 4,000 Soviet advisors and technicians were sent to help reconstruction.

However, communist attempts to follow the Soviet model and create an industrialised economy had mixed results – a common experience for countries in the developing world in their immediate post-colonial phase. In particular, the economy lacked several of the raw materials and the capital and skills required to complete such an ambitious task. While the USSR provided aid to its ally, the Soviet model still proved difficult to establish in Vietnam.

In the countryside the communists attempted to repeat the collectivisation of agriculture that they had accomplished in the North, but the peasantry resisted collectivisation. The Mekong Delta was the rice basket of Indochina, and these unpopular policies prompted passive resistance by the peasants. They preferred to leave land uncultivated rather than hand over their produce to the government, and they were prepared to slaughter their own livestock for the same reason. The peasants resorted to a **black market** for their goods. The net effect of this was to cause food shortages on a massive scale.

These economic problems had not been so widespread when the North turned to communism, because it was essentially an agrarian society. In the South, with a more developed commercial and manufacturing base, the problems were much greater. The economy slowly ground to a halt, and shortages and hyper-inflation led to austerity measures in the early 1980s.

Doi Moi

The leadership was divided. Reformers wanted a shift towards **market socialism** to overcome the stagnating economy, while hardliners feared that any moves towards economic liberalism would lead to the erosion of socialism. The reformers won the debate and, in 1986, a 'renovation' of the economy began. This was known as Doi Moi. Several of the policies were similar to those being introduced in both China and the USSR. The regime allowed small-scale private businesses to produce consumer goods, while the peasants were given a free hand in the production of food. From 1990, Vietnam's economy began to improve.

Vietnam experienced an increase in gross domestic product (GDP) of 8 per cent a year during the period 1990–7, while foreign investment rose by 300 per cent. A relaxation of state control also encouraged tourism, and Vietnam now gains a substantial proportion of

Comecon: the Council for Mutual Economic Assistance, set up in 1949 between the USSR and the Eastern European countries as a Soviet response to the Marshall Plan. At first the terms of trade were advantageous to the USSR, but were later equalised under Nikita Khrushchev.

Black market: secret trading without the knowledge of the government.

Market socialism: an economic system in which enterprises are owned by the state or by public co-operatives, but production and exchange of goods are determined mainly by market forces rather than by state planning.

its income from this source. In 1993, the US granted diplomatic recognition to Vietnam, and in 1995 normalised its relations, lifting all sanctions.

Immediately after the 1979 war against China, the Soviet Union gave more training and aid to build up the Vietnamese army, but this came to an end in 1989–91 when the USSR and the Eastern European regimes collapsed. The loss of aid and trading partners caused problems for the Vietnamese economy.

Despite these issues, and after nearly sixty years of turmoil, conflict and suffering, Vietnam has developed a stable and independent government. Although it has moved towards a form of capitalist economy, it has followed China's example in attempting to keep communist political control, and the Communist Party remains the only political party in Vietnam.

End of unit activities

- Draw up a table to summarise the challenges involved in reuniting the two Vietnams after 1975. Include sections on political, social and economic challenges.

- Find out what you can about the 'boat people', and make notes on the following: who they were; why they were leaving Vietnam; how many people were involved; what problems they encountered; and how successful their mission was.

- Use the information in this chapter to write notes on Vietnam's relationship with China, the United States and Cambodia since 1975.

- Use the information on the websites below, together with information from books and other websites, to prepare an oral presentation on Pol Pot, the Khmer Rouge and the Cambodian genocide, and to discuss its connection to the situation in Vietnam.

  www.edwebproject.org/sideshow/khmeryears/index.html

  www.time.com (enter the above terms into the search box)

- 'Although American policy in Southeast Asia was designed to prevent the domino effect, American actions instead caused such an effect.' Prepare an argument to oppose or support this statement.

- Find out what is meant by the terms 'social freedoms' and 'political freedoms'. Then write a letter from a Vietnamese Communist Party official to a Vietnamese refugee living in the US, explaining why social freedoms are more important than political freedoms. Finally, write a reply from the refugee, which counters those arguments.

KEY CONCEPTS QUESTION

Change and continuity: How far did the Doi Moi economic policies followed in Vietnam after 1986 mark a fundamental change from those pursued before then?

Remember, to answer questions like this, you need to address both change and continuity, in order to show how they were different and similar.

End of chapter activities

Paper 1 exam practice

Question

With reference to its origin, purpose and content, analyse the value and limitations of **Source A** below for an historian studying the Vietnam War.   [4 marks]

SOURCE A

The war in Vietnam is a new kind of war, a fact as yet poorly understood in most parts of the world. Vietnam is not another Greece, where indigenous guerrilla forces used friendly neighbouring territory as a sanctuary. Vietnam is not another Malaya, where Communist guerrillas were, for the most part, physically distinguishable from the peaceful majority they sought to control. Vietnam is not another Philippines, where Communist guerrillas were physically separated from the source of their moral and physical support. Above all, the war in Vietnam is not a spontaneous and local rebellion against the established government... In Vietnam a Communist government has set out deliberately to conquer a sovereign people in a neighbouring state.

A US government document describing the war in Vietnam in 1965.

Skill

Value and limitations (utility/reliability) of sources.

Utility/reliability questions require you to assess one source over a range of possible issues/aspects – and to comment on its value to historians studying a particular event or period of history.

Examiner's tips

The main areas you need to consider in relation to the sources and the information/view they provide, are:

- **origin**, **purpose** and **content**
- value and limitations.

These areas need to be linked in your answer, showing how the value and limitations of the source to historians relates to the source's origin and purpose.

For example, a source might be useful because it is primary – the event depicted was witnessed by the person producing it. But was the person in a position to know? Is the view an untypical view of the event? What is its nature? Is it a private diary entry

Origin: the 'who, what, when and where?' questions.

Purpose: this means 'reasons, what the writer/ creator was trying to achieve, who the intended audience was'.

Content: this is the information or explanation(s) provided by the source.

(therefore possibly more likely to be true), or is it a speech or piece of propaganda intended to persuade? The value of a source may be limited by some aspects, but that doesn't mean it has no value at all. For example, it may be valuable as evidence of the types of propaganda put out at the time. Similarly, a secondary source – or even a tertiary source – can have more value than some primary sources: for instance, because the author might be writing at a time when new evidence has become available.

Before you write your answer, draw a rough chart or spider diagram to show, where relevant, these various aspects. Make sure you do this for the correct source!

Remember: a source doesn't have to be primary to be useful. Remember, too, that content isn't the only aspect to have possible value. The context, the person who produced it, and so on, can be important in offering an insight.

Common mistakes

Don't just comment on content and ignore the nature, origin and purpose of the source. Don't say 'a source is/isn't useful because it's primary/secondary'.

Simplified mark scheme

Band		Marks
1	**Explicit/developed** consideration of **BOTH** origin, purpose and content **AND** value and limitations.	3–4
2	**Limited** consideration/comments on origin, purpose and content **AND** value and limitations. **OR more developed** comments on **EITHER** origin, purpose and content **OR** value and limitations.	0–2

Student answer

One problem or limitation of Source A is that it is a US government document, so it might be biased – although this would depend on whether it was intended for publication (in which case it might be propaganda); or whether it was an internal document, which would be likely to be more reliable.

Examiner's comments

There is some relevant analysis of **Source A**, referring explicitly to both value and limitations, and origin and possible purpose. The comments are valid and are clearly linked to the question. The candidate has thus done enough to get into Band 2, and so be awarded two marks. However, as there are no comments about the source's content, and because the overall assessment is rather limited, this answer fails to get into Band 1.

Activity

Look again at the source, the simplified markscheme, and the student answer. Now try to write a paragraph to push the answer up into Band 1, and so obtain the full four marks. As well as commenting on what content/information the source provides, try to make comments on value and limitations that relate to what the historian might be trying to study – for example, are they looking for information, or trying to discover US government thinking/motives?

Summary activity

Copy this diagram and, using the information in this chapter, make brief point form notes under each heading.

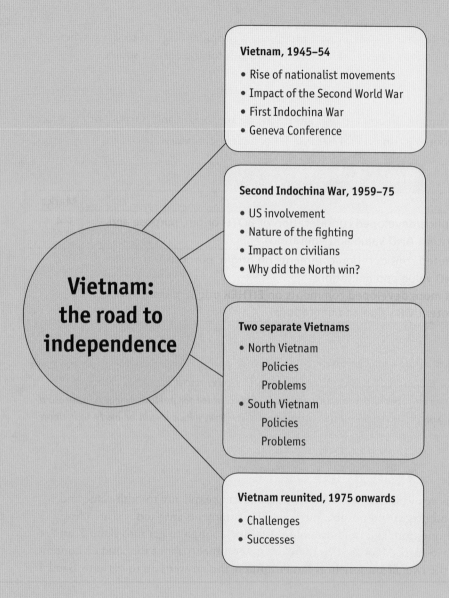

Vietnam: the road to independence

Vietnam, 1945–54
- Rise of nationalist movements
- Impact of the Second World War
- First Indochina War
- Geneva Conference

Second Indochina War, 1959–75
- US involvement
- Nature of the fighting
- Impact on civilians
- Why did the North win?

Two separate Vietnams
- North Vietnam
  Policies
  Problems
- South Vietnam
  Policies
  Problems

Vietnam reunited, 1975 onwards
- Challenges
- Successes

Paper 2 practice questions

1 Evaluate the reasons for opposition to colonial rule in Indochina.
2 Examine the role of the Viet Minh in the struggle for independence between 1941 and 1954.

3 Evaluate the reasons for the emergence and development of the Viet Cong in South Vietnam in the period 1957–68.

4 'The leadership of Ho Chi Minh was the key factor in the defeat of French colonialism in Indochina by 1955.' To what extent do you agree with this statement?

5 Evaluate the significance of the Cold War on the development of the independence struggle in Vietnam.

6 Compare and contrast the main consequences of the Vietnam War on North and South Vietnam.

Further reading

Try reading the relevant chapters/sections of the following books:

Anderson, David L. (2005), *The Vietnam War*, Basingstoke: Palgrave Macmillan.

Duiker, William J. (2000), *Ho Chi Minh: A Life*, New York: Hyperion.

Herring, George C. (2001), *America's Longest War: The United States and Vietnam, 1950–1975*, Maidenhead: McGraw-Hill Higher Education.

Karnow, Stanley (1994), *Vietnam: A History*, London: Pimlico.

Kolko, Gabriel (1985), *Anatomy of a War*, New York: Pantheon.

McAlister, John T. (1970), *Viet Nam: The Origins of Revolution*, London: Allen Lane.

Pike, Douglas (1991), *Viet Cong: The Organization and Techniques of the National Liberation Front of South Vietnam*, Cambridge, MA: De Capo Press.

5 Cuba

Introduction

The Caribbean island of Cuba had a long struggle to achieve full independence. For more than 300 years – from the 16th century until the end of the 19th century, it was a Spanish colony. In fact, it was just one of the many states in the Americas that were part of the long-lasting Spanish empire. From the mid-18th century onwards, the growing importance of sugar turned Cuba into one of Spain's wealthiest colonies in the Americas.

Spanish Cuba was ruled by a captain-general who, in turn, was supervised by the Spanish viceroy based in Mexico. Cuba's captain-general and the rest of Cuba's administrators were Spaniards, appointed by the Spanish government and sent out to the island. As they were poorly paid, corruption as a way of obtaining wealth soon became widespread.

While the indigenous Amerindian population tried to resist the often-brutal Spanish colonisation, the first serious independence movements in Cuba did not appear until the early 19th century. Before then, uprisings in Cuba tended to be small-scale slave rebellions that aimed to end slavery on the island. However, a successful slave rebellion that began in 1791 in the French colony of Saint-Domingue (present-day Haiti) acted as an inspiration to the later independence movements in Cuba. As early as 1812, the Aponte Conspiracy – in imitation of the successful rebellion in Saint-Domingue, which finally achieved independence from France in 1804 – attempted to achieve an independent Cuba.

One factor that made it difficult to develop an independence movement in Cuba was the way Cuban society was organised. As in Spain's other colonies in the Americas, Cuba's population was socially and racially divided into distinct racial castes. At the top were the *peninsulares* – these were Spanish-born Spaniards who had come to Cuba as administrators or to seek their fortune. Then there were the *criollos* – these were those born in Cuba to Spanish parents. Below them were the *mestizos* and the *mulattos*: these were, respectively, those whose ancestry was Spanish-Amerindian or Spanish-African. Cuba also had a significant population of free blacks and *mulattos* – below them were the black slaves.

From the 1820s – as Simón Bolívar's 'Liberation' campaigns won independence from Spanish control for several mainland Latin American countries – an increasing number of Cubans began to take steps to achieve independence for Cuba. The first serious attempt, an explicitly Bolívarian uprising, came in 1823. Although this was unsuccessful, in the second half of the 19th century, there were two Wars of Independence against Spanish rule. The first one, from 1868–78, was unsuccessful; but the Second War of Independence, which began in 1895, was ultimately successful and ended Spanish control in 1898.

However, it seemed to many Cubans in 1898 that they had merely exchanged Spanish control for US domination. This was because in 1898, just as it seemed the Cuban rebel Liberation Army seemed about to achieve victory, the US intervened and declared war on Spain in April 1898. The Spanish–American War was very brief; and it resulted in the US taking control of Spain's remaining colonies in the Americas – including Cuba. From 1898 until 1902, Cuba was under US military rule. Although Cuba became officially independent in 1902, its economy was increasingly dominated by US businesses in the decades that followed. In addition, the US intervened militarily several times in Cuba politics. As a result, many Cubans feel their island did not become fully independent until Fidel Castro's Revolution of 1959.

Fact: The US also took over two other Spanish colonies in the Pacific: the Philippines and Guam. At the same time, the US also annexed another Pacific territory – Hawaii. This US expansion in the Pacific would later be a serious cause of tension between the US and Japan.

Figure 5.1 Colonial Latin America and the Caribbean

1 Unit | The origins and rise of independence movements in Cuba

KEY QUESTIONS

- What political factors led to the development of an independence movement in Cuba?
- What economic and social factors contributed to the development of an independence movement?
- What external factors influenced the rise of the independence movement?
- What other factors influenced the rise of the independence movement?

Overview

- In many ways, the year 1492 was an important turning point for Cuban history – and for both the Americas and the rest of the world.
- Not only did it open the Americas up to what soon became a brutal and murderous conquest by powerful European states, it was also an important first step in the process now known as globalisation.
- By 1514, Cuba had been conquered by Spanish forces, despite resistance from the indigenous Amerindian population.
- From the mid-18th century, Spanish control of Cuba was threatened by other powers – in particular, by the US, which began to consider plans for annexation.
- A slave revolt in 1791 in the French colony of Saint-Domingue, which ended in achieving independence in 1804, inspired the first serious independence rebellion in Cuba in 1812.
- The successes of Bolívarian independence movements in Latin America in the early 1820s inspired another unsuccessful Cuban independence rising in 1823.
- In the 1860s, those Cubans wanting independence were further encouraged by evidence of Spain's declining imperial power.

5.1 What political factors led to the development of an independence movement in Cuba?

Before 1800, the main political factors that contributed to the rise of an independence movement in Cuba were connected with Spanish rule and the system of slavery.

Establishing Spanish control

In 1492, during his first voyage on behalf of the Spanish monarchy to establish a sea-route to the East Indies, Cristoforo Colombo (a.k.a Cristobal Colon or Christopher Columbus) 'discovered' the 'New World'. This voyage turned out to have enormous repercussions for the Americas and for Europe – and for Cuba. When Colombo landed on Cuba, he declared it to be a Spanish possession. By 1509, Spanish adventurers had completed the mapping of Cuba's coastline. In 1511, Diego de Velasquez sailed from the west of the Spanish island of **Hispaniola** and landed on the coast of eastern Cuba, where he established a settlement at Baracoa. He arrived with a sizeable force, and orders to conquer the whole island. The conquest – mostly conducted by Pánfilo de Narváez – was brutal. After several massacres, which were part of a genocidal plan designed to crush the determined guerrilla resistance of the indigenous populations, the Spanish conquest was completed by 1514, and the Spanish settlement of Havana was established. Velasquez then became the governor of both Hispaniola and Cuba.

> **Hispaniola:** this had already been brutally conquered by Spanish forces, which, from 1493 to1503, had virtually wiped out the indigenous Taino population. Today, the island contains two states: Haiti in the west, and the Dominican Republic in the east.

SOURCE A

When the locals had come … from a large settlement in order to receive us… – and had given us loaves and fishes and any other foodstuffs they could provide – the Christians [Pánfilo de Narváez's Spanish troops] …, without the slightest provocation, butchered, before my eyes, some three thousand souls – men, women and children – as they sat there in front of us. I saw that day atrocities more terrible than any living man has ever seen, nor ever thought to see.

Extract from an account by Las Casas, a Spanish Dominican priest, of the massacre of the inhabitants of Caonao in Cuba. Quoted in R. Gott (2005), *Cuba: A New History*, New Haven: Yale Nota Bene, p.15.

> **Fact:** The most determined resistance came from the Taínos (part of what became known as the Arawak people), initially led by their chieftain (*cacique*) Hatuey. He was originally from Hispaniola, but had left there for Cuba, after witnessing a brutal Spanish massacre of Indians there in 1503. He was eventually captured by the Spanish forces in 1512, and was burned alive at Yara de Baracoa. Later leaders, such as Caguax, were either killed, or captured and suffered a similar fate.

However, a more limited Indian resistance continued for several more decades, with attacks on Spanish settlements still taking place throughout the 1520s and into the early 1530s.

Slavery in Cuba

Once part of the Spanish empire, the local inhabitants were ruthlessly exploited – mainly as forced labour in gold and copper mines; or on the land, which was distributed by the king of Spain to those Spaniards willing to colonise the new territory. However, Cuba's

Figure 5.2 A monument to Hatuey, which is located in Baracoa, where the first Spanish forces landed in 1511. Today, he is celebrated as Cuba's 'First National Hero'. The inscription reads: *Hatuey – first American rebel slain in the Yara de Baracoa*

local native populations – decimated by massacres, Western diseases and suicide – often fled to remote and inaccessible places, to avoid their new 'responsibilities' to the Spanish settlers.

Initially, the Spanish began to search for slaves from other parts of Latin America and the Caribbean. Later, they began to import slaves from Africa. Over the next 300 years, almost one million West Africans were taken to Cuba. At first, the numbers were relatively small but, by the 17th century, Africans formed almost 50 per cent of Cuba's population. However, the vast majority of slaves (possibly as high as 85 per cent) arrived in the 19th century, to work on the sugar and tobacco plantations that, from the 17th century, had come to replace cattle ranching as Cuba's main economic activity. From 1821–31 alone, it is estimated that 600,000 slaves were imported. Even after the slave trade had been banned, small numbers of Africans were still brought to Cuba illegally – this did not end until the abolishment of slavery in 1886. Slavery had an important impact on Cuba's developing society, culture and economy. In particular, many white settlers feared slave rebellions – as early as 1532, there was a rebellion in a gold mine; in 1538, blacks and native Cubans joined together against the white landowners. As became increasingly evident after 1800, the experience of slavery eventually resulted in black Cubans forming the bulk of the military forces that successfully fought to end Spanish control of Cuba.

Fact: Several thousand native Cubans survived in the swamps, mountains and small islands of Cuba – especially in the more remote eastern regions. In the late 16th and 17th centuries, these natives were often joined by runaway black slaves. They then formed independent villages – and even towns – known as *palenques*. These later formed resistance support centres for the independence movements that began to emerge in the 19th and 20th centuries.

Fact: Before 1886, slavery had already been abolished in most other countries in the Americas. But Spanish Cuba – along with Brazil and the US – was among the last to retain it. The reason it lasted so long in Cuba was largely the result of the demands of the extremely wealthy sugar plantation owners.

5.2 What economic and social factors contributed to the development of an independence movement?

During the 19th century, developments within Cuba – especially economic developments – significantly contributed to the emergence of a movement aiming for independence from Spain.

Spanish Cuba's economy before 1800

Initially, the main economic activity was the growing of tobacco; in addition, there were cattle ranching and sugar plantations. Until the second half of the 18th century, most sugar plantations were relatively small. However, from about 1750, Cuba quickly developed into a prosperous sugar colony. This was partly the result of the emergence in Cuba of a class of landowners who wanted to increase their wealth by adopting more modern methods; and by a decision to significantly increase the importation of black slaves to work on these larger plantations. During the second half of the 18th century, the number of slave ships arriving in Cuba rose from six to 200 a year. The number of sugar plantations in Cuba increased fivefold, and the amount of land given over to sugar production doubled between the 1770s and the 1790s. By 1800, sugar was Cuba's biggest single export. The wealth this generated soon turned Cuba into Spain's most valuable colony.

5

5.3 What external factors influenced the rise of the independence movement?

As well as developments within Cuba, there were also some external factors that contributed to the development of an independence movement in Cuba after 1800. The two most significant factors were the slave revolt in Saint-Dominque in 1791, and the independence movements associated with Simón Bolívar.

External challenges to Spanish control

By the 18th century, Spanish territories in the Americas – including Cuba – seemed well-established. However, from the mid-18th century, Spanish control of Cuba was increasingly challenged. At first, the main threat came from Britain. As Spain grew weaker, Britain took advantage – for instance, briefly seizing Guantanamo in 1741, even taking Havana in August 1762, and then occupying Cuba itself until February 1763. Once Spain was able to resume control of Cuba in 1763, following the Treaty of Paris, it began to introduce some reforms regarding education, taxation and the landholding system. Various bodies were established that gave the landowning white élites some limited involvement in Cuba's future economic development.

QUESTION

What was the significance of the Napoleonic Wars as regards the ability of Spain to retain control of its colonies in the Americas?

Another external threat to Spanish control of Cuba soon came from the United States of America which gained independence from Britain in 1783. Within a short space of time, US politicians and business people began to think about either the purchase of Cuba from Spain, or even outright annexation by the US. The French Revolution and then the Napoleonic Wars that began in 1803 also had serious implications for Spanish control: the former mainly because of its ideas of liberty and equality; the latter because contact between Spain and Cuba was seriously disrupted – especially when Napoleon's forces invaded Spain itself.

The Saint-Domingue slave rebellion, 1791–1804

Ideals of the French Revolution: these had been announced at the start of the French Revolution in 1789, in the Declaration of the Rights of Man, which had stated that all men were free and equal. The Revolution's three main slogans were: 'Liberty', 'Equality' and 'Fraternity'. In 1794, Robespierre had persuaded the French Convention to vote for the abolition of slavery.

The event that had the first serious impact on the emerging independence movement in Cuba was the slave revolt that broke out in the wealthy French colony of Saint-Domingue (present-day Haiti) in April 1791. Saint-Domingue had been a French colony since 1659, and was only sixty miles from Cuba. Inspired by the **ideals of the French Revolution**, more than half a million black slaves – who comprised 90 per cent of the island's population – rose up against their white 'owners', in what became a revolutionary upheaval that continued until 1804. They were led by **Toussaint L'Ouverture**, and the uprising soon turned into what became known as the Haitian Revolution. With the defeat of a sizeable French force at the end of 1803, the leaders of the rebellion changed Saint-Domingue's name to Haiti and, on 1 January 1804, declared it to be an independent country – the first independent country in the whole of Latin America and the Caribbean.

Economic and social impact of the Haitian Revolution

About 30,000 French refugees – many of them former plantation owners – left Saint-Domingue and settled in Cuba. They brought the remains of their considerable wealth and agricultural expertise, and soon set about improving the Cuban economy. In just a few decades, large sugar and coffee plantations were established in Cuba, and soon came to dominate the economy. These then contributed to an increased demand for slaves in Cuba. While cattle ranches and tobacco farms continued to be important, it was sugar and coffee that came to dominate in the 19th century. These economic developments resulted in a greatly increased demand for black slaves in Cuba. By 1791, the slave population in Cuba had been 85,000 – according to the census of 1841, there were by then 436,000 slaves: about 45 per cent of the total population. In addition, there were free blacks – these numbered 153,000 by 1841. Taken together, these two groups formed almost 60 per cent of Cuba's population. However, Cuba's white élites, who feared the possibility of a rebellion in Cuba similar to the one in Haiti, increasingly adopted racist attitudes towards Cuba's black population. In particular, they believed that remaining a Spanish colony would offer military protection against any slave revolt.

Thus a conspiracy in 1809, led by the *crillo* Ramon de la Luz, to achieve independence from Spain, failed to gain the support of Cuba's plantation owners.

The impact of the Haitian Revolution on Cuba's blacks

However, many of Cuba's black slaves – unlike Cuba's whites – found the events in Haiti very inspiring. In Cuba's early years as a Spanish colony, free blacks were not particularly discriminated against, and were even allowed to carry weapons and form a black militia in Havana. Since the late 16th century, blacks – both slaves and free 'coloureds' – had been allowed to form societies known as *cabildos* (later known as 'fraternal societies'). However, the Haitian Revolution changed the attitudes of white settlers to this state of affairs. In fact, it was from among Cuba's 'free people of colour' that Cuba's first rebel leaders came. The first attempt to gain independence and the ending of slavery was in 1795, led by Nicolas Morales, a free black. A more serious separatist revolt took place in 1810, at a time when the Spanish government was having to deal with Napoleon's invasion of Spain.

The Aponte Conspiracy, 1812

The first real Cuban independence uprising came in February 1812 – and was explicitly in imitation of the rebellion in Haiti. It was led by **Jose Antonio Aponte**, who had earlier been the commander of the Havana black militia. He admired both Toussaint L'Ouverture and Henri Christophe and, believing that Spain was about to end the slave trade and even slavery itself, he and his followers – and various organisations of black slaves – aimed to overthrow Spanish control and set up an independent Cuba. Several whites also supported the aims of this planned rebellion. However, some plans were betrayed to the Spanish authorities and, although there were several slave revolts on sugar plantations, the Spanish forces were able to crush it. In April 1812, Aponte was hanged, along with five other 'free men of colour' and three slaves – their heads were then cut off and displayed as a warning to others. A severe repression was then unleashed by the authorities.

Toussaint L'Ouverture (1743–1803)

He had been a slave until his early thirties, but had been freed in 1776. His considerable military abilities earned him the nickname of 'The Black Napoleon'. He was able to gain control of the whole of Saint-Domingue, and then successfully invaded the neighbouring Spanish colony on the eastern side of Hispaniola. In 1801, he declared himself governor and did much to improve the island's economy; but in 1802, he was forced to resign when Napoleon sent forces by to restore French control. Toussaint was arrested and deported to France; he was then sent to prison, where he died in 1803. After his deportation, leadership passed to Jean-Jacques Dessalines, a former slave. It was Dessalines who defeated the French forces in 1803 and proclaimed the independence of Haiti in 1804. Another former slave who rose to prominence during the Haitian Revolution was Henri Christophe.

Jose Antonio Aponte (?–1812)

He was a black carpenter, and had been an officer in Havana's black militia. In 1810, he became the leader of a *cabildo*, and it was with this group that he plotted what became one of Cuba's largest independence uprisings in the early 19th century.

Cuba

Simón Bolívar (1783–1830)

He was born in Venezuela, and came from the wealthy and aristocratic *crillo* upper class. He became a military and political leader, and soon came to play the central role in the successful struggle of Latin America countries for independence from the Spanish empire. His military victories earned him the nickname 'El Libertador' ('The Liberator'). The new independent republic of Bolivia – that, before 1823, had previously been the northern part of Peru – was named after him in 1825.

ACTIVITY

Find out more about the Bolívarian movements in the early 1820s. Why would these developments have inspired those Cubans wanting independence?

The Bolívarian movement

Another external development that had inspired Aponte's unsuccessful uprising was the growing number of anti-Spanish insurrections on the mainland of Latin America. These were in large part the result of Napoleon's occupation of Spain in 1808, and his replacement of Spain's king with his own brother. The first to rebel and claim independence from the new French-dominated government in Spain were Argentina and Venezuela. In the latter, one of the important participants had been **Simón Bolívar**.

In 1811, Venezuela proclaimed its independence – although this first attempt was defeated by Spanish forces, Bolívar raised a new army and briefly liberated Venezuela again in 1813. However, Venezuela was finally liberated in 1821; in 1822, he also freed Colombia and Ecuador from Spanish control. The following year, he liberated Peru and Bolivia.

Bolívar and Cuban independence in the 1820s

In the 1820s, the Cuban independence movement was inspired by Bolívar's achievements – even though he did not extend his campaign to Caribbean islands such as Cuba as he feared it might become 'another Republic of Haiti'. The Cuban section of Bolívar's movement – the Soles y Rayos de Bolívar (Suns and Rays of Bolívar) – was led by Jose Francisco Lemus and Jose Maria Heredia. Their independence plot centred on a force of 3,000 Bolívarians from Venezuela, which was to invade in support of an uprising in Cuba. However, the authorities uncovered the plot in November 1823, and the invasion force never arrived. Although the Cuban conspirators were arrested and sent into exile, Cuban politics continued to be influenced by Enlightenment ideas, and by events such as the American, French and Haitian Revolutions.

The response of the Spanish authorities in Cuba was to repress even more harshly than previously any signs of revolt amongst the black population. Following the Soles y Rayos conspiracy, Francisco Dionisio Vives (1755–?), was sent out in 1823 as captain-general of Cuba, with strict orders to maintain Spanish control. One of those who became a victim of the repression that followed was Felix Varela, who supported both Latin American independence from Spain and the abolition of slavery. He became an exile, staying in Spain and then the US. From there, he wrote many articles that had a big influence on the next generation of Cuban intellectuals and progressives who would lead the struggle for independence.

5.4 What other factors influenced the rise of the independence movement?

Other important factors behind the emergence of an independence movement in Cuba were economic and political developments in the 1850s and 1860s, along with evidence of Spain's declining power.

The Cuban élites and independence from Spain

Initially, most of Cuba's white élites were opposed to the idea of independence from Spain. However, for several reasons, this began to change in the 19th century – some of the leaders of Cuba's independence movement eventually came from this social layer.

Cuban independence in the 1830s

Most of Cuba's white economic élites were reluctant to support independence from Spain, as they feared both losing Spanish support of the slavery system, and the economic impact of cutting trade links with Spain, which had just recently given greater benefits to the Cuban economic élites. In addition, they also feared the possible influence the black population of Cuba might have in an independent Cuba.

However, this fear of the blacks receded somewhat as the 19th century moved on. This was because there was significant white immigration to Cuba – in part, this was linked to the aim of ensuring that the black population in Cuba would never equal, never mind exceed, that of whites. During the 1820s, several white immigrants had settled from the USA, Latin America, Spain and the Canary Islands. These *peninsulares* did not want to separate from Spain. Although they were Cuban nationalists, their vision of Cuba was of a Cuba that would still be part of the Spanish empire – and of a Cuba where the blacks had no real future.

In the 1830s, a group of intellectuals, led by the journalist José Antonio Saco, pushed forward the campaign for a 'white Cuba'. These, too, while wanting more autonomy from Spain, did not want full independence. When Britain abolished slavery in its Caribbean colonies after 1833, Saco and his group became further concerned that the blacks of Jamaica and Haiti might join forces with Cuba's black population, and that an independent Cuba might be dominated by blacks. They then began to advocate the idea that the US – still a slave-owning state – should annex Cuba and make it part of the USA.

> **QUESTION**
>
> Why did some white Cubans favour annexation by the US rather than independence?

Spanish repression and Cuban independence

From 1823 until 1832, Vives was responsible for one of the longest and most repressive regimes of any Spanish ruler. In 1824, he set up a special military tribunal – the Comision Militar Executiva y Permanente – specifically designed to suppress any signs of revolt – whether by black slaves or by those wanting to achieve the independence that had been achieved by Spain's colonies in Central and Latin America by 1824. This tribunal placed Cuba under martial law for the next fifty years. One of the tribunal's first actions was the discovery and repression, in 1829, of the 'Black Eagle' conspiracy – another unsuccessful attempt at securing independence from Spain. Vives went so far as to suggest that, because of the danger that free blacks and *mulattos* might make common cause with Cuba's slave population, all members of such groups should be expelled from Cuba.

> **SOURCE B**
>
> The existence of free blacks and mulattoes in the middle of the enslavement of their comrades is an example that will be very prejudicial some day, if effective measures are not taken in order to prevent [the slaves'] constant and natural tendency towards emancipation.
>
> Comments made by Vives in 1832. Quoted in R. Gott (2005), *Cuba: A New History*, New Haven: Yale Nota Bene, p. 56.

When Vives left in 1832, he was replaced by General Miguel Tacón y Rosique. He, too, ruled Cuba with an iron hand – although there were other unsuccessful conspiracies or risings in 1837. Tacón also fuelled the early independence movement by often refusing to implement progressive reforms which the Spanish government introduced in the 1830s for its remaining colonies. For instance, he refused to abolish the Comision Militar, and would not allow elections to take place in Cuba in 1836. When the governor of Oriente province protested, Tacón sent troops to take control of the province.

However, these repressive actions resulted in Cuba's intellectuals turning against Spain. Once again, the alternatives of independence, or annexation by the US, were the two main options considered. Saco – an early advocate of annexation by the US – was sentenced by the Comision Militar in 1834 to internal exile. He felt that the harsh repression was pushing Cuba towards revolution, and believed only the US would be strong enough to prevent this. While this did not gain much support within Cuba itself, there were many more powerful and influential supporters of this option within the US itself.

Cuba's economic problems

Cuba began facing serious economic problems from the mid-19th century. The prolonged economic growth that, from the late 18th century, had turned Cuba into the world's biggest single producer of sugar, had begun to slow down. Increasingly, Cuba's sugar industry faced competition from European and North American sugar beet and the development of new sugar-cane producing regions. Furthermore, Spain's economic problems meant that it could not absorb all of Cuba's sugar production.

Fact: By 1860, the number of slaves in Cuba had declined from a peak in 1841 of almost 500,000 (44 per cent of Cuba's population), to almost 370,000 (less than 30 per cent of Cuba's total population of 1.4 million).

An additional problem related to the question of slavery that, for centuries, had been a crucial element in Cuba's sugar production. In 1817, the slave trade had, at least officially, been declared illegal as a result of treaties that Britain had pressurised Spain into signing. Although the trade had, nonetheless, continued for another two decades, in 1835 Britain forced Spain to sign another treaty, which made the Spanish authorities take even greater steps to prevent evasions of the law – from then on, the numbers of slaves imported into Cuba declined considerably. By 1860, this trade had virtually ceased.

During the 1840s and 1850s, because of Spain's growing problems, many *hacendados* (owners of sugar mills) began to modernise their sugar production in order to be less dependent on slave labour. They also increasingly turned to the idea of annexation by the US, which was still based on slavery – some had even helped organise armed US expeditions to Cuba. However, the abolition of slavery in the US during the American Civil War meant that an alternative to slavery was needed even more urgently. Cuba's plantation owners increasingly tried to delay the eventual abolition of slavery and to obtain guarantees of compensation once it did end.

Opposition to Spanish rule

Cuba's *criollo* plantation owners also wanted reforms to the administrative system in Cuba, so that they could have greater influence. Many became convinced that Spain would not grant such reforms, so they came to support some sort of independence. Some – influenced by the nationalist ideas of philosophers and poets – thought a fully independent Cuba would then be able to form close economic links to the US. Others favoured the 'Texas option' – where, in the 1840s, once Texas had rebelled against the Mexican government, the leaders of the rebellion had then obtained annexation by the US.

However, these demands were resisted by the majority of *peninsulares* (Spanish emigrants) who dominated the colonial administration and trade. They saw the reforms demanded by the plantation owners as being a first step towards independence, which they strongly opposed. One reason for their stance was that many of them believed that any rebellion against Spanish rule in Cuba would result in the same thing as had happened in Haiti in the 1790s. Numerically, however, the Cuban *criollos* outnumbered the Spanish *peninsulares* twelve to one in the western provinces, and twenty-three to one in the east of the island.

In the second half of the 19th century, opposition to Spanish rule increased among most sections of Cuba's population. In part, this was the result of a high and increased tax burden – mainly to pay for Spain's military campaigns in Mexico (1862) and her naval campaigns against Peru and Chile (1866), and for all Spain's diplomatic corps in Latin America. In addition, Cuba's white *criollo* population increasingly resented the often arbitrary rule of Spanish bureaucrats and the haughty and discriminatory behaviour of many of the *peninsulares*, who looked down on the Cuban-born whites. In addition, the free blacks – now roughly 16 per cent of the population – were also beginning to express their discontent and frustration.

Hopes of reform

In 1865, those Cubans wanting reform were encouraged by internal developments in Spain, where a liberal government came to power. This new government proposed a Junta de Information, composed of members elected in Cuba, Puerto Rico and the Philippines, to meet in Madrid to discuss constitutional reforms and the difficult issue of slavery. However, Cubans were angered by the abrupt dismissal of this Junta in 1867, and by the new government's refusal to listen to its recommendations. Instead, martial law was reconfirmed, political gatherings were banned, and the press was censored and controlled.

To make matters worse, an international economic crisis impacted negatively on Cuba's sugar industry. This, combined with the disappointment over possible reforms, led to the emergence of pro-independence groups – some of which were prepared to take to armed struggle. However, the majority of Cuba's population (some 80 per cent of the total) lived in the western regions, where almost 90 per cent of the sugar plantations were – these *hacendados* were in favour of reform, but did not want to risk a military conflict with Spain. In the east, there were relatively fewer sugar plantations and slaves, and the economy there was weaker than in the west. Here, the *hacendados* were more inclined to take Spain on in a war of liberation.

Declining Spanish power

The growing independence movement in Cuba was also encouraged to take military action by Spain's lack of success in **Santo Domingo**, and by France's eventually failed expedition to Mexico. It seemed to many Cuban nationalists that European powers in general – and Spain in particular, which had serious internal political problems and seemed to be in decline – were no longer able to resist a determined independence movement. In addition, many of those who had had military experience in the struggles in Santo Domingo moved to the eastern provinces in Cuba, bringing their military expertise with them.

Santo Domingo: now the Dominican Republic – the central and eastern parts of Hispaniola, had declared its independence from Spain in 1821, inspired by the actions of Bolívar on the Latin American mainland. However, it was then occupied by Haiti until 1844, when it regained its independence. Briefly a Spanish colony once more from 1861, it became permanently independent in 1865.

Thus, by the mid-19th century, this combination of important political and economic developments had led to increasingly serious attempts amongst sections of Cuban society to achieve complete independence from Spanish rule. As study of the next unit will show, further developments over the next fifty years would eventually result, in 1902, in the emergence of an independent Cuba – or, at least, of a Cuba independent from Spain.

End of unit activities

1   Using information from this book, and any other resources available to you, draw a timeline to show the successes of the Bolívarian movement in Latin America in the early 1820s.

2   Then list the ways these Bolívarian independence successes were significant for developments in Cuba before 1860.

3   Working in pairs, draw up a list showing the differences and similarities between the Aponte Conspiracy of 1812, and the Soles y Rayos movement of 1823.

4   Write two letters to a Cuban newspaper: one presenting the arguments in favour of Cuban independence from Spain; and one arguing for annexation by the US.

KEY QUESTIONS

- What methods were used in the struggle for independence?
- What was José Martí's role in the struggle for independence?
- Why did the independence movement succeed?

Overview

- After 1840, Cuba experienced some more serious armed uprisings – the two most important ones, in 1868 and 1895 respectively, were clearly independence movements.

- From 1848, the US made offers to Spain for the purchase of Cuba – but Spain refused. This led some politicians in the US to consider the annexation of Cuba, which was increasingly seen as being important for US interests.

- The first serious armed uprising for Cuban independence broke out in 1868 and was at first led by Carlos Manuel de Céspedes. This First War of Independence lasted ten years, but ended in defeat in 1878. One reason for this was divisions over aims between rebel leaders.

- During the 1880s, José Martí began to organise another armed rebellion for Cuban independence. To help in this, he formed the Cuban Revolutionary Party in 1892.

- The Second War of Independence broke out in 1895 and, although Martí was killed early on, by 1898 the rebels' Liberation Army seemed on the point of total victory.

- However, in that year, the US decided to intervene and declared war on Spain. After Spain's defeat in the short Spanish–American War, the US took over Spain's remaining colonies in the Americas – including Cuba.

TIMELINE

1823 Dec: US announces the Monroe Doctrine.

1843 Mar: La Escalera Rebellion in Cuba.

1848 US offers Spain $100 million for Cuba.

1854 US offers Spain $130 million for Cuba.

1868 Oct: Carlos Manuel de Céspedes begins First Independence War; Grito de Yara.

1869 Apr: Rebel Constituent Assembly proclaims 'Republic of Cuba in Arms'; Céspedes elected president.

1873 Céspedes deposed as president.

1874 Feb: Céspedes killed by Spanish troops.

1877 Dec: Estrada captured.

1878 Feb: Pact of Zanjon.

Mar: Protest of Baragua.

1879 Aug: Guerra Chiquita.

1892 Jan: Martí forms the Cuban Revolutionary Party.

1895 Feb: Start of Second Independence War.

Mar: Rebels issue their Manifesto of Montecristo.

May: Martí killed by Spanish troops.

Sept: Rebel Constitution announced.

1896 Oct: Valeriano Weyler orders first concentration camps set up.

Dec: Antonio Maceo and Francisco Gómez killed by Spanish troops.

1898 Feb: The Maine incident.

Apr: US declares war on Spain; Teller Amendment.

Dec: Treaty of Paris ends Spanish–American War.

QUESTION

Why did the rebellion of 1843–4 present problems for those Cubans trying to build support for independence from Spain?

5.5 What methods were used in the struggle for independence?

Before Cuba finally achieved independence – or at least a form of independence – in 1902, there were three military struggles related to ending Spanish rule and/or slavery in the second half of the 19th century.

La Escalera Rebellion, 1843–4

The first broke out in March 1843: this was a black rebellion, known as **La Escalera Rebellion**. It was a joint rebellion of slaves and 'free people of colour', and some of their leaders believed they would have Britain's support.

This rebellion was the most significant one between Aponte's 1812 rebellion, and the First War of Independence that began in 1868. The rebellion spread quickly across western Cuba. One of the uprisings, in November 1843, took place in Matanzas province – and was led by a black female slave known as '**La Negra Carlota**'.

Figure 5.3 The monument erected to commemorate the role of Carlota, and the two other leaders, of the uprising on the Triumvirato sugar plantation in the Rebellion of 1843-44. Carlota is the figure in the centre

Cuba's captain-general, Leopoldo O'Donnell, and the Comision Militar, responded quickly, carrying out a ferocious repression from January to March 1844 against all whites, slaves and free people of colour who had played leading roles in the rebellion. The Cuban authorities then exiled all free blacks not born in Cuba – as O'Donnell assumed they had stirred up the black slaves. However, this rebellion was essentially one of blacks and *mulattos* wanting to end slavery and achieve equal rights, rather than a clear struggle for Cuban independence.

Many white Cubans who favoured independence were worried by the La Escalera Rebellion, as the 1841 census had shown that, for the first time, the number of slaves outnumbered that of whites. Out of Cuba's total population of just over one million, whites numbered 418,000, slaves 436,000 and free people of colour 153,000. Thus whites wanting independence now seemed unlikely to make common cause with blacks wanting an end to slavery. Instead, Cuba's white intellectuals were divided about whether to declare independence and rely on British forces to end slavery; or to accept US support to achieve an independent Cuba that still retained slavery. Nonetheless, just over twenty years later, Cuba's first major armed attempt to gain independence from Spain broke out.

The First War of Independence, 1868–78

This armed struggle for independence – also known as the Ten Years' War – began in the east of Cuba, where there were fewer railways and roads – making it more difficult for the Spanish authorities to transport troops to deal with any rebellion. This knowledge made pro-independence groups there more prepared to take armed action, and a serious conspiracy began to take shape, centred on the town of Bayamo, in Oriente province.

Early actions

Their main leaders were *criollos*, and included **Carlos Manuel de Céspedes**, Salvador Cisneros Betancourt, Ignacio Agramonte and Francisco Vicente Aguilera.

During the summer of 1868, the plotters organised a widespread refusal to pay taxes, while also spreading independence literature in the region, and trying to get pro-reform Cubans in the west to support an independence rebellion. Although Céspedes wanted the rebellion to begin in July 1868, the majority decided on December. However, rumours that the authorities in Havana had discovered their plot and were about to crush it – led Céspedes to take unilateral action and, on 10 October, he began the revolt on his own plantation. There, he freed all his slaves and announced the independence of Cuba.

Because of the uncertainty in Spain, Cuba's strongly conservative captain-general, General Francisco Lersundi y Hormaechea, took little action early on and, on 18 October, Céspedes was able to capture the town of Bayamo. He then officially declared the independence of Cuba in what became known as the Grito de Yara (Cry of Yara) – the 'cry' referred to the shout that had launched the independence movements in Latin America in the 1820s. When news of this spread, other risings against Spain broke out in the eastern provinces of Oriente and Camaguey. In addition, several younger reformists in Havana decided to join him. By early 1869, the colonial authorities were faced with a rapidly expanding rebellion that lasted for ten years.

While soon outnumbered – Spain eventually sent more than 100,000 troops to crush this rebellion – the insurgents were helped by the support they gained from peasants, who had a good knowledge of the local landscape. This enabled them to move quickly through the countryside, have forewarning of troop movements, conceal their forces and pick favourable sites for combat. The rebels were also aided by the fact that, unlike the Spanish troops, they were used to Cuba's tropical climate. As a result, Cuba experienced an increasingly bitter ten years' war.

Theory of Knowledge

History and ethics:
Slavery is a very contentious issue. Can – or should – historians avoid making moral judgements about past practices when writing about slavery and slave plantations? Draw up a list giving the main arguments for and against moral relativism. Do you think there are any universal moral absolutes?

Carlos Manuel de Céspedes (1819–74)

He was a Cuban plantation owner and lawyer who, on 10 October 1868, began what was Cuba's First War of Independence. After freeing all his slaves, he urged them to join with his fellow conspirators in a war to achieve independence from Spain and to end slavery. In April 1869, he was elected as president of the 'Republic of Cuba in Arms'. But leadership differences led to him being deposed in 1873, and in 1874 he was killed by Spanish troops. He famously refused to end his struggle in return for the return of his son Oscar, who had been captured by Spanish forces. As a result, his son was executed by the authorities. He is known as the Padre de la Patria (Father of the Country) in Cuba, and a statue to him now stands in the square of Bayamo.

Figure 5.4 The statue of Céspedes in Bayamo

QUESTION

Using information from this section, discuss how effective the *trocha* was in combating the independence insurgence of 1868–78?

Spanish tactics

In order to restrict the rebel areas to the east and centre of Cuba, and so preventing any serious unrest in the west, Lersundi ordered the building of a defensive military trench, more than 50km (30 miles) long – the *trocha militar* – across the middle of the island, from Moron in the north to Jucaro in the south. It was built between 1869 and 1872, by black slaves and Chinese coolies, and was defended by a line of more than forty forts.

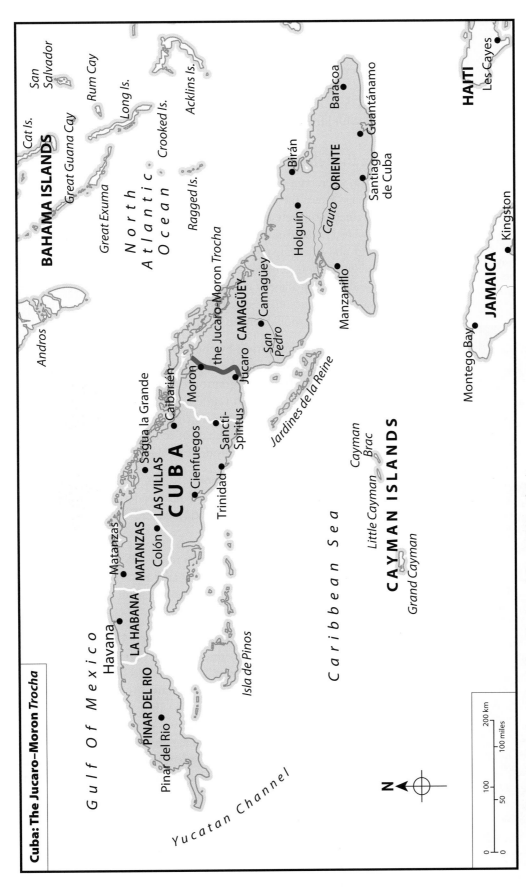

Figure 5.5 Map showing the Jucaro–Moron *Trocha* and the provinces of Cuba

Máximo Gómez (1836–1905)

He came from a wealthy family in Santo Domingo, and had been a commander in the Spanish army there. When civil war broke out in Santo Domingo in 1865, he lost his lands and fled to Cuba, where he became a farmer. He quickly joined Céspedes' rebellion and became one of his most able military leaders. After the end of the Ten Years' War, he remained a supporter of Cuban independence. He ended up as Cuba's military commander in Cuba's Second War of Independence (1895–8) and did much to develop a form of guerrilla warfare, based on methods used by Spaniards resisting Napoleon's invasion. His combination of insurgency and insurrection had a big influence on the tactics later used by Fidel Castro and Che Guevara in the rebellion against Batista.

In addition, to counter the rebels' guerrilla activities, Lersundi also ordered the forcible removal of people from rural areas into concentration camps and towns controlled by the government; and young men who were found outside their home area were arrested and executed. However, probably the main reason why the *trocha* proved so effective was because of divisions within the rebel leadership about whether to spread the rebellion to the west. For, in 1875, when Máximo Gómez was finally allowed to take forces to the west, he crossed it with little difficulty.

Divisions within the rebels

Divisions soon began to emerge within the ranks of the rebels, which resulted in the loss of their early advantage. It was these divisions, as much as the military campaigns waged by Spanish forces, which ultimately led to the failure of this First Independence War. These differences were a combination of regionalism, conflicting class interests, arguments over military strategy and emerging racial and nationalist tensions. In April 1869, a rebel Constituent Assembly met in Guaimaro, officially proclaimed the birth of the new 'Republic of Cuba in Arms' and drew up a liberal constitution. But the attempt to reach a compromise over the slavery issue pleased no one: it stated that all inhabitants of the new republic were free – but that the freed slaves should remain as paid employees on the plantations.

The meeting also called for annexation by the US, and set up a system by which military leaders could not act without the approval of the civilian leadership. This latter move was suggested by Ignacio Agramonte who – like several others – had begun to worry about the authoritarian tendencies being shown by Céspedes. In 1873, Céspedes was deposed as president and briefly replaced by Betancourt. In February 1874, Céspedes was killed in a skirmish with Spanish troops and in 1875, Tomás Estrada Palma became the new president of the rebel republic.

By then, many of the early leaders – drawn mostly from Cuba's *criollo* élites – were either dead or in exile. Meanwhile, younger and more radical leaders had become military leaders: these included the Dominican **Máximo Gómez** and the Cuban *mulatto* **Antonio Maceo**.

However, funds for the struggle from Cuban exiles in the US began to dry up when the rebel agenda became more radical; while, after 1876, the restoration of political peace in Spain meant the Spanish authorities in Cuba could once again concentrate on defeating the rebels.

This situation convinced the new military leaders of the rebel forces that it was necessary to take the independence war into the wealthier western regions of Cuba. They argued that, by destroying the region's many sugar mills, they would simultaneously deprive the Spanish administration of vital funds and leave thousands of slaves and peasants free to join the struggle for independence. In this war, they believed Spain would soon be forced to give independence to Cuba. This was opposed by the *criollo* political leaders, who feared this would alienate the *peninsulares* who owned most of the big sugar plantations in the west, and who opposed independence. As a result, Gómez was deprived of his command. As the war continued, most rebel military leaders were either removed from their commands, or resigned in the face of constant interference from the civilian leaders. As a consequence, the rebels failed to make any significant breakthrough, and a stalemate soon developed.

Figure 5.6 A modern poster in Cuba, showing Maceo (on the left) alongside Che Guevara – another famed guerrilla leader, who played a prominent part in the Cuban Revolution of 1959, which finally established the full independence of Cuba

The end of the war

The newly appointed captain-general in Cuba, General Arsenio Martínez-Campos y Antón, took advantage of these divisions within rebel ranks, and promised reforms and an amnesty. Spain also sent reinforcements, enabling him to increase counterinsurgency measures. In December 1877, Estrada was captured and Gómez called for a ceasefire. The war was finally ended in February 1878 by the Pact of Zanjon. As well as granting an amnesty to all rebels, it gave Cuba limited autonomy rights and also freed all slaves and Chinese who had fought in the rebel Liberator Army.

However, not all rebels were happy with this, as they wanted complete independence and the abolition of slavery. Led by Antonio Maceo, they rejected the treaty at Baragua in March 1878 and announced their intention of continuing the independence war. However, with most rebels having abandoned the struggle, Maceo's 'Protest of Baragua' had limited impact, and the remaining rebel forces were eventually forced to give up and sign the treaty in May 1878 – Gómez, Maceo and several other leaders then went into exile. Despite a short-lived uprising in August 1879 – known as the Guerra Chiquita (Little War) – another armed struggle for Cuban independence did not break out until 1895.

The Second War of Independence, 1895–8

The first shots in this war – which eventually resulted in Cuban independence from Spain – came on 24 February 1895, when several small groups rose up in arms in various places. As in the First Independence War, their greatest successes were in the eastern regions. On

Antonio Maceo (1845–96)

He was known as 'The Bronze Titan', a title given him by his mainly black troops. He was extremely able, charismatic and popular. Although willing to receive money and weapons from outside countries, he was, like Martí, totally opposed to the idea of direct military intervention by the US. His troops were disparagingly referred to by white Spanish troops as the *mambi* (based on the African word *mbi*), implying they were just black bandits and criminals. In modern-day Cuba, these *mambises* Cubans are still seen as heroes of Cuba's struggle for independence. The date of Maceo's death during the Second Independence War, 7 December 1896, later became a National Day of Mourning in Cuba for all those heroes who had died in Cuba's struggle for independence.

ACTIVITY

Draw up a list of the issues that soon began to divide the rebels in the First War of Independence. Then try to put them in order of importance, and write a short paragraph to justify your first choice.

José Martí (1853–95)

After Cuba's First War of Independence (also known as the Ten Years' War), Martí spent fifteen years in exile in New York, raising money to re-launch the struggle for Cuban independence and racial equality. He was a revolutionary and democratic political thinker and activist, poet and lawyer – and became known as the 'Apostle'. He felt the US party system was corrupt, with big business able to use their great wealth to get governments to do their bidding. In particular, he saw US imperialism as a threat to Cuban independence. He was also anti-capitalist and supported the labour movement. Although he set up the Cuban Revolutionary Party in 1892, he was critical of several aspects of Marx's ideas. Because of his inspirational role in Cuba's struggle for independence from both Spain and the US, he became a hero to independence movements across Latin America, not just in Cuba.

1 April 1895, its main leaders, **José Martí** and Maximo Gómez, landed with a small band of revolutionaries on the southern coast of Cuba. At the same time, Antonio Maceo – and his brother, José – landed with a small force on the north coast of Oriente province, to support the February uprising. However, for Martí and his fellow independence revolutionaries, this Second War of Independence produced an outcome that failed to meet their aspirations. Although Spanish control ended in 1898, it was replaced by a US military occupation, followed by the long-lasting dominating influence of the US.

Early actions

Although not a trained soldier, Martí took part in military actions. However, only six weeks into the war, on 19 May, Martí was killed in a Spanish ambush. As Martí was the rebels' most distinguished and respected civilian political leader, his death so early on in the rebellion was to have serious repercussions for the rebellion – and for Cuba itself – in the years to come. In part, this was because earlier divisions within the ranks of independence movement had already begun to re-emerge before Martí's death. In fact, Martí had already clashed with Maceo over the question of civilian control over military leaders. After Martí's death, Gómez and Maceo – although they saw the need for a political organisation that could obtain international recognition and military supplies – soon began to organise a revolutionary government closer to their views about the need for military leaders to have more independence.

In September 1895, rebel leaders formed a constituent assembly which then approved a constitution. Gómez and Maceo were able to get this to include a clause that made it clear that the civilian authorities could only intervene in military operations if 'absolutely necessary' to achieve important political ends. The constituent assembly then chose Salvador Cisneros Betancourt, a wealthy aristocrat who had fought in the First Independence War as president; while Tomás Estrada Palma (the last president of the Republic in 1878) was appointed as the foreign representative of the 'Republic in Arms'. Gómez was then appointed as commander-in-chief, with Maceo as second in command.

Ordinary Cubans – especially blacks – gave the rebels considerable support; as a result, the rebellion spread rapidly during 1895. By the end of the year, Gómez and Maceo commanded a force of more than 30,000 rebels – 80 per cent of them were black, and were referred to by white Spanish troops as the ***mambises***.

At this time, Spanish forces in Cuba numbered under 20,000. However, the number of black rebels strengthened the determination of some whites to remain under Spanish control, or to turn to the US: either option was seen as preventing Cuba becoming a black republic similar to that established much earlier in Haiti.

Despite Martí's early death, the rebels had considerable success. However, as in the First Independence War, divisions soon began to appear among rebel leaders: these were over the question of US involvement, and whether the rebel forces should take the war into the rich sugar lands of central and western Cuba. Unlike last time, however, Gómez and Maceo decided to take matters into their own hands. They quickly crossed the old *trocha* line in October 1895 and, by the end of the year, their forces were threatening Matanzas.

There were no serious battles, but many cane fields, mills and plantation houses were set on fire. This rebel strategy – of burning 'everything that could provide income to the enemy' – became known as *la tea* (torch or firelighter). Martínez-Campos was sent back by Spain as captain-general of Cuba, with extra troops. At first, he hoped he could – as in 1878 – bring an end to the rebellion by obtaining a political resolution. However, he soon realised that there was much more support for the rebels than in the First War.

Figure 5.7 Some of Maceo's *mambi* troops

KEY CONCEPTS QUESTION

Change and continuity: In what ways had the issues dividing the rebels in 1895–6 changed from the divisions that had emerged in the First War of Independence, and in what ways were they the same?

Valeriano Weyler (1838–1930)

He had fought in the First Independence War, and had been in the US during the American Civil War – while there, he had admired General Sherman's destruction of fields, railways and mansions in Georgia in 1864, which was designed to break the morale of civilians who supported the Confederate Army of the South.

By January 1896, rebel forces under Gómez marched to the outskirts of Havana itself, proving this war of independence to be much more successful than the first one. Martínez-Campos, who refused to resort to severe repression of the civilian population, resigned as captain-general and returned to Spain. Thus it seemed as though the rebels were on the point of total victory.

Spanish repression

However, the new captain-general sent out to replace him was General **Valeriano Weyler**. Unlike his predecessor, he was more than prepared to impose a harsh repression and to follow a scorched-earth policy in order to keep Cuba for Spain. Weyler was determined to push the rebel forces back to the east, behind the *trocha* constructed during the First Independence War. This was strengthened, and he also built a new one west of Havana, from Mariel to Majana. His actions forced the rebels to fight in the open, and Maceo's forces suffered many casualties in February 1896 as they tried to join up with Gómez's troops. Soon, Weyler had more than 60,000 troops at his disposal, and he also set up a communications system to give advance warning of rebel troop movements. Nonetheless, Maceo was able to join up with Gómez, and in March the rebel forces received fresh weapons delivered by Calixto García, who then took command of the entire eastern region.

However, Weyler then began a counterinsurgency strategy which made the Second Independence War infamous. This was the widespread use of concentration camps and strategic hamlets – both of these became techniques widely used in many 20th-century conflicts. Weyler had first used them in the First Independence War, but only

Cuba

on a limited scale. Now he was determined to make full use of this *recontrado* method of intimidating and controlling the civilian population. The idea was for the forcible removal of the populations from entire towns and villages in those areas where the rebels were active. These civilians would then be concentrated (*reconcentracion*) in centres that could be defended easily by his troops. This was designed to deprive the rebels of support and food. Ideally, these new population centres would be provided with food grown in special zones of cultivation. However, if this was not possible, then Weyler was prepared to accept that these *reconcentrados* might starve.

He also insisted that the entire population had to be registered – those refusing military orders were found guilty of treason and executed. The first concentration orders were issued in October 1896, in the western area of Pinar del Rio, where Maceo's forces were still active. However, his harsh methods were often unsuccessful as many civilians, rather than passively accept possible disease or even starvation in the concentration camps, decided to join the rebels in the mountains.

KEY CONCEPTS QUESTION

Significance: In what ways were Weyler's methods of repression important in aiding the independence rebels?

The rebels on the defensive

By the end of 1896, the rebels were facing real problems. Weyler had retaken control of the west; while, in the east, Gómez was once again having difficulties with the civilian leadership of the war. A particular problem was over the tactic of *la tea*, which increasingly angered the sugar and coffee plantation owners. The civilians also objected to Gómez promoting lower-middle-class and black people to officer appointments, simply on the basis of proven military skill. Instead, he was told, he should promote members of the white professional classes – even if they lacked military experience. To help him deal with this growing political crisis, Gómez ordered Maceo to come to the east to support him.

Maceo's forces had recently been reinforced by the arrival of a boatload of new recruits – including Francisco Gómez (the son of Máximo) – along with more weapons and ammunition. He managed to evade Weyler's new *trocha* and established his camp outside Havana. But there, in December 1896, he was surprised by a larger Spanish force, and was – along with Gómez's son – killed in a small skirmish. Maceo's death was a serious loss to the rebels – not only was he an extremely able military leader, but he was also very popular. However, the shock of Maceo's death led the civilian leaders to leave Gómez's military independence intact.

Weyler took advantage of Maceo's death to launch an attack on Gómez's forces. Almost 40,000 fresh Spanish troops were sent to central Cuba and, although Gómez's forces were outnumbered by about ten to one, they fought determinedly. Using guerrilla tactics, they not only eluded Weyler's main forces for some time, but carried out surprise attacks on Spanish columns, which inflicted heavy losses. As a result, by May 1897, Weyler's offensive had lost its momentum. Nonetheless – despite some victories by Calixto García – the Liberation Army seemed unable to launch a new offensive.

QUESTION

How did events in the Philippines help the struggle for independence in Cuba?

Spain's reaction

The Second Independence War had been extremely costly for Spain – more than 200,000 troops had been sent to Cuba since 1895. Furthermore, since August 1896, Spain had also faced another rebellion in the Philippines. With so many troops tied up in Cuba, Spain had been forced to open negotiations with the rebels in the Philippines and reach a compromise. In June 1897, a more liberal government came to power in Spain that decided to end hostilities against the Cuban rebels. Spain then granted dominion status (a form of home rule) to Cuba, and a 'home rule' government – under José María Gálvez, an Autonomist leader from the 1870s – was allowed to come to power in Cuba. Weyler was outraged and resigned in protest. In January 1898, the *peninsulares* began organising violent demonstrations in Havana against the new government.

Gómez – who knew that the 'home rulers' were a relatively small group – rejected the reforms and all offers of negotiations with Spain. The fighting thus continued, with the rebels determined to achieve complete independence from Spain. It seemed to many that the rebels would soon achieve this.

QUESTION

Why did Gómez refuse to negotiate with Spain about autonomy or 'home rule' for Cuba?

5.6 What was José Martí's role in the struggle for independence?

Although Martí was killed very early on in the Second War of Independence, he nonetheless played a significant role in forging a movement that, unlike the one behind the unsuccessful First Independence War, was finally able to achieve Cuban independence.

He also continued to act as an inspiration for those Cuban movements that, during the 20th century, struggled against US domination of Cuba.

José Martí's early actions

With the bulk of Cuba's white independence leaders in exile after the end of the First War of Independence in 1878, it soon became apparent that unity between white and black needed to be restored within the independence movement if it was to have any chance of ending Spanish control. It was in these circumstances that José Martí became the main inspiration for and leader of Cuba's later independence movement. When Cuba's First Independence War broke out in 1868, he was still at school in Havana but quickly helped set up a newspaper called *Patria Libre*, which supported the rebels. As a result, he was arrested by the *voluntarios* and sentenced to six years in prison but, in 1871, he was exiled to Spain. From 1875, he travelled through Europe before living in Mexico and then Guatemala. His time there, and his study of the role of Maximo Gómez in the First Independence War, made him convinced that a civilian democracy, not a military *caudillo* (dictator), should be the way forward for Cuba.

SOURCE A

The hands of every nation must remain free, for the untrammelled development of the country, in accordance with its distinctive nature and its individual elements.

Extract from various writings by Martí in 1891. Quoted in H. Thomas (2001), *Cuba, or the Pursuit of Freedom*, London: Picador, p. 301.

Although he spent most of his life in exile in the US, Martí was a firm believer that Cuba should achieve its independence from Spain on its own, and he was strongly opposed to any union with the US – which he later came to see as the 'monster' because of its determination to dominate and control countries in the Americas.

SOURCE B

Crucial to the realization of these goals [sovereignty and social justice] is the work of Jose Marti (Cuba's national hero)… Marti's thinking was decisively shaped by his experience in the United States. His observations of the US political system inured him against multi-party arrangements and the politics that ensued. His succinct summarization of the system was:

'Elections are quite costly. The capitalists and the large companies help the needy candidates with their campaign expenses; once the candidates are elected, they pay with their slavish vote for the money which the capitalists lay out in advance.'

I. Saney (2004), *Cuba: A Revolution in Motion*, London: Zed Books, pp. 46–7.

After the Pact of Zanjon, he was able to return to Cuba from exile and quickly joined, along with Juan Gualberto Gómez, the Cuban Revolutionary Committee (CRC) that had been set up by Calixto García in New York. However, he was again sent into exile in Spain for his part in planning the Guerra Chiquita in 1879.

Martí's years of exile

He quickly travelled back, via Venezuela, to New York in 1881, where he stayed for fifteen years and began planning to re-launch Cuba's independence movement. While in Venezuela, his earlier sympathy for black slaves and indigenous peoples was confirmed by what he saw. He was also determined that an independent Cuba should avoid a form of government that saw the military, wealthy white landowners and the church join together to dominate the rest of the population.

Once in New York, he was soon appointed as president of the CRC, and in July 1882 sent an outline of his views to Gómez and Maceo, who were both in exile in Honduras. Although he had no immediate plans of renewing the military struggle, he worked hard – via meetings and journalism – to unite the Cuban exiles behind an independence movement that rejected both Spain and the US, and a Cuba where there would be racial harmony. In 1884, Gómez and Maceo came to New York – but their insistence that the independence struggle be controlled by military commanders rather than civilians led to Martí temporarily abandoning some of his political work.

However, he continued to see expressions of US sympathy for Cuba as just a mask for the fact that powerful groups in the US were simply looking for ways to add Cuba to their 'empire'. In 1887, at a meeting in New York to celebrate the nineteenth anniversary of the Grito de Yara, he began to resume his political activities within the independence movement as, by then, most had come to accept his insistence on the need for civilian control of the movement. He contacted Gómez again, asking him to get involved – although Gómez was generally supportive, neither he nor Martí thought a new independence war could be launched just then. In particular, this was because Cuban society was still divided on racial lines, and many wealthy plantation owners still looked to annexation by the US as the preferred option.

The Cuban Revolutionary Party

For Martí, awareness of these divisions led him to conclude that only the ordinary people of Cuba could achieve real independence. For that, he came to believe that the Cuban nation needed one political party that would be dedicated to the vast majority of Cubans – and especially for the ordinary working classes. This party was his Cuban Revolutionary Party, which he formed in January 1892. He thus explicitly rejected a political system in which different political parties would vie for votes, with the main aim of keeping themselves in power, rather than working in the interests of ordinary Cubans. The political experience of Cuba from 1902 to 1959 meant that many increasingly disenchanted Cubans began to return to Martí's ideas many decades after his death.

SOURCE C

The Cuban Revolutionary Party does not aim to deliver to Cuba a victorious group of people who look on the island as their prey and property, but to prepare, through every effective means afforded us by the freedom we have found abroad, the war we must wage for the dignity and wellbeing of all Cubans, and to deliver to Cubans a liberated homeland.

Extract from Article 5 of the Cuban Revolutionary Party. Quoted in Havana Times, 20 January 2014.

Another reason for setting up his Cuban Revolutionary Party was to avoid dependence on a small number of wealthy donors who tried to use their money to limit the more radical aspects of the new independence movement. Instead, individual members of the new party were to contribute 10 per cent of their earnings. With this change, he was able to persuade both Gómez and Maceo to re-join the movement – as both had, during the First Independence War, resented the more cautious approach of the landowners. Martí then quickly ensured that Gómez was appointed overall military commander.

> **QUESTION**
>
> What were the main reasons for Martí setting up the Cuban Revolutionary Party in the way he did?

Planning the Second War of Independence

To plan for the next attempt at achieving Cuban independence, he then gave up all his paid employment, and devoted himself full-time to raising funds and preparing for what, in April 1895, became the Second Independence War.

However, the rebels' plans suffered a severe setback on 14 January 1895, when US authorities seized the ships and weapons which were just about to go to Cuba, to launch three simultaneous expeditions to Cuba. Martí had hoped that, by doing this, a long-drawn-out war could be avoided, which he feared would lead to the emergence of military *caudillos*, the destruction of economic assets and, especially, US intervention.

With the prospects of surprise attacks, a mass rebellion and a quick victory now dashed, Martí desperately gathered together new supplies, and then travelled to the Dominican Republic to meet up with Gómez. There, on 25 March, they issued their first political manifesto, the Manifesto of Montecristo, proclaiming how the new Cuban Republic would be won and run by whites and blacks acting in unison. The Manifesto was adopted, along with the slogan: '*La Victoria o el Sepulcro!*' ('Victory or the tomb!'). As well as wanting Cuban independence, he was very aware of the threat the US posed: not just to Cuban independence, but also to the independence of other states in the region.

Theory of Knowledge

History and the role of individuals:
'The history of the world is but the biography of great men' (Thomas Carlyle, 1795–1881). How significant do you think Martí's role was in achieving Cuban independence? Are there any factors you think were more important?

SOURCE D

[It is my duty] … to prevent, by the independence of Cuba, the United States from spreading over the West Indies and falling, with that added weight, upon other lands of our America. All I have done up to now, and shall do hereafter, is to that end… I have lived inside the monster and know its insides.

Extract from a letter sent by Martí the day before he was killed. Quoted in American People, 15 March 2008, http://americanpeople2.blogspot.co.uk/2008/03/jos-marti-cuban-revolution-ary-party.html.

5.7 Why did the independence movement succeed?

Cuban independence was finally achieved: not just by the rebels, but also by a combination of internal and external factors.

The impact of the First War of Independence

Not surprisingly, the ten years of war from 1868 to 1878 had several significant impacts on Cuba – the main ones being economic and political. These were to play important roles in the outbreak of the Second War of Independence in 1895, which finally succeeded in ending Spanish rule.

Economic impact of the First Independence War

The destruction of many sugar mills in the east led to more modern technologies and machinery being introduced – the same happened in the west, where many large *hacendados* began to build larger and more efficient mills, even though they had not suffered any significant damage during the war. In addition, many of those who had suffered big losses or could not afford to invest in larger sugar mills, became *colonos* (planters) who sold their sugar to the mills. In many cases, owners were forced to sell their lands and sugar mills – increasingly often these were bought up at very low prices by US investors and businesses. From 1878 onwards, US economic penetration of Cuba became increasingly significant, and the US soon came to displace Spain as the economic focus of Cuba's sugar trade.

The following table shows Cuban sugar exports to Spain and the US, 1850–96 (figures are in million pesos).

	1850	1860	1890
Spain	7	21	7
USA	28	40	61

As a consequence, there were many wealthy US businesses that were increasingly keen for the US government to take a greater interest in developments in Cuba.

However, these developments made the Cuban sugar industry – and the Cuban economy in general – very dependent on developments in the US. One factor behind the Second Independence War was the decision by the US government in 1894 to put tariffs on sugar imports. Very quickly, Cuban sugar exports to the US dropped from 800,000 tons in 1895 to just over 225,000 tons in 1896. By then, Cuba's sugar industry was already struggling – in part because of increased international competition. These economic problems helped create a political and social atmosphere favourable to a new rebellion.

Political impact of the First War of Independence

The most significant political impacts of the First War of Independence in Cuba over the next twenty years were the rise and fall of the Autonomist Party; and the growing influence of Jose Martí and his Cuban Revolutionary Party (see Section 5.6, The Cuban Revolutionary Party).

A few months after the end of the First Independence War, leading reformists, along with many Cubans wanting to see a rapid process of reconstruction and the restoration of prosperity, met in Havana to found the liberal Autonomist Party. Their aim was to achieve autonomy for Cuba by peaceful means. Those who wanted independence were opposed to this party – but so, too, were most *peninsulares* who were essentially conservatives, and who feared autonomy would soon lose them influence and lead, eventually, to independence.

Initially, the divisions among independence veterans and the immediate prospects of reform being allowed by Spain gave the *autonomistas* some significant support. Their achievements over the next twenty years, however, were limited. While Spain did eventually abolish slavery in 1886 and grant some political rights to Cubans, significant inequalities remained – and many liberals were angered in 1890 when Spain specifically excluded Cuba from the universal suffrage proclaimed in that year. Further Spanish promises of reforms and greater autonomy in 1893 were resisted by the *peninsulares* and disbelieved by many Cubans. By then, the Autonomist Party was seriously weakened and many Cubans gave their support to Martí's new Cuban Revolutionary Party, which campaigned for full independence.

Yet, despite the failure of the First Independence War, it had strengthened those feelings of a collective Cuban identity which had begun to emerge in the early 19th century – by 1878, a clear national consciousness had emerged among many Cubans. Memories of Cuban heroes and victories – and of acts of Spanish brutality – stirred up nationalist and patriotic feelings, which would remain strong in many Cubans. Although those opposed to independence would continue to warn of a race war similar to what had happened in Haiti, the independence struggle had shown that most blacks were more than willing to join whites in a common struggle. Ultimately, it proved to be an important example and inspiration for the next movement that did, finally, achieve independence for Cuba. In many ways, this First War of Independence was just the first battle in an on-going

KEY CONCEPTS QUESTIONS

Causation and consequence: Why did US ownership of land and business assets in Cuba increase after the First War of Independence?

What were the main consequences of these developments for Cuba?

thirty-year war for independence, which didn't come to an end until 1898, when US intervention finally ended Spanish rule in Cuba.

However, this First Independence War resulted in most *peninsulares* fearing an independent Cuba and thus strengthened their determination to support continued Spanish rule. In addition, the brutal actions of pro-authority 'killer battalions' of *peninsulares* against the rebels led to the emergence of a tradition of violent resistance to authority, that was an important characteristic of all later Cubans rebellions – including the Second War of Independence.

The role of the US

Ironically, the role played by the US – which had had an interest in Cuba for many decades – was one of the most significant reasons why Cuba's independence movement was eventually successful in ending Spanish rule.

The US and Cuba, 1800–50

The US had had a significant interest in Latin America and the Caribbean – and especially in Cuba – since the early 19th century. As Spain lost its colonies on the Latin and Central American mainland in the early 1820s, the US began to take a greater interest in developments in Cuba. In fact, ever since 1776, groups within the US had begun to consider what actions the US should take in relation to Cuba.

In April 1823, US secretary of state John Quincy Adams made it clear that the US should not allow Britain – or any other foreign power – to replace Spanish control with their own. In October, former US president Thomas Jefferson wrote to US president James Monroe, about the value of the US acquiring one or more of the Spanish provinces in the Americas. In particular, he discussed the pros and cons of either annexing Cuba, or 'allowing' it to become independent. His ideas were later enshrined in the Monroe Doctrine, which was announced to the US Congress on 2 December 1823. This declared that the US had the right to 'oversee' the Americas.

Thirty-year war for independence: because of US domination of Cuba after 1898, many Cubans believe true independence wasn't achieved in Cuba until the Cuban Revolution of 1959.

Fact: These *voluntarios* were funded by Spanish merchants, landowners and slave traders – i.e. those groups which had long dominated Cuba's institutions. These volunteer militia quickly expanded – before long, numbers had risen from 10,000 to possibly as many as 70,000 men. They were undisciplined and often devoted more time to punishment, reprisals and repression than to fighting the rebels, which was mainly left to the regular Spanish troops. In many towns, they rounded up those believed to sympathise with the aims of the rebels and executed them without trial.

Fact: When the US acquired Spanish Florida in 1821, the discussions about Cuba, and Spain's other possessions in the region, soon came to be linked with questions of the 'national security' of the US.

Fact: When US governments considered what should and should not be allowed to happen in Central and Latin America and the Caribbean, they did not acknowledge that the US itself was also a 'foreign power' in the region – albeit a North American one.

SOURCE E

These islands are natural appendages of the North American continent, and one of them [Cuba] – almost in sight of our shores – from a multitude of considerations has become an object of transcendent importance to the commercial and political interests of our Union… Cuba, forcibly disjoined from its own unnatural connection with Spain, and incapable of self-support, can gravitate only towards the North American Union.

Extract from a letter sent by John Quincy Adams to the US minister in Madrid, 23 April 1823. Quoted in: R. Gott (2005), *Cuba: A New History*, New Haven: Yale Nota Bene, p. 58.

SOURCE F

The intellectual father of Manifest Destiny, John Quincy Adams, predicted that Cuba would eventually drop into US hands by the laws of 'political gravitation' just as 'an apple severed by a tempest from its native tree cannot but choose to fall to the ground'. By the end of the century, the laws of political gravitation had come to apply, as Adams had predicted.

N. Chomsky (2010), *Hopes and Prospects*, London: Penguin Books, p. 49.

For the time being, however, the question of Cuba lay relatively dormant in US politics. It re-emerged in the 1840s, following the **US invasion of Mexico** in 1846, and its annexation of half its territory at the end of 1847. This was confirmed by the Treaty of Guadalupe Hidalgo in February 1848, with the US giving Mexico financial compensation for the **loss of its territories**.

The success of its war against Mexico led to renewed interest in the US for further 'imperial' expansion. Several people in the US spoke of either purchasing Cuba from Spain, or sending a military force to simply take the island, along the lines of the USA's invasion of Mexican territory. One such was Cristóbal Mádan, a wealthy Cuban planter living in exile in New York. By then, the US had become Cuba's main trading partner – the vast majority of Cuba's sugar was exported to the US, while the US supplied most of Cuba's manufactured imports. In addition to sugar, Cuba also exported large quantities of its tobacco, coffee and cocoa. These close economic links between the US and Cuba continued to strengthen after 1845. In addition, a growing number of US citizens settled in Cuba; while Cuba's exiles – such as Mádan – increasingly chose the US rather than European countries as their preferred destination.

In 1848, US president James Polk offered Spain $100 million for Cuba; in 1854, US president Franklin Pierce increased this to $130 million. Both offers were rejected by Spain; but, significantly, US ambassadors advised that, should Spain continue to refuse, the US would be 'justified' in simply taking the island from Spain if the US had the military strength to do so. Initially, the US government did not think a possible war against Spain was viable.

The US and Cuba's Second War of Independence

Initially, US president Grover Cleveland believed the interests of US businesses were best served by Spain remaining in control of Cuba – as Spain paid compensation for damage done to US-owned properties. However, almost from the beginning, Weyler's methods of counterinsurgency were reported outside Cuba by Cuban exiles and US journalists. *The New York Journal* – a jingoistic newspaper, owned by William Randolph Hearst – in particular gave considerable hostile coverage to Weyler's methods. In addition, US businesses were coming to the view that Spain was no longer able to protect their properties in Cuba – so they began to call for US intervention and annexation. Soon, US politicians began to argue either for US intervention to set up an 'independent' Cuban government acceptable to US interests or for outright US annexation. President Cleveland had tried to get Spain to negotiate over Cuba in April 1896, but Spain had rejected the offer. Almost immediately, the US Office of Naval Intelligence asked for war plans to be drawn up against Spain.

Nonetheless, in the 1896 presidential elections, Cleveland was accused by the press of doing nothing about Cuba and, in the atmosphere created by further reports of Spanish brutality in Cuba, the election resulted in the victory of the Republican candidate, William McKinley. Unlike his Democrat opponent, William Jennings Bryan (who was against US intervention in Cuba), McKinley was very much in favour of intervention. He appointed the openly expansionist Theodore Roosevelt as assistant secretary of the navy and told the US ambassador to Spain to warn that, if they did not end the war in Cuba, the US would act unilaterally.

The *Maine* incident, February 1898

Hearst had done much, via his papers, to stir up public opinion – and pressure the US government – to support US intervention in the Cuban Independence War. Other

US invasion of Mexico: in 1821, Mexico had gained independence from Spain. During 1835–6, US landowners in Texas – which had been part of Mexico – had fought a war of independence, which became known as the Texas Revolution. In 1836, Mexico had been forced to accept the independence of the new Republic of Texas. Then, in 1845, Texas accepted the US offer of annexation. However, the 1836 treaty had not specified exactly where the border between Texas and Mexico was to be. Disputes over this border issue led, in 1846, to the US–Mexican War, which lasted from 1846 to 1848. In February 1848, the Treaty of Guadalupe Hidalgo ended the war.

Loss of territories: Mexico was forced to accept its loss of New Mexico, California and Texas (and several other states) to the US.

QUESTION

Why was the war against Mexico significant as regards US policy towards Cuba?

Cuba

Fact: That the incident was, after all, an accident was first seriously suggested in 1910. Then, in the 1970s, US Admiral Hyman Rickover examined the evidence and concluded that it was the result of an internal coal fire, in a bunker next to the magazine, which had caused the explosion. He stated that similar fires – although not so serious – had previously occurred on other US ships.

Volunteer forces: these included Theodore Roosevelt's 'Rough Riders' (also known as 'Teddy's Terrors'). Officially, they were the First US Volunteer Cavalry. They were commanded by General Leonard Wood, who later became the ruler of Cuba following Spain's defeat. They received much publicity because both Theodore Roosevelt and William Hearst fought with them – and Hearst made sure their exploits were widely reported back in the US in his papers.

Fact: US senator Henry Cabot Lodge was an early supporter of US intervention in Cuba in 1898 – in one speech, he praised the USA's record of 'conquest, colonization and territorial expansion' so far in the 19th century, and argued that it should 'not be curbed now'.

newspapers, in competition with Hearst, had done the same. Their opportunity came on 15 February 1898, when the US battleship *Maine* was blown up in Havana harbour, killing 258 US sailors. Theodore Roosevelt blamed the Spanish authorities and placed the navy on full alert, while the press said the disaster had been because of a Spanish mine. The US government later held an official inquiry, which confirmed the view that Spain was to blame. Spain, however, claimed it was an accidental internal explosion and nothing to do with them. Despite this, and urged on by the press, the US government insisted on negotiations with Spain.

The *Maine* incident stirred up public opinion in the US, and the slogan 'Remember the *Maine*!' soon led to a rush to join **volunteer forces** and regular US army units.

The US government portrayed its role relating to Cuba in 1898 as a 'humanitarian intervention', intended to liberate Cuba from Spanish repression. However, according to historian Louis Perez, the Cubans' guerrilla forces had just about defeated the Spanish troops by the time the US decided to intervene.

SOURCE G

[The US military campaign] was ostensibly against Spain, but in fact [was] against Cubans… The intervention changed everything, as it was meant to. A Cuban war of liberation was transformed into a US war of conquest.

L. Perez (1998), *The War of 1898*, Chapel Hill, NC: University of North Carolina Press. Quoted in N. Chomsky (2010), *Hopes and Prospects*, London: Penguin Books, p. 50.

With Gómez refusing to call off the war of liberation, Spain was in a very difficult position, even before the *Maine* incident. Spain's desperation is shown by the fact that the authorities in Cuba even suggested to Gómez, three days before the US declared war, that they join forces against the impending US invasion – even promising to supply him with weapons.

This Spanish offer was rejected by Gómez for several reasons – one of which was that he (unlike Martí and Maceo) did not think a US intervention would necessarily be bad for Cuba's independence. The attitude of Calixto García, the commander of the rebel forces in Oriente, was also unclear. He had had little warning about the imminence of US intervention and, when it happened, wasn't sure of how to react. In the end, he made a pragmatic decision on the spot to help the US forces, as he concluded that the US would respect Cuban sovereignty. Maso, the rebels' political leader, actually welcomed the prospect of US intervention, and saw it as allowing Martí's Cuban independence aims to be finally achieved. Before too long, however, they had all come to regret their passive or active acceptance of US intervention that, as Leonard Wood stated in a letter, would start a new era for US foreign policy: not just with Cuba but, more importantly, with the rest of the world.

Although other European nations pleaded for a peaceful resolution, the US decided to declare war on Spain on 25 April. The US military command was then told to prepare for invasion – not just of Cuba, but also of Spain's other colonies in the

Caribbean and even in the Pacific. Thus Puerto Rico, the Philippines and Guam all became targets for US annexations. Thus the war that began in 1898 was not the 'war of liberation' of Cuba that had been talked about earlier in the US for some time. In fact, **Elihu Root**, who was Secretary of War from 1899 to 1904, later stated that, as regards Cuba, 'we intend to rule and that is all there is to it'.

The Teller Amendment

In deciding their attitude to the possibility of US intervention, many rebel leaders, and many ordinary Cubans, had been influenced by the Teller Amendment, which had been added to the declaration of war in April 1898, and ratified by the US Congress. This stated that the US occupation of Cuba should not be 'permanent'. This Amendment had been pushed for by Cuban exiles, and was seen as a clear rejection by the US of any imperialist intentions as regards Cuba.

SOURCE H

The United States hereby disclaims any disposition or intention to exercise sovereignty, jurisdiction or control over [Cuba] except for pacification thereof, and asserts its determination, when that is accomplished, to leave the government and control of the island to its people.

Extract from the Teller Amendment. Taken from www.loc.gov/rr/hispanic/1898/teller.html.

As soon became clear, however, US policy in Cuba turned out to be more than a disinterested humanitarian action, designed simply to help liberate a neighbouring people from colonial repression.

The Spanish–American War, 1898

The first serious actions of the war took place not in Cuba, but in the Philippines in May 1898, when the US destroyed Spain's Pacific fleet in Manila Bay, and then, in August, when it occupied Manila itself – these steps turned out to be just the first steps in what became a bloody invasion of the Philippines, which was fiercely resisted by various nationalist groups. By then, however, the US had turned its attentions to Cuba.

When the war began, Spain sent its Atlantic fleet to the Caribbean to defend Cuba. It arrived in May and based itself in the bay of Santiago de Cuba – but was then kept there for more than a month by a large US fleet. This allowed a small force of US troops to land and link up with Cuban rebels. The bulk of US forces, some 15,000 strong and under the command of General William Shafter, began landing near Santiago on 22 June. These US armed forces were instructed to do nothing to recognise any Cuban political authority. While rebel forces could be aided and used, this was only to be on a limited scale and for military purposes only.

There was little Spanish resistance, and Shafter's quickly force met up with almost 5,000 rebel troops, including 3,000 led by Calixto García. Almost from the beginning, the US commanders concluded that García's forces, which controlled most of Oriente province, were the most significant of the rebel army and, although Gómez did receive some supplies, their communications with Gómez and other

Elihu Root (1845–1937)
As secretary of war under US presidents William McKinley (1899–1901) and Theodore Roosevelt (1901–4), Root played a big part in drawing up the terms under which the US would rule the new colonial possessions it had acquired following its defeat of Spain in 1898. He was in charge of the brutal suppression of an independence movement in the Philippines, and for the Platt Amendment of 1901, which stated the US had the right to intervene in Cuba in the future, in order to maintain 'stable government'.

Historical debate:
Historians such as Perez and Saney are convinced that, by the time the US intervened in Cuba in 1898, the rebel forces were on the point of victory. Carry out some additional research on this issue, and then decide which interpretations you find most plausible.

Cuba

SOURCE I

With the mambises – Cuban liberation fighters – on the verge of victory, the United States, with a keen eye on its economic and strategic interests, intervened. At the defeat of Spain, Washington extracted a peace treaty 'that effectively transferred sovereignty over Cuba to the United States'. Thus, a period of American domination of Cuba was initiated, lasting until the triumph of the Cuban Revolution in 1959. During this six-decade period, Cuban economics and politics were controlled by US corporate and financial interests.

I. Saney (2004), *Cuba: A Revolution in Motion*, London: Zed Books, p. 9.

---

rebel leaders were virtually non-existent. The US was helped in their refusal to recognise the rebel government by the fact that Garcia and Gómez had increasingly ignored the civilian branch of the 'Republic in Arms' – something that Martí had tried so hard to prevent.

However, relations between the two military forces were somewhat strained – in large part because the mostly white US soldiers were disconcerted by the fact that most of the Cuban insurgents were black. On 1 July, the Battle of Luma San Juan took place. This was the only significant land battle involving US troops of the entire US intervention in Cuba: more than 3,000 US troops faced fewer than 1,000 Spanish defenders. Despite this, the US troops – which included Roosevelt's 'Rough Riders' – took a whole day to overcome the defenders. This was despite the fact that US commanders had asked Calixto García to take his 3,000 soldiers to create diversions, to prevent Spanish troops in other garrisons from coming to the aid of the besieged Spanish forces in Santiago. Once taken, the US military authorities refused to allow rebel forces to enter the city.

Although there were a few more clashes after 1 July, the land war in Cuba was over in less than three weeks. It is thus difficult to deny the fact that the defeat of Spanish forces in Cuba probably owed more to the three years of war waged by Cuban rebels than to the short-lived US intervention.

With Santiago in US hands, the Spanish admiral decided to leave the harbour of Santiago, so that he would not suffer the fate of Spain's Pacific fleet. But when they sailed out on 3 July, they were met by the US fleet, which inflicted heavy losses on the Spanish ships. By 17 July, Spain had agreed surrender terms – by then, Spain had been defeated in Manila and the US had already occupied Puerto Rico. Significantly, the flag that was raised over the governor's palace in Santiago was the US flag, not the Cuban one. Even more significantly, US General Wood – not one of the rebel leaders – took over as the city's new governor.

This Spanish–American War was ended by the Treaty of Paris, signed on 10 December 1898 – significantly, as far as Cuba was concerned, there were no Cuban representatives present. The terms of the treaty saw the US take possession of several Spanish colonies: Cuba and Puerto Rico in the Americas, and the Philippines and Guam in the Pacific. In return, the US paid Spain compensation of $20 million for the loss of its former colonies.

QUESTION

Does the Battle of Luma San Juan show that the US intervention was not really necessary, as far as achieving Cuban independence was concerned?

Fact: Despite the years of insurgency, Cuban troops were not allowed by the US commanders to take part in the victory celebrations that took place later. To the rebels, it seemed that just as they were about to secure independence for Cuba, their victory had been taken away by the US.

End of unit activities

1 Reread the accounts above of the First and Second Wars of Independence. Then produce a chart summarising the way these two independence struggles show continuity and/or change as regards methods and outcomes.

2 Find out more about Maximo Gómez and Antonio Maceo. Then write a couple of paragraphs to explain their contributions to the struggle for Cuban independence.

3 Carry out some additional research on the *Maine* incident. How important do you think this was in leading to US intervention, in comparison to other factors?

KEY QUESTIONS

- What political challenges did Cuba face after independence?
- What economic and social challenges did independent Cuba face after 1902?
- How did Cuba's governments respond to these challenges after 1902?

Overview

- Although Spain no longer ruled Cuba after 1898, the island was not independent. Instead, for the next four years, Cuba was under US military rule – with US General Wood as its governor.
- As well as disbanding the rebel army, the US then began to create a political system for Cuba, based on the US model.
- Although Cuba became nominally independent in 1902, when US forces withdrew, the Platt Amendment of 1901 – which the Cubans had to incorporate in their new 'independence' constitution – gave the US the right to intervene militarily to ensure 'stability'. This angered many Cuban nationalists.
- For the next twenty years, Cuban politics was dominated by corruption and electoral fraud – sometimes resulting in armed uprisings by the parties that felt they had been cheated out of victory.
- At the same time, US investments in Cuba greatly increased, and the Cuban economy became closely tied to that of the US.
- In order to protect these economic assets, the US used the terms of the Platt Amendment to send troops back into Cuba on three occasions between 1902 and 1925. For many Cubans, such developments seriously undermined Cuban independence.

5.8 What political challenges did Cuba face after independence?

Although Cuban nationalist forces had played a crucial part in the defeat of Spanish forces in Cuba by 1898, they were not the ones who shaped the nature of the new political regime that was to replace Spanish rule in

Cuba. Instead, this process was carried out by the US and, for the next four years, Cuba was ruled by what was effectively a US military dictatorship.

The US military government, 1898–1902

The US administration, as it only talked to the white élites – the majority of whom favoured annexation by the US – was convinced a long US occupation would be popular with Cubans. Despite the Teller Amendment, US President McKinley told Congress in December that US forces would continue to occupy Cuba until there was no unrest and a 'stable' government was established.

Establishing US control

General John Brooke initially took over as the first US governor of Cuba; then, in December 1898, he was replaced by General Wood – like Brooke, he believed the US should stay in control of Cuba for many years. One of the first steps taken by the US occupation forces was to disband the Cuban rebel force that, by 1898, numbered 33,000. In part, this was because of US fears that the rebel forces might eventually turn against Cuba's 'liberators'. So, in May 1899, the rebel Liberation Army was disbanded, with $75 being paid to all rebels who handed in their weapons. This removed the only potential source of serious opposition to US rule and influence. The US authorities then set up the **Rural Guard**, a paramilitary force intended to deal with the problem of banditry after the war. The US administration appointed an almost exclusively white officer corps, and introduced racial segregation in the ranks – this angered former rebels.

Political settlement

Elihu Root began to work on an electoral system for Cuba that would ensure the victory of those Cuban whites who favoured the option of US annexation. Root's aim was to create a system that, by excluding ordinary people, would avoid an outcome that might conflict with US plans and interests. So a limited franchise was drawn up which gave the vote to men over the age of twenty-one who were either able to read and write or who owned property worth at least $250. Very reluctantly, Root also included Cuban males who had fought in the rebel army. In all, some 100,000 men were entitled to vote – the poor, most blacks and all women were denied the vote. In June 1900, municipal elections were held – the small number of voters choosing from three parties: the Republican Party, the Cuban Nationalist Party and the Democratic Union Party. The first two favoured outright independence; the Democratic Unionists (which included several supporters of the old Autonomist Party), however, were a conservative group that favoured annexation by the US.

Despite this carefully drawn-up franchise, the parties favouring independence won – General Wood was appalled by this 'wrong' result. Root, however, was less concerned – his main object was that the blacks should be kept out of the political process, in case Cuba went the way of Haiti and Santo Domingo and produced a black republic. He thus instructed Wood to begin to prepare Cuba for independence – but to ensure that, after the transfer of power, the US was still left with considerable control. In particular, Root pointed out that, since the 1820s, the US had been determined that no foreign power – other than Spain – should control Cuba. This, he stated in 1901, should remain the aim for the 20th century – even if Cuba demanded its right to independence. The task, as he saw it, was to ensure US control until such time as elections produced a 'better' result: i.e. a Cuban government that, according to US definitions, would be 'stable'.

Fact: Fears of instability were not unfounded – in 1899, Emilio Aguinaldo, the Filipino leader who had become a hero in the struggle against the Spanish in the Philippines, rebelled against US forces that had occupied the islands after the Treaty of Paris. Furthermore, it soon became apparent to the US authorities in Cuba that nationalist feelings remained strong after 1898. Although García died in 1899, Gómez remained popular and came to oppose the US military occupation of Cuba.

The Rural Guard: provided employment for the many rebels who found it hard to find jobs after the war. However, not all US officers approved of the way the Guard was established. General James Wilson, a more progressive officer, worried they would lead to the emergence of an eventual military dictatorship in Cuba – similar to those that had already appeared in other parts of the Americas.

QUESTION

Why did the US authorities draw up such a limited franchise for Cuba after 1898?

5

The Cuban constitution

To achieve this, Root ensured the new republican constitution for Cuba would include guarantees that would bind Cuba closely to the US. In particular, he wanted the US to have veto powers over Cuba's foreign, defence and economic policies. He also wanted the US to have the 'right of intervention' if it considered that either Cuban independence or 'stable government' were under what the US saw as a 'threat' or a 'breakdown of order'.

In September 1900, elections were held for a Cuban Constitutional Convention that, in November, began to draw up a new constitution – modelled on that of the US – and to determine US–Cuban relations. Many Cubans saw this as an election that would finally result in genuine independence for Cuba. However, in January 1901, once a constitution had been drawn up, General Wood then presented the US demands that Root had drafted. Many of the delegates were appalled at the severe restriction on Cuban sovereignty these conditions would impose.

The Platt Amendment

Although Cuba sent a delegation to see Root in the US to protest against these terms, US demands remained and were achieved by the **Platt Amendment**; this had been adopted by the US Congress in March 1901, and was finally incorporated into 'independent' Cuba's constitution, which came into effect in 1902.

The main points of the Platt Amendment gave the US oversight of Cuba's public finances, the right to intervene in Cuba, and the right to establish military bases on

QUESTION

What is the figure on the right of the cartoon in Figure 5.8 meant to represent?

Figure 5.8 A Cuban cartoon commenting on the implications of the Platt Amendment for Cuba's independence. *'El hierro'* refers to the branding iron

Cuba. Many Cubans who had shared Martí's view of independence – both from Spain and the US – saw it as reducing Cuba's independence to nothing more than a myth. Many others, however, reluctantly accepted it as a less worse outcome than continued US military occupation.

The Republic of Cuba 1902

The 'independent' Republic of Cuba was officially proclaimed on 20 May 1902, and its first president – elected unopposed on 31 December 1901 – was Tomás Estrada Palma. He represented the Moderate Party, but was backed by the Republican Liberal Party (headed by José Miguel Gómez) and the National Liberal Party (led by Alfredo Zayas). Maximo Gómez, a strong supporter of independence, refused to stand; while Bartolome Maso, strongly opposed to the Platt Amendment – and more popular than Estrada – withdrew after Wood had deliberately rigged the electoral commission to ensure Estrada's victory.

Most of Cuba's small white élite backed Estrada, who was a Cuban-born US citizen who was happy to have a close relationship between Cuba and the US. In fact, Estrada favoured **outright annexation** by the US. In this, he was typical of much of the Cuban élite who, by 1902, saw little advantage for themselves within a genuinely independent Cuba. It was people like them who provided most of the leading politicians and administrators in the early years of the Republic of Cuba. Nonetheless, once Estrada had been installed as president, the US flag was replaced by the new Cuban flag, and the US began to withdraw its troops from Cuba.

Politics in the republic, 1902–6

From the very start, a serious political problem in the new Republic of Cuba was that of corruption, which had often been the norm under Spanish control. Because jobs in the state sector provided income for many thousands of people – at a time when unemployment in Cuba was a problem – and because such jobs were distributed by whichever party won the election, electoral fraud quickly became widespread.

Corruption and electoral fraud, 1902–6

Under Spanish and then US rule, Cubans had had no experience in self-government or of party discipline before 1902; for many, politics was just a way of obtaining economic advantage in various ways. Although Estrada took some steps to reduce corruption, little actually changed. One example was related to the compensation for veterans of the Independence War. Instead of the land that had been promised, the Cuban government decided to raise a foreign loan in order to give the ex-combatants cash payments. But fraud and corruption ensured that many soldiers received very little – while some politicians became very rich.

During elections, the different political parties often placed their own armed guards outside polling stations to ensure their candidates won. Consequently, serious disputes developed after most elections – often, under the terms of the Platt Amendment, those aggrieved would call for US intervention. In February 1904, elections were held for the new National Congress – but electoral fraud was widespread, and the country was deeply divided between the centralist Conservative Republican Party (CRP) and the National Liberal Party, which supported local autonomy. The results showed the CRP had 'won' most seats, but the National Liberals refused to accept the results and withdrew

Platt Amendment: this set down seven conditions for the withdrawal of US troops from Cuba, and clearly showed the unequal nature of the relationship between Cuba and the US. At first, the Cuban constituent assembly rejected the Platt Amendment; and it was only adopted by fifteen votes to fourteen. In 1903, Cuba signed a Treaty of Relations with the US, which confirmed the seven guarantees set down in the Platt Amendment – this treaty remained in force until 1934 when, as part of Franklin Roosevelt's 'Good Neighbor' policy towards the Americas, the US agreed to remove three of the seven pledges. Both at the time, and subsequently, many Cubans deeply resented this serious and humiliating erosion of their independence, which essentially turned Cuba into a semi-colony or protectorate of the US.

Outright annexation: this attitude of Estrada and the Cuban élites meant they were not angered by later US encroachments on Cuban sovereignty. However, such attitudes – and subsequent US actions – soon revived interest in Martí's dream of a Cuba free from 'Yankee' dominance.

from the Congress. Then, in December 1905, there were presidential elections. Estrada – angered by the widespread corruption and backed by the US minister in Havana – put himself forward for re-election as the Moderate Party candidate; the Liberal Party put forward José Miguel Gómez as their candidate to oppose Estrada. The elections took place in an atmosphere of distrust and violence and, in view of the widespread rigging, Gómez withdrew from the contest, allowing Estrada to be returned unopposed.

The Liberals then organised an armed insurrection to remove the government. In August 1906, 24,000 rebels – many of them black – began a march on Havana. Several provincial leaders joined them in what became known as the Guerrita de Agosto (the August War). Faced with a rebellion of this size, Estrada was in a very weak position, as the US had ensured that Cuba had no standing army, while the Rural Guard numbered only about 3,000, and was moreover spread across the island. Thus, to ensure he was not overthrown, he appealed to the US for intervention. US president Theodore Roosevelt said he would only send troops if it looked like Cuba was going back to the chaos of the Independence Wars. So Estrada simply resigned and got his cabinet to do the same. With no effective government in Cuba to protect US investments there, the US somewhat reluctantly sent in 6,000 marines to establish 'peace and order' so that elections for a new government could be held. Charles Magoon, a US lawyer, was then appointed governor of Cuba.

QUESTION

Why was Cuban politics so often corrupt after 1902?

The Second US occupation, 1906–9

Magoon stayed to rule Cuba for three years, with much of the work overseen by US Colonel Enoch Crowder. Under Magoon's rule, the electoral, administrative and legal systems were reformed. The US also allowed Cuba to form a small professional army to help maintain order in the future. On 1 August 1908, under new rules drawn up mainly by the US and designed to limit electoral fraud, municipal and provincial elections took place – these were won by the new Conservative Party, which had largely been created by Magoon to replace the now-discredited Moderate Party. The Liberals were divided for these elections but, in the presidential elections held in November 1908, they united behind Gómez again and won the election – Gómez remained as president until 1913. Gómez, although respectful of democratic institutions and keen to avoid further US intervention, proved to be a very corrupt politician. Many politicians and administrators followed his example.

Nonetheless, on 28 March 1909, Magoon officially transferred power to the new president of Cuba, and US troops once again withdrew from Cuba. One effect of these regular appeals to the US by Cuba's white élites was to make clear the political differences between those élites and ordinary Cubans still loyal to Martí's vision of nationalism and independence.

5.9 What economic and social challenges did independent Cuba face after 1902?

Although the idea of Cuba being incorporated into the US remained popular with some US administrators in both Washington and Havana – as it did with most of the small white Cuban élite – concerns about the cost of occupation began to be raised. By

1902, the US had decided the time had come to 'give' Cuba its independence; so US occupation troops were gradually withdrawn. Nonetheless, the new republic of Cuba faced several problems in the period 1902–25.

The US and Cuba's economy

The Second War of Independence had pushed Cuba's economy almost to the point of collapse – 80 per cent of the sugar estates were in ruins, and the 1898 harvest (*zafra*) was only 60 per cent that of 1895. Additionally, communications were badly damaged, about 90 per cent of Cuba's cattle had been lost and the tobacco industry was virtually non-existent. However, within two years, the economy had begun to revive. The tobacco industry recovered quite quickly; but the sugar industry's revival was slower – in part, this was the result of US tariffs, as well as low international prices. As a result, despite significant US and British investments, the total sugar crop value in 1902 was still well below the level of 1894.

Although Brooke appointed white Cubans who had been exiles in the US to be ministers for several government departments, he made sure the Department of Customs was placed under US military control. After 1898, the Cuban economy was quickly dominated by US businesses. These did not limit themselves to taking over the bulk of Cuba's sugar and tobacco industries – they also began to take control of the railways, public utilities and minerals. As a result, a powerful business lobby quickly developed in the US, pushing for even closer commercial relations with Cuba. Thus as early as 1902, US president Roosevelt was suggesting a reciprocity treaty between the US and Cuba, on the basis that US interests would best be served by having 'control' of the Cuban market.

The economy

Despite the various political problems in the years after 1902, Cuba's economy experienced a significant recovery over most of the next twenty years. Continued US intervention, and closer economic ties with the US, were supported by US businesses and settlers who poured into Cuba after 1898, as well as by most of the white Cuban élite.

The Cuban–American Reciprocity Treaty, 1903

In December 1903, Cuba signed a reciprocity treaty with the US – this gave Cuban sugar preferential treatment in the US market, but it also reduced duties on US imports, which restricted industrial and manufacturing development in Cuba. This reciprocity treaty also did more to encourage even greater US investment in Cuba, thus tying the island's economy even closer to the US market. Large amounts of US money were invested in the sugar industry, the railways, the mining and tobacco industries, textile and other consumer-goods factories. As a result, sugar production rose from under 300,000 tons in 1900 to just over one million tons in 1905; while the cattle, tobacco and other industries also recovered quickly from the effects of the recent war.

The Cuban currency was made interchangeable with the US dollar, and Cuba's monetary policy was set by a US bank. By 1905, more than 13,000 US citizens had bought land in Cuba – soon, 60 per cent of rural properties were owned by US corporations or individuals. Those Cubans who could take advantage of the wealth such developments brought to Cuba in the early years of the republic were happy about this state of affairs.

Cuba

Impact of the First World War

Cuba's economy was also helped by the First World War, which broke out in 1914, because the war disrupted world supplies of sugar from European sugar beet – this led to a massive demand for Cuban sugar. In 1912 the price of sugar had been 1.96 cents per pound – the lowest since 1900; but, after 1914, the price of sugar rose steadily: from 1914 to 1916, income from sugar almost doubled. By 1920, it had reached a high of 23 cents per pound. To meet the new demand, land was purchased, peasants were evicted and forests were cut down – all to create more sugar plantations and mills. In addition, newer technologies were introduced. This rapid expansion of the Cuban economy helped Mario García Menocal, the Conservative president who ruled from 1913 to 1921. In 1915, he created a National Bank and issued a national currency – the Cuban peso – which was initially based on a par with the US dollar.

The following graph shows sugar production in Cuba, 1880–1925.

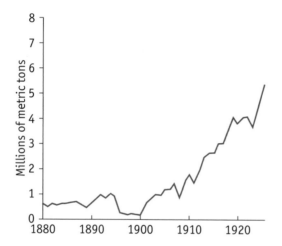

The 1920–1 economic crisis

In 1919 – following the end of the First World War in 1918 – controls on the price of sugar, which had been fixed at a low level in the last year of the war, were lifted. Consequently, world sugar prices rose dramatically during early 1920, and US sugar companies in Cuba made immense profits. However, by the end of the year, the prices dropped just as dramatically – and soon reached 3.5 cents per pound. This caused real problems: bankruptcy for many Cuban owners of sugar mills, and thus serious repercussions for Cuban banks, which soon ran out of money. The resultant financial crisis – accompanied by a political crisis – caused the National Bank to close its doors in April 1921. In June, Cuba's entire banking system collapsed – although US and other foreign banks profited from this by buying at cheap prices the sugar mills belonging to bankrupted owners.

To get out of this, Zayas (who became president of Cuba in 1921) appealed to the US banks for a large loan. A loan of $50 million was eventually agreed – but on very harsh terms. Crowder told Zayas that the government budget needed to be cut and should, in future, be subject to greater controls. Once agreed, the US loan was made in 1922. This form of US intervention had, in the long term, much more influence on Cuba than the various US military interventions between 1906 and 1917. However, its object was the same as the military option – to protect and increase US investments in Cuba. In addition, Cuban plantation and business owners also increasingly looked to the US for protection of their assets. Thus, in a very real sense, Cuba had become a virtual colony, effectively controlled by the USA's economic power.

Dependence on the US economy

By as early as 1914, Cuba's export industry was dependent on just two commodities: out of Cuba's total exports that year, sugar accounted for 77 per cent and tobacco for 16 per cent. For most of this time, sugar exports amounted to about 80 per cent of Cuba's entire foreign exchange. Increasingly, Cuba's economy was in practice, integrated into the US economy. By the mid-1920s, 75 per cent of Cuba's sugar production was foreign-owned. These developments made Cuba's economy very dependent on external factors. In addition, increasing numbers of Cubans came to feel that 'independence' was little more than US 'economic annexation'. As Cubans themselves continued to be divided along lines of class and race, they found it very difficult to influence economic developments. This domination of the Cuban economy by US businesses continued to increase, right up to the Cuban Revolution of 1959.

SOURCE A

The sugar boom, and the absence of European competition, also intensified American penetration of the Cuban economy (US investments in Cuba rose from $205 million in 1911 to $1200 million in 1924), increased Cuba's dependence on the USA for its imports as well as sugar exports (51% of Cuba's imports came from the USA in 1914, 83% in 1915) and deepened the trend to a single-crop economy.

L.E. Aguilar in L. Bethell (ed.) (1993), *Cuba: A Short History*, Cambridge: Cambridge University Press, pp. 47–8.

SOURCE B

In the years leading up to the Revolution [of 1959], US investment in Cuba comprised more than 11 percent of the total US investment in Latin America and the Caribbean. By 1959, US corporations controlled 40 percent of sugar production and 75 percent of arable land; they also owned more than 90 percent of electric and telephone utilities, 50 percent of the railways, 90 percent of mines, 100 percent of oil refineries and 90 percent of cattle ranches. They dominated the transportation, manufacturing and tourist sectors. Moreover, US banks held more than one quarter of bank deposits.

I. Saney (2004), *Cuba: A Revolution in Motion*, London: Zed Books, p. 9.

QUESTION

What problems, if any, did the Cuban economy's close connections with that of the US cause for newly independent Cuba?

191

5

Social divisions

After 1902, Cuban society was divided along lines of both class and race – both issues contributed to the problems Cuba faced in the first two decades after independence.

Cuba's labour movement

One of the impacts of the increasing US domination of the sugar industry was that the small and medium-sized independent growers – who, before the 1870s, had produced most of the cane – sold out (for various reasons) to the big US sugar companies. By 1912, these owned or controlled more than 10 per cent of all land in Cuba. Similarly, the number of sugar mills declined: from 1,190 in 1877, to 207 in 1899, to 184 by 1925. In their place were huge modern mills known as *centrales*. In 1906, such US concerns produced only 15 per cent of Cuba's sugar – by 1928, this reached 75 per cent.

Because these concerns required large labour forces, Cuba saw the rise of a sizeable rural working class that, for much of the year, had little or no employment. These people were obviously concerned about wages. They also maintained links with the working classes in Havana and Cuba's other cities. Many migrated to urban areas in search of work – but often found themselves forced to live in slums.

SOURCE C

The technology of sugar production affected labor as well as ownership and management. Cultivation came to require a large-scale work force, especially at harvest time. Cane needs to be replanted only periodically, at intervals of 5 to 25 years. Therefore the principal need for labor is for the harvest, or *zafra*, a feverish three-month period of intense activity, mostly spent on the arduous cutting of cane with machetes. The rest of the year was known in Cuba as the *tiempo muerto*, the 'dead season' of widespread unemployment and underemployment.

But workers had nowhere to go. Because of the enormous plantations they could not lease or purchase small-scale plots of land for their own use.

T.E. Skidmore and P.H. Smith (1984), *Modern Latin America*, New York: Oxford University Press, pp. 259–61.

Fact: Many of these workers from Haiti were only employed for the harvest, and were sent back once it ended – thus saving the plantation owners from having to pay wages throughout the year. Those from Jamaica, however, tended to stay – in part, because US settlers felt they made better servants.

However, the expanding economy soon faced a labour shortage. In part, this was because dispossessed peasants were often reluctant to become labourers, while former black slaves were not keen to return to plantation work and were still hugely resentful about the massacres of 1912 (see Section 5.9, The republic and blacks). The plantation owners – determined to make huge profits out of the high prices being paid for sugar – resisted the attempts by Cuban workers to achieve better wages. Instead, the answer of the *hacendados* was to try to recruit cheap black labour from other Caribbean islands, especially Haiti and Jamaica. Although this had been forbidden by General Wood in 1902, the ban was lifted in 1912. In part, this was because of pressure from the bigger US companies which had invested in Cuba since 1898. For instance, United Fruit, which owned the Nipe Bay Company, got Cuba's government to agree that it could import almost 1,500 black workers from Haiti. From then on, nearly 300,000 black workers from Haiti and Jamaica were brought into Cuba. In addition, after the fall of the Manchu Dynasty in China in 1911, employers also began once again to import Chinese workers.

The economic boom and then the 1920–1 economic crisis – both of which occurred under Menocal's presidencies – created significant problems for working-class Cubans. These led to the first labour Congress being held in Havana – an early sign of emerging working-class movements and trade unions. These developments were helped by the policy of encouraging white immigration from Spain, as some of those who came from Spain were anarchists or anarcho-syndicalists. Several were trained agitators who quite soon became active in Cuba's emerging trade union movement. As early as October 1917, there was a great strike in the sugar industry, which demanded higher wages and the eight-hour day. The president then decreed that all foreign-born workers who had been on strike should be expelled from Cuba. The fact that both rural and urban working classes had connections was to prove important for the nationalist movement from the 1920s onwards.

White immigration

White immigration had been encouraged by the Spanish administrators in Cuba before 1898, and those who had come – unlike what had happened in Spain's other lost colonies in the Americas – remained after Spanish imperial rule had ended. Cuba's Spanish-born population – the *peninsulares* – was still large in the early 20th century; soon, their numbers were increased by further white immigration from Spain, which continued at a steady pace throughout the first decades of the Republic.

By 1898, whites formed more than 50 per cent of Cuba's population, and the US census of 1899 showed that white male foreigners formed 20 per cent of the entire male population of Cuba – most of them were from Spain. The policy of encouraging white settlers from Spain was continued by General Wood when he was in control of Cuba, who hoped they would run the island. He also took steps to ensure the individual and property rights they had enjoyed under Spanish rule would continue in the new Republic. Over the next thirty years, almost one million settled in Cuba – more than had come during 400 years of Spanish control. While Cuban-born whites tended to dominate Cuba's politics, the Spaniards controlled commerce and industry, and were also well-represented in the professions.

Racial tensions

Many Cubans who had either fought in the independence war, or had supported those who had, were disturbed by the attitude of the new 'colonial' rulers of their island. The US authorities were often disparaging about the rebel forces, and were openly contemptuous of Cuba's black population. However, US administrators were happy to import black contract workers from other islands in the region – such as Haiti and Jamaica – to help with the work of economic reconstruction. However this influx of black labourers made the white élites fearful and they objected. So, in 1900, the US authorities began to advocate a 'white only' immigration policy.

Additionally, US occupation forces decided to keep the whites who had been administrators during Spanish rule in post after 1898 – in fact, many of them continued in these posts even after formal independence was finally permitted by the US in 1902. They retained their attitudes and methods, so Cuba continued to be ruled much as it had been under Spanish colonial control. This angered those Cuban veterans who had fought in the Second War of Independence, as many felt they should have those jobs now Spain no longer ruled Cuba. Their campaign to expel what the veterans called the 'enemies' of Cuba worried the US, and Gómez was warned to take action to control these veterans.

Fact: The 1920–1 economic crisis also caused problems for the *colono* system, which had expanded since the end of the 19th century. Almost 18,000 out of the estimated total of 50,000 *colonos* lost their land as a result of the crisis. Most of those who survived became almost totally dependent on the wealthy sugar-mill owners – thus ending any chance of Cuba developing a sizeable and influential middle class between the wealthy élite and poor workers and peasants.

Fact: One of the white settlers from Spain who came after 1898 was Angel Castro, the father of Fidel and Raul Castro. This migration from Spain continued until 1933 when, after the revolution of that year, Cuba no longer welcomed Spanish migrants.

Cuba

Thus, for many US administrators and politicians, the Cubans were a racially mixed population unfit to govern themselves. The preference of Cuba's US rulers to deal only with the white Cuban élites, and those exiles who now returned from the US, also angered large numbers of blacks who had fought in the independence war. Furthermore, thousands of white US citizens now flocked to Cuba to start a new life in this new US 'colony'. The combination of these developments began to create significant racial tensions in Cuba after it finally became independent in 1902.

But, apart from the all-pervading influence of the US, another problem for the new Republic of Cuba was the continuing role played by those administrators who had been in post under Spanish rule. Most decided to stay and thus took new oaths of allegiance – first to the US and then, after 1902, to the new Republic of Cuba.

The republic and blacks

At the same time as encouraging white immigration, Wood had also taken steps to keep black and Chinese immigration down to a minimum. In May 1902, just before returning to the US, he had signed a law forbidding the import of contract labour – the law specifically mentioned the Chinese. These racist laws, and the old Spanish colonial attitudes, were retained by Estrada and his governments. The US census of 1899 had revealed that Cuba's black population had declined to only 32 per cent of a total population of 1.5 million. Overall, Cuba's population had declined by about 200,000 – from 1.85 million in 1894 to 1.7 million by 1898. Much of this was the result of war, the impact of Weyler's 're-concentration', and hunger and disease. While the government did what it could to increase white immigration, and an atmosphere of 'white supremacy' prevailed in Cuba, it was clear that Cuba also contained a large number of discontented blacks. They had formed almost 85 per cent of the fighters during the Independence Wars but, unlike the whites, had received no significant rewards. As their leaders – those who had not died during the wars – began to die, they were replaced by middle-class 'men of colour' returning from exile, whose main aim was to enter politics as members of the Liberal Party.

Some leaders – such as Juan Gualberto Gómez and Martín Morúa Delgado – tried to promote the education and integration of blacks. Both tried, unsuccessfully, to end racial segregation in public places and racial discrimination in employment. Their failed attempts did nothing to reduce the disillusionment felt by many blacks.

QUESTION

Why were many Cubans angered by the system of administration set up after 1898, under the auspices of the US?

SOURCE D

During the colonial days of Spain, the Negroes were better treated, enjoyed a greater measure of freedom and happiness than they do today. Many Cuban Negroes were welcomed in the time of oppression, but in the days of peace … they are deprived of positions, ostracized and made political outcasts. The Negro has done much for Cuba. Cuba has done nothing for the Negro.

Comments made by Arthur Schomburg, the black American historian (originally from Puerto Rico), after a visit to Cuba in 1905. Quoted in L. Perez (1999), *On Becoming Cuban: Identity, Nationality and Culture*, London: University of North Carolina Press, p. 323.

Much of their dissatisfaction led to revived memories of how racist even many of the white liberals who had fought alongside them for independence had been. It was this discontent that led many of them to join the ranks of the Liberal Party's army in 1906, which was raised against Estrada's election rigging. More importantly, as Magoon had begun to consider how, after 1906, to reform the electoral system, some blacks began to think about forming their own political party. An important role was played by Evaristo Estenoz, an ex-slave who was an Independence War veteran and who had been deeply disappointed by the Liberals and their failure to reward the blacks who had played such an important role in the liberation of Cuba from Spain. Estenoz and many other veterans were still committed to Martí's ideas about nationalism and independence. In 1908, he formed the Partido de Independiente de Color (PIC, Independent Party of Colour). Its politics were mainly progressive, and he pushed for more jobs in public administration to be given to blacks. They published their own newspaper, *Prevision*, and began to develop an early form of what later would be called 'black consciousness'. The PIC also called for the end to the whites-only immigration policy, and called on Magoon and the US to support their programme.

Figure 5.9   A photograph of the PIC leaders

However, the fact that they began to erode the support for the Liberals among black voters soon led to a campaign of vilification in the white-owned newspapers. In particular, Estenoz was accused of 'black racism', and articles began to raise the old fear of a Haitian black republic in Cuba. In 1910, he was arrested, the PIC was threatened with closure and the newspaper was closed down. The government then ordered the arrest of hundreds of black activists on the pretext of ending 'threats against whites' and preventing an uprising. But no evidence of such a conspiracy and no weapons were found. Estenoz was released from prison at the end of the year, and those put on trial were found not guilty and released. However, the Congress then passed the so-called 'Morua Law', which outlawed the formation of a party based on colour – as a consequence, the PIC was banned.

Estenoz, however, refused to give up. After failing to get José Miguel Gómez to agree to repeal the law and give secure jobs to blacks, in return for delivering the black vote again to the Liberals, he wrote to US president William Taft, to see if the US would extend the Platt Amendment's guarantees to Cuba's black citizens. There was no reply from the president, and the US minister in Havana estimated that, without white leadership, Estenoz's movement presented no real threat to the stability of Cuba. However, on Independence Day, on 20 May 1912, Estenoz began an armed protest movement, with about 5,000 rebels in order to be legalised in time for the November elections. The US now decided to respond, and troops were sent to Cuba – officially, to protect US-owned sugar plantations. However, the US warned that it would take further steps if this revolt was not crushed.

Cuba's President Gómez was annoyed by the arrival of US marines, and was confident of crushing this uprising unaided. An atmosphere of white fear and hatred had already been whipped up by the press, and white militia were quickly formed and martial law declared. Gómez's white troops then carried out a fierce repression, and more than 3,000 blacks were massacred in what many historians later concluded was a thinly disguised race war. Among those killed was Estenoz himself. Although memories of this massacre of 1912 remained for decades later among the black population, its effect was to turn most away from politics. However, several eventually ended up in the lower ranks of the police and the army – the only white-dominated institutions to which they had any real access. It was from these security groups that, after the dictatorship of Machado in the 1920s, Fulgencio Batista was to emerge and eventually become the last dictator of Cuba before the 1959 Revolution.

Fact: The US intervened in the Americas many times in the first decades of the 20th century. Even under the presidency of Woodrow Wilson (1913–21) – often portrayed as a liberal and democratic idealist – the US carried out seven military interventions in the Caribbean and Latin America in defence of US economic and strategic interests in the region. Apart from Cuba, other countries to which US troops were sent included the Dominican Republic, Haiti, Mexico, Honduras and Guatemala.

5.10 How did Cuba's governments respond to these challenges after 1902?

One of the main challenges facing newly-independent Cuba was how to reduce or even end US military influence over Cuban affairs after 1902.

Continuing US military influence

US military interventions in the Americas, 1890–1920, had a very negative impact on Cuba's political development. In particular, it allowed unpopular governments to ask for US military intervention against any opposition that was becoming a powerful rival. The US was usually willing to assist – especially when the 'threat to stability' came from Cuba's poor. On several occasions after 1902, the US either intervened militarily or manipulated Cuban domestic politics to ensure that governments malleable to US control were established. As the chart shows, US troops intervened in Cuba three more times between 1902 and 1923: in both 1906 and 1917, they stayed for several years.

DATES	COUNTRIES
1890	Argentina
1891	Chile, Haiti
1894	Nicaragua
1895	Panama
1896	Nicaragua
1898	Cuba, Puerto Rico, Nicaragua
1899	Nicaragua
1903	Honduras, Dominican Republic (1903–4)
1906–9	Cuba
1907	Nicaragua, Honduras
1908	Panama
1910	Nicaragua
1911	Honduras
1912	Cuba, Panama, Honduras, Nicaragua (1912–25)
1914	Dominican Republic, Mexico (1914–18), Haiti (1914–34)
1916–30	Dominican Republic
1917–23	Cuba
1918–20	Honduras
1920	Guatemala

Table to show US military interventions in the Americas, 1890–1920

Politics and uprisings, 1909–24

Despite Magoon's reforms, Cuban politics continued to be marked by corruption and electoral fraud – with further examples of both violently-contested results and US intervention.

In the 1912 elections, the Conservative **Mario García Menocal** was opposed by Alfredo Zayas for the Liberal Party. However, the Liberals soon split into two factions and, as those who had supported Gómez decided to throw their weight behind Menocal, Zayas was easily defeated. Menocal ruled in a very arbitrary way, and increased the power of the president by merging the Rural Guard with the army and modernising the new unified force.

For the presidential elections in November 1916, Menocal was opposed by Zayas, the candidate of the now-reunited Liberal Party. Despite Menocal's professed attempts to limit electoral fraud, he resorted to the usual bribery, vote-rigging and even violence. When the first 'results' of the voting were announced, it seemed as though Zayas would win by a large margin. However, as further results were announced by the administration, Menocal's votes began to increase: the final results showed more votes had been cast than there were eligible voters! At first, Cuba's Supreme Court tried to arbitrate; but, in

ACTIVITY

Carry out some additional research on the reasons for US military intervention in Cuba between 1902 and 1920. Do you think these interventions were just for the stated reasons? Or were other considerations also involved?

Mario García Menocal (1866–1941)

He was once described as 'more American than Cuban' and formed a close relationship with US president Woodrow Wilson. He fought in the Second War of Independence under Calixto García. After 1898, he served in the US military government as chief of police in Havana. After US troops left in 1902, he worked as a manager for the newly formed Cuban American Sugar Corporation. He became a millionaire but, despite being incredibly wealthy, he still stole large amounts of money from the Cuban treasury.

Cuba

February 1917, Zayas, along with several leading Liberals such as **Gerardo Machado**, led an armed revolt – known as La Chambelona. Gómez, still the leader of the Liberals, then appealed to US president Woodrow Wilson for US intervention, as had happened in 1906.

However, Wilson condemned the uprising and gave his support to Menocal. Although 2,000 marines were immediately sent, their main role was to protect US plantations and businesses. Nonetheless, they remained in Cuba for six years. Menocal was able to defeat the Liberal uprisings – Gómez was captured and imprisoned for several months before being released. Once again, government forces then carried out a harsh repression.

Before the presidential elections due in 1920, Menocal asked the US general Crowder to suggest some amendments to the electoral system. In these elections, the main contenders were Gómez for the Liberals, and Alfredo Zayas – now the leader of the Partido Popular Cubano. Menocal backed Zayas and, during the election campaign, there was yet again considerable fraud and violence. The US decided to take action to prevent another uprising. From January 1921, negotiations took place under US supervision, and fresh elections were called for 15 March 1921. However, convinced there would be the usual corruption and vote-rigging, the Liberals withdrew. Gómez then went to the US, to ask the new US president Warren Harding to intervene. Harding refused, and Zayas was returned as president of Cuba in May 1921 – once secure, he decided to ignore several of the reforms Crowder had recently introduced. Although Zayas then went back to a more corrupt way of ruling again, he subsequently lost the 1924 election to General Gerardo Machado, the leader of the Liberals. Machado was sworn in as Cuba's fifth president on 20 May 1925.

Cuban nationalism in 1925

All these economic and social problems had the effect of increasing the attraction of a more independent Cuba in some political quarters. Initially, this revived Cuban nationalism focused on reforming the political system, ending corruption and passing laws to protect Cuban economic interests from growing US domination – including one to restrict the purchase of Cuban land by foreigners. After 1921, however, Cuban nationalism began to take a more radical twist. Of particular importance were developments among students at Havana University. They began to agitate – taking many ideas from Martí's as-yet unfulfilled dreams – for a 'new Cuba' that would be free of corruption and '**Yankee**' domination and imperialism. They were increasingly joined by young radical intellectuals and labour movement leaders who also began to demand serious reform. In 1923, a Veterans and Patriots Association was formed, which called for votes for women, workers' participation in running industries and the ending of the Platt Amendment. In 1925, the Cuban Communist Party was formed. It was from developments like these that, after 1925, the main struggles for a truly independent Cuba would emerge over the next three decades, and would finally result in the Cuban Revolution of 1959.

End of unit activities

1 Carry out some further research on the presidential election results in Cuba between 1902 and 1924. Then make a chart giving the names of those who became president, and which political party they represented.

2 Find out more about Cuba's racial divisions in the first quarter of the 20th century. Then write a couple of paragraphs to explain why these developed.

3 Reread this unit, and then summarise the various political, economic and social challenges faced by Cuba after 1902. Which one do you think was the most serious?

Fact: The continuing problem of corruption and electoral fraud inspired two radical student movements against Zayas and then Machado in 1923 and again from 1927 to 1933. These movements also wanted to end Cuba's economic subservience to the US, and were based on Martí's radical anti-imperialism and egalitarianism. Despite increased repression after 1927, their opposition continued.

'Yankee': this term was originally used by British forces during the American War of Independence to describe their opponents in a disparaging way. At first, it tended to be associated with those from New England, but soon came to mean anyone from the US. In the context of relations between the US and the rest of the Americans – including Cuba – it soon came to be associated with what was called 'Yankee imperialism'.

End of chapter activities

Paper 1 exam practice

Question

How, according to **Source A**, how has the position of black people in Cuba altered since the gaining of independence in 1902?   [3 marks]

> **SOURCE A**
>
> During the colonial days of Spain, the Negroes were better treated, enjoyed a greater measure of freedom and happiness than they do today. Many Cuban Negroes were welcomed in the time of oppression, but in the days of peace … they are deprived of positions, ostracized and made political outcasts. The Negro has done much for Cuba. Cuba has done nothing for the Negro.
>
> Comments made by Arthur Schomburg, the black American historian (originally from Puerto Rico), after a visit to Cuba in 1905. Quoted in L. Perez (1999), *On Becoming Cuban: Identity, Nationality and Culture*, London: University of North Carolina Press, p. 323.

Skill

Comprehension of a source.

Examiner's tips

Comprehension questions are the most straightforward questions you will face in Paper 1. They simply require you to understand a source and extract two or three relevant points that relate to the particular question. As only three marks are available for this question, make sure you don't waste valuable time that should be spent on the higher-scoring questions by writing a long answer here. All that is needed are a couple of short sentences giving the necessary information to show that you have understood the source. Basically, try to give one piece of information for each of the marks available for the question.

Common mistakes

When asked to show your comprehension/understanding of a particular source, make sure you don't comment on the wrong source! Mistakes like this are made every year – remember, every mark is important for your final grade.

Simplified mark scheme

For each item of **relevant/correct information** identified, award one mark, up to a maximum of three marks.

Student answer

Source A says black people in Cuba have become political outcasts.

Examiner's comments

The candidate has selected one relevant and explicit piece of information from the source – this is enough to gain one mark. However, as no other points have been identified, this candidate fails to gain the other marks available for the question.

Activity

Look again at the source and the student answer. Now try to identify other pieces of information from the source, and also try to make a general comment about the message of the source, in order to obtain the other two marks available for this question.

Summary activity

Copy this diagram and, using the information from this chapter and any other materials that you have available, make notes under each of the headings. Where there are differences of opinion and interpretation about certain aspects (such as causes and consequences, or significance), try to mention the views of different historians.

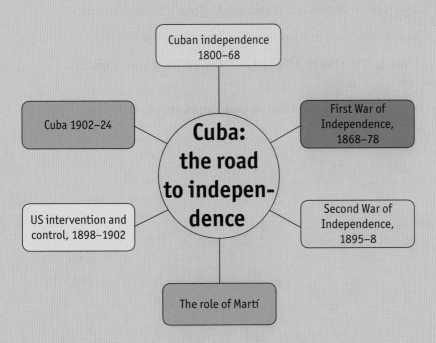

5

Paper 2 practice questions

1 Examine the factors which led to the emergence of independence movements in Cuba in the 19th century.

2 'The main reason why Cuba failed to obtain independence before 1902 was because rebel leaders were divided.' To what extent do you agree with this statement?

3 Evaluate the contribution made by Martí to Cuban independence.

4 'The role of the US was the most important factor in Spain's defeat in Cuba in 1898.' To what extent do you agree with this statement?

Further reading

Try reading the relevant chapters/sections in the following books:

Bethell, L. (ed.) (1993), *Cuba: A Short History*, Cambridge: Cambridge University Press.

Childs, M.D. (2006), *The 1812 Aponte Rebellion in Cuba*, Chapel Hill, NC: University of North Carolina Press.

Gott, R. (2004), *Cuba: A New History*, New Haven: Yale University Press.

Kirk, J.M. (1983), *José Martí: Mentor of the Cuban Nation*, Gainesville: University of Florida Press.

Perez, L. (2008), *On Becoming Cuban*, Chapel Hill, NC: University of North Carolina Press.

Perez, L. (2010) *Cuba: Between Reform and Revolution*, Oxford: Oxford University Press.

Saney, I. (2004), *Cuba: A Revolution in Movement*, London: Zed Books.

Skidmore, T.E. and Smith, P.H. (1984), *Modern Latin America*, New York: Oxford University Press.

Thomas, H. (1971), *Cuba: The Pursuit of Freedom*, London: Harper & Row.

Ireland

Introduction

Ireland was in many ways England's first real colony. Between 1171 and 1250, most of Ireland fell under English rule. An Irish parliament was established in 1264; and, in 1541, Henry VIII got this Irish parliament to declare him king of Ireland. However, there was considerable opposition to his Protestant Reformation, as the majority of the population in Ireland remained loyal to Catholicism.

Despite some serious revolts, Elizabeth I had successfully completed the English conquest of Ireland by 1601. A serious revolt that broke out in 1641 under Charles I was eventually crushed by Oliver Cromwell in 1649. He then abolished the Irish parliament; in addition, he confiscated almost eleven million acres of land in northern and central Ireland from those who had revolted and/or had supported Charles I in the English Civil War. This land was then given to his Protestant English and Scottish soldiers and supporters. From then on, a '**Protestant Ascendancy**' was clearly established in Ireland.

Although a separate Irish parliament was re-created by Charles II, and the Catholic religion was tolerated, he did not undo Cromwell's land settlement. A further revolt during the reign of James II was crushed in 1690 by William III.

'**Protestant Ascendancy**': this was the political, economic and social domination of Ireland by a small number of large Anglo-Irish landowners, the Protestant Church of Ireland and its clergy, and professionals who had to be members of the Anglican Church of Ireland.

Historical Provinces of Ireland

Figure 6.1 The four historic provinces of Ireland

Boundary of the Province of Ulster
Boundary of the state of Northern Ireland
Boundary of Irish provinces

KEY QUESTIONS

- What social and economic factors led to the development of an independence movement in Ireland?
- What political factors led to the development of an independence movement in Ireland?
- What external factors influenced the rise of the independence movement?

Overview

- After the 1800 Act of Union, which made Ireland a part of Britain, an independence movement gradually began to emerge in Ireland as a result of various social, economic and political problems.

- The first major issue was religion. Although the vast majority of the Irish population were Catholics, Ireland and its land were effectively owned and controlled by a Protestant élite. This was often known as the 'Protestant Ascendancy'.

- In 1823, Daniel O'Connell formed the Catholic Association to campaign for Catholic Emancipation. This was achieved in 1829 and, in 1838, the issue of tithes was partially reformed by a Tithe Commutation Act.

- However, there were also problems connected to economic underdevelopment, landownership and poverty. In particular, Ireland remained essentially a rural economy, with the vast majority involved with agriculture. In 1840, O'Connell formed the Repeal Association to obtain the repeal of the Act of Union, so that an Irish parliament could solve these problems.

- This campaign was, however, interrupted by the Great Famine, which began in 1845. Apart from the sufferings and deaths of millions of Irish people, the Great Famine ultimately led to a split in 1846 within the Repeal Association between the constitutionalists against the use of force as a way of achieving their aims, and Young Ireland militants who refused to rule out the use of force.

- In 1847, these Young Irelanders formed the Irish Confederation and, in July 1848, began a rebellion. This was a failure, and many of its leaders were either imprisoned or fled abroad.

- From 1850, with the formation of the Irish Tenant League, some of these Young Ireland leaders began to campaign on the issue of landownership and tenants' rights.

- However, this failed to achieve any real success and, in 1858, the Irish Republican Brotherhood (IRB) was formed in Dublin, committed to achieving a totally independent Ireland by the use of force.
- Preparations for an uprising in Ireland were disrupted by the British authorities arresting hundreds of IRB members in February 1866. Attacks on British North America (Canada) by Fenian supporters in the US in April 1866 also failed to achieve their aims. So the IRB began to make new plans for actions in Ireland and Britain.

6.1 What social and economic factors led to the development of an independence movement in Ireland?

Ultimately, the continuing 'British connection' after 1690 was the main cause of the developing independence movement in Ireland. This political 'British connection' became stronger in 1800, following the passing of the Act of Union. This act was passed by Britain following a serious rebellion mounted by **Wolfe Tone's United Irishmen** in 1798 (see Section 6.3, Wolfe Tone's rebellion, 1798). However, the rebellion was quickly defeated, and the British government responded with the Act of Union, which came into effect in 1801. This abolished Ireland as a separate kingdom: from then on, Ireland became an integral part of the United Kingdom. However, there were several specific social and economic issues that were also important contributory factors.

Social divisions within Ireland

An early important factor in the development of an independence movement in Ireland was religion.

Catholic Emancipation

After 1800, Irish reformers focused on the question of Catholic Emancipation, demanding full civil and political rights for all Roman Catholics, to give them equality with Protestants. Despite an understanding that this would be part of the Act of Union settlement, this did not happen. Many Irish people thus felt cheated and, during the 1820s, a mass movement emerged, led by **Daniel O'Connell**.

O'Connell believed that the various problems that Ireland suffered from – including high land rents and poverty – could not be solved until Catholics, who formed the vast majority of the population, had the right to be elected to parliament. Initially, Catholic Emancipation was an upper-middle-class issue; O'Connell, however, decided to widen the appeal of this cause to include ordinary Irish tenants.

In 1823, he set up the Catholic Association that, in addition to campaigning for equal political rights for Catholics, also called for better rights for tenants. In order to increase its effectiveness, O'Connell managed to gain the support of the Catholic clergy who, previously, had not been overtly political. Support for his organisation also grew because of its opposition to the increasing number of **Orange Order** demonstrations and meetings.

Wolfe Tone's United Irishmen: this rebellion had been a non-sectarian movement, which had drawn support from both Protestants and Catholics who wanted to see an independent Ireland. However, during the four decades after its defeat, religious divisions – linked to the political questions of reform and independence – became increasingly obvious in Ireland. By 1845, questions of political reform – and especially of greater autonomy and outright independence for Ireland – became ever more closely connected to Catholicism.

Daniel O'Connell (1775–1847)

He was a lawyer, who belonged to a once-wealthy Roman Catholic family. He was drawn to radical democratic politics from an early age, and decided to campaign for equal rights and religious tolerance in Ireland. However, he did not support the use of force, arguing that the Irish should instead try to achieve their rights through political action. Thus his constitutional form of Irish nationalism meant he did not support Wolfe Tone and the United Irishmen in 1798. He campaigned on several issues – especially the linked issues of Catholic Emancipation and the repeal of the Act of Union – and, after 1829, became known as 'The Liberator' (or 'The Emancipator').

Initially, the Association's membership fee was high, but O'Connell wanted it to be open to all Catholics, including the poor. So, in 1824, he created an associate membership that was only one penny a month – this became known as the 'Catholic Rent'. This enabled even the poorest to join: as a result, the Catholic Association became a mass movement. In order to collect the Catholic Rent fees, O'Connell established a national network of agents. This, in turn, helped the Association to grow, and made ordinary people feel they were part of an effective movement that would deliver the reforms they wanted. It also helped make O'Connell the most important of Ireland's Catholic leaders.

The 1826 election

O'Connell then decided to force the issue during the 1826 general election. Although Catholics had been given the vote in 1793, the franchise was limited to those who owned or rented property over a certain value. In most Irish counties, the bulk of the electors were Catholic tenants but, because there was no secret ballot, these tenants were usually pressured into voting for the candidates favoured by their landlords who, in the main, were Protestants. O'Connell decided to try to reduce the influence of the landowners by persuading their tenants to vote for candidates who favoured Catholic Emancipation – even if this was against the landlords' wishes. To help tenants take such a risk, the Catholic Association promised financial compensation to any tenants evicted for going against the wishes of their landlords. The Catholic Association also persuaded the local Catholic clergy to encourage Catholic voters to support pro-Emancipation candidates, even if they were Protestants. As a result, candidates opposed to Catholic Emancipation were defeated by pro-Emancipation candidates in four of Ireland's counties.

The 1828 by-election

Whilst the results of the Catholic Association's intervention in the 1826 election were not enough to end the ban on Catholics being able to stand in parliamentary elections, a new opportunity to exert political pressure arose two years later. In 1828, the MP for County Clare, William Vesey-FitzGerald, was appointed to the British cabinet. This required him to stand for election again – and O'Connell argued that the Catholic Association should oppose him.

Although he could not take a seat in parliament, there was no law against a Catholic standing in a parliamentary election. The full resources of the Catholic Association were used for O'Connell's election campaign and, on 28 June 1828, he defeated Vesey-FitzGerald by 2,057 votes to 982.

O'Connell's victory caused much excitement among Catholics, and increased support for the cause of Emancipation – although O'Connell repeatedly stressed the need to use only peaceful methods. However, many new political clubs were then formed to help spread support for Emancipation. These 'Liberal Clubs', in turn, provoked the creation of political clubs – known as 'Brunswick Clubs' – to oppose this. With the prospect of serious sectarian violence in Ireland, the British government finally decided that Catholic Emancipation should be granted, in order to avoid a general rebellion breaking out.

The 1829 Catholic Emancipation Act

On 13 April 1829, the British parliament passed an Act granting Catholic Emancipation. Under its terms, Catholics were finally allowed to sit in the parliament in Westminster. In addition, the Act allowed Catholics to be appointed to even the highest military ranks and to hold all but the highest government posts. However, in order to reassure Protestants in Ireland that their Ascendancy would not be too greatly undermined, the property qualifications for voting were raised. The effect of this was to disenfranchise a large number of lower-middle-class Catholics. Yet, despite this compromise, the Emancipation of 1829 was seen as a great victory, and O'Connell was hailed as 'The Liberator'. Having been elected as MP for Clare in 1828, he refused to take the oath of loyalty, so a new election was held in July 1829. He was re-elected unopposed and finally took his seat in February 1830. Later, several of his supporters were also elected as MPs.

The main significance of O'Connell's campaign to win Catholic Emancipation was that it created a new type of Catholic political movement. The campaign – and its eventual victory – raised the political consciousness of Catholics, and began to create the idea that Catholicism, Irish nationalism and independence were virtually one and the same thing. Yet, despite Catholic Emancipation, religion continued to be an important factor behind the emergence of an independence movement in Ireland. One particularly important factor was the Tithe War, which began in 1831.

The Tithe War, 1831–6

After 1829, the question of **tithes** remained. In the aftermath of O'Connell's success over Catholic Emancipation, many Catholics decided to take action over tithes. This was done independently of O'Connell and his Catholic Association. The Tithe War really began in March 1831, and consisted of peaceful non-payment by resisters. Sometimes, however, when the police attempted to seize goods to the value of the unpaid tithes, violence did break out. The first serious instance came in June 1831, when police killed twelve resisters and injured twenty others. As opposition grew, more clashes resulting in deaths took place. In December 1831, resisters ambushed a police patrol in County Kilkenny: in all, twelve of the forty constables were killed – including the chief constable. As a consequence, British soldiers were at times ordered to assist the police. This use of British soldiers alienated many Catholics, who began to see full independence as the only way of obtaining justice in Ireland.

Although this Tithe War was supported by the Catholic clergy, O'Connell did not favour the complete abolition of tithes. This lost him some support among Catholics – and helped prepare the way for those who supported using violence in order to achieve full independence from Britain. As the Tithe War continued, the authorities soon realised the cost of collecting payment in kind far outweighed the value of the unpaid tithes. Eventually, in 1836, the government suspended the collections and, in August 1838, the Tithe Commutation Act for Ireland reduced the amount directly payable by 25 per cent, and transformed the remainder into part of the rent payable by tenants to their landlords, who were to pass this element on to the church. However, it was not until 1869, when the Irish Church was disestablished (see Section 6.4, The Fenians and Home Rule), that tithes were finally ended.

Economic factors

Unlike England, and several other European countries, Ireland saw relatively little industrialisation in the period 1750–1850 and, instead, remained overwhelmingly rural and agricultural. More than 80 per cent of the population was rural, and almost three-quarters of males were engaged in some form of agricultural work.

Tithes: these were the annual payments that all Irish people had to pay to the established Protestant Church of Ireland for its upkeep – including the payment of the salaries of the Anglican clergy, many of whom did not live in their parishes. However, Anglicans were only a small minority of Ireland's population – most were Catholics, and there was also a large Presbyterian population. Catholics in particular objected to paying tithes to the Church of Ireland.

QUESTION

Why did Roman Catholics in Ireland object to paying tithes?

6

Ireland

Ireland's economy before the Great Famine

Initially, the outbreak of war with revolutionary France had had a positive impact on Irish agriculture, as prices had risen. However, when the wars ended in 1815, there was a dramatic collapse in prices: as much as 60 per cent compared to pre-1815 prices. For most of the next thirty years, agricultural prices increased only slightly. As a result, there was much economic hardship – especially for more than one million landless labourers, who lived at just about subsistence level.

At the same time, Ireland experienced a rapid population growth far higher than in other European countries. In 1800, there were five million people in Ireland; this had increased to almost 8.5 million by 1845. This was despite the fact that more than 1.5 million Irish people had emigrated to North America since 1800. This led to overpopulation and high unemployment in some areas, making the 1820s and 1830s a time of considerable hardship for many Irish people.

Those involved in Ireland's various industries also found the first half of the 19th century a difficult time. There were several general recessions in the textile industries during the 1820s and, during the 1830s, the wool and cotton industries declined. In addition, changes in production methods saw linen manufacture move from rural cottages to factories in urban areas – many of these factories were located in the province of Ulster. As a result, many rural families lost an important part – if not all – of their income. Furthermore, Irish artisans faced increasing competition from cheap manufactured goods from Britain; while unskilled labourers were regularly hard-hit by fluctuations in the economy. The urban poor suffered from high unemployment, and were often worse off than the rural poor, with many living at almost starvation-level.

Landownership

The general economic situation of many Irish people before 1845 was also affected by the nature of landownership. By the mid-17th century, Britain's conquest and confiscations had resulted in the bulk of Ireland's cultivated land being owned by a small class of Protestant landowners. During the 18th century, most of these large landowners began to carve up their estates into smaller units, which they then rented out to middlemen tenants on long-term leases at fixed rents. This new class of tenant-farmers – who often lived as absentee landlords in England – then sublet these farms to smaller farmers at high rents. These cottiers, in their turn, then often subdivided their holdings in order to provide land for their sons. For many Irish families, possession of a plot of land was vital for their survival.

Because of the population increase, there was often a surplus of labour in some parts of Ireland. Those who did find work were often paid a combination of money and small plots of land, on which to grow potatoes. By 1845, about three million people relied on the potato, which was grown on almost two million acres of the six million acres under cultivation in Ireland. Overall, Ireland was one of Europe's poorest countries. By 1845, it was estimated that half the population in Ireland were living in real poverty. Events after 1845 led increasing numbers of Irish people to link their poverty to the 'British connection' – and to see independence as the only way to end their poverty.

The Great Famine

In 1845, a potato **blight** destroyed the potato crop in Ireland. By mid-November, almost one-third of the crop was lost; while previously harvested potatoes were found to be

Fact: Ireland's poor became so dependent on the potato as it was easier to grow – even on poor soil – and yielded three times the crop of any grain. It could be fed to livestock, and 1.5 acres of potatoes could feed a family of five or six for a year. It was also nutritional and so was a good subsistence food. Furthermore, it could be sold for cash: in the more prosperous east, farmers could feed their families on potatoes, and then grow other crops for cash. As a result, the Irish ate more potatoes than any other nation. However, the downside was that the potato was more perishable and not as easily stored as grain.

Blight: this was a fungus that attacked the potato leaves and then worked down to the potato itself, causing it to rot. It had first appeared in the US in 1843, and had spread to Europe in 1845.

affected. This developed into the worst crop failure in more than a century, and made a widespread famine in Ireland distinctly likely. As the crops failed, poor tenants were often unable to pay the rents: as a result, there were many evictions, which caused even more hardship. These evictions led to growing resentment at the British authorities and also raised the whole question of landownership – and Irish independence.

The British response

The first reaction of Robert Peel's Conservative government in Britain was to buy £100,000 worth of maize from the US – partly to limit hunger in Ireland, but also to stabilise food prices. However, Peel stuck closely to the **liberal view** that it was not really the role of government to intervene in the economy or society. Instead, local charities and committees were given funds to distribute cheap food to the poor. In early 1846, Peel launched a public works project, to provide temporary work for the poor and unemployed. As a result, the number of deaths from hunger and disease was limited during the winter of 1845–6.

However, in June 1846, Peel pushed through the repeal of the **Corn Laws**, arguing that free trade would result in cheaper grain, which would benefit the poor in Ireland and in Britain generally. However, he refused to act on the request of Irish MPs to ban the export of grain from Ireland. The repeal of the Corn Laws split the Conservative Party, and Peel's government fell when he tried to introduce an Irish Coercion Bill to deal with potential food riots. He was replaced by a Whig government headed by Lord Russell.

The Whigs were also strong believers in **laissez-faire**, so Russell decided to drop some of Peel's interventions. The direct purchase and distribution of food was stopped, and no plans were made for any possible crop failure in 1846. Yet these steps took place in a year where the general food-supply situation across Europe was much worse than it had been in 1845. Nonetheless, assuming that the problems of blight were over, the public works schemes were closed down in August 1846. In addition, Russell's government believed that poverty in Ireland was mainly due to the actions of the Irish landowning class – who were thus expected to finance and carry out the bulk of any relief themselves. Some – such as Lord Clarendon – even blamed the Irish people themselves for their poverty.

'Black 47'

However, the 1846 potato harvest was virtually a complete failure, with more than three-quarters of Ireland's potato crop being destroyed. Local relief work schemes were unable to cope with the massive numbers seeking relief: by December, numbers had risen to almost 500,000. In addition, those who were given work were paid wages that were so low that workers couldn't afford to buy food – some even collapsed and died from hunger while working on these schemes.

To make things worse, the winter of 1846–7 was very harsh. Although some grain was held back from export, and some was imported, the amount exported was still large. By early 1847, there was massive starvation and death, and the year became known as 'Black 47'. Those who did not starve to death were made weak by malnutrition and fell victim to disease – especially typhus. By the spring of 1847, more than 750,000 men were employed on various private and public work schemes – but their low wages meant they could not afford the high and rising prices charged by merchants for the imported grain and flour, or for the prices for Irish grain demanded by Irish landlords.

> **QUESTION**
>
> Why did the potato blight, which hit Ireland in 1845, have such a serious impact on so many Irish people?

Liberal view: this view was based on the concept of 'laissez-faire': that government should not interfere with the economy, which should be left to industrialists and bankers. Since the 1980s, it has once again become the dominant political and economic 'orthodoxy' in many developed countries. This 'free market' attitude is accompanied by a belief in unregulated capitalism, and is often referred to now as 'neo-liberalism'.

Corn Laws: the first law had been passed in 1815, after the end of the wars against France. They had been introduced to protect British farmers' incomes from the importation of cheaper grain from abroad. The Corn Laws achieved this by placing a tax on foreign grain imports: this ensured that corn prices in Britain would remain high, thus benefiting British farmers.

Laissez-faire: as part of the government's belief that the operation of the market and free trade was the best way to regulate the economy, it was decided that food should not be provided for free or sold at below-market prices. To do so was seen as damaging the economic interests and profits of merchants, retailers and traders. The new lord-lieutenant of Ireland stated quite clearly that it was not up to the government to feed the Irish people.

> ### SOURCE A
>
> The landlords made a raid upon the grain crops and sold them for their rents, leaving the producers of those crops to starve or perish or fly the country… People now allude to those years as the 'famine' in Ireland: There is no famine in any country that will produce in any one year as much food as will feed the people who live in that country… There was no famine, but plunder of the Irish people by the English government of Ireland.
>
> Comments made by Jeremiah O'Donovan Rossa after the Great Famine. Quoted in P. Adelman and R. Pearce (2005), *Great Britain and the Irish Question*, London: Hodder Education, p. 56.

Fact: Very few accepted the arguments of Irish nationalists who believed that the Act of Union meant that the whole of Britain – not just Ireland – should give financial assistance to help Ireland cope with the Great Famine.

Fact: As the poor rates were based on the number of tenants a landlord had, this was one way to reduce outgoings. In addition, it proved increasingly difficult to collect rents when so many tenants were poor – this was another reason for the evictions.

Fact: The blight did return on several occasions – in 1860, 1879, 1890 and 1897 – but it lasted for much shorter periods and did not affect all areas. Although there were serious food shortages and, in some areas, some starvation, there was nothing like the suffering seen in the period 1845–52.

In response, the government turned to the direct provision of relief, via soup kitchens – although, once again, these were to be provided by the Irish authorities from local rates. By August 1847, more than three million people were being fed in this way. Although the potato harvest of 1847 was much smaller than usual, it was largely free from blight. Consequently, the government stopped the soup kitchen scheme in September 1847. Instead, the poor were told to apply to workhouses for relief. However, the numbers applying – almost a quarter of a million – overwhelmed the workhouses, and the cramped living conditions resulted in the rapid spread of disease among the malnourished applicants. Soon, many of the Poor Law Unions were bankrupt. As a result, this method was abandoned in favour of providing 'outdoor relief': more than 800,000 victims of the famine began to receive relief in their own homes.

Things were made worse by the fact that some landlords and farmers, faced with rising rate demands to fund this Poor Law system of famine relief, decided to evict many of their tenants, and to move from arable to pastoral (animal)/farming. In addition, many smallholders gave up their land in order to receive poor relief. These evictions made the suffering of famine victims even worse, as they lost the chance to grow any food. As a result, there were several instances of intimidation of such landlords, and even acts of violence.

Then, in 1848, the blight returned, and resulted in that year – and especially the winter of 1848–9 – being the worst time of all in the Great Famine. Despite the painfully obvious suffering, the British government did nothing more. Although the worst was over by 1849, it was not really until 1852 that the situation began to improve – although the high yields of pre-famine years were not reached. Slowly, the pressure on poor relief began to decline, and Irish agriculture began to recover. However, the emigration rate continued at a high level – in part, because many feared that the blight, and famine, might return at any time.

The impact of the Great Famine

The most immediate effect of the Great Famine was on Ireland's population. Approximately one million people died between 1845 and 1850 – either from starvation, or from disease closely linked to malnutrition. As well as this loss of life, almost 1.5 million Irish people emigrated – mostly to the USA, but also to Australia and New Zealand. Overall, therefore, the Irish population declined by almost 25 per cent during this period: between the two censuses of 1841 and 1851, the total population dropped from eight million to six million. By 1900, the Irish population was only about half of the figure for 1845. The death toll – and the mass emigration to the US – left a great

Figure 6.2 A poor Irish family searches for potatoes during the Great Famine

bitterness and resentment against British rule. The Great Famine thus raised questions about the ways in which Ireland was governed by Britain.

6.2 What political factors led to the development of an independence movement in Ireland?

Despite Catholic Emancipation, there remained serious divisions and resentments in Ireland over questions of landownership and religion. In particular, the bulk of the land was owned by Protestant Anglo-Irish families, while the Catholic majority

Fact: In fact – unlike with Catholic Emancipation – there was little support generally within the Commons as a whole for repeal. Most Whigs – as well as most Conservatives – were reluctant to restore a separate Irish parliament that, when it had existed, had been very corrupt. Thus O'Connell's strategy of trying to put pressure on the British parliament to repeal the Act of Union was unlikely to succeed in the way that Catholic Emancipation had.

'Monster Meetings': these were often held at sites of great historical importance as regards past events in Irish history. In the long term, this helped the growth of Irish nationalism and the desire for complete independence. For instance, Clontarf – where the cancelled Dublin meeting was to have met in October 1843 – was where, in 1014, the Irish king Brian Boru had defeated his Viking rival, briefly leading to a united Ireland.

Young Ireland (*Eire og***):** was a term first used by their opponents, and was intended to mark them out from the more moderate 'Old Ireland' section of the Repeal Association headed by Daniel O'Connell.

were tenants or labourers and were treated as second-class citizens. Tensions over these issues increasingly led to the emergence of an Irish nationalism that, at first, campaigned peacefully for reforms but, eventually, began to demand complete independence.

The Repeal Association

Once Catholic Emancipation had been achieved, O'Connell turned his attentions to the Act of Union. O'Connell began to call for its repeal, and for Ireland to have its own parliament once again. In 1840, he founded the Repeal Association, modelled on his earlier Catholic Association. To fund it, he created a 'Repeal Rent', which brought in even more money than the Catholic Rent had. Its first meeting was on 15 April 1840, in Dublin. As before, one reason for the rapid growth of this repeal movement was that O'Connell once again obtained the support of the Catholic clergy who, in turn, helped the movement gain popular support. However, in 1841, the Conservatives returned to power, and Robert Peel was not sympathetic to the idea of repeal. In addition, O'Connell and the Repeal Association met with much opposition in the province of Ulster.

Believing that it might be some time before the Whigs were back in power, O'Connell tried to put pressure on Peel by stirring up public opinion. This peaceful method, he believed, would force the government to grant repeal – as had happened with Catholic Emancipation. Thus, in 1843, he launched a big campaign for repeal, based on organising a series of large gatherings – called '**Monster Meetings**' – across most of Ireland. Most of these rallies attracted crowds of up to 100,000. These were much larger than the meetings that had been organised for Catholic Emancipation, greatly alarming the British authorities. In August 1843, the largest meeting to date took place at Tara. In October 1843, O'Connell planned one for Clontarf, just outside Dublin. However, when the British government banned it a few hours before it was due to take place, and ordered British troops to suppress it if it did take place, O'Connell called the meeting off rather than risk the outbreak of violence. This decision lost him significant support within the Repeal Association, which soon became divided over what to do next. Nonetheless, O'Connell – along with a few other repeal leaders – was arrested for conspiracy and subsequently sent to prison in May 1844 for one year.

However, in September 1844, the sentence was quashed by the House of Lords and O'Connell was able to retake his seat in parliament. His return, however, coincided with the impact of the Great Famine (see Section 6.1, The Great Famine). His calls for financial aid for the Irish people were ignored or even ridiculed in Britain. Although he did organise a few more meetings, they were generally poorly attended. In addition, his time in prison – although brief – had seriously undermined his health. By the time he died in 1847, the repeal movement had all but faded away.

Young Ireland

Although O'Connell's repeal movement had been unsuccessful, it inspired new generations of Irish nationalists who increasingly aimed for full independence for Ireland. One such nationalist group became known as **Young Ireland**.

This group initially operated within the Repeal Association. Its three most important leaders were Thomas Davis, John Blake Dillon and Charles Gavan Duffy. In 1842, they began to produce *The Nation*: a newspaper that initially promoted O'Connell's repeal movement, and was very successful. Davis – who was a Protestant – believed that what Ireland needed was a strong national identity, shared by all Irish people, regardless of class or religion. Dillon believed that all Irish nationalists should work together and that – at least initially – they should use peaceful methods. Duffy, the editor, was a Catholic journalist and political organiser – he believed the Irish MPs in parliament should act independently; in particular, he argued they should only form alliances with those who supported repeal.

In 1844, after O'Connell's imprisonment and the virtual collapse of the Repeal Association, the Young Irelanders were joined by John Mitchel. He was a Protestant lawyer who strongly believed that complete independence for Ireland was necessary if its various social, economic and political problems were ever to be solved. Unlike the other three, Mitchel advocated the use of physical force. Another influential member who joined this Young Ireland grouping was James Fintan Lalor – he argued that, in order to gain mass support for independence, it was necessary to link it to the various problems relating to the land question. Also important by then was William Smith O'Brien, who acted as head of the Repeal Association during O'Connell's imprisonment and who belonged to Young Ireland from 1846. However, the attitude of the Young Irelanders to the use of violence became hardened as a direct result of the growing distress caused by the Great Famine. In 1848, this would lead to an unsuccessful Young Ireland Rebellion, which attempted to seize independence from Britain (see Section 6.3, The Young Ireland Rebellion, July 1848).

> **ACTIVITY**
>
> Try to find out more about the reasons for the growing differences within the Repeal Association between O'Connell and the 'Old Ireland' faction and the Young Ireland group.

The land question after 1850

One consequence of the Great Famine was to focus attention on the issue of landownership in Ireland. After 1845, the 'land question' became an increasingly important political factor in the emergence of an independence movement in Ireland.

As well as its huge impact on Ireland's population, the Great Famine also had a big impact on landholding in Ireland. The starvation and emigration of the famine wiped out most of the cottier class of smallholders. As a result, the more affluent larger landowners bought up the smaller plots: in all, about 200,000 smallholdings – constituting almost 25 per cent of Irish farms – disappeared. During the 1850s, almost 3,000 estates – totalling about five million acres – were sold. Most of the new owners were either members of the old landowning class, or speculators who – via a method known as 'rack-renting' – raised rents to extremely high levels.

However, these changes in landownership resulted in the increased prominence of owners of medium-sized holdings. This increasingly confident middle-class soon became concerned with the politically-loaded question of landownership. Towards the end of the Great Famine, Irish tenant leagues began to emerge in several local areas. In part, this was a response to the evictions that some landlords were imposing on tenants of smallholdings.

EJECTMENT OF IRISH TENANTRY.

THE EJECTMENT.

Figure 6.3 Irish tenant Daniel Downe and his family being evicted from their farm and home, published in the *London Illustrated Times*, on 16 December 1848

SOURCE B

The terrible clearances of the late 1840s and early 1850s were not sustained throughout the period; of the 90,000 evictions apparently recorded from 1847 to 1880, 50,000 took place between 1847 and 1850. From 1854 to 1880 the annual rate of actual eviction dropped to 1.36 per 1000 holdings; the annual number of houses levelled usually stayed below one hundred. Statistics were always problematic, raising difficulties of definition as well as actual occurrence;... The image of the ruthlessly clearing landlord remained in the mind of the public;... But where they did occur, the decisions were as often taken by large land-leasing farmers who were farming an estimated 75 per cent of Irish land by 1854.

R.F. Foster (1989), *Modern Ireland 1600–1972*, London: Penguin Books, p. 374.

The Irish Tenant League and the Independent Irish Party

After the failure of the 1848 Young Ireland Rebellion, those Young Irelanders who remained in Ireland returned to the land question, which became increasingly important in the following decades. Duffy revived *The Nation* and, in August 1850, persuaded the local tenant leagues to unite and form the Irish Tenant League.

By then, these local tenant leagues had come to include farmers with larger holdings. They became increasingly influential during the 1850s, and were more concerned with social and economic issues rather than the wider questions of Irish nationalism and independence.

They demanded fair rents, and compensation for evicted tenants for any improvements they had made. Although the League did not last long, its campaign for the '**Three Fs**' gave greater prominence to the question of land reform.

After the general election of 1852, the League gained the support of a small group of Irish MPs – of all political affiliations. The League was then effectively wound up, and a new organisation was formed: the Independent Irish Party. However, social and religious differences – especially those between Protestant Ulster and the rest of Ireland – soon began to undermine unity. Then, following a slump in farming prices in 1859, this tenants' movement collapsed. However, although the Irish Independent Party broke up, it had raised important issues that would later be largely resolved.

'Three Fs': These were

Free sale: being able to sell the 'interest' in a holding, and obtaining compensation for improvements made.

Fair rent: a low rent fixed by a tribunal rather than landlords.

Fixity of tenure: guaranteed tenure of land for a certain period of time.

6.3 What external factors influenced the rise of the independence movement?

War and political developments abroad were also important factors in the development of the early Irish independence movement. The three main factors before 1900 were:

- political revolution in France, and then war between Britain and Revolutionary France;
- the series of revolutions which broke out across Europe in 1848;
- the emergence of militant republicanism among the Irish communities in the USA.

Wolfe Tone's rebellion, 1798

The first external catalyst influencing the development of an independence movement in Ireland was provided by the French Revolution of 1789. Its ideals inspired Wolfe Tone. In 1791, he – along with several liberal and radical Protestants and Catholics who resented English rule and who wanted to achieve a completely independent Irish republic – founded the Society of United Irishmen. When Britain became involved in war with revolutionary France, they felt this presented Ireland with a good opportunity to seize independence. Although this rebellion – which broke out in the spring of 1798 – was quickly defeated, Wolfe Tone came to be seen by many as the founding inspiration behind Irish republicanism. His rebellion was also an early example of the application of a belief that proved very significant later on: that any serious difficulties faced by Britain could provide an opportunity to obtain Irish independence.

The Young Ireland Rebellion, July 1848

Many Irish people blamed the British government and British landowners for the Great Famine. By 1848, some Young Irelanders had come to believe that Irish independence from Britain would only be achieved by the use of violent methods. These members of Young Ireland criticised the methods favoured by O'Connell and his supporters. After his release from prison in 1844, O'Connell had continued to favour renewing support for the Whigs, in the hopes that they would repeal the Act of Union. This was opposed by those associated with *The Nation* and Young Ireland. In July 1846, O'Connell's supporters introduced the 'Peace Resolutions', which explicitly forbade the use of physical force in order to achieve repeal of the Act of Union. Most Young Irelanders then resigned from the Repeal Association.

The Irish Confederation

These 'seceders' decided to form their own organisation: the Irish Confederation. Their main aim was for a national parliament for Ireland, with full legislative and executive powers. Their first official meeting took place in Dublin, on 13 January 1847. The main leaders were John Mitchel, James Fintan Lalor, Charles Gavan Duffy, William Smith O'Brien and John Blake Dillon. Although membership eventually reached over 10,000, most members were relatively poor, so funds were limited. At this stage, they still hoped to achieve their aims by peaceful methods; and they based their new organisation on the principles of freedom, tolerance and truth. However, the Irish Confederation refused to rule out 'other means' if necessary.

As the Great Famine continued unabated, Mitchel decided that the more restrained approach of *The Nation* was no longer tenable. So, inspired by Wolfe Tone's rebellion of 1798, he formed his own newspaper, *The United Irishmen*, towards the end of 1847. Its first issue appeared in February 1848. He believed the failure of the repeal movement, and the growing horrors of the famine, showed that peaceful agitation for reform was now useless. Instead, he argued for civil disobedience and, eventually, an uprising against England to achieve an independent Irish republic.

He also agreed with Lalor, who argued that, as the land had been forcibly taken from the Irish people in previous centuries, the entire landlord system in Ireland should be swept away. In its place, he envisaged an Ireland where the land belonged to independent peasant farmers. According to Lalor, only such a change in landownership would allow a truly free and independent Ireland to emerge.

The 'Year of Revolutions', 1848

The attitude of these Young Irelanders to the use of violence was influenced by a series of popular revolutions and uprisings that broke out in many European countries in 1848: soon to be termed the 'Year of Revolutions'. The first revolution broke out in France in February 1848; then other revolutions broke out in many parts of the Austro-Hungarian and Russian empires. The most significant of these were in Hungary, Poland and various Italian states. In addition to demanding political reforms, these revolutions also called for national independence. Not surprisingly, this had an impact on the Young Irelanders who had set up the Irish Confederation.

Mitchel and O'Brien thus began to make plans for a similar revolution in Ireland. At public meetings, and through the pages of his newspaper, Mitchel openly agitated for ending the Act of Union. In April 1848, the authorities in Dublin arrested several of the plotters: including Mitchel and O'Brien. The British government then passed the Treason Felony Act, which turned sedition – punishable by a short prison

QUESTION

Why did the Young Ireland leaders decide to organise a rebellion in 1848?

sentence – into a felony, which was punishable by death or transportation for life. Although O'Brien was found not guilty, Mitchel was found guilty of treason and sentenced to fourteen years' transportation.

The failed rebellion

Despite this setback, O'Brien and a few others – including Meagher and Dillon – decided to press on with their plans, and fled to the south where their rebellion began at the end of July 1848. However, it was poorly organised, and most potential supporters were half-starved and demoralised as a result of the Great Famine. In addition, the Catholic Church did not support the rebellion. After only a few weeks, the small force of rebels was defeated in a skirmish with police at a farmhouse belonging to Margaret McCormack.

Although Dillon managed to escape, and sporadic risings continued until late 1849, the rebellion was effectively over. Most of the main Young Ireland leaders were eventually arrested, found guilty of treason and sentenced to death. In the end, however, because of popular support, the death sentences were commuted to transportation.

Although Young Ireland and their Irish Confederation – along with their form of Irish nationalism – collapsed in the 1850s, their journalism in *The Nation* and *The United Irishmen* succeeded in creating a clear form of Irish nationalism that proved influential over the coming decades. Furthermore, despite its failure, the rebellion of 1848 was nonetheless a significant event in the development of an independence movement in Ireland. As well as seriously raising the ideal of fighting for an independent Irish republic, Young Ireland also contributed the tactic of tenants waging a land war against landlords as an important part of the liberation struggle for Irish independence. As has been seen, the issue of landownership became an increasingly important political issue in Ireland after 1850.

Fact: Opponents of the rebels called the skirmish 'the battle of the widow McCormack's cabbage patch'. For many years, the house was known as 'The Warhouse'; then, in 2004, the Irish government made it a national heritage monument, known officially as the 'Famine Warhouse 1848'.

SOURCE C

The Young Ireland rebellion was considered pathetic by many, including *The Times*, which called it 'a cabbage-garden revolution'. What the Young Irelanders did accomplish, however, was the provision of a succinct propaganda for future nationalists. Not only did their journalism argue an easily understood nationalism, they produced a 'Library of Ireland', a series of biographies and histories which became a sort of extensive textbook for nationalists … [while] Charles Gavan Duffy lived until 1903, and was able to influence opinion through his retrospective writings about the 1840s and 1850s.

J. Coohill (2014), *Ireland: A Short History*, London: Oneworld Publications, p. 51.

The US and the Fenians, 1858–66

The independence movement in Ireland was also influenced by developments in the US where, as a result of the Great Famine, there were large numbers of Irish immigrants. In fact, even after the end of the Great Famine, many Irish people continued to emigrate to the US. Many of these Irish settlers blamed Britain for their sufferings.

Ireland

Fenian Brotherhood:
O'Mahony, who had gone to the US in 1856, was a Celtic scholar, and based the name of his organisation on the 'Fianna', who were a legendary band of Irish warriors led by Fionn mac Cumhaill, a mythical Celtic figure.

Rival factions: eventually, in 1867, a new organisation was set up, called Clan-na-Gael ('Family of Gaels'). By the early 1870s, this group, led by John Devoy, had replaced the Fenian Brotherhood as the main Fenian organisation in the US.

Fact: Hopes for an alliance with the US were raised by the outbreak of the American Civil War in 1861 as, at first, it looked as though Britain might enter the war on the side of the Confederates.

Fact: As with those Irish emigrating to the US, poverty in Ireland – and especially the Great Famine – had forced many Irish people to emigrate to the British mainland. Although the census of 1861 showed that only 3.5 per cent of the total population had been born in Ireland, there were many more who had been born of Irish descent in Britain. Almost 200,000 lived in the north-west of Britain, where they had sought work in the cotton factories in and around Manchester, and in the port of Liverpool. Among these Irish communities in Britain, there was often strong support for the aims of the Fenians. By 1865, it is estimated that there were more than 80,000 Fenian supporters in Britain.

The Fenian Brotherhood and the Irish Republican Brotherhood

In 1858, John O'Mahony – one of the 'Men of 1848' who, along with James Stephens, had escaped to France after the defeat of the Young Ireland Rebellion of 1848 – founded the **Fenian Brotherhood** in New York. Stephens returned to Ireland and, on 17 March (St Patrick's Day) 1858, formed the Irish Republican Brotherhood (IRB) in Dublin. The IRB was linked to the Fenians in the US. Its main aim – inspired by the rebellions of 1798 and 1848 – was to raise funds for political and military actions in order to end British rule of Ireland and so achieve an independent Irish republic. In particular, its members thought that Ireland's various problems – including the question of land reform – should take second place to the struggle for independence. Other leading Fenian members were Jeremiah O'Donovan Rossa, John O'Leary and Thomas Clarke Luby.

Although **rival factions** began to emerge in the US, O'Mahony continued to run Fenian affairs there. He issued bonds – payable within six months of Ireland gaining its independence – in the name of the 'Irish Republic', in order to raise money. Many Irish immigrants in the US bought these bonds: the money raised was then used to buy large quantities of weapons.

As previously, Irish nationalists were encouraged by Britain's various military difficulties in the 1850s: its poor military performance in the Crimean War of 1853–6, and the Indian Mutiny in 1857. In addition, at one point it looked as though war might break out with France. However, this did not happen, and many Fenians then began to consider the US as a possible ally.

The IRB in Ireland

Although the IRB focused on the issue of independence, they were helped by the economic crisis that hit rural Ireland in 1859. This was the worst crisis since the Great Famine, and lasted until 1864 – by 1863, there had been three failed harvests, causing serious hardship for many, especially for the smaller and poorer farmers. It formed an important backdrop to the emergence and rise of the Fenian movement in the late 1850s and early 1860s.

In Ireland, in 1863, Stephens founded a Fenian newspaper, the *Irish People*, and, by 1864, the IRB had more than 54,000 members. These were mostly drawn from the lower middle classes, journalists, artisans and shopkeepers. The Catholic Church, however, was opposed to the IRB, and banned its members from joining it: in part, because as well as being non-sectarian, it was also a secret organisation. Nonetheless, the IRB continued to attract members. Fenian groups in the US and in Britain sent significant financial help and, by 1865, Fenian leaders in Ireland believed it was time to plan a rising. In that year, funds of almost $250,000 had been raised in the US alone. The Fenians now had more than 5,000 weapons, and possibly as many as 50,000 men willing to fight: some of these were men who had fought during the American Civil War and so had military training and experience. The IRB decided that it would launch a rebellion in 1866.

However, the British government was aware – through its many spies and informers – of Fenian activities and, in September 1865, it closed down the *Irish People*, confiscated funds that had been sent from the US and arrested many of the IRB's main leaders: including Stephens, O'Leary and Rossa. Although Stephens later escaped from Richmond Gaol, the authorities then suspended habeas corpus in February 1866, and hundreds of Fenian activists were arrested. At the same time, some of the British army's units in Ireland were moved to England, as many of the Irish soldiers serving in the British army were sympathetic to the Fenian cause. Nonetheless, despite these setbacks to their plans, the IRB continued to plan an uprising in Ireland.

Developments in North America, 1866

Meanwhile, in the US, a Fenian convention in 1865 decided to attack Britain's North American possessions (which later became Canada). In April 1866, and with the tacit support of the US government, Fenians in the US launched attacks on parts of Canada. Their aim was to put pressure on the British government to grant Irish independence by attacking British strongholds, and capturing parts of Canada's transport system and territory. The most significant of the 1866 raids took place in June, but all were unsuccessful and, although a few similar raids took place until as late as 1871, nothing was achieved. As a result, attention focused once more on a rebellion in Ireland itself.

End of unit activities

- Using information from this book, and any other resources available to you, produce a chart to summarise the various religious reforms achieved in Ireland in the period 1800–38.
- Then write a couple of paragraphs to show the relative significance of the role played by Daniel O'Connell.
- Working in pairs, produce a newspaper article to outline Ireland's economic problems before 1845, and the social and economic impact of the Great Famine.
- Write a letter from a member of the IRB in Ireland, explaining how Wolfe Tone's rebellion of 1798, the Great Famine and the Young Ireland Rebellion of 1848 inspired the formation of the IRB in 1858.

Fact: Many in the US government had been angered by the failure of the British government to support the unionist side in the American Civil War (1861–5). In addition, the US had long had the desire to extend its territory by annexing Canada. Unsuccessful attempts had been made during the American War of Independence, and during the Anglo–American War of 1812–15. However, after 1815, the US gradually began to abandon any lingering plans for annexation and, by the Treaty of Washington in 1871, had effectively given up this aim.

QUESTION

Why was the connection within Fenian organisations in the US important for the IRB in Ireland?

TIMELINE

1867 Feb: Fenian uprisings in Ireland and Britain.

1869 Jul: Irish Church Act.

1870 First Irish Land Act.

1873 Nov: Isaac Butt forms Home Rule League.

1878 Oct: 'New Departure' agreed between Charles Stewart Parnell and the IRB.

1879 Oct: National Land League of Ireland formed by Parnell and Michael Davitt; start of the 'Land War'.

1881 Second Irish Land Act.

1882 Apr: 'Kilmainham Treaty'.

May: Phoenix Park assassinations.

Oct: Parnell forms the Irish National League.

1886 Apr: First Home Rule Bill.

1893 Feb: Second Home Rule Bill.

1905 Nov: Sinn Féin formed.

1912 Apr: Third Home Rule Bill.

Sep: Unionists form Solemn League and Covenant to oppose home rule.

1913 Nov: Irish Volunteers formed.

1916 Apr: Easter Rising.

1918 Dec: Sinn Féin's victory in general election.

1919 Jan: Declaration of Irish Independence; start of the 'War of Independence'.

1921 Oct: Start of the London Conference.

1922 Jan: Anglo–Irish Partition Treaty ratified.

KEY QUESTIONS

- What methods were used in the struggle for independence?
- What were the roles of Michael Collins and Éamon de Valera in the struggle for independence?
- Why did the independence movement succeed?

Overview

- Although there were attempts by the IRB in 1867 to achieve Irish independence by force, these were unsuccessful. For the next four decades, most Irish nationalists – including those who favoured a totally independent Irish republic – focused on achieving peaceful reform of the outstanding issues of landownership and home rule.

- Individuals such as Isaac Butt, Charles Stewart Parnell and Michael Davitt formed various organisations to achieve these reforms. The land question was eventually settled by a series of Land Acts between 1870 and 1903.

- This left the other issue of home rule or self-government still to be resolved. In 1882, Parnell formed the Irish National League – but attempts to pass Home Rule Bills in 1886 and 1893 failed. Partly because of these disappointments, differences soon began to emerge between those who wanted to use more militant methods in order to achieve complete independence.

- In 1905, Sinn Féin was formed, and this began to attract members of the IRB and others who were prepared to use force in order to obtain independence. The Third Home Rule Bill of 1912 eventually brought matters to a head.

- Because of the Parliament Act of 1911, the 1912 Home Rule Bill would eventually become law in 1914. This alarmed Ulster's unionists who, in 1912, began to form a paramilitary organisation – the Ulster Volunteers – to oppose this. This led Irish nationalists to form the Irish Volunteers to counter this.

- However, the outbreak of the First World War in August 1914 led to the Home Rule Act being suspended until after the war. This angered many Irish nationalists and, in April 1916, a small group launched the Easter Rising, hoping to take advantage of Britain's involvement in the First World War.

- Although this rising was rapidly crushed, the decision by the British authorities to execute the leaders who survived led to increased sympathy for the rebels. As a result, Sinn Féin won a landslide victory in the general election of 1918. Instead of taking their seats in Westminster, in January 1919 they declared Irish independence and began the 'War of Independence'.

- After two years of fighting between the Irish Republican Army (IRA) and British forces, a truce was agreed and discussions took place in London. These resulted in the Anglo–Irish Partition Treaty, which was ratified in January 1922.

6.4 What methods were used in the struggle for independence?

By 1867, events in Ireland had seen both peaceful and violent methods used to achieve reform and greater autonomy – and even complete independence from Britain. After 1867, these two methods continued – with violence, although often short-lived, becoming more frequent. Increasingly, towards the end of the 19th century, the aim shifted from reform to independence. This period, however, began with violence from the Fenians.

The Fenian Risings of 1867

Urged on by veterans of the American Civil War, and by radicals in England who were keen to support a republican movement, the IRB leadership decided to launch a series of uprisings in early 1867. These took place in February and March 1867, and were planned by Thomas Kelly. Yet, although these were supposed to be coordinated, they were poorly organised. As a result, they were easily contained by the authorities, which had been kept up-to-date by the informers they had within the Fenian movement. Kelly and some other Fenians in England tried – unsuccessfully – to capture the arsenal of Chester Castle, in order to gain weapons for the rebellion in Ireland. Instead, Kelly and Timothy Deasy were arrested and sent for trial in Manchester.

The Manchester Martyrs

On 18 September 1867, as Kelly and Deasy were being taken to court, a group of thirty Fenians – led by Edward O'Meagher Condon – staged a daring rescue. However, in the attack on the prison van, a policeman was accidentally killed. Most of the Fenians involved in the rescue were arrested, and five – including Condon – were tried for murder. All five were found guilty and sentenced to death; but the death sentences of two were overturned. However, the remaining three – Michael Larkin, William Philip Allen and Michael O'Brien – were hanged outside Salford Gaol on 23 November 1867, in front of a crowd of almost 10,000. These three – who had shouted '**God save Ireland**' as they were led from the court – became known as the 'Manchester Martyrs'. Many people in Ireland, including many Catholic priests – although not the Catholic leadership – felt that the decision to hang these three Fenians was too harsh for an act that was not premeditated. This event thus won many more supporters for the IRB and for the cause of Irish independence.

'God save Ireland': a song, entitled 'God Save Ireland', was written after their executions: this was the Irish national anthem until 1926, when it was replaced by 'The Soldier's Song'.

Ireland

Fact: Barrett was hanged outside the walls of Newgate Prison, before a crowd of more than 2,000 people. This was an historic execution, as Barrett was the last person to be publicly hanged in Britain.

Fact: Karl Marx, the communist economist and philosopher, who stated that England would never be free until Ireland was free, was one of those who criticised the Clerkenwell explosion. In part, this was because he saw the explosion as likely to weaken English working-class support for Irish independence and, instead, drive them into supporting the actions of the British government. Nonetheless, he – along with Engels, his fellow communist collaborator – continued to support the cause of Irish independence.

Figure 6.4 (top) A poster commemorating the three Manchester Martyrs produced in 1867 by Fenian supporters in the US. (bottom) A photograph, taken in 2008, of a mural in Belfast, which calls for the remains of the three Manchester Martyrs to be returned to Ireland

These new supporters included many more moderate nationalists – often known as constitutionalist nationalists – who were often prepared to work with the more revolutionary Fenians to achieve reforms. At the same time, many Fenians became involved with these constitutionalists in later campaigns for Land and Home Rule.

The Clerkenwell Outrage

Initially, however, the Fenians soon lost some of this support as a result of what happened in London on 13 December 1867. A group of Fenians, organised by Michael Barrett, attempted to rescue Richard O'Sullivan-Burke – a senior Fenian prisoner who had been caught trying to purchase weapons in Birmingham – by blowing up an external wall of Clerkenwell Prison. Unfortunately, too much explosive was used and twelve working-class people, living in tenement houses opposite the prison, were killed; more than fifty others were injured. Barrett was arrested and tried for the deaths caused by the explosion.

Although he produced witnesses who testified that he had been in Scotland at the time, he was found guilty. On 26 May 1868, Barrett was executed.

Although Barrett also became a martyr for the Fenian cause, there was much revulsion and anger in London and the rest of England at the Clerkenwell explosion – this anger was directed against not only the Fenians, but also all Irish people living in England.

By 1867, the impetus of the Fenian movement had declined, and Irish nationalists who favoured the use of peaceful methods to achieve reforms became more prominent again. However, the Fenian movement did not disappear, and it would reappear in the coming decades. In addition, the rise of the Fenian movement was one of the factors that led William Gladstone, in the 1870s and 1880s, to decide 'to pacify Ireland'. He attempted to do this by a series of reforms that he hoped would appease most Irish groups.

The Fenians and Home Rule

Though the Fenian Rising in 1867 was a failure, it did influence several later developments. In December 1868, the Liberal leader William Gladstone became prime minister and was determined to 'pacify' Ireland by passing significant reforms. Initially, he wished to end the 'Protestant Ascendancy'. His first step was to disestablish the Anglican Church of Ireland. The **Irish Church Act of 1869** removed one Irish grievance by ending tithes – as a result, Irish Catholics no longer had to pay money to the Church of Ireland.

A much more important issue, which was to have greater importance towards the end of the century, was the growing appeal of a movement for home rule. After the Fenian Risings, a United Amnesty Association was formed, which campaigned for the release of the Fenian prisoners. In 1869, **Isaac Butt** became the president of that association. He was a barrister who had previously defended some of the Young Ireland rebels of 1848 and then some of the Fenian prisoners of 1867. In May 1870, he launched the Home Government Association in Dublin, to campaign peacefully for home rule for Ireland. This was after discussions with some leading members of the IRB, who were prepared to give support to this initiative. As a result, six Fenians were present at the foundation of this association, which held its first public meeting in September 1870.

The Home Rule League

In November 1873, the Home Government Association became the Home Rule League and, although Butt saw it more as a pressure group than a political party, fifty-nine of its members were elected in the general election of 1874. However, Butt's aim of achieving home rule was frustrated by fact that Benjamin Disraeli's Conservative Party, which had won a large majority in 1874, refused to grant any significant reforms on Irish issues. Butt's influence within the league was also reduced by the fact that most of the home rulers elected were Liberal landowners.

Soon, a more radical wing amongst the Home Rule League emerged which impacted on Butt's leadership. Joseph Biggar, for instance, used the tactic of 'obstructionism' to talk out government legislation as a protest at Disraeli's refusal to consider reform. Also, in 1874, Charles Stewart Parnell joined the League and managed to get elected as an MP the following year. He immediately adopted a directly confrontational approach in the House of Commons. From then on until his death in 1879, Butt – who disagreed with the actions of both Biggar and Parnell – saw his influence decline further, while that of Parnell increased.

Irish Church Act of 1869: the Act, which was passed in July 1869 but did not come into force until January 1871, also removed Church assets (for which £10 million compensation was paid), and made it a voluntary body, with provision to look after the clergy.

Isaac Butt (1813–79)

He was a Conservative from Dublin who, initially, had been an Orangeman in favour of maintaining the Union with Britain. Consequently, he had opposed Daniel O'Connell's attempt to get the Act of Union of 1800 repealed. However, events during the Great Famine convinced him that Ireland needed a federal system that would restore an Irish parliament, and give Ireland control of its domestic issues. He favoured using peaceful and legal methods to get reforms passed in the British parliament; but his failure to do so eventually led to his loss of influence within the home rule movement.

Fact: The election of so many 'home rulers' was partly the result of the Secret Ballot Act that had been passed in 1872 by Gladstone's government. This Act – which ended voting in public – made it impossible for landowners to force their tenants to vote in a certain way.

6

The land question, 1870–91

The Fenian Uprisings of 1867 also helped persuade Gladstone that, as well as religion in Ireland, the land issue needed to be reformed. In particular, the execution of the three Manchester Martyrs had led many of those who favoured using peaceful methods for achieving reform of Ireland's problems to have some sympathy with the Fenian cause.

> **SOURCE A**
>
> The Fenian conspiracy has been an important influence with respect to Irish policy.
>
> Comments made by William Gladstone in the House of Commons on 31 May 1869.

John Gray (1815–79)

Although a Protestant, Gray was sympathetic to the nationalist views of Young Ireland, supported O'Connell's call for the repeal of the Act of Union and was involved in the Repeal Association. He had been imprisoned, along with O'Connell, for conspiracy and sedition in February 1843. Released on appeal, he distanced himself from the use of violence, and so did not get involved in the 1848 rebellion. Instead, he helped establish the Irish Tenant League. Disappointed by the limited reforms Gladstone was prepared to concede, he eventually left the Liberal Party and, in 1874, was elected as a Home Rule League MP.

'Fixity of tenure': this clause of the Act was largely down to Gray, who had to work hard to convince Gladstone to go even this far. One of the problems facing Gladstone was that many members of the Commons and especially of the Lords were substantial landowners in Ireland.

As has been seen, the Great Famine had had serious economic impacts on those Irish peasants who survived. Most of these were tenant farmers, renting land from landowners. By 1870, a small minority of these landowners – 302 (1.5 per cent of all landowners) – owned almost 34 per cent of the land in Ireland, and roughly a quarter of the land was owned by landlords who did not even live in Ireland. Many people held the view that land in Ireland was owned by an uncaring – and often remote – landlord class. For many in Ireland, the question of land reform thus became entwined with that of Irish nationalism and independence.

As a result, the Fenians were prepared to work alongside constitutionally minded reformers on the questions of land reform and home rule. Gladstone was concerned by this loose alliance, and so tried to address the first of these issues. Another reason for Gladstone's decision to reform the land question was an economic downturn in the 1860s. This had led to the revival of the Irish Tenant League, under the leadership of **John Gray**.

Gray's paper, the *Freeman's Journal*, took up the call for the 'Three Fs' and land reform. In February 1870, he organised a well-attended Land Conference that approved these demands. His campaigning activities helped provide the information that eventually persuaded Gladstone of the need for land reform in Ireland. Although, for various reasons, it would take several attempts to achieve the degree of radical reform desired by an increasing number of Irish people, a first step was taken in 1870, via the Irish Land Act.

The First Irish Land Act, 1870

The main aim of this Act, which came into force in 1871, was to deal with the growing demand in Ireland for the 'Three Fs' – although some issues were only dealt with partially, and others not at all. The Act gave evicted tenants the right to compensation for any improvements made – provided the reason for their eviction was not non-payment of rent. Under the terms of the 'Bright Clauses', tenants were also offered thirty-five-year loans (at 5 per cent interest), to enable tenants to buy their holdings from their landlords. However, the landlords were not compelled to sell, and most farmers were unable to afford to borrow such amounts. In addition, although rents were not to be 'exorbitant', no independent tribunals were established to fix rent levels or control unfair rent increases. Also, although **fixity of tenure** was given to those tenants with leases less than thirty-one years, tenants having longer leases were not covered: many landlords then tried to extend the length of leases in order to evade the new law. Finally, tenants still lacked protection against eviction.

Not surprisingly, many were disappointed, and violent protests erupted in some rural areas. In response, Gladstone's government passed the Peace Preservation Act, which gave extra powers to the police and military to repress outbreaks of violence. The following year, the Westmeath Act allowed police to arrest those suspected of being members of secret societies: this was mainly aimed at Fenians and the IRB. As a result of the disappointments over the Land Act and the increased repression by the authorities, some of those who had favoured using only peaceful means of obtaining reform became disillusioned, while others began to move closer to those arguing that home rule was more necessary than ever.

The 'Land War', 1879–82

Despite Gladstone's limited land reforms, which had done something to address the main problems, a **new agricultural crisis** hit the Irish countryside in the late 1870s. In 1877 and 1878, there were poor harvests; while cheap food imports from the US led to a significant drop in the price of agricultural goods in Ireland. In western Ireland, potato production dropped by almost 75 per cent.

As a result of the hardship, the issues of rents and evictions came to the fore once again. In April 1879, a mass protest – or 'Monster Meeting' – took place in Irishtown, County Mayo, against a Catholic priest and landlord who had threatened to evict tenants who would not – or could not afford to – pay their rents. **Michael Davitt** took up the cause of the tenant farmers. His campaigning – and that of others – on this issue finally persuaded the landowner to cut his rents by 25 per cent. Elsewhere, there were sporadic outbreaks of protests and violence. This was used by Davitt and Parnell as a way to gain support for more radical measures.

In October 1879, Davitt and Parnell formed the National Land League of Ireland, which campaigned for all the 'Three Fs' to be fully granted. In many ways, however, the National Land League was a loose coalition: Parnell, although seeking and welcoming support from the Fenians, never supported their idea of a violent nationalist revolution. In addition, Davitt wanted to go much further than Parnell as regards the land question – Parnell never supported Davitt's call for land nationalisation and redistribution.

Despite this, the new organisation gained support from a wide cross-section of the Irish population. At its height, it had more than 200,000 members and, for a time, it looked as if civil war might break out in some parts of rural Ireland.

Many agreed that further land reform was needed, while the Fenians and their supporters welcomed the 'direct action' tactics – such as a rent strike – which the Land League soon adopted. In addition, the Land League's calls for direct action could be interpreted as threatening violence.

As part of its campaign, the Land League used public meetings and rallies, slogans and posters, rent strikes and **boycotts**.

Unpopular landlords and their agents were shunned: people refused to trade with them, and even to talk to them. The tactic was also applied to policemen and their families, and to those tenants who refused to join the rent strikes. In the small villages and towns of rural Ireland, it made life very difficult – for instance, people found it almost impossible to buy food or other goods. Many were faced with joining the rent strike, or leaving

New agricultural crisis: this was part of the crisis, known as the 'Long Depression', which hit Europe in 1874.

Michael Davitt (1846–1906)

He had joined the IRB in 1865, and had been involved in the 1867 rising. In 1870, he was imprisoned for gun-running – while in prison, he changed his attitude to the use of violence, and decided to focus on achieving the redistribution of land by peaceful and legal means. Although he remained firm in his non-violent approach after 1870, many of his demands were politically radical.

Boycotts: this form of protest took its name from Charles Boycott, the agent of two unpopular landlords in County Mayo. In September 1880, he served eviction orders on eleven tenants in rent arrears. As a result, he and his family were totally 'boycotted' – or ostracised – by the local inhabitants of his community. At the end of the year, he left Ireland for England.

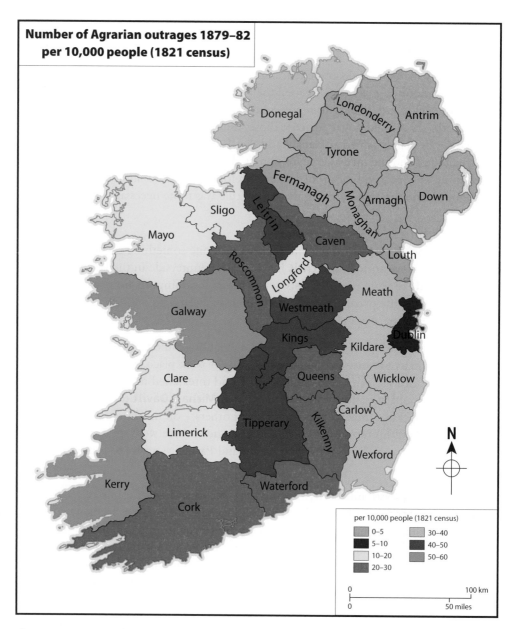

Number of Agrarian outrages 1879–82 per 10,000 people (1821 census)

per 10,000 people (1821 census)

- 0–5
- 5–10
- 10–20
- 20–30
- 30–40
- 40–50
- 50–60

0   100 km

0   50 miles

Figure 6.5   A map of rural violence during the Land War, 1879–82

their communities. In the main, this legal tactic was peaceful – although sometimes there were individual acts of intimidation and violence.

The Second Irish Land Act, 1881

Partly to deal with the growing unrest, Gladstone passed a Second Land Act in 1881, in order to address outstanding elements of the 'Three Fs'. Tenants were given the right of 'free sale' of holdings and 'fixity of tenure' – provided they abided by certain conditions. However, the Act left the setting of 'fair rents' to an Irish Land Commission, and those in rent-arrears were excluded from the fair-rent clause. Parnell and Davitt used their newspaper, *United Ireland* – published by O'Brien – to attack the inadequacies of the new Act and, instead, to call for a rent strike. Gladstone responded by getting Parnell interned in Dublin's Kilmainham Gaol, on 12 October, under the **Irish Coercion Act of 1881**, for 'sabotaging the Land Act'. On 14 October, the Land League and its paper were banned, and several other leaders were interned – although not Davitt, who was already in prison in England.

Irish Coercion Act of 1881: this was passed specifically to deal with the protest campaign of the National Land League. In particular, it gave the British government in Ireland the right to intern (arrest and imprison) people 'reasonably suspected' of crime and conspiracy.

Figure 6.6 Poster of the Irish Land League, advertising a meeting on 24 July 1880. This attempted to link up urban working-class radicals with the struggle of small tenant farmers in the countryside

Figure 6.7 Cartoon about the passing of the Second Land Act of 1881. Gladstone is shown signing it, while Parnell stands behind him

QUESTION

What is the message of the cartoon in Figure 6.7?

The rent strikes

Although imprisoned, on 22 October 1881, Parnell and Davitt issued their 'No Rent Manifesto', drafted by O'Brien. This urged small tenant farmers to stage a rent strike in order to obtain the rent abatements promised by the Second Irish Land Act. This manifesto was then published in the *United Ireland* – which O'Brien, still imprisoned, edited and had published in London and Paris. Although the ability of the National Land League to organise rent strikes was severely limited by the repression, acts of violence (including the murder of some landlords, their agents and members of the Royal Irish Constabulary) increased in many rural areas. This was despite the Land League discouraging violence. From March to December 1880, there were almost 2,500 'outrages' in rural areas; for the same period in 1881, with the Coercion Act in force, the number rose to almost 4,000; the figure for 1882 was even higher.

Consequently, Gladstone held talks with Parnell and, in April 1882, the 'Kilmainham Treaty' was agreed. In return for the government agreeing to extend the 1881 Land Act to those tenant farmers in rent arrears, and to phase out coercion, Parnell agreed to withdraw the 'No Rent Manifesto', and to take steps to end the violence. In May, all the Land League prisoners were released and in Dublin, on 17 October 1882, Parnell announced the formation of a new organisation: the Irish National League.

Land reform, 1885–1892

Fact: There was another important Irish Land Purchase Act in 1903. This was the Wyndham Act, which was passed after pressure from O'Brien and others. Although there was no compulsory sale (although this was added by the 1909 Land Act), the scheme was attractive to both tenants and landlords, as the government agreed to pay the difference between the price landowners demanded and that offered by tenants. This did away with the problem of loans and, by 1914, almost nine million acres had been bought by tenants. This Act essentially finished off 'landlordism' in Ireland.

From the mid-1880s until 1892, the Conservatives were in power. As a combination of economic problems and unrest persisted after the 1881 Land Act, the Conservatives attempted to follow up Gladstone's reforms with other steps to stem unrest. In 1885, the Irish Land Purchase Act (also known as the Ashbourne Purchase Act) provided £5 million in long-term and low-interest loans to help tenants buy the land they rented.

However, in 1886, when the agricultural economy began to suffer further problems, the National Land League was revived under the leadership of John Blake Dillon and William Smith O'Brien. In October 1886, they announced their 'Plan of Campaign' that, by collective direct action, was intended to force down rents. It centred on all tenants coming together to agree what rents they thought were fair – if the landlords refused to agree, then the tenants would enforce a rent strike. However, this was not very successful. Nonetheless, the Conservative responded with the usual 'carrot and stick' approach. Another Land Act in 1887 allowed tenants to take part in the rent arbitration scheme. However, the new Conservative chief secretary for Ireland, Arthur Balfour, who was appointed in 1887, quickly showed he intended to use force to suppress the activities of the Land League and its 'Plan of Campaign'. On 9 September 1887, the Royal Irish Constabulary (RIC) opened fire on a demonstration in Mitchelstown in County Cork: three people were killed and many more wounded. Because of the strict way he enforced the Irish Crimes Act of 1887, Balfour soon earned the nickname 'Bloody Balfour'.

Nonetheless, further Irish Land Purchase Acts were passed, in 1888 and 1891, to provide extra loans for tenants to buy the land they leased. As a result of the various land reforms between 1870 and 1891, the land question in Ireland was more or less settled.

The campaign for land reform had become closely intertwined with the causes of both home rule and Irish independence. With the Irish land question almost sorted by 1892, the focus thus shifted to the calls for either home rule or complete independence. Although, initially, the important roles were played by home rulers like Parnell, within twenty years the impetus had shifted to those who – like Éamon de Valera and Michael Collins – wanted complete independence – and were prepared to fight for it.

Home rule, 1879–1914

After his election as an MP in 1875, Parnell had quickly become the leading light in the Home Rule League. His more radical approach included attempts to work more closely with the Fenians in the campaign for the home rule. Unlike Butt, he had sufficient political skill to get the different elements of Irish nationalism – constitutionalists and 'physical force' nationalists wanting independence – to work together: initially for land reform but, in the long term, for home rule.

However, this plan then suffered a setback. As a result of Butt's failure to obtain any home rule reform, the IRB – reorganised in 1873 under the leadership of Charles Kirkham – concluded that Butt's constitutional approach had failed and that, in order to guarantee the purity of the republican independence doctrine, it should stop supporting the constitutionalist campaign for home rule. So, in September 1876, the Fenians in Ireland withdrew their support from Butt's Home Rule League.

Joseph Biggar, who – along with fellow Home Rule League MP John O'Connor Power – was also a Fenian, opposed this line. Biggar and Power were supported by several members of the IRB's Supreme Council, who continued to argue that the attempt to work through parliament should be continued – if only as a way to keep members and supporters active. Those opposed to the new line taken by Kirkham were either expelled or forced to resign from the IRB. However, in August 1877, with the aid of IRB supporters, Parnell replaced Butt as president of the **Home Rule Confederation**.

The 'New Departure'

Almost at once, Parnell held private meetings with leading members of the IRB's Supreme Council. These concluded that, with the right kind of support behind him, and a group of committed nationalists in the House of Commons, Parnell could bring public opinion in Ireland to support more progressive and militant actions. The result was that Clan-na-Gael stated that the Fenians would, once again, consider supporting the home rule campaign. In October 1878, following meetings between Parnell, other leading constitutionalists and leaders of the IRB, John Devoy (the leader of Clan-na-Gael) sent a telegram to Parnell. This offered Parnell the support of the IRB – provided that certain conditions were met. This agreement is known as the 'New Departure'.

Fact: Parnell was helped in this after he had stated in parliament in June 1876 that he did not think the Fenians had committed murder in Manchester in 1867. In fact, some historians think that, after the signing of the 'Kilmainham Treaty' in 1882, he took the IRB oath. Although, as he was essentially a constitutionalist – and was not a supporter of total separation from Britain – this would have been done for purely tactical reasons.

Home Rule Confederation: this was a home rule organisation that Butt had established to complement the work of the Home Rule League in Britain, as opposed to Ireland.

Fact: By 1876–7, the IRB's total membership in Ireland was just under 20,000. However, despite this relatively small membership, their close connections to wealthy Irish revolutionary organisations in the US meant they had a disproportionately large political significance in Irish politics. Consequently, they were a powerful political force that had to be taken into account by any practical politician wishing to achieve reform in Ireland.

SOURCE B

Nationalists here will support you on the following conditions:

First: Abandonment of the Federal demand and substitution of a general declaration in favour of self-government.

Second: Vigorous agitation of the Land Question on the basis of a peasant proprietary, while accepting concessions tending to abolish arbitrary evictions.

Third: Exclusion of all sectarian issues from the platform.

Fourth: Irish members to vote together on all Imperial and Home Rule questions, adopt an aggressive policy and energetically resist coercive legislation.

Fifth: Advocacy of all struggling nationalities in the British Empire and elsewhere.

Telegram from John Devoy to Charles Stewart Parnell, 25 October 1878. Quoted in M. Collier (2008), *Britain and Ireland 1867–1922*, Harlow: Heinemann, p. 51.

Parnell, too, argued that, with the right kind of support in Ireland, he believed a more aggressive campaign in parliament could achieve real reform. However, he interpreted the 'New Departure' differently from Devoy: instead of the land question being used by nationalists to build up support for an independence movement, Parnell saw he could use those wanting independence to achieve significant land reform. One result of the 'New Departure' was the Land War, which broke out in 1879 (see Section 6.4, The 'Land War', 1879–82). This had seen Parnell work closely with Devoy and Michael Davitt – the latter made several attempts to persuade Parnell to join the IRB. Although, as has been seen, the Land War persuaded Gladstone to agree to modifications of the 1881 Land Act, this was not enough for those wanting independence.

SOURCE C

The New Departure was the term soon to be given by extremist republicans in the United States, headed by Devoy, to a new public policy of their own. This consisted of temporarily shelving the single uncompromising goal of an Irish Republic to be won by force of arms, and substituting a more gradualist approach of short-term objectives to be won at Westminster under the leadership of Parnell. The theory was that this would help activate popular nationalist feeling, and parliamentarians were in turn to accept as a final goal a totally independent Ireland...

Devoy ... [who] had received favourable personal reports on Parnell and his attitude... finally swung the full force of his Irish-American organization, the Clan-na-Gael, over to the principle of such an alliance.

R. Kee (1972), *The Green Flag: A History of Irish Nationalism,* London: Penguin Books, p. 368.

The move to violence, 1882–1914

The 'New Departure' had been opposed by those members of the IRB wanting to concentrate on achieving independence via a revolutionary uprising. One of the groups that had split away as a result of Devoy's alliance with Parnell was 'The Invincibles'. On 6 May 1882, members of this group murdered the chief secretary and the under-secretary for Ireland in Dublin's Phoenix Park. This had several impacts on Irish politics: it immediately led the government to introduce repressive legislation, including the Prevention of Crimes Act, which suspended trial by jury and gave the RIC the power to search and arrest on suspicion. In addition, it caused problems for Parnell who, despite condemning the murders, was blamed by the media and by many people.

More importantly for the struggle for independence, it drove a wedge between Parnell and the more radical Fenians such as Davitt who wanted nationalisation and redistribution of the land. So, in October 1882, Parnell set up the Irish National League (INL) to focus on obtaining home rule; the sixty-three members who were MPs formed the Irish Parliamentary Party (IPP) in the House of Commons. Not surprisingly, this move was attacked by those nationalists wanting complete independence. Nonetheless, by the end of 1882, the INL soon had more than 200 branches in Ireland – by 1885, it had almost 600 branches. However, Parnell's '*ne plus ultra*' speech, which he made on 21 January 1885, did please some of those wanting independence.

'Ne plus ultra': this Latin phrase means: 'no more beyond'. By it, Parnell meant that it was not possible to say that, in relation to Ireland's 'national question', home rule would be the final reform. However, he also made it clear elsewhere that his goal was the restoration of an Irish parliament in Dublin, which could then decide all domestic issues. Those wanting independence wanted to go further as, under home rule, the British government would retain control of taxation, foreign policy and the military.

SOURCE D

I do not know how this great question [home rule] will eventually be settled. I do not know whether England will be wise in time, and concede to constitutional arguments and methods the restitution of that which was stolen from us towards the close of the last century… We cannot ask for less than the restitution of Grattan's Parliament… But no man has a right to fix the boundary to the march of a nation. No man has a right to say to his country, 'thus far shalt thou go and no farther'.

An extract from the speech Parnell made in Cork in January 1885. ('Grattan's Parliament' was the name of the Irish parliament which was abolished by the 1801 Act of Union.) Quoted in P. Adelman and R. Pearce (2008), *Great Britain and the Irish Question*, London: Hodder Education, p. 101.

In order to build support for his National League, Parnell also obtained the backing of the Catholic Church in 1883.

When Gladstone's government lost a vote over the budget in June 1885, Parnell tried to use the size of the IPP vote to play off the Liberal and Conservative parties against each other in order to obtain home rule. In the general election at the end of 1885, he encouraged voters in England to vote for Conservative candidates.

Fact: Parnell encouraged voters to back the Conservatives because the Conservatives had a built-in majority in the House of Lords. At this time, the Lords had the power to block any legislation, no matter how many times it was passed in the House Commons. Thus, if home rule was ever to become law, the Conservatives needed to support it.

Fact: In 1884, Parnell had made sure his control of this new organisation was strong by introducing the 'pledge', by which all INL MPs – who were part of the Irish Parliamentary Party (IPP) – had to agree to support the party on all votes on which a majority of the party had agreed.

THE IRISH FRANKENSTEIN.

Figure 6.8 A cartoon by John Tenniel published in *Punch* magazine on 20 May 1882. Parnell is shown as the 'Irish Frankenstein'. Readers in 1882 would have been very familiar with Mary Shelley's novel, *Frankenstein*, first published in 1818

In that election, the number of seats won by the Liberals in Ireland dropped from thirteen to none, while the INL won eighty-six out of Ireland's 103 seats. This showed the amount of support for Parnell's call for home rule. As no party won an overall majority, Parnell's influence increased, as the IPP MPs held the balance of power.

The First Home Rule Bill, 1886

Gladstone at last decided to support home rule and, on 8 April 1886, he introduced the Home Rule (Government of Ireland) Bill. Prophetically, Gladstone expressed the hope that parliament would pass the bill and grant home rule now, rather than be forced to do so at some later date. The bill was introduced on 16 April, but was a disappointment for many Irish nationalists, as executive power would rest with a lord-lieutenant of Ireland, who would not be answerable to the assemblies in Ireland. In addition, while the British parliament would control some aspects of Irish taxation, the eighty MPs in Ireland would be entitled to would lose their representation at Westminster.

Even so, many in Gladstone's Liberal Party – who had already been made uneasy by his Land Acts – were opposed to this, and about fifty Liberal MPs eventually joined forces with the Conservatives to defeat it.

Gladstone called new elections for July 1886, but the result was a disappointment for Parnell, as the Conservatives were able to form a government with the support of those Liberals opposed to home rule. As the Conservatives supported the Protestants in Ulster, any chance of achieving home rule was temporarily over; consequently, Parnell's influence suffered a slight decline.

However, although the question of home rule persisted, it was clear now that any chance of home rule rested with the Liberal Party rather than the Conservatives. At the same time, more radical nationalist began to challenge Parnell's control: one example of this was the 'Plan of Campaign' that began in 1886 over the question of rents and evictions. This seemed likely to lead to a second Land War, and made Parnell vulnerable to accusations that he supported the violent actions of nationalists who clearly saw independence as their final goal. During 1886–7, '**Establishment**' newspapers such as *The Times* began to publish letters that they claimed showed that Parnell supported violence. Although these were proved to be forgeries in 1889, Parnell's influence was eventually ended as a result of being named in a divorce petition in November 1890. Parnell refused to resign as leader of the IPP – but this split the IPP (which numbered seventy-three) in two: into twenty-nine Parnellites and forty-four anti-Parnellites. The anti-Parnellites – led by MPs such as Tim Healey – then officially resigned from the INL and the IPP. They formed the Irish National Federation (INF) in 1891; eventually, this was led by John Blake Dillon. As well as Dillon and Healey, William O'Brien and Justin McCarthy were other important leaders.

Although Parnell was supported by the remaining members of the INL/IPP – eventually led by John Redmond – and by the Fenians, and began to adopt a more radical line once more, his political influence was effectively ended and he died in 1891. However, in 1898, the INF itself split, with O'Brien setting up the United Irish League in order to achieve unity with the INL. In 1900, this merged with the INF under the leadership of John Redmond and a new reunified IPP was formed. This resumed the struggle for home rule.

'Establishment': in British politics, this refers to the dominant élites and groups that effectively control the broad thrust of economics and politics. In the main, this means the large landowners, bankers and industrialists – along with the political élite that largely shared the outlook, interests and even social and educational backgrounds of the wealthy élites.

Parliament Act of 1911: this had been introduced when the Lords rejected the 1909 'People's' Budget, which would have increased taxes on wealthy industrialists and landowners to help pay for old age pensions to be paid to poor people. The Lords had rejected this, and two elections had been fought in 1910 over the Lords' veto. The Liberals won both – but with very slim majorities. As a result, they were dependent of the votes of the IPP and other Irish nationalists which, between them, had won eighty-two seats.

The Second Home Rule Bill 1893

During the general election of 1892, Gladstone campaigned on the issue of home rule. He was able to form a majority government and introduced a new Home Rule Bill in February 1893. The Second Home Rule Bill, unlike the first, stated that Irish MPs would remain in Westminster and would be allowed to vote on all bills affecting Ireland. Although it was passed by MPs, the large Conservative majority in the Lords voted it down.

The Liberals lost power in 1895, and the Conservatives – in alliance with those Liberals opposed to home rule – were in government for the next ten years. Although the Conservatives were prepared to introduce reforms regarding land tenure and education, home rule was off the agenda. However, the Liberals returned to power in 1906, so home rule once again became a possibility. This was especially so after the **Parliament Act of 1911**.

This had ended the power of the House of Lords to permanently block any legislation they did not like. It proposed that, as long as a bill passed in the Commons in three successive sessions in two years, it would automatically become law, regardless of the Lords. The Lords reluctantly agreed to pass this law as the Liberal government had got the king to agree that, if they won the second 1910 election, he would create enough Liberal peers to end the Conservative majority there.

6.5 What were the roles of Michael Collins and Éamon de Valera in the struggle for independence?

The move into a new century saw influence pass from the constitutionalists who favoured peaceful methods to those republicans prepared to use violence to achieve full independence.

The Third Home Rule Bill, 1912

Once the Parliament Act had become law, the Irish nationalist MPs expected to be rewarded with home rule. So, in April 1912, H.H. Asquith (the Liberal prime minister) introduced the Third Reform Bill.

This was very similar to the Second Home Rule Act. Although it was strongly opposed by the Conservatives, it passed its final stage in the House of Commons in May 1914 and, despite the Lords once again rejecting it, it would pass into law under the terms of the 1911 Parliament Act. However, with the outbreak of the First World War in August 1914, the British government rushed through the **Suspensory Act**, which postponed the implementation of the Home Rule Act until the end of the war. These developments also led to the emergence of outright revolutionaries such as **Padraic Pearse, James Connolly**, Michael Collins and Éamon de Valera.

The Suspensory Act also put on hold Conservative proposals – reluctantly agreed in principle by Asquith – that Ulster might be temporarily excluded from the operation of home rule.

Padraic Pearse (1879–1916)

Also known as Padraig or Patrick, Pearse became interested in Irish history and culture from an early age and, in 1900, joined the Gaelic League in which he found several radical and militant nationalists. He was a teacher, barrister and poet, and soon came to believe that a revolutionary uprising was the only way to gain Irish independence. He shared James Connolly's belief that independence was the only way to achieve economic and social justice in Ireland. In August 1915, at the funeral of the Irish revolutionary Jeremiah O'Donovan Rossa, his oration included the phrase: 'Ireland unfree, shall never be at peace'. He helped plan the Easter Rising, and was commander-in-chief of the 1916 rebels: he was executed on 3 May 1916.

James Connolly (1868–1916)

He was born in Scotland to Irish immigrant parents, and moved to Ireland in 1895. He set up the Irish Socialist Republican Party and, alongside James Larkin, later became a leader of the Irish Transport and General Workers' Union. He was a revolutionary socialist and a respected Marxist writer. He wanted Ireland to become a socialist republic and supported Irish independence as part of that struggle. He set up the Irish Citizen Army (ICA) in November 1913, initially to provide protection for union pickets from police and troops during the Dublin Lockout, which had begun in August. He accepted women as well as men as members of the ICA: the ICA's flag was the 'Plough and Stars'.

Figure 6.9   A postcard showing John Redmond, the leader of the Irish nationalist MPs, leading H.H. Asquith, David Lloyd George and Randolph Churchill by the nose

Revolutionary nationalism and Irish independence 1914–16

This postponement served, in the end, to give the initiative to those who wanted to achieve complete independence from Britain – and were prepared to use force to do so. Even before postponement, however, revolutionary Irish republicans had been pushed in the direction of armed revolt by developments concerning Ulster.

Once it had become clear that the Third Home Rule Bill would eventually become law, the unionists decided to act. Fearing that an Irish parliament with a Catholic majority would eventually result in a totally independent Ireland, they decided to use force to resist. Led by the Ulster Protestant Sir Edward Carson – and supported by several leading Conservatives, including Randolph Churchill – they organised huge demonstrations protesting against the Bill. On 27 July 1912, the unionists organised a meeting at Blenheim Palace (Randolph Churchill's home), where Bonar Law, the Conservative Party's leader, spoke to a crowd of more than 3,000 unionists.

Later, unionists drew up the Solemn League and Covenant, by which unionists could swear an oath to oppose home rule. Carson was the first to sign it, on 28 September – followed by almost 500,000 unionists. They then set up the Ulster Volunteer Force (UVF), and began open military training. By the summer of 1914, they had more than 100,000 members and, with more than £1 million in donations from Orange Order members and sympathisers in Ireland and Britain, began to buy large supplies of guns and ammunition, mainly from Germany. This was despite a government ban, issued in December 1913, on importing weapons. In fact, despite the ban, the army and police did nothing to prevent the UVF unloading large shipments of weapons and ammunition at several of Ulster's coastal towns at the end of April 1914.

Figure 6.10   Armed unionists march through Portadown in protest against home rule, September 1912

This alarmed both the constitutionalist nationalists and those radicals who wanted a totally independent Irish republic. The latter began to make plans of their own. On 25 November 1913, Eoin MacNeill held a nationalists' meeting in Dublin to form the Irish Volunteers (IV) to oppose the Ulster Volunteers. Although this move was initially condemned by Redmond and other leading members of the IPP, many ordinary members joined. Redmond's stance also gave an opening to the more radical IRB, which had been relatively side-lined for some time. Now it was reactivated, and many of its members also joined the IV and soon obtained leadership positions. By May 1914, the IV had about 80,000 members and began undertaking military training. In June 1914, Redmond attempted to take control of the IV's ruling Provisional Committee, by insisting that its existing twenty-five members be joined by twenty-five of his own supporters. By July, the IV had doubled in size to almost 160,000 and decided to obtain more weapons.

However, on 16 July, the British army killed three unarmed civilians at Howth in Dublin, while attempting to prevent an attempt by nationalists to land weapons. After

Historical debate:
In 1998, historian Alan O'Day's *Irish Home Rule* presented a new interpretation, arguing that previous perspectives on the home rule movement, which concentrated on establishing the differences between constitutionalists like Butt and revolutionaries like Davitt, had missed an important point. This was that, within the Irish nationalist movement, there were two distinct groups: those who sought home rule on political and moral justice grounds; and those who wanted home rule for material reasons, arguing that home rule was necessary for Ireland to secure its future economic development. He also concluded that the failure of home rule was significant as it showed the limitations of parliamentary/constitutional approaches for dealing with Ireland's problems.

Fact: Unionist paramilitary groups had been buying weapons and holding military drills since 1911. Then, in January 1913, the Ulster Unionist Council decided to bring these together as one organisation.

August 1914, however, because the British government's main priority was to ensure Irishmen would continue to enlist, the authorities in Dublin tended to turn a blind eye to most of the activities of the Irish Volunteers. Thus war – in this case, the First World War – once again gave an opportunity that revolutionary republicans were able to exploit in their struggle for Irish independence.

At the same time as the Irish Volunteers were being formed, another more left-wing group, the Irish Citizen Army, led by James Connolly, also armed itself and was prepared to fight.

Figure 6.11 Members of the ICA. The anti-war banner of the Irish Citizens' Army drapes from Liberty Hall, the headquarters of the Irish Transport and General Workers' Union. The slogan in the bottom corner of the photograph was used by James Larkin, but is often attributed to the French philosopher P.J. Proudhon

SOURCE E

We have no foreign enemy except the treacherous government of England – a government which even whilst it is calling us to die for it, refuses to give a straight answer to our demand for Home Rule.

Comments made at the start of the First World War in 1914, by James Connolly, leader of the Irish Citizens' Army. Quoted in A. Todd (2001), *The Modern World*, Oxford: Oxford University Press, p. 17.

Also significant for the republican cause and the fight for Irish independence was a new political organisation that had been set up in November 1905. This was the **Sinn Féin Party**, which favoured total independence for Ireland, and was led by **Arthur Griffith**.

Initially, Sinn Féin attracted little support from the Irish people who, until events after 1912, tended to support the position of the IPP and the struggle for home rule.

The Curragh Mutiny, 1914

Both the nationalist moderates and the more militant republicans were especially angered in March 1914 by what became known as the Curragh Mutiny, in which Protestant officers at the British army's headquarters in Dublin were allowed to temporarily 'resign' their commissions rather than enforce the Home Rule Act. This idea had been put forward by the opposition Conservative Party, which argued that the army should not be used to deal with any resistance to home rule. Eventually, John Seeley, the Liberal government's secretary of state for war, informed the army's commander-in-chief in Ireland that any soldier wishing to absent himself from duty in Ulster could do so. Following some misunderstandings, Asquith finally informed army leaders that the army would not be used against Ulster unionists. Ireland seemed on the point of civil war but, in August 1914, Britain declared war on Germany and, as has been seen, the Act was suspended until the end of the war.

Most Irish people – Catholic and Protestant – supported the British government in the war, and many men, both unionists and nationalists, volunteered to join the British army. By 1916, more than 150,000 had volunteered. However, the nationalists were angered when Carson became a member of the wartime coalition government, and the army recruits from Ulster were allowed to form a special Ulster Division.

On 20 September 1914, Redmond, who supported Britain's involvement in the First World War, promised that the Irish Volunteers would fight for Britain. Most members of the IV accepted this and formed the National Volunteers.

However, the more radical members of the IV – influenced by people such as Eoin MacNeill and by the IRB – were outraged by Redmond's actions and about 10,000 refused to participate in the National Volunteers. A meeting then took place between Connolly, Pearse and other Fenian republican leaders. On 24 September 1914, these Irish Volunteers issued a statement in Dublin, which made clear the split between the Redmondite and non-Redmondite Irish Volunteers.

SOURCE F

At the next meeting of the Provisional Committee [of the Irish Volunteers] we shall propose:…

3. To [oppose] any diminution of the measure of Irish self-government which now exists as a Statute on paper and which would not now have reached that stage but for the Irish Volunteers.

4. To repudiate any undertaking, by whomsoever given, to consent to the legislative dismemberment of Ireland; and to protest against the attitude of the present Government, who under the pretence that 'Ulster cannot be coerced', avow themselves prepared to coerce the Nationalists of Ulster.

5. To declare that Ireland cannot, with honour or safety, take part in foreign quarrels otherwise than through the free action of a National Government of her own; and to repudiate the claim of nay man to offer up the blood and lives of the sons of Irishmen and Irishwomen to the service of the British Empire, while no National Government which could speak and act for the people of Ireland is allowed to exist.

Extracts from the statement to the Irish Volunteers, 24 September 1914. Amongst those signing were Eoin MacNeill, Padraic Pearse and James Plunkett. From: Eoin MacNeill papers, School of History and Archives, University College Dublin Archives, IE UCDA LA 1/H/1 (6-7), www.ucd.ie/archives/html/collections/macneill-eoin.htm.

Arthur Griffith (1871–1922)

After involvement with cultural organisations, Griffith became more political and, in 1899, set up the newspaper *United Irishman*. In this, he argued that Ireland needed to be self-sufficient politically and economically. He worked with other separatist movements, and joined the Irish Volunteers in 1913. However, he did not favour the use of force, and left the IRB in 1910. Instead, he argued for 'abstentionism' – refusing to participate in or cooperate with any British institution; although he also believed in retaining links to the British crown. He opposed Irish people fighting in the First World War: as a result, in December 1914, the newspaper *Sinn Féin* was banned. He did not take part in the 1916 Easter Rising but was imprisoned nonetheless by the British. In 1919, he became president of the first Irish parliament, and headed the Irish delegation at the negotiations in London that led to the Anglo–Irish Partition Treaty of 1921.

Fact: Redmond had hoped the National Volunteers would also be allowed to fight as a distinct army corps. But Lord Kitchener, the secretary of state for war, who distrusted Irish Catholics, refused to allow this.

ACTIVITY

Watch the video clip of the entire poem being read, accompanied by images of the Easter Rising, on www.youtube.com. Enter 'The Rebel – Padraig Pearse' into the search box.

Then write a couple of sentences to explain why this poem might have influenced Irish people to support the struggle for Irish independence.

SOURCE G

And I say to my people's masters: Beware,

Beware of the thing that is coming, beware of the risen people,

Who shall take what ye would not give.

Did ye think to conquer the people,

Or that Law is stronger than life, and than men's desire to be free?

We will try it out with you, ye that have harried and held,

Ye that have bullied and bribed.

Tyrants … hypocrites … liars!

The final lines of Padraic Pearse's poem, 'The Rebel'. Quoted at www.ucc.ie/celt/published/E950004-024/index.html.

Roger Casement (1864–1916)

He was an Irish diplomat and poet, who became an anti-imperialist as the result of his experiences as a consul in British colonies in Africa, and of his investigations into atrocities committed against indigenous peoples by colonial powers. During his trial, when some people were arguing for clemency for him, the British government circulated pages of what became known as the 'Black Diaries'. These appeared to reveal details of his private life as a gay man. Although historians remain divided on how genuine the diaries are, the publication of these extracts effectively undermined support for him; he was hanged as a traitor on 3 August 1916.

It was this smaller and more revolutionary group of Irish Volunteers that, less than two years later, would have a dramatic impact on the struggle for Irish independence. Meanwhile, in 1915, members of the IRB were able to take control of the Gaelic League – its new head was Thomas Clarke, who was a leading member of the IRB's Military Council. The year before, Padraic Pearse, who was a founder member and already an important leader of the Irish Volunteers, had joined the IRB in 1913. He was soon co-opted onto the IRB's Supreme Council and its Military Council by Tom Clarke.

From 1914 onwards, militant republicans and socialists worked increasingly closely together, and many members of Connolly's ICA also joined the IRB. In January 1916, with Connolly's support, the Military Council of the IRB decided on a military uprising for later in the year. However, the Military Council was divided: Eoin MacNeill believed it should only take place when the conditions were right; but Pearse and Connolly felt that a political and military example should be given. Even if it was doomed to end in failure in the short-term, they believed it could provide a spark for a future nationwide uprising against British control.

The Easter Rising, 1916

More importantly, a minority of Republicans saw Britain's involvement in a major war as an opportunity to grab full independence for Ireland. A shipment of arms for the Republicans, carried by a German ship, the *Aud*, was intercepted by the British navy off the coast of County Kerry, and **Roger Casement**, an important Irish nationalist, was arrested. Since 1914, he had been in Germany, trying to get Irish prisoners of war to join an 'Irish Brigade' to fight for Irish independence, which he hoped Germany would support. Although this failed, he had succeeded in purchasing weapons and ammunition for the revolutionary republicans.

Despite this setback, on Easter Monday, 24 April 1916, a small group of about 2,000 from the Irish Volunteers and the Irish Citizens' Army, led by Padraic Pearse and James Connolly, took over important buildings in Dublin, including the General Post Office,

POBLACHT NA H EIREANN.

THE PROVISIONAL GOVERNMENT
OF THE
IRISH REPUBLIC
TO THE PEOPLE OF IRELAND.

IRISHMEN AND IRISHWOMEN   In the name of God and of the dead generations from which she receives her old tradition of nationhood, Ireland, through us, summons her children to her flag and strikes for her freedom.

Having organised and trained her manhood through her secret revolutionary organisation, the Irish Republican Brotherhood, and through her open military organisations, the Irish Volunteers and the Irish Citizen Army, having patiently perfected her discipline, having resolutely waited for the right moment to reveal itself, she now seizes that moment, and, supported by her exiled children in America and by gallant allies in Europe, but relying in the first on her own strength, she strikes in full confidence of victory.

We declare the right of the people of Ireland to the ownership of Ireland, and to the unfettered control of Irish destinies, to be sovereign and indefeasible.   The long usurpation of that right by a foreign people and government has not extinguished the right, nor can it ever be extinguished except by the destruction of the Irish people.   In every generation the Irish people have asserted their right to national freedom and sovereignty, six times during the past three hundred years they have asserted it in arms.   Standing on that fundamental right and again asserting it in arms in the face of the world, we hereby proclaim the Irish Republic as a Sovereign Independent State, and we pledge our lives and the lives of our comrades-in-arms to the cause of its freedom, of its welfare, and of its exaltation among the nations.

The Irish Republic is entitled to, and hereby claims, the allegiance of every Irishman and Irishwoman.   The Republic guarantees religious and civil liberty, equal rights and equal opportunities to all its citizens, and declares its resolve to pursue the happiness and prosperity of the whole nation and of all its parts, cherishing all the children of the nation equally, and oblivious of the differences carefully fostered by an alien government, which have divided a minority from the majority in the past.

Until our arms have brought the opportune moment for the establishment of a permanent National Government, representative of the whole people of Ireland and elected by the suffrages of all her men and women, the Provisional Government, hereby constituted, will administer the civil and military affairs of the Republic in trust for the people.

We place the cause of the Irish Republic under the protection of the Most High God, Whose blessing we invoke upon our arms, and we pray that no one who serves that cause will dishonour it by cowardice, inhumanity, or rapine.   In this supreme hour the Irish nation must, by its valour and discipline and by the readiness of its children to sacrifice themselves for the common good, prove itself worthy of the august destiny to which it is called.

Signed on Behalf of the Provisional Government,
THOMAS J. CLARKE,
SEAN Mac DIARMADA,   THOMAS MacDONAGH,
P. H. PEARSE,   EAMONN CEANNT,
JAMES CONNOLLY.   JOSEPH PLUNKETT.

Figure 6.12   The Proclamation of the Irish Republic, read by Pearse outside the General Post Office on 24 April 1916, at the start of the Easter Rising. This was mainly written by Pearse, although Connolly and Plunkett also contributed

Ireland

ACTIVITY

For more information –
and a documentary
film – about those
who led or took
part in the Easter
Rising, visit http://
todayinirishhistory.
com/tag/padraic-
pearse. Then produce
a chart outlining both
the value and the
limitations of this film
for historians wishing
to find out about the
Easter Rising.

Fact: There were supposed
to be risings elsewhere in
Ireland but, as a result of
the opposition of MacNeill,
and some poor planning,
only a few of these actually
took place.

Fact: People living near
Kilmainham Gaol could hear
the gunfire as each rebel
was shot and, on the day of
Connolly's execution, a large
and angry crowd gathered
outside the prison. Connolly
had been so badly injured
in the fighting that a doctor
judged he only had a day
or two to live. Nonetheless,
the authorities proceeded
with his execution on 12
May. He had to be carried
to the prison courtyard and
then strapped to a chair, in
case he fell over. A further
ninety-seven were due to
be executed, but Asquith,
the British prime minister
intervened to get these
commuted to varying terms
of imprisonment.

which became their headquarters. Although they had no chance of success, they proclaimed the independence of Ireland and raised the green, white and orange tricolour flag over the Post Office.

For the next six days, fighting between the rebels and British troops took place across Dublin. Connolly and Plunkett were the main military commanders, but their rebellion ended when the British shelled the occupied buildings from a warship on the River Liffey. Eventually, Pearse arranged the surrender of those rebels still alive – many of these, including Connolly, were seriously wounded. The death count was 450 – with 250 of these being civilian casualties: some of the latter included those shot by troops for looting shops. The surviving rebels were arrested and marched to prison.

At that point, most Dubliners were angry with the rebels for the damage they had caused, and for betraying their countrymen who were fighting in Europe on Britain's side.

Figure 6.13 Death by firing squad after the Easter Rising

Yet the British authorities then made a serious political miscalculation. Although as recently as 1915, Padraic Pearse had publicly spoken of the political significance of Fenian martyrs, the British authorities began to try the prisoners by military tribunals.

When the first group of prisoners were found guilty of treason, fifteen of them were sentenced to death by firing squad. These were then executed in batches of one to three a day, from 3 to 12 May; their bodies were then put into a mass grave, without coffins. Later, in August, Roger Casement was hanged.

SOURCE H

The Defenders of this Realm have worked well in secret and in the open. They think that they have purchased half of us and intimidated the other half. They think that they have foreseen everything, think that they have provided against everything; but the fools, the fools, the fools! – they have left us our Fenian dead, and, while Ireland holds these graves, Ireland unfree shall never be at peace.

Extract from a speech made by Padraic Pearse at the funeral of Jeremiah O'Donovan Rossa in 1915. Taken from http://irishhistorian.com/Quiz/FamousQuotations.html.

The rise of Sinn Féin, 1916–18

Before these executions, Sinn Féin had not been a very significant party – but the executions turned the Easter rebels into national heroes, and resulted in a massive increase of support for Sinn Féin.

Figure 6.14   Commemorative posters, showing the seven signatories of the Proclamation of 1916, all of whom were executed

This support increased further when the British government put Ireland under martial law and – apparently believing that the Easter Rising had been planned by Sinn Féin – imprisoned almost 3,500 nationalists. These included the Sinn Féin

KEY CONCEPTS

Change and continuity: How far were the Fenian Rising of 1867 and the Easter Rebellion of 1916 similar as regards their historical contexts and their outcomes?

Fact: One of these seats was won by Count George Plunkett, whose son Joseph had been one of the 1916 Rising leaders executed by the British. His other sons, George and Jack, both took part in the Rising, and went on to be important members of the IRA. The other seat was won by Joseph McGuinness – he had also fought in the Rising.

Fact: This impacted on the moderate nationalists who, in 1916, led a walk-out from Parliament in London in protest at Britain's first attempt to introduce conscription in Ireland (the second one was in 1918) – against the advice of the chief secretary for Ireland, Henry Duke. The IPP MPs then joined Sinn Féin in an anti-conscription campaign. After a series of strikes and the signing of a National Pledge, Lloyd George dropped the plan. By then, however, large sections of the Irish population had been further radicalised – as a result, the influence of the moderate home rulers was seriously weakened.

leader, Arthur Griffith. As with the executions of the rebels, the wide-scale nature of these arrests pushed many Irish people into a more radical view concerning Irish independence.

By 1917, Sinn Féin was committed to the creation of a totally independent Ireland. In February and March, it won two by-elections in what had been safe seats for the more moderate Nationalist Party. Éamon de Valera, another Sinn Féin leader – who had been released in June 1917 – then won the East Clare seat in July 1917.

Figure 6.15 Éamon de Valera after his surrender, at the end of the Rising. He had been commandant of one of the IV's military units. However, unlike the other commandants, his death sentence was immediately commuted to imprisonment

In October 1917, Sinn Féin held its tenth conference (*ard-fheis*). This proved to be an important point as, up until then, Sinn Féin had been mainly concerned with cultural nationalism. Although it had not played an important part in the Easter Rebellion, Sinn Féin decided to try to unite – as had Parnell – in one organisation, the violent separatist wing and the parliamentary wing of Irish nationalism. From this point on, Sinn Féin was committed to the cause of an independent Irish republic. At this conference, de Valera was elected president of Sinn Féin, while Arthur Griffith became vice-president. Griffith, still against the idea of further military uprisings, instead pushed for a campaign to persuade other countries that Ireland should be a sovereign, free and independent country.

By the end of 1917, the rise in nationalist sentiment resulted in Sinn Féin gaining more than 250,000 members. Then, in the December 1918 general election (in which, for the first time, women – provided they were over thirty – could also vote), Sinn Féin – by now openly committed to a separatist republicanism that argued that Ireland was not a part of England – won seventy-three out of Ireland's 105 seats, with the moderate Irish Nationalist Party only winning seven seats. One of the Sinn Féin candidates elected in 1918 was **Countess Markievicz**.

This Sinn Féin victory in practice ended the influence and significance of Redmond's Irish Party in Ireland.

The struggle for Irish independence 1918–19

Having won an overwhelming victory in Ireland, the Sinn Féin MPs, led by Éamon de Valera, refused to go to Westminster and, in 1919, set up their own all-Ireland parliament in Dublin, called the Dáil Éireann (Parliament of Ireland). At its first meeting on 21 January 1919, the MPs passed the Irish Declaration of Independence.

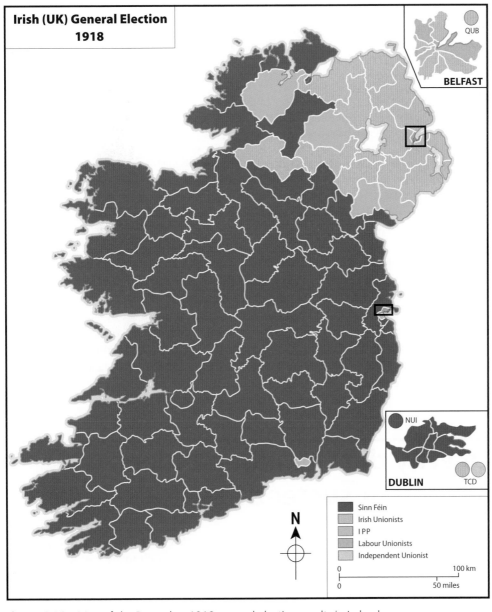

Figure 6.16 Map of the December 1918 general election results in Ireland

Countess Markievicz (1868–1927)

She was a suffragette and socialist who had commanded a section of the Irish Volunteers during the Easter Rising and had been imprisoned by the British for her involvement in the rebellion. Her election in December makes her the first woman to be elected to the British House of Commons. She was also one of the first women in the world to have a senior ministerial post: she acted as minister for labour in the Irish Republic from 1919 to 1922. However, because – like all Sinn Féin MPs – she refused to go to London, she was not the first woman to take a seat in parliament.

Fact: De Valera was one of seventy-three Sinn Féin leaders arrested in May 1918 as part of the authorities' attempt to deal with what was called the 'German Plot'. This was the claim that the current anti-conscription campaign in Ireland was part of a German plot calculated to deprive Britain of extra troops, and to increase membership and support for Sinn Féin.

Figure 6.17   Michael Collins (1890–1922)

Born in County Cork, Collins moved to London in 1906, and was soon attracted to the cause of Irish nationalism. In 1908, he joined Sinn Féin, and the following year became a member of the IRB. Collins believed that, for Ireland to gain independence, nationalists would have to use force: in 1914, he joined the Irish Volunteers. He acted as Joseph Plunkett's aide-de-camp during the Easter Rising, and fought alongside Pearce and Connolly. He was imprisoned in England; on his release in December 1916, he returned to Ireland and the cause of independence. In 1920, the British government offered a reward of £10,000 (worth about £300,000 in 2014) for information leading to his capture or death. He helped negotiate the Partition Treaty of 1921, which led to a civil war in southern Ireland. He was assassinated by anti-Treaty IRA members on 22 August 1922.

SOURCE I

Whereas the Irish People is by right a free people:

And Whereas for seven hundred years the Irish people has never ceased to repudiate and has repeatedly protested in arms against foreign usurpation.

And Whereas English rule in this country is, and always has been, based on force and fraud and military occupation against the declared will of the people:

And Whereas the Irish Republic was proclaimed in Dublin on Easter Monday, 1916, by the Irish Republican Army acting on behalf of the Irish people:…

And Whereas at the threshold of a new era in history the Irish electorate has in the General election of December 1918, seized the first occasion to declare by an overwhelming majority its firm allegiance to the Irish Republic:

Now, therefore, we, the elected Representatives of the ancient Irish people in National parliament assembled, do, in the name of the Irish nation, ratify the establishment of the Irish Republic and pledge ourselves and our people to make this declaration effective by every means at our command:

We ordain that the elected Representatives of the Irish people alone have the power to make laws binding on the people of Ireland, and that the Irish parliament is the only parliament to which that people will give its allegiance:

Extracts from the Declaration of Independence, 1919. For the full text of the Declaration of Independence, see http://rsfnational.wordpress.com/miscellaneous/rsf-policies/declaration-of-independence-1919.

In April 1919, de Valera – who had been arrested again in May 1918 and had then escaped from his English prison in February 1919 – was elected president, while Griffith became vice-president and **Michael Collins** became minister of finance. This new unofficial Irish 'government' then began to collect taxes, and also set up a new system of local government based on town and county councils – Sinn Féin won most of the seats on these councils. Griffith, however, had been somewhat surprised by the decision to set up a separate state, as he still believed that the total separation of Ireland from Britain should be postponed for a while.

6.6 Why did the independence movement succeed?

The Irish independence movement was eventually successful as a result of employing a combination of tactics: war, propaganda and diplomacy. Although many nationalists felt that, in fact, the independence struggle had not been successful – and still isn't, given that Ireland remains divided into two separate states.

The 'War of Independence', 1919–21

This Sinn Féin rebellion quickly resulted in a guerrilla war – also known as the Anglo–Irish War – between the British army and the newly formed Irish Republican Army (IRA). The IRA was led by Michael Collins who, although often on the run, managed to fulfil his duties as finance minister, as well as to mastermind the activities of the IRA.

The IRA's first attack was on two members of the RIC in January 1919. Although Sinn Féin's leadership had not authorised this action, the IRA saw it as the first shots in the 'war of independence'. On 31 January 1919, the Dáil officially declared that a **state of war** existed between Ireland and Britain. Britain responded by banning the Dáil and Sinn Féin.

In July 1919, Collins formed a special assassination unit, which was known as 'The Squad' or 'The Twelve Apostles'. In September 1919, he became director of intelligence for the IRA. He was determined to try to avoid direct military clashes between the IRA and the larger and better-trained British army. Instead, he adopted the tactics of guerrilla war, using a mixture of ambushes, assassinations and occasional skirmishes. The main targets were members of the RIC: during 1919 and the early part of 1920, the IRA killed 176 policemen and fifty-four soldiers, and destroyed or damaged forty-five RIC barracks. One result was that many members of the RIC resigned rather than risk being shot – and it became increasingly difficult to recruit new officers.

The Auxiliaries and the Black and Tans

As the fighting continued into 1920, the police increasingly lost control of the country. To strengthen the police, the British government recruited and sent over to Ireland almost 10,000 'special troops' from ex-officers and unemployed ex-soldiers – and even from certain categories of prisoners. The Auxiliaries were mostly ex-officers, and were attached to the RIC; the other special force, mostly drawn from ordinary ex-soldiers, was known as the '**Black and Tans**'.

The first Black and Tan units arrived in Ireland during March 1920. During 1920, both sides were responsible for several atrocities, reprisals and counter-reprisals, but the British atrocities only tended to push more and more Irish people into supporting Sinn Féin and even the IRA.

From the summer of 1920, the IRA resorted increasingly to the use of mobile 'active service units', usually known as 'Flying Columns'. These attacks and ambushes scored several notable successes over the next twelve months. As with other guerrilla wars – both previous and later – the IRA was able to operate as it did because it had the active or passive support of many Irish people. There were also a significant number of sympathisers within the British administration in Ireland.

'Bloody Sunday', 21 November 1920

In fact, Collins had several spies in Dublin Castle, the headquarters of the British authorities. This enabled him to avoid capture on many occasions, and also to discover the existence and identities of a group of deep-cover British agents: these were later called the 'Cairo Gang'. After getting approval from the Sinn Féin minister for defence, Collins ordered members of 'The Squad' and the Dublin Brigade of the IRA to eliminate these British agents. On Sunday 21 November 1920, these IRA units killed twelve **British Army undercover agents** who had recently arrived in Dublin with orders

---

KEY CONCEPTS QUESTION

Significance: How significant was the rise of Sinn Féin in the period 1916–18 in the struggle for Irish independence?

State of war: in theory, this implied that any actions by the IRA were acts of war, not terror.

'Black and Tans': they were given this nickname because a lack of uniforms meant they tended to use a mixture of the regular army's khaki uniforms and the dark-green uniforms worn by the RIC.

British Army undercover agents: these included some MI5 officers who had been drafted into Dublin during the summer and late autumn by Field Marshall Sir Henry Wilson. Their brief was to destroy Collins's organisation using any methods they considered necessary. These had included assassinating Sinn Féin members not involved in military operations as a way of flushing out IRA leaders. Briefly an Irish unionist politician, Wilson had encouraged senior army officers to resign in the Curragh Mutiny of 1914. On 22 June 1922, Wilson was assassinated outside his London house by two IRA men.

Figure 6.18 Two members of the Black and Tans search a suspected Sinn Féin supporter. Another suspect lies dead in the background

ACTIVITY

Watch the clip from the film *Michael Collins* at www.youtube.com. Enter 'Bloody Sunday 1920' into the search box. Then carry out further research on the incident portrayed, and explain how accurate you think the film clip is.

to eliminate Collins and his spies. Two Auxiliaries were also unintentionally killed that day, and this led to the Auxiliaries and RIC retaliating by killing thirteen spectators (including a woman and a child) and one player at a Gaelic football match at Croke Park in Dublin. In addition, two IRA men (and an innocent civilian), who had been arrested the day before, were killed by Auxiliaries in the guard room in Dublin Castle – allegedly for 'trying to escape'. As a result of all these deaths, this day became known as 'Bloody Sunday'.

In retaliation for the actions of the Auxiliaries, the IRA then launched attacks on the Auxiliaries: including an ambush on an Auxiliary convoy in Kilmichael, in County Cork, on 28 November 1920, in which eighteen Auxiliaries were killed. The IRA also attacked an Auxiliary unit in Cork. So, on 11–12 December, a combined force of Auxiliaries, Black and Tans and British troops burnt down the centre of Cork – even attacking firefighters who tried to put out the fires. Thereafter, several Auxiliary units wore burnt corks in their hat bands.

After December 1920, the independence war became even more violent, reaching a peak in the summer of 1921. Yet, by mid-1921, despite several spectacular successes, the IRA was beginning to face serious problems in Dublin and elsewhere. In particular, the IRA was running short of both men and weapons. This was despite the fact that a trip by de Valera to the US in 1920 had resulted in him raising $5 million, which had been used to buy Thompson machine guns, which were then smuggled into Ireland. Even Michael Collins was one of those thinking that the IRA could not continue for much longer.

Figure 6.19 A photograph of the centre of Cork, taken on the morning of 12 December 1920

The propaganda war

Sinn Féin was also quite effective in its use of propaganda. The *Irish Bulletin* – the official paper of the government of the Irish Republic – produced by Desmond Fitzgerald and Erskine Childers, detailed atrocities committed by British forces. Most of the official British and Irish press were generally reluctant to cover these actions, so Sinn Féin printed the paper in secret and, as well as distributing the paper within Ireland, also ensured that copies were given to international press agencies. The impact of this Sinn Féin propaganda was twofold. First, it helped gained sympathy – and funds – for the independence campaign from supporters across the world. Second, regular stories about the actions of the Auxiliaries and the Black and Tans made it increasingly difficult for the British government to increase repressive measures in Ireland.

The truce

By the autumn of 1919, the British government had begun to consider implementing the Third Home Rule Act of 1912. Consequently, in September 1919, it introduced a revised version – sometimes called the Fourth Home Rule Bill. This proposed establishing two separate home rule governments in Ireland: in Northern Ireland (Ulster) and in Southern Ireland. This Government of Ireland Act, which proposed proportional voting to protect the rights of minorities, eventually became law on 23 December 1920. Although this was supported by the Ulster unionists, Sinn Féin opposed the idea of a divided Ireland. They thus rejected the Act, and the fighting continued. By then, with most Irish nationalists committed to complete independence, the British government began to believe it would be unable to defeat the IRA.

However, by June 1921, a military stalemate had been reached and both sides had had enough of the bitter fighting. Thus Lloyd George suggested to de Valera that

Fact: Both sides used propaganda – especially during the summer of 1921. The British government – in an attempt to encourage loyalism among Irish Protestants and to win support for their tactics in Ireland – regularly issued reports when the IRA killed spies or collaborators who were also Protestants, but tended not to mention religious affiliations if those killed (the overwhelming majority) were Catholics. From August 1920, Dublin Castle had its own Propaganda Department that regularly 'planted' stories in the press to influence public opinion in Britain, where an increasing number were becoming concerned about the actions of the security forces in Ireland.

a conference should be held in London to discuss a settlement. Collins was in part taken by surprise by this move, as he felt the IRA wasn't able to carry the fight on to a victorious conclusion. In addition, as a result of the Government of Ireland Act of 1920, Northern Ireland, as a separate entity, had come into existence in May 1921. The unionists' victory in the subsequent general election undermined Sinn Féin's claim to speak for all of Ireland. However, Sinn Féin and its forces were also politically strengthened by these elections, as they won virtually every seat in the south – and even six seats in Northern Ireland.

The London Conference

A truce was agreed, which came into force on 11 July 1921 and, in October 1921, talks began in London between the British government, led by Lloyd George, and four Sinn Féin leaders, led by de Valera and Griffith.

Lloyd George offered **dominion status** to the southern counties – provided that the province of Ulster, to be known as Northern Ireland, remained part of the UK. Lloyd George also said that, if the majority of the people in Ulster voted to join the rest of Ireland, this would be allowed. This seemed to suggest that permanent partition of Ireland was unlikely. Even so, de Valera and several other leading Sinn Féiners were opposed to splitting Ireland or accepting anything less than a fully sovereign independent Irish republic. Consequently, de Valera refused to attend further talks in what became the London Conference and, instead, sent Collins in his place. Collins, like Griffith – and the majority of Sinn Féin – believed these terms should be accepted, as they offered a way, eventually, of peacefully achieving complete independence for the whole of Ireland.

Their belief that this was possible was based on the fact that the 1920 Government of Ireland Act had included two promises that seemed significant. These were to set up a Boundary Commission to decide the exact boundaries between Northern and Southern Ireland, and to create a Council of Ireland to work for reunification. Assurances about these were repeated by Britain during the discussions. Collins and his supporters believed that, over time, it would be possible to persuade some Catholic-dominated areas in the north to join the south – this would then make Northern Ireland unviable. Lloyd George himself did not think Northern Ireland would be able to exist for very long.

Dominion status: this offered slightly more independence than home rule. The south would be a self-governing territory within the British Empire – like Canada or Australia, for example. But this would still mean that Irish MPs would have to swear an oath of loyalty to the British crown, and that the south would have to help Britain in any future wars.

SOURCE J

Although at the beginning there are to be two parliaments and two governments in Ireland, the Act contemplates and affords every facility for union between north and south, and empowers the two parliaments by mutual agreement and joint action to terminate partition and set up one parliament and one government for the whole of Ireland.

An extract from the Government of Ireland Act, 1920. Quoted in A. Todd (2001), *The Modern World*, Oxford: Oxford University Press, p. 68.

However, the Irish delegation was under strict orders not to sign anything without full consultation with the Irish government. After several journeys between London and Dublin, the British delegation made it clear that, if an agreement was not signed – with no further discussions with the Dáil – the war would resume, with a much larger number of British troops being deployed. Aware that the IRA was not really able to fight such a serious conflict, Collins and Griffith – both of whom wanted peace after so many years of bitter conflict – finally signed in the early hours of 6 December 1921.

SOURCE K

When you have sweated, toiled, had mad dreams, hopeless nightmares, you find yourself in London's streets, cold and dank in the night air. Think – what have I got for Ireland? Something she has wanted these past seven hundred years. Will anyone be satisfied at the bargain? Will anyone? I tell you this: early this morning I signed my death warrant. I thought at the time how odd, how ridiculous – a bullet may just as well have done the job five years ago.

Comments made by Michael Collins in a letter to his friend, John Kane, on 6 December 1921. Quoted in M. Collier (2008), *Britain and Ireland, 1867–1922*, London: Heinemann, p. 158.

Theory of Knowledge

History: the relationship between social and natural sciences:
According to Steven Pinker (b. 1954), *'History is a kind of experiment, albeit an imperfectly controlled one.'* How far do you think this view applies to the Irish 'War of Independence' of 1919–22 and its outcome? Do you think there is a hierarchy of validity between the social and natural sciences?

The Partition of Ireland, 1921

The Irish cabinet accepted the treaty by four votes to three. There then followed a bitter argument in the Dáil about accepting the proposals: both those concerning the partition of Ireland, and those relating to dominion status. Eventually, though, the Dáil voted sixty-four to fifty-seven to accept. So, on 7 January 1922, the Anglo–Irish Partition Treaty was ratified. This formally brought the 'War of Independence' to an end. As a result of the Partition Treaty, the south of Ireland became the Irish Free State (Saorstat Eireann), with its own parliament, but still having to swear an oath of loyalty to the British crown. The new Free State government then formed the Irish National Army – initially from the ranks of those members of the IRA that supported the Treaty.

End of unit activities

1 Using the information in this unit, and any other resources available to you, produce a chart (a) listing the various organisations set up in Ireland between 1867 and 1900 to achieve reform of the Land and Home Rule issues; and (b) summarising the various reform acts passed during this period that relate to these two issues.

2 Find out more about Charles Parnell and Michael Davitt. Then write a couple of paragraphs to evaluate their contributions to the struggle for Irish independence.

3 Carry out some additional research on the Easter Rebellion. How significant do you think this was, in comparison to other factors in the period 1912–2, in relation to the creation of the Irish Free State in the south of Ireland?

4 Write a newspaper article comparing the roles of Michael Collins and Éamon de Valera in the 'War of Independence' from 1919 to 1922.

KEY QUESTIONS

- What political challenges did the Irish Free State face after independence?
- What economic and social challenges did the Irish Free State face after 1922?
- How did Ireland's government respond to these challenges in the period 1922–32?

Overview

- Almost as soon as the Anglo–Irish Partition Treaty had been ratified, Sinn Féin split into pro- and anti-Treaty factions. De Valera was anti-Treaty and so resigned from the Irish Free State government.

- The Irish Civil War then broke out, but de Valera's IRA 'Irregulars' were soon defeated, and the Civil War ended in April 1923.

- The Free State government – led by William Cosgrave and his new Cumann na nGaedheal party – then attempted to restore law and order. A new police force – An Garda Síochána – was formed; and an attempted army mutiny by anti-Treaty IRA officers in 1924 was easily defeated.

- The new government then followed essentially conservative economic and social policies between 1922 and 1932. These included avoiding protectionism, cutting old age pensions and keeping other social benefits low, and outlawing divorce and birth control.

- For most of the period 1922–32, Cosgrave's party faced no serious political opposition. However, in 1926, de Valera formed a new party – Fianna Fáil – which was prepared to take the oath of loyalty to the British crown, as required by the Partition Treaty of 1922.

- In 1932, Fianna Fáil won the general election, and de Valera became prime minister. He immediately began to renegotiate the constitutional relationship with Britain and, in 1949, a completely independent Irish republic – the Republic of Ireland – came into existence. However, as Northern Ireland continued to exist, Ireland remained disunited.

6.7 What political challenges did the Irish Free State face after independence?

Almost immediately, the new Irish Free State was faced with several problems. In particular, it was faced with a Civil War between those who supported the 1922 Treaty and those who did not. The pro-Treaty forces were led by Michael Collins, the interim prime minister and commander of the Free State forces, while the anti-Treaty forces – known as the 'Irregulars' – were led by de Valera. Thus the first task of the new Irish Free State was to survive and win the Civil War.

QUESTION

Why did Sinn Féin split into two factions at the beginning of 1922?

Partition and the Republicans

After the signing of the Partition Treaty, the nine counties of Ulster were reduced to the six most Protestant ones; the three overwhelmingly Catholic ones were then transferred to the Irish Free State. However, the new administration of Northern Ireland then refused to participate in the promised Boundary Commission. This disappointed those who had signed the Treaty, as the prospects of a peaceful reunification now seemed very unlikely.

In January 1922, de Valera resigned as president in protest, and Griffith took his place, while Collins became prime minister in a provisional government. Sinn Féin fought the general election in the south, in June 1922, as a united party, and pro-Treaty candidates won a clear victory, gaining almost 80 per cent of the votes. The government then attempted to transform the IRA into the Irish National Army (INA), with additional new recruits.

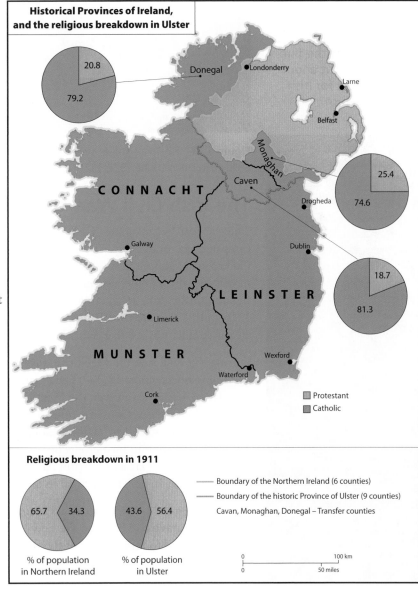

Figure 6.20 The four historic provinces of Ireland, and the religious breakdown in Ulster (1911 census figures). This map also shows the three counties of Ulster that were transferred to the Irish Free State in 1922

251

Ireland

ACTIVITY

Watch the film *Michael Collins* (1996), then answer the following questions:

Was Collins a terrorist? What are the values and limitations of the film for finding out about the struggle for Irish independence?

William Cosgrave (1880–1965)

He was an early member of Sinn Féin, and joined the Irish Volunteers in 1913. He played a prominent part in the Easter Rising of 1916: although sentenced to death, his sentence was later commuted to life imprisonment. He agreed with Collins and Griffith over the signing of the Partition Treaty and, after Collins's assassination in August 1922, took Collins's place. He was president of the Executive Council from 1922 to 1932, and represented the Free State's conservative rural middle classes. He preferred to concentrate on issues related to the Civil War, and to follow a conservative policy in relation to taxation and public expenditure.

However, de Valera's anti-Treaty IRA supporters – known as the 'Irregulars' or republicans – refused to be bound by either the partition terms of the Treaty, or the oath to the British crown. These 'Irregulars' called themselves the IRA and, in June, anti-Treaty forces took over the Four Courts in Dublin. The Irish Free State then came under intense pressure from Britain to deal with the anti-Treaty faction. Eventually, using weapons borrowed from Britain, Collins ordered the bombardment of the Four Courts.

Figure 6.21 Pro-Treaty forces shell anti-Treaty forces in the Four Courts building in Dublin, June 1922

The Irish Civil War, 1922–3

These actions began a bitter Civil War, as the anti-Treaty forces took up arms in a guerrilla campaign against the new Irish government. Although they managed to assassinate Michael Collins in an ambush in August 1922, the anti-Treaty forces were outnumbered and the new INA, which eventually numbered almost 60,000 troops, soon defeated the rebels. The fighting finally came to an end on 30 April 1923, when a ceasefire was agreed. Between 1916 and 1923, more than 10,000 people had been wounded or killed, but the outcome of all this conflict was less than what had been desired by many republicans.

During this civil war, the Free State government executed seventy-seven Republicans, and imprisoned almost 12,000. These actions effectively neutralised the bulk of the anti-Treaty leaders. However, the Free State government thus lost the support of most of their Sinn Féin party. Consequently, in April 1923, the pro-Treaty Sinn Féiners set up a new party: Cumann na nGaedheal (Society of the Gaels). As de Valera and his supporters refused to take part in further elections until 1927, and other parties were generally small and weak, the pro-Treaty Cumann na nGaedheal was able to rule Ireland as effectively a one-party state. In general, it ruled in an authoritarian way.

In December 1922, with Sinn Féin's main leaders – Collins and Griffith – dead, **William Cosgrave** had become the new leader of the Free State. During the next decade, he tried to repair some of the damage done during the Anglo–Irish War and the Civil War that had followed.

Figure 6.22   Armed anti-Treaty members of the IRA, in Grafton Street, Dublin

Law and order

After the civil war, it was necessary to re-establish law and order. In September 1922, An Garda Síochána (Guardian of the Peace) was established to replace the army as the Free State's policing arm. The recruits came from the pro-Treaty IRA and soon gained the support of the bulk of the population. At the same time, the INA was greatly reduced – to about 15,000 by 1924. This angered many soldiers as there was considerable unemployment in the Free State in the 1920s. In addition, many old IRA members within the army (known as the IRA Organisation) were only partly reconciled to the Free State. They wanted to see the Free State return to Collins's tactic of using the Treaty as a stepping stone towards obtaining a completely independent and united Ireland. These tensions eventually sparked off an attempted mutiny in March 1924. The IRA Organisation wanted to remove those army commanders not in sympathy with the aim of a united independent republic. Although the mutiny was quickly neutralised by the government, the IRA Irregulars – from this point on simply referred to as the IRA – carried out sporadic attacks on police stations and assassinations of Free State politicians.

Political opposition after 1926

De Valera had, since 1925, begun to reconsider his relations to the Free State. In May 1926, he persuaded many of his followers in Sinn Féin to form a new party, Fianna Fáil (Warriors of Ireland), which would contest elections and be prepared to enter the Dáil and take the Oath of Fidelity to the British crown. This was the first serious political opposition the Free State government had faced since 1922. Although he lost the support of the Sinn Féin/IRA 'Irreconcilables', Fianna Fáil gradually increased its support. In the September 1927 elections, de Valera's new party won forty-four seats to the government's forty-seven. After some hesitations, Fianna Fáil agreed to take the oath – although making it clear that they saw it as an empty gesture.

> **QUESTION**
>
> What was the significance of de Valera's decision to form Fianna Fáil in 1926?

Historical debate:
Much 20th-century historical work has shown that there were strong and significant differences between the two main political groups in the Free State. These resulted from serious divisions over what the nature of the new Ireland should be. According to Jeffrey Prager (1986), the main differences between the pro- and anti-Treaty factions was to do with political ideology dating back to the 1790s, rather than specific issues to do with the 1922 Treaty and the 'national question'. Richard Dunphy (1995) also sees the national question as often being less important after 1922 than issues of party organisation and politics.

SOURCE A

The strength of the political tension between pro- and anti-treaty sides during this period [1922–32] meant that the ideological division in Irish politics was largely based on ideas of the nation, rather than on economic or social theories as in other European nations. Throughout the rest of the twentieth century, it became nearly impossible to talk about Irish politics in left/right or conservative/socialist terms. The long struggle for some sort of independence, combined with limited social and economic reforms brought in by the British, meant that it was the sovereignty question that preoccupied Irish political minds for nearly fifty years.

J. Coohill (2014), *Ireland: A Short History*, London: Oneworld Publications, p. 141.

6.8 What economic and social challenges did the Irish Free State face after 1922?

After six years of conflict, neither Irish unity nor full independence had been achieved. In addition, the Free State delivered little in the way of economic improvement or social justice. Thus economic and social inequalities remained.

The economy

The Free State had to deal with the economic results of partition, which deprived it of the industry in the north, which had long been the most industrialised part of Ireland. On top of this, it had to cope with the economic impacts of the fighting since 1916, which had seen considerable destruction of transport and property. The response of the new government was to follow a conservative economic policy that focused on low taxation and low government expenditure. It avoided protectionism, and instead opted for free trade, and there was little direct state aid for industry. Instead, Cosgrave's government focused on agriculture.

Agriculture

In 1923, the government passed the Land Purchase Act, which set up the Land Commission. This speeded up the land purchase process: by 1932, 450,000 acres had been distributed to 24,000 families. As a result, most of the farms south of the new border were eventually owned by those who farmed them. However, the larger landowners and the cattle farmers benefited most from these policies. Irish farmers in particular, were dependent on the British market – by 1926, more than 50 per cent of the population were involved in agriculture. The trend was to continue the consolidation of medium-sized farms; tillage declined, cattle-raising remained dominant and the redistribution of land by purchase continued. Despite some state help in livestock breeding and poultry farming, agricultural productivity remained extremely low. The main aim of the government was to protect the interests of the farmers by helping to maximise their incomes. In order to do this, the government decided to use any revenue balances to reduce or keep low income tax.

Industry

The Free State's economy was to a large extent still strongly influenced by its continuing connection to Britain. In 1924, 98 per cent of all Irish exports went to the UK. As with agriculture, it was the bigger industrial firms which benefited from free trade. Generally, the lack of sufficient coal and iron reserves, and the massive competition from British goods, limited industrial expansion. The worst-hit smaller firms were helped by some limited protectionist tariffs placed on goods such as shoes and soap. In addition, the loss of Ulster meant the Free State had little industry to begin with. Despite some limited forms of protectionism and tariffs on imported industrial goods, the Free State did little to help promote the development of new industries. Productivity was low and industrial exports actually declined – even though, overall, exports rose to a peak of nearly £50 million in 1929 (paying for almost 80 per cent of all imports).

Social welfare

Cosgrave's government was opposed to any kind of meaningful social welfare policies: in 1924, old age pensions were actually cut, and unemployment and other labour benefits remained low, and were kept at pre-1922 levels. In part, this was the result of the fact that the Free State economy could not afford the social welfare reforms passed by the British Liberal government in the period 1906–14.

However, these actions also reflected the conservative political and economic views of the government.

Religion

Although the Free State's population was overwhelmingly Catholic, the religious and educational rights of the Protestants in the Free State were protected by law, and they were given weighted representation in the Senate. In 1926, they formed 28 per cent of farmers with more than 200 acres, and 18 per cent of the professional class – yet they were only 8.5 per cent of the population. Nonetheless, many left and, by 1930, the proportion of Protestants in the twenty-six counties had fallen to 7.5 per cent.

Although the constitution insisted on the separation of the Catholic Church and state, the Free State government worked closely with the Church hierarchy. This impacted on the possibility of welfare reform, as the Church wished to keep its traditional dominant role in matters of health and welfare. This alliance also meant that divorce was forbidden in 1925, birth control was outlawed and children of 'mixed' marriages had to be brought up as Catholics. There was also a strict censorship of books and films. However, most ordinary Catholics generally supported such policies during the 1920s.

> **QUESTION**
>
> Why do you think the Free State government did so little as regards social and health care during the decade after 1922?

SOURCE B

The professionalism of the Free State government, and the political stability that ensued from its regime, is impressive; future generations owed them much. But looked at another way, the lopsidedness of developments south as well as north of the new border is striking: and if post-1917 Sinn Féin and its successor organizations had effectively won the Anglo-Irish war, it is tempting to conclude that on other levels they lost the peace.

R.F. Foster (1989), *Modern Ireland 1600–1972*, London: Penguin Books, p. 535.

6.9 How did Ireland's government respond to these challenges in the period 1922–32?

'Colonial' connection: according to constitutional experts at the time, the new constitution was essentially a republican one, with only very limited references to monarchical authority and membership of the British Commonwealth. Thus several of these experts concluded that it was flexible enough to lead, eventually, to a complete republic.

Fact: Following the 1932 elections, Cosgrave's party merged, in September 1933, with some other political parties, to form Fine Gael (the United Irish Party) – compared to de Valera's Fianna Fáil, this was a right-wing party.

Fact: The oath of loyalty was abolished in 1932 and, in 1936, the External Relations Act took charge of foreign policy – although the Free State remained within the Commonwealth. In 1937, a new constitution changed the name of the Irish Free State to Éire (Ireland), which, in all but name, became a republic. The final step towards complete independence came on 18 April 1949 (St Patrick's Day), when the Republic of Ireland Act of 1948 came into force. This ended all remaining connections with Britain, with Éire being renamed as the Republic of Ireland.

The economy

The results of the government's economic policies were mixed. Although agriculture accounted for 50 per cent of all jobs in the 1920s, it only contributed about 30 per cent of the national income. However, in 1927, the state-sponsored Agricultural Credit Corporation was established to help farmers make improvements by advancing capital, with their farms as security for the loans.

Despite generally giving limited state help for industry, in 1927, the government set up a semi-state company to oversee the production and distribution of electricity. In 1929, this company commissioned the building of a hydroelectric dam. This provided jobs for 4,000 construction workers, and also eventually transformed the living and working conditions in rural areas. Generally, however, industrial production remained low in the 1920s. Because it did little to promote new industrial employment schemes, the problem of emigration continued. Yet the Wall Street Crash and the subsequent economic panic did not immediately impact on the Free State.

Social welfare

Partly because of its conservative economic and taxation policies, the Free State had, by 1929, avoided the problems of hyper-inflation that afflicted several countries during the 1920s. However, the price for this was paid by those struggling on low incomes, and dealing with the poverty arising from unemployment and underemployment. Smaller farmers, working on generally uneconomic lands, and the labouring poor, were angered by the lack of welfare reform. Spending on welfare remained low – and proposals for general unemployment benefit were rejected. Only a few workers received any unemployment assistance – and then only for six months. Hospitals and the health care systems, which were generally poor before 1922, were neglected. Old people who were ill were often cared for in the former workhouses, and the old and ill generally relied on the care provided traditionally by Church bodies and organisations. Even when spending on defence declined after 1929, the government did not spend the surplus on social welfare. Thus, as in Ireland before 1922, poverty forced many to leave the country.

Women

During the 1920s, the position of women declined. Previously, in the period 1914–23, many women – such as Countess Markievicz and Maud Gonne – had played prominent roles in the struggle for Irish independence. But the increased influence of the Catholic Church undermined this. Issues such as the banning of divorce and birth control did nothing to improve the lot of Irish women.

Moving towards a republic

Constructing an Irish identity

To deflect criticism from anti-Treaty organisations, which continued to accuse the government of selling out the dream of a fully independent Irish republic, the Irish Free State government tried to construct a clear national identity. Thus it pushed the teaching of the Gaelic language. By 1932, compulsory teaching of the 'national language' had been introduced into the educational system. In addition, proficiency in the language was made a necessary qualification for a wide variety of state administrative and civil service posts.

The British connection

Instead of economic and welfare reform, the Irish Free State government focused its attentions on ending the **'colonial' connection** with the British Empire. It campaigned for separate representation in the new League of Nations, and worked with other British dominions in order to achieve greater autonomy. This was largely achieved in December 1931 by the Statute of Westminster.

The question of the land annuities that the Free State had to pay to Britain remained politically important in the 1920s. In practice, it was Irish farmers making repayments of the loans – received under the Land Acts of 1891 and 1909 – to allow them to buy the land they farmed. Because of rural poverty in the 1920s, some farmers found it impossible to keep up these payments, and the IRA took up the cause.

De Valera's Fianna Fáil party also championed such farmers – it was this that played a significant role in his victory in the February 1932 elections.

During those elections, de Valera promised to rewrite the constitutional relationship between the Free State and Britain, and proclaimed the aim of achieving a united thirty-two-county Ireland. Once prime minister, he immediately began to try to renegotiate the terms of the Anglo–Irish Partition Treaty.

End of unit activities

- Carry out some further research on the Irish Civil War between 1902 and 1924. Then make a chart outlining the main causes and events, and explaining why the Irish Free State was able to defeat the rebels.

- Reread this unit, and then summarise the various political, economic and social challenges faced by the Irish Free State after 1922. Which do you think was the most serious challenge?

- Find out more about the Free State's economic and social policies between 1922 and 1923. Then write a couple of paragraphs to explain why the Free State adopted these policies.

KEY CONCEPTS ACTIVITY

Significance: Carry out some additional research on developments in the Free State from 1926 to 1932. Then draw up a chart to show the main issues raised during the 1932 general election.

Finally, write a couple of paragraphs to explain which factor you think was the most significant one as regards de Valera's victory.

Theory of Knowledge

History, bias and selectivity of perception:
T.E. Lawrence (1888–1935) once wrote: '*No man ever yet tried to write down the entire truth of any action in which he was engaged.*' Do you think this is why Éamon de Valera never attempted to write an autobiography? Are all autobiographies mainly attempts at self-justification and cover-up? Can you think of any that are not?

End of chapter activities

Paper 1 exam practice

Question

What is the message of **Source A**? [2 marks]

SOURCE A

THE IRISH FRANKENSTEIN.

Skill

Comprehension of a source's message.

Examiner's tips

Write a concise answer. Just a couple of brief sentences are needed, giving the information necessary to show that you have understood the message of the source.

Try to include some brief overall comment about the source's message.

Common mistakes

Make sure you don't comment on the wrong source! (Mistakes like this are made every year. Remember – every mark is important for your final grade.)

Simplified markscheme

For each **relevant point/comment**, award one mark – up to a maximum of two marks.

Student answer

Source A shows Parnell with the monster that he has created but can't control.

Examiner's comments

The candidate has selected one relevant and explicit piece of information from the source – this is enough to gain one mark. However, as no other point has been identified, this candidate fails to gain the other mark available for the question.

Activity

Look again at the source and the student answer above. Now try to identify one or two other relevant points about the source's message, and so obtain the other mark available for this question. For instance, what had prompted the cartoon, what does the 'monster' represent or what is the cartoon's overall message?

Summary activity

Copy this diagram and, using the information from this chapter and any other materials that you have available, make notes under each of the headings. Where there are differences of opinion and interpretation about certain aspects (such as causes and consequences, or significance), try to mention the views of different historians.

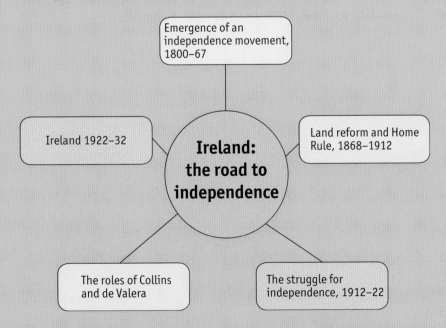

Paper 2 exam practice

1 Examine the social and economic factors that led to the emergence of an independence movement in Ireland before 1900.

2 Compare and contrast the relative significance of Young Ireland and the IRB in the struggle for Irish independence before 1900.

3 Evaluate the role and importance of Michael Collins in the struggle for Irish independence after 1914.

4 'The main challenges facing the Irish Free State after 1922 were economic.' To what extent do you agree with this statement?

Further reading

Try reading the relevant chapters/sections in the following books:

Adelman, P. and Pearce, R. (2008), *Great Britain and the Irish Question*, London: Hodder Education.

Collier, M. (2008), *Britain and Ireland 1867–1922*, Harlow: Heinemann.

Coogan, T.P. (1995), *De Valera: Long Fellow, Long Shadow*, London: Arrow.

Coohill, J. (2014), *Ireland: A Short History*, London: Oneworld Publications.

English, R. (2007), *Irish Freedom: The History of Nationalism in Ireland*, London: Pan Books.

Foster, R.F. (1989), *Modern Ireland 1600–1972*, London: Penguin Books.

Kee, R. (2000), *The Green Flag: A History of Irish Nationalism*, London. Penguin Books.

O'Connor, U. (2001), *Michael Collins and the Troubles: The Struggle for Irish Freedom*, New York and Edinburgh: Mainstream Publishing.

Pelling, N. (2003), *Anglo–Irish Relations 1798–1922*, London: Routledge.

Exam practice

Introduction

You have now completed your study of the origins and rise of independence movements in Zimbabwe, India and Pakistan, Vietnam, Cuba and Ireland, the challenges that each faced and how they responded to them. In the previous chapters, you have had practice at answering some of the types of source-based questions you will have to deal with in Paper 1. In this chapter, you will gain experience of dealing with:

- the longer Paper 1 question, which requires you to use both sources and your own knowledge to write a mini-essay;
- the essay questions you will meet in Paper 2.

Exam skills needed for IB History

This book is designed primarily to prepare both Standard and Higher Level students for the Paper 2 *Independence Movements* (World History Topic 8). However, by providing the necessary historical knowledge and understanding, as well as an awareness of the key historical debates and perspectives, it will also help you prepare for Paper 1. The skills you need for answering both Paper 1 and Paper 2 exam questions are explained in the following pages.

Paper 1 exam practice

Paper 1 skills

This section of the book is designed to give you the skills and understanding to tackle Paper 1 questions. These are based on the comprehension, critical analysis and evaluation of different types of historical sources as evidence, along with the use of appropriate historical contextual knowledge. For example, you will need to test sources for value and limitations (i.e. their reliability and utility, especially in view of their origin, purpose and content) – a skill essential for historians. A range of sources has been provided, including extracts from official documents, tables of statistics, memoirs and speeches, as well as visual sources such as photographs and cartoons.

Exam practice

In order to analyse and evaluate sources as historical evidence, you will need to ask the following 'W' questions of historical sources:

- **Who** produced it? Were they in a position to know?
- **What** type of source is it? What is its nature – is it a primary or secondary source?
- **Where** and **when** was it produced? What was happening at the time?
- **Why** was it produced? Was its purpose to inform or to persuade? Is it an accurate attempt to record facts, or is it an example of propaganda?
- **Who** was the intended audience – decision-makers, or the general public?

You should then consider how the answers to these questions affect a source's value.

The example below shows you how to find the information related to the 'W' questions. You will need this information in order to evaluate sources for their value and limitations.

address WHAT? (type of source)

John Foster Dulles WHO? (produced it)

11 June 1954 WHEN? (date/time of production)

situation in Indo-china WHY? (possible purpose)

World Affairs Council WHO? (intended audience)

Origins: the 'who, what, when and where' questions.

Purpose: this means 'reasons, what the writer/ creator was trying to achieve, who the intended audience was'.

Content: this is the information or explanation(s) provided by the source.

Remember: a source doesn't have to be primary to be useful. Remember, too, that content isn't the only aspect to have possible value. The context, the person who produced it, and so on, can also be important in offering an insight.

SOURCE A

The situation in Indo-china is not that of open military aggression by the Chinese Communist regime. Thus, in Indo-china, the problem is one of restoring tranquillity in an area where disturbances are fomented from Communist China, but where there is no open invasion by Communist China. This task of pacification, in our opinion, cannot be successfully met merely by unilateral armed intervention. Some other conditions need to be established. Throughout these Indo-china developments, the United States has held to a stable and consistent course and has made clear the conditions which, in its opinion, might justify intervention.

Extract from an **address** by US secretary of state **John Foster Dulles**, **11 June 1954** on the **situation in Indo-china**, delivered to the **World Affairs Council**.

This approach will help you become familiar with interpreting, understanding, analysing and evaluating different types of historical sources. It will also aid you in synthesising critical analysis of sources with historical knowledge when constructing an explanation or analysis of some aspect or development of the past. Remember, for Paper 1, as for Paper 2, you need to acquire, select and deploy relevant historical knowledge to explain causes and consequences, continuity and change. You also need to develop and show (where relevant) an awareness of historical debates, and different perspectives and interpretations.

Paper 1 questions will thus involve examining sources in the light of:

- their **origins**, **purpose** and **content**;
- their value and limitations.

The value and limitations of sources to historians will be based on the origins, purpose and content aspects. For example, a source might be useful because it is primary – the event depicted was witnessed by the person producing it. But was the person in a position to know? Is the view an untypical view of the event? What is its nature? Is it a private diary entry (therefore possibly more likely to be true), or is it a speech or piece of propaganda intended to persuade? The value of a source may be limited by some aspects, but that doesn't mean it has no value at all. For example, it may be valuable as evidence of the types of propaganda put out at the time. Similarly, a secondary – or even a tertiary – source can have more value than some primary sources, for instance, because the author might be writing at a time when new evidence has become available.

Finally, when in the exam room, use the information provided by the Chief Examiner about the four sources, as it can give some useful information and clues to help you construct a good answer.

Paper 1 contains four types of question. The first three of these are:

1 **Comprehension/understanding of a source** – some will have two marks, others three marks. For such questions, write only a short answer (scoring two or three points); save your longer answers for the questions carrying the higher marks.

2 **Assessing the value and limitations of a source**. Remember to deal with all the aspects required: origins, purpose, content, and value and limitations (four marks).

3 **Cross-referencing/comparing or contrasting two sources** – try to write an integrated comparison; for example, comment on how the two sources deal with one aspect, then compare/contrast the sources on another aspect. This will usually score more highly than answers that deal with the sources separately. Try to avoid simply describing each source in turn – there needs to be explicit comparison/contrast (six marks).

These three types of questions are covered in the chapters above. The other, longer, type of Paper 1 question will be dealt with in this section.

Paper 1 – judgement questions

The fourth type of Paper 1 is a judgement question. Judgement questions are a synthesis of source evaluation and own knowledge.

Examiner's tips

- This fourth type of Paper 1 question requires you to produce a mini-essay – with a clear/relevant argument – to address the question/statement given in the question. You should try to develop and present an argument and/or come to a balanced judgement by analysing and using these four sources and your own knowledge.

- Before you write your answer to this kind of question, you may find it useful to draw a rough chart to note what the sources show in relation to the question. This will also make sure you refer to all or at least most of the sources. Note, however, that some sources may hint at more than one factor/result. When using your own knowledge, make sure it is relevant to the question.

- Look carefully at the simplified markscheme below – this will help you focus on what you need to do to reach the top bands and so score the higher marks.

Common mistakes

Don't just deal with sources or your own knowledge! Every year, some candidates (even good ones) do this, and so limit themselves to – at best – only five out of the nine marks available.

Simplified markscheme

Band		Marks
1	**Consistently focused** on the question. **Developed and balanced** analysis, with **precise use** of **BOTH** sources **AND** relevant/accurate own knowledge. Sources and own knowledge are used **consistently** and **effectively** together, to **support argument/judgement**.	8–9
2	**Mostly focused** on the question. **Developed** analysis, with **relevant use** of **BOTH** sources **AND some** detailed own knowledge. But sources and own knowledge **not always combined** to support analysis/judgement.	6–7
3	**Some focus** on the question. **Some analysis**, using some of the sources **OR** some relevant/accurate own knowledge.	4–5
4	**No/limited focus** on the question. **Limited/generalised comments** on sources **AND/OR** some **limited/inaccurate/irrelevant** own knowledge.	0–3

Student answers

The student answers below have brief examiner's comments in the margins, as well as a longer overall comment at the end. Those parts of the answers that make use of the sources are **highlighted in purple**. Those parts that deploy relevant own knowledge are **highlighted in red**. In this way, you should find it easier to follow why particular bands and marks were – or were not – awarded.

Question 1

'The NVA/VC had won the Vietnam War by 1975 because of their guerrilla warfare tactics.' Using Sources A, B, C and D, and your own knowledge, to what extent do you agree with this statement? [9 marks]

SOURCE A

Figure 7.1 Viet Cong guerrillas

SOURCE B

The Pentagon was recommending that the US mobilize for virtually total war and this in an election year. The war had already exacerbated the rate of inflation, and taxes would have to be increased. It was a fact that opinion polls during the Tet crisis indicated that the American public favoured a stronger military response, but it was also the case that Johnson's standing with the people was plummeting. Americans wanted to win, but the president seemed incapable of delivering. The scene was set for the most dramatic turnabout in the war.

T.E. Vadney (1987), *The World Since 1945*, London: Penguin, pp. 327–8.

SOURCE C

The US military never successfully resolved the tension between 'clearing and holding' and 'searching and destroying'. The effort against the VC was largely successful, however, and pacification programmes did show some effectiveness over the medium term. Operational errors on the part of the VC (most notably, the Tet Offensive) also contributed vitally to erosion of the internal rebellion; over time, the NLF became an enormously less important part of the military equation in South Vietnam. These successes were, however, undermined by US willingness to undertake a serious effort to control infiltration into South Vietnam: as the VC withered, the NVA took responsibility for fighting the communist ground war in South Vietnam.

C.D. Walton (2005), *The Myth of Inevitable US Defeat in Vietnam*, London: Frank Cass, p. 56.

SOURCE D

The US can go on increasing aid to South Vietnam. It can increase its own army. But it will do no good. I hate to see the war go on and intensify. Yet our people are determined to struggle. It is impossible for westerners to understand the force of the people's will to resist and to continue.

Comments made by North Vietnamese politician Pham Van Dong in 1964. Quoted in M. Chandler and J. Wright (1999), *Modern World History*, Oxford: Heinemann, p. 110.

Student answer

There are a number of reasons why the NVA/VC had won the Vietnam War by 1975, and these four sources offer a range of examples. First, Source A shows that the NVA/VC did fight a guerrilla rather than a conventional war. The US found this very difficult to counter. However, some historians believe that the US had found an effective military answer to the nationalist guerrillas, as Source C demonstrates. So it was not purely military factors – such as guerrilla warfare – that led to communist victory. The events on the ground had a seriously negative effect on US domestic opinion, as Source B shows. This finally forced the US to withdraw from Vietnam, allowing a victory for the North and the Viet Cong.

EXAMINER'S COMMENT BOX

This is a good, well-focused, start. Sources A, B and C are referred to, interwoven and used, along with a little own knowledge, to set up a sustainable line of debate.

EXAMINER'S COMMENT BOX

All four sources are clearly referred to and used, showing a good understanding of their content, as well as a little own knowledge. There is also a comment at the end that hints at a wider understanding of the developments in Vietnam and develops the initial line of debate.

EXAMINER'S COMMENT BOX

As before, sources (C and B) are clearly used and, in this case, linked. There is also relevant own knowledge and evidence of a high-level response pointing to the way in which historians revise their views of the past, and how the same events can be interpreted in radically different ways.

EXAMINER'S COMMENT BOX

The conclusion shows that the student has kept the question in mind and has attempted to make a judgement.

Sources A, B and C all relate to each other. Source A shows that the guerrilla offensive in the South was effective because of the support of communist China, which supplied military material. Source D, however, shows the determination of the Vietnamese people to resist whatever actions the US took. The US claimed the struggle in Vietnam was part of a worldwide communist conspiracy, and this was one of the reasons that the US resorted to a full-scale military reaction to the guerrilla threat in the South. In the long term, this tied the USA's hands and created the domestic pressures to withdraw as shown in Source B.

Finally, Source C is a revisionist theory that challenges the impact of the guerrilla strategy on the outcome of the war. Because of the nature of the war and its high media profile, the US was often depicted in sources and, hence, modern histories of the conflict, as incapable of checking the guerrillas. Source C challenges this, arguing that actually the US military reaction was both well thought out and effective. It argues that, militarily, the Tet Offensive of 1968 was a massive military setback for Hanoi. This 'truth', however, was not reflected in the media coverage of the war in America, and led the US public to come to the wrong conclusions, prompting the political opposition to the war outlined in Source B. This both lends weight to the original line of debate and shows how perspectives can be affected by depictions of events on television.

In conclusion, these four sources show that guerrilla warfare was only one of the reasons why the NVA / VC won the Vietnam War by 1975. Overall, the main reason was probably the one shown in Source B – the impact of events in Vietnam on US domestic opinion. The other sources are interlinked, thus showing that, although reasons for historical change can be laid out in an order of hierarchy, in reality factors are linked to each other to produce historical change.

Overall examiner's comments

There is good use of most of the sources, with clear references to them. However, Source D is not used extensively. The response displays a good grasp of the historical process. There is some use of own knowledge, mainly integrated with comments on the sources. There are, however, some omissions. For example, the strong willingness to resist – and the methods used – by the Viet Cong and the North Vietnamese are not really explored. Also, the unstable political situation in South Vietnam is not mentioned by the sources nor brought in by the candidate. Hence, although this might just get into Band 2, it definitely fails to get into Band 1.

Activity

Look again at all the sources, the simplified markscheme and the student answer. Now try to write a few paragraphs to push the answer up into Band 1, and so obtain the full nine marks.

Question 2

Using Sources A, B, C and D, and your own knowledge, evaluate the success of the Cuban independence movement by 1898. [9 marks]

SOURCE A

[It is my duty] ... to prevent, by the independence of Cuba, the United States from spreading over the West Indies and falling, with that added weight, upon other lands of our America. All I have done up to now, and shall do hereafter, is to that end ... I have lived inside the monster and know its insides.

Extract from a letter sent by Martí the day before he was killed. Quoted in American People, 15 March 2008, http://americanpeople2.blogspot.co.uk/2008/03/jos-marti-cuban-revolutionary-party.html.

SOURCE B

SOURCE C

The Cuban Revolutionary Party does not aim to deliver to Cuba a victorious group of people who look on the island as their prey and property, but to prepare, through every effective means afforded us by the freedom we have found abroad, the war we must wage for the dignity and wellbeing of all Cubans, and to deliver to Cubans a liberated homeland.

Extract from Article 5 of the PRC. Quoted in the Havana Times, 20 January 2014.

SOURCE D

[The US military campaign] was ostensibly against Spain, but in fact [was] against Cubans... The intervention changed everything, as it was meant to. A Cuban war of liberation was transformed into a US war of conquest.

L. Perez (1998), The War of 1898, Chapel Hill, NC: University of North Carolina Press. Quoted in N. Chomsky (2010), *Hopes and Prospects*, London: Penguin Books, p. 50.

Exam practice

EXAMINER'S COMMENT BOX

This is a good introduction, showing a clear understanding of the topic and the question.

EXAMINER'S COMMENT BOX

There is some clear use of Source A, and some brief use of Source B, with a little own knowledge – but this is not very extensive.

EXAMINER'S COMMENT BOX

There is explicit use of Source C – which is also linked to Source A. But, although the question is kept in mind, there is limited precise own knowledge.

EXAMINER'S COMMENT BOX

There is explicit use of Source D, with some precise own knowledge, which is integrated with the source to produce a synthesis.

EXAMINER'S COMMENT BOX

All four sources have been clearly referred to and used, along with some own knowledge. The conclusion shows that the student has kept the question in mind and has attempted a judgement.

Student answer

In one way, the Cuban independence movement had been very successful by 1898. This was because Spanish rule was ended in that year. However, the reality was much more complicated – in many ways, US rule merely replaced Spanish rule for many years after 1898.

Source A, which is a letter written by Martí, shows how the whole question of Cuban independence was closely connected to US ambitions in the region. He makes it clear that the United States wants to spread and fall 'upon other lands of our America'. He wrote this letter just the day before he was killed in 1895. This was right at the start of the Second War of Independence – the First War of Independence against Spain, from 1868 to 1878, had been unsuccessful.

Source B shows some of the guerrilla fighters which fought against Spanish troops. These mambi troops fought against the Spanish troops in both the independence wars and, during the Second War of Independence, were able to hold out against the much stronger armies commanded by General Weyler. By 1898, they had almost ended Spanish control over large parts of Cuba.

Source C is from the Cuban Revolutionary Party's articles, and shows they wanted to achieve complete independence for Cuba – and a free Cuba which was for all Cubans. It is not surprising that Article 5 says this, because the Cuban Revolutionary Party was set up by José Martí in 1892 – this therefore links to Source A, and shows his aims for Cuban independence were consistently the same. However, although these were his aims, this isn't what happened in 1898.

Finally, Source D is the one that really refers to how successful – or unsuccessful – the Cuban independence movement was by 1898. This source is a secondary source and shows what happened: 'A Cuban war of liberation was transformed into a US war of conquest.' This happened because the US had always wanted to rule Cuba and, using the Maine incident of 1898 as an excuse, declared war on Spain in 1898. Spain was quickly defeated, but the US then excluded the rebel forces and instead ruled Cuba for four years. Although the US 'allowed' Cuba to be independent in 1902, it really dominated the country until Castro's revolution of 1959.

In conclusion, these four sources show that the Cuban independence movement was not very successful. Despite Martí's aims and fears, the US ended up dominating Cuba for fifty years.

Overall examiner's comments

There is good and clear use of the sources throughout. However, the use and integration of precise own knowledge to both explain and add to the sources is limited at times. Nonetheless, the answer is clearly focused on the question, and the candidate has done enough to get into Band 2 and be awarded six or seven marks.

Activity

Look again at all the sources, the simplified markscheme and the student answer. Now try to write a few paragraphs to push the answer up into Band 1, and so obtain the full nine marks. In particular, try to add some precise details about the various successes of the independence movement's forces before 1898, and make some extra points with the sources.

Paper 2 exam practice

Paper 2 skills and questions

For Paper 2, you have to answer **two** essay questions – chosen from two **different** topics from the twelve options offered. Very often you will be asked to comment on two states from two different IB regions of the world. Although each question has a specific markscheme, you can get a good general idea of what examiners are looking for in order to be able to put answers into the higher bands from the general 'generic' markscheme. In particular, you will need to acquire reasonably precise historical knowledge in order to address issues such as cause and effect, or change and continuity, and to learn how to explain historical developments in a clear, coherent, well-supported and relevant way. You will also need to understand and be able to refer to aspects relating to historical debates, perspectives and interpretations.

Make sure you read the questions carefully, and select your questions wisely. It is important to produce a rough essay plan for **each** of your essays **before** you start to write an answer, and you may find it helpful to plan both your essays before you begin to write. That way, you will soon know whether you have enough own knowledge to answer them adequately.

Also remember to keep your answers relevant and focused on the question. For example, don't go outside the dates mentioned in the question, or answer on individuals/states different from the ones identified in the question. Don't just describe the events or developments – sometimes, students just focus on one key word or individual, and then write down all they know about it. Instead, select your own knowledge carefully, and pin the relevant information to the key features raised by the question. Also, if the question asks for 'causes/reasons' and 'consequences/results', or two different countries/leaders, make sure you deal with **all** the parts of the question. Otherwise, you will limit yourself to half marks at best.

Examiner's tips

For Paper 2 answers, examiners are looking for clear/precise analysis, and a balanced argument, linked to the question, with the use of good, precise and relevant own knowledge. In order to obtain the highest marks, you should be able to refer, where appropriate, to historical debate and/or different historical perspectives interpretations, or historians' knowledge, making sure it is both relevant to the question **and** integrated into your answer.

Common mistakes

- When answering Paper 2 questions, try to avoid simply describing what happened. A detailed narrative, with no explicit attempts to link the knowledge to the question, will only get you half marks at most.
- If the question asks you to select examples from **two** different regions, make sure you don't chose two states from the same region. Every year, some candidates do this, and so limit themselves to – at best – only eight out of the fifteen marks available for each question.

KEY CONCEPTS

Remember – when answering essay questions, you will often need to consider aspects of one or more of the six Key Concepts. These are:

Change

Continuity

Causation

Consequence

Significance

Perspectives

Simplified markscheme

Band		Marks
1	**Consistently clear focus** on the question, with **all main aspects addressed**. Answer is **fully analytical** and **well-structured/organised**. There is **sound understanding** of historical concepts. The answer also integrates **evaluation** of different historical debates/perspectives, and reaches a **clear/consistent judgement/conclusion**.	13–15
2	**Clear understanding** of the question and **most of its main aspects are addressed**. Answer is **mostly well-structured and developed**, with supporting own knowledge mostly relevant/accurate. Answer is **mainly analytical**, with **attempts at a consistent conclusion**; and shows **some understanding** of historical concepts and debates/perspectives.	10–12
3	**Demands of the question are understood** – but **some aspects not fully developed/addressed**. Relevant/accurate supporting own knowledge, but attempts at analysis are **limited/inconsistent**.	7–9
4	**Some understanding** of the question. **Some relevant own knowledge**, with some factors identified – but with **limited explanation**. **Some attempts at analysis**, but answer is mainly **description/narrative**.	4–6
5	**Limited understanding** of the question. **Short/general answer**, with very **little accurate/relevant** own knowledge. Some **unsupported assertions**, with **no real analysis**.	0–3

Student answers

Those parts of the student answer which follow will have brief examiner's comments in the margins, as well as a longer overall comment at the end. Those parts that are particularly strong and well-focused will be **highlighted in red**. Errors/confusions/loss of focus will be **highlighted in blue**. In this way, you should find it easier to follow why marks were – or were not – awarded.

Question 1

Examine the reasons why India and Pakistan were granted independence in 1947. [15 marks]

Skill

Analysis/argument/evaluation.

Examiner's tip

At first sight this question seems straightforward, but it conceals a major potential pitfall. The combination of two states, India and Pakistan, effectively makes this a dual question.

Student answer

India and Pakistan were granted independence in 1947 essentially for three main reasons. First, even before the First World War, Britain had become uncomfortable with retaining its colonial possessions in India, and had made tentative constitutional reforms. A second factor was the growth and activities of the Indian nationalist movement. Finally there was the impact of the Second World War. Prior to this, there were elements of the British establishment that could not, for ideological or economic reasons, tolerate the loss of their Indian empire. It took the Second World War to so weaken Britain as a colonial power that it had little choice but to grant independence. The fact that the British were forced to give up India as a result of the pressures of the Second World War explains why two states emerged in 1947.

Even before the First World War Britain introduced constitutional reforms that allowed for limited Indian representation, a first tentative step towards eventual self-government. In 1909, the British minister John Morley introduced political concessions in the subcontinent, and in 1910, when the first elections were held, 135 Indians took their places as legislators. But Morley's reforms were motivated by the desire to maintain British control over this most important part of the empire, rather than the granting of full independence.

The First World War, however, showed both Congress and the British just how dependent the colonial power was on India in terms of military power and finance. This increased the pressure on Britain to meet certain demands and grant India increasing autonomy. In 1917 the government announced its intention of encouraging 'the gradual development of self-governing institutions'. Thus, by the end of the First World War it was clear that Britain intended to modify its relationship with India. The problem, however, was that once the crisis of the First World War passed there was less incentive to actually carry out these plans. The First World War, therefore, had two effects on the process of Indian independence. First, it had shown the strength of India as a potential sovereign state. Second, it had resulted in a grudging willingness of the colonial power to grant India a level of autonomy.

However, the slow pace of constitutional reform stimulated the rise of the Indian independence movement. At the core of the movement was the Indian National Congress. This organisation had its origins in the late 19th century. Before the First World War, Congress had sought a negotiated solution to the question of independence. However, when Britain did not implement any form of self-government after the First World War, despite its announced intention in 1917, it became clear to Congress leaders that more militant tactics would have to be adopted to force the British out. This development was encouraged by the 1918–19 influenza epidemic, which killed more than twelve million Indians, and by the bloodshed in the holy city of Amritsar in 1919, when British troops fired on a protest meeting, killing 379 people and wounding more than 1,000 more.

Congress, however, was composed of a middle-class élite who were wary of radicalism and instability. Congress had to balance militant action against the real threat of the development of new forms of nationalist agitation so extreme that they would create a post-colonial India under the control of radicals rather than the traditional Indian élite. Evidence of this was the formation of the Indian Communist Party, which championed armed struggle against the British – a development that would only succeed after considerable bloodshed and would probably destabilise India and result in chaos. Thus, Congress had to tread very carefully if it was to achieve its objectives.

EXAMINER'S COMMENT BOX

This is a clear and well-focused introduction, showing a good grasp of the key requirements of the question.

EXAMINER'S COMMENT BOX

There is a clear line of debate being developed here, with both supporting accurate own knowledge and a sense of critical judgement.

EXAMINER'S COMMENT BOX

There is accurate supporting own knowledge here, with explicit development of the original line of debate. Once again the answer displays both control and a sense of critical judgement.

Exam practice

EXAMINER'S COMMENT BOX

There is more analysis here, with supporting accurate own knowledge. The response extends the debate.

Into this situation stepped Gandhi. He was in many ways the solution to Congress's dilemma. His political tactic of satyagraha and his public image had a devastating effect on Britain's legitimacy as a colonial power. Acts of satyagraha exposed the inherent injustice of colonial rule. A good example of this is the Salt March of 1930. Secondly, Gandhi became a world figure. His image of a quasi-holy man who was resisting the might of the British Empire with reasonableness and dialogue was very appealing to both the more liberal elements of the British élite and the wider world, especially the USA. Gandhi presented the Indian nationalists with a middle way – resistance to colonial rule through non-violent action – which exposed the ridiculousness of a liberal democracy like Britain maintaining its grip on India. To some extent, this neutralised the more radical elements in Congress, such as Subhas Chandra Bose, and also the extreme left. To a great degree it also created a stable environment for political change. In this Gandhi proved to be a unique historical figure.

The key event was, however, the Second World War. This conflict bankrupted Britain and made maintenance of its empire impossible. Thus, in the immediate post-war period, the British rushed to meet Congress's demands. By 1947, independence had been granted to the subcontinent. This period was characterised by British mismanagement, which both allowed for the emergence of two states in the region, India and Pakistan, and led to massive inter-communal violence.

EXAMINER'S COMMENT BOX

Here the student extends the debate to cover Pakistan as well, as required by the question. However, the relationship between Britain and the Muslim League lacks detail, and the concluding sentence is unfocused.

The emergence of Pakistan was, in many ways, inevitable. The Muslim League had been formed before the First World War and its leader, Jinnah, had long since come to the conclusion that an independent Muslim state had to be created if Muslims were to retain political independence from the Hindu majority. The British, however, connived with the Muslim League in an attempt to control the situation and, as a result, when the two-state solution came into existence it was in an unsatisfactory form. The solution of dividing Pakistan into East and West was unworkable in the long run, and the mass movement of population resulted in killing on a huge scale.

Thus, Indian and Pakistani independence came about due to a combination of three factors. First, the British had indicated they were willing to make serious concessions to the nationalists by the time the First World War had ended. Second, the Indian nationalists had set in train a very effective political campaign in the 1920s and 1930s, in which Gandhi played a key part. Third, the Second World War had forced Britain to grant independence. It was the circumstances associated with this final factor that led to the specific form of independence adopted in the subcontinent, a region divided along religious grounds in the form of India and Pakistan. This unsatisfactory solution led to mass bloodshed at the time and has created instability both in Pakistan and between Pakistan and its neighbour ever since.

EXAMINER'S COMMENT BOX

This is a punchy and focused conclusion that finishes with a flourish.

Overall examiner's comments

This is a good, well-focused and analytical answer, with very specific and relevant own knowledge that supports the points made without obscuring them. The answer is thus good enough to be awarded a mark in Band 1 – probably thirteen marks. However, not all aspects are given equal weight. In particular, the Pakistan part of the answer is unbalanced. More importantly, it would have been very useful to have some mention of **relevant specific historians/historical interpretations**.

Activity

Look again at the simplified markscheme and the student answer. Now try to write a few extra paragraphs to push the answer up to the top of Band 1 and obtain the full fifteen marks available.

Question 2

Evaluate the role and significance of Michael Collins in the struggle for Irish independence between 1900 and 1922.   [15 marks]

Skill

Analysis/argument/evaluation.

Examiner's tip

Look carefully at the wording of this question, which asks for the role **and** significance of Michael Collins during the period 1900–22 to be evaluated. If high marks are to be achieved, answers will need to **do more than just describe** what he did.

Student answer

Michael Collins was an important revolutionary leader in the struggle for Irish independence, and played an important part in this struggle in several different ways. These ranged from his roles as the leader of the IRA to his political role as negotiator and minister after 1918.

Michael Collins became a Irish nationalist at an early age and, after moving to London for a while, became a member of the Irish Republican Brotherhood (IRB) in 1909. This was a body dedicated to the achievement of Irish independence. It had been set up in 1858, and was greatly inspired by the Young Ireland rebellion of 1848. It was linked to the Fenian organisations in the US, and began to take violent action to end British rule in 1867. Although their various risings failed to achieve their aims, the IRB continued to exist – even when various British governments began to introduce land reforms that addressed some of the problems connected with landownership in Ireland. The IRB later developed a mixed reaction to the question of home rule – tending to see support of it as a tactic that would help them build support for the achievement of a totally independent Ireland.

Collins soon became an important organiser for the IRB when he returned to Ireland, and played an important role in the Irish Volunteers, a para-military group that had been formed to counter the Ulster Volunteers, a para-military group set up by Protestants to block the implementation of the Third Home Rule Bill of 1912. Along with a section of the Irish Volunteers, and members of the Irish Citizens' Army (led by James Connolly), Michael Collins took part in the Easter Rebellion in 1916. Although he was one of those arrested after the Rising, he was not executed. While he was imprisoned, he began to plan for a better-organised military campaign. He then joined Sinn Féin and began to work with Arthur Griffith and Éamon de Valera. In the 1918 elections, in which Sinn Féin won a landslide victory, Collins was one of those elected. The Sinn Féin MPs then refused to go to the British parliament in London and instead set up their own Irish parliament, called the Dáil. They then declared Irish independence.

Collins soon came to take charge of the Irish Republican Army (IRA) – which is what the Irish Volunteers were called after 1919. In addition, he was also appointed by de Valera as minister of finance in the rebel government. However, Sinn Féin's actions led to the Irish War of Independence, which lasted until 1921. During this war, Collins – like many other Sinn Féiners – was on the

---

EXAMINER'S COMMENT BOX

This is a brief but clear and well-focused introduction, showing a good grasp of the key requirements of the question.

EXAMINER'S COMMENT BOX

There is quite a bit of accurate supporting own knowledge – unfortunately, it is mostly focused on the period **before** 1900! This is thus irrelevant to the question.

EXAMINER'S COMMENT BOX

This is better, in that the answer is now focused on the period after 1900. However, despite some references to the significance of Collins's role, the answer is beginning to become rather descriptive.

EXAMINER'S COMMENT BOX

Again, there is plenty of accurate – and relevant – own knowledge. But there is little evaluation or analysis of relative importance – instead, the descriptive/narrative approach is continued.

run. However, he had a good network of spies and informers and was able to run the intelligence and planning side of the IRA's campaigns, which he felt should concentrate on assassinations and guerrilla warfare, as the British army was large and better-armed and trained. The IRA soon began to attack members of the police and the British army, and, in September 1919, Collins formed a special assassination squad known as the 'Twelve Apostles'. In 1920, the 'Twelve Apostles' killed twelve British undercover agents who had been sent to Ireland, with instructions to use any methods needed to destroy the IRA leadership. This action was followed by reprisals, making this day known as 'Bloody Sunday'.

EXAMINER'S COMMENT BOX

This is still an essentially descriptive answer – which is a shame, as the candidate clearly has a good overall grasp of developments, and some relevant precise own knowledge.

The independence war became increasingly bitter – especially when the British government sent in the Auxiliaries and the Black and Tans to support the police and the regular army. However, by 1921, a military stalemate had been reached, and the British government suggested negotiations. As soon as de Valera realised that Britain would not agree to a completely independent and united Ireland, he left the negotiations to Collins. Eventually, Collins agreed to the Anglo–Irish Partition Treaty – this included an oath to the British crown, and the splitting of Ulster from the rest of Ireland. Collins knew the IRA was not strong enough to face an enlarged British army in Ireland, which is what Britain threatened if the fighting continued. He – like Griffith – had had enough of the death and destruction, and believed the treaty offered a way to peacefully achieve within a generation their aim of an independent Irish republic. Although this was narrowly approved by the Sinn Féin government and the Dáil, de Valera and others resigned in protest. There then began a civil war in the Irish Free State, with some anti-Treaty members of the IRA and Sinn Féin fighting against the IFS government and forces. This Civil War lasted from 1922 to 1923 – and during it, Collins was assassinated.

EXAMINER'S COMMENT BOX

This is a brief but reasonably well-focused conclusion – which at last shows an awareness of what should have been done throughout the answer.

In conclusion, Collins played an important role in the struggle for Irish independence – and would no doubt have continued to do so if he had not been killed in 1922. This is mainly for two reasons: his leadership of the IRA from 1918 to 1921, and his negotiating skills during 1921–2. In both of these roles, it can be argued that he was more important than Éamon de Valera.

Overall examiner's comments

In the main, the candidate seems to have understood the demands of the question, and there is plenty of mostly relevant detailed own knowledge. However, the overall approach is descriptive rather than evaluative/analytical. In addition, the first part of the answer was mostly irrelevant, as it dealt with the period before 1900.

The answer has thus only done enough to be awarded Band 4 – although probably at the top end, thus gaining six marks. To reach Band 1, the answer would need to explicitly evaluate/assess Collins's role, by explaining **why** his actions were important, and by placing them in context – for example, by dealing with the roles of other people/ factors (for instance, de Valera's role, as mentioned in the conclusion).

Activity

Look again at the simplified markscheme and the student answer. Now try to write a few extra paragraphs to push the answer up into Band 1, and so obtain the full fifteen marks available. As well as making sure you address all aspects of the question, try to integrate some reference to **relevant historians/historical perspectives**.

Question 3

Compare and contrast the independence movements in **two** developing states – one in Africa and the other in Asia. [15 marks]

Skill

Analysis/argument/evaluation.

Examiner's tip

This question once again seems to be fairly straightforward. It allows the candidate to select the case studies to use in support of the question, and the demands of the question will be met as long as the essay discusses Asia and Africa. The potential pitfall lies in the open-ended nature of the question. What exactly is meant by 'compare and contrast'? Before embarking on the essay, therefore, you will need a clear plan, based on themes if possible. Thus, you might look at the basis of support, the historical context of each case study, the methods of achieving independence and so on. In this way, you will be able to interweave the two case studies into the text to meet the demands of the upper bands of the markscheme.

Student answer

In Indo-china, the independence movement was called the Viet Cong (VC). They were helped by the army of North Vietnam. They were guerrillas and fought a guerrilla war against the Americans. In Rhodesia, the independence movement was ZANU and ZAPU, who were also guerrillas but who did not receive any help from outside people.

The VC had fought the French and had been able to set up an independent North Vietnam, but when the Americans helped the South Vietnamese, the war began again. The VC fought as guerrillas and this defeated the Americans because US troops were not used to fighting in the jungle.

In Rhodesia, the whites had total control and the black people were little more than serfs. By 1965, the whites had set up an independent Rhodesia on their own. They would not give independence or political rights to the blacks. The white leader was Ian Smith and he was an extremist. The black nationalists were so upset by this that they set up their own armies, called ZAPU and ZANU. Robert Mugabe led the nationalists and they fought a guerrilla war against the whites. The nationalists had a hard time of it because of the powerful Rhodesian army, and it was only after a long time that they were successful.

In Vietnam there was a big battle called Tet. The VC won Tet and they captured the US embassy in the South Vietnamese capital Saigon. This was shown to the Americans on television and it so upset them that they turned against their president, Lyndon Johnson, and forced him to step down. Because of this battle the VC won. There were no battles like this in Zimbabwe.

So, the Zimbabwean and Vietnamese independence movements were the same because they were both guerrilla wars. They also had good leaders like Mugabe and Ho Chi Minh, which allowed them to win. There were many similarities, but some factors were different. The Vietnamese had a jungle to hide in, whereas the Zimbabweans did not. So there were differences and similarities between the two movements.

EXAMINER'S COMMENT BOX

The first paragraph is a very basic start, which addresses the question set only on a superficial level. There is a very limited attempt at comparison. The student fails to identify the outside support for the Zimbabwean independence movements.

EXAMINER'S COMMENT BOX

Some relevant knowledge is displayed in the second paragraph, but it is not focused on the question except by inference.

EXAMINER'S COMMENT BOX

The third paragraph shows some relevant knowledge, but it is even more generalised than the previous one. There are also inaccuracies – for example ZANU and ZAPU were the organisations themselves, not the military wings.

EXAMINER'S COMMENT BOX

Some relevant knowledge is displayed in the fourth paragraph but it is not moulded to the question set. Some of this is on the brink of being inaccurate – Tet was in fact a big setback for the VC. Note the crude failed attempt at a comparative analysis at the end.

Overall examiner's comments

This is a weak response that barely engages the question set. It does display some valid own knowledge but has problems moulding this to the question. It flags up some interesting points but fails to develop them. It has real problems of control. It shows limited relevant own knowledge and would thus enter the markscheme in Band 4. The short length of the response, however, would place it at the bottom of this band, gaining four marks.

Activity

Look again at the simplified markscheme and the student answer. Now try to write a more detailed response to push the answer up to a higher level.

Further information

Sources and quotations in this book have been taken from the following publications.

Afigbo, A.E. et al. (1986), *The Making of Modern Africa, Volume 2: The Twentieth Century*, London: Longman.

Arnold, G. (2006), *Africa: A Modern History*, London: Atlantic Books.

Berend, I.T. (1996), *Central and Eastern Europe, 1944–93*, Cambridge: Cambridge University Press.

Blake, R. (1977), *History of Rhodesia*, London: Methuen Publishing.

Bose, S. and Jalal, A. (1998), *Modern South Asia*, London: Routledge.

Bottaro, J. et al. (2001), *Successful Human and Social Sciences Grade 9*, Cape Town: Oxford University Press.

Burke, P. (1995), *Revolution in Europe, 1989*, London: Wayland.

Buss, C.A. (1958), *Southeast Asia and the World Today*, Princeton: D. Van Nostrand.

Cannon, M. et al. (2009), *20th Century World History*, Oxford: Oxford University Press.

Chandler, M. and Wright, J. (1999), *Modern World History*, Oxford: Heinemann.

Chandra, B. et al. (2000), *India after Independence: 1947–2000*, London: Penguin.

Cole, A.B. (ed.) (1956), *Conflict in Indo-China and International Repercussions*, New York: Cornell University Press.

de Bary, W. (1958), *Sources of Indian Tradition*, New York: Columbia University Press.

Demma, V.H. (1989), *American Military History*, Washington, DC: US Army.

Documents from the Military Archives of Former Warsaw Pact Countries (2000), Historical Office, Office of the Secretary of Defence and Joint History Office.

Dubček, A. (1992), *Hope Dies Last*, Tokyo: Kodansha International.

Fisher, P. (1985), *The Great Power Conflict After 1945*, London: Basil Blackwell.

Galbraith, J.K. (1994), *A Journey Through Economic Time: A Firsthand View*, Boston: Houghton Mifflin.

Garton Ash, T. (2002), *The Polish Revolution: Solidarity*, New Haven: Yale University Press.

Gates, R. (1997), *From the Shadows*, New York: Simon & Schuster.

Geary, P.J. (2003), *The Myth of Nations*, Princeton: Princeton University Press.

Gott, R. (2004), *Cuba: A New History*, New Haven: Yale University Press.

Guha, R. (2007), *India after Gandhi: The History of the World's Largest Democracy*, London: Macmillan.

Havel, V. (1990), *Living in Truth, Essays on Politics and Conscience*, London: Faber and Faber.

Hayslip, L.L. (1993), *When Heaven and Earth Changed Places*, New York: Plume.

James, L. (1997), *Raj: The Making and Unmaking of British India*, London: Abacus.

Karnow, S. (1984), *Vietnam: A History*, Harmondsworth: Penguin.

Kelly, G.A. (1968), *Addresses to the German Nation*, New York: Harper Torch.

Leaver, D. (2004), *Encyclopedia of African History II*, London: Routledge.

Longworth, P. (1992), *The Making of Eastern Europe*, London: Macmillan.

Meredith, M. (2005), *The State of Africa*, London: Free Press.

Metcalf, B. and Metcalf, T. (2006), *A Concise History of Modern India*, Cambridge: Cambridge University Press.

Nehru, J. (1946), *The Discovery of India*, London: Meridian Books.

Nkrumah, K. (1965), *Neo-colonialism: The Last Stage of Imperialism*, London: Thomas Nelson & Sons.

Ost, D. (2005), *The Defeat of Solidarity*, New York and London: Cornell University Press.

Pollock, A. (1995), *Vietnam: Conflict and Change in Indochina*, Melbourne: Oxford University Press.

Raftopoulos, B. and Mlambo, A. (2009), *Becoming Zimbabwe*, Harare: Weaver Press.

Santoli, A. (1985), *To Bear Any Burden*, New York: E.P. Dutton.

Talbot, I. and Singh, G. (2009), *The Partition of India*, Cambridge: Cambridge University Press.

Vadney, T.E. (1987), *The World Since 1945*, London: Penguin.

Walsh, B. (2001), *Modern World History*, London: John Murray.

Walton, C.D. (2005), *The Myth of Inevitable US Defeat in Vietnam*, London: Frank Cass.

Zhai, Q. (2000), *China and the Vietnam Wars, 1950–1975*, Chapel Hill: University of North Carolina Press.

Index

Index

Index

Acknowledgements

The author and publishers acknowledge the following sources of copyright material and are grateful for the permissions granted. While every effort has been made, it has not always been possible to identify the sources of all the material used, or to trace all copyright holders. If any omissions are brought to our notice, we will be happy to include the appropriate acknowledgements on reprinting.

Images

Cover NARINDER NANU/AFP/Getty images; 1.1 Keystone/Getty Images; 2.3 TopFoto; 2.4 James Burke/The LIFE Picture Collection/Getty Images; 2.6 AFP/Getty Images; 2.7 Central Press/Getty Images; 2.8 © Gallo Images/Alamy; 2.9 © peter jordan/ Alamy; 2.11 Keystone-France/Gamma-Keystone via Getty Images; 2.12 AFP PHOTO/ ALEXANDER JOE (Photo credit should read ALEXANDER JOE/AFP/Getty Images; 2.13 Jim Barber/Shutterstock; 2.14 © BRIAN HARRIS/Alamy; 2.15 STR/ AFP/Getty Images; 2.16 © PHILIMON BULAWAYO/Reuters/Corbis; 3.2 Central Press/Getty Images; 3.3 Mary Evans Picture Library; 3.4 PNA Rota/Getty Images; 3.5 Popperfoto/Getty Images; 3.6 Mansell/The LIFE Picture Collection/Getty Images; 3.7 © Dinodia Photos/Alamy; 3.8 Margaret Bourke-White/The LIFE Picture Collection/ Getty Images; 3.10 Keystone/Getty Images; 3.11 Howard Sochurek/The LIFE Picture Collection/Getty Images; 4.2 © ITAR-TASS Photo Agency/Alamy; 4.3 AFP/AFP/ Getty Image; 4.4 Keystone-France/Gamma-Keystone via Getty Images; 4.6 AFP/AFP/ Getty Images; 4.7 © Tim Page/CORBIS; 4.8 Keystone/Hulton Archive/Getty Images; 4.9 AP/Topfoto; 4.10 © Bettmann/CORBIS; 4.11 Rolls Press/Popperfoto/Getty Images; 4.12 Ronald S. Haeberle/The LIFE Images Collection/Getty Images; 4.13 AFP/ Getty Images; 4.14 Rolls Press/Popperfoto/Getty Images; 5.2 © Luca Barbieri/Alamy; 5.3 Michael Leo Owens; 5.4 Callelinea; 5.6 © DESMOND BOYLAN/Reuters/Corbis; 6.2 Illustrated London News/Getty Images; 6.3 © Lordprice Collection/Alamy; 6.7 © Pictorial Press Ltd/Alamy; 6.8 © Pictorial Press Ltd/Alamy; 6.10 Topical Press Agency/ Getty Images; 6.11 National Library of Ireland; 6.12 © Pictorial Press Ltd/Alamy; 6.13 National Museum of Ireland; 6.14 National Library of Ireland; 6.15 © Tallandier/ Bridgeman Images; 6.17 © Hulton-Deutsch Collection/CORBIS; 6.18 FPG/Hulton Archive/Getty Images; 6.20 Walshe/Getty Images; 6.21 Walshe/Getty Images; Source A © Pictorial Press Ltd/Alamy; 7.1 Three Lions/Hulton Archive/Getty Images.